IFIP Advances in Information and Communication Technology 374

Editor-in-Chief

A. Joe Turner, Seneca, SC, USA

Editorial Board

Foundations of Computer Science
Mike Hinchey, Lero, Limerick, Ireland

Software: Theory and Practice
Michael Goedicke, University of Duisburg-Essen, Germany

Education
Arthur Tatnall, Victoria University, Melbourne, Australia

Information Technology Applications
Ronald Waxman, EDA Standards Consulting, Beachwood, OH, USA

Communication Systems
Guy Leduc, Université de Liège, Belgium

System Modeling and Optimization
Jacques Henry, Université de Bordeaux, France

Information Systems
Jan Pries-Heje, Roskilde University, Denmark

ICT and Society
Jackie Phahlamohlaka, CSIR, Pretoria, South Africa

Computer Systems Technology
Paolo Prinetto, Politecnico di Torino, Italy

Security and Privacy Protection in Information Processing Systems
Kai Rannenberg, Goethe University Frankfurt, Germany

Artificial Intelligence
Tharam Dillon, Curtin University, Bentley, Australia

Human-Computer Interaction
Annelise Mark Pejtersen, Center of Cognitive Systems Engineering, Denmark

Entertainment Computing
Ryohei Nakatsu, National University of Singapore

T0224142

IFIP – The International Federation for Information Processing

IFIP was founded in 1960 under the auspices of UNESCO, following the First World Computer Congress held in Paris the previous year. An umbrella organization for societies working in information processing, IFIP's aim is two-fold: to support information processing within ist member countries and to encourage technology transfer to developing nations. As ist mission statement clearly states,

> *IFIP's mission is to be the leading, truly international, apolitical organization which encourages and assists in the development, exploitation and application of information technology for the bene t of all people.*

IFIP is a non-profitmaking organization, run almost solely by 2500 volunteers. It operates through a number of technical committees, which organize events and publications. IFIP's events range from an international congress to local seminars, but the most important are:

- The IFIP World Computer Congress, held every second year;
- Open conferences;
- Working conferences.

The flagship event is the IFIP World Computer Congress, at which both invited and contributed papers are presented. Contributed papers are rigorously refereed and the rejection rate is high.

As with the Congress, participation in the open conferences is open to all and papers may be invited or submitted. Again, submitted papers are stringently refereed.

The working conferences are structured differently. They are usually run by a working group and attendance is small and by invitation only. Their purpose is to create an atmosphere conducive to innovation and development. Refereeing is less rigorous and papers are subjected to extensive group discussion.

Publications arising from IFIP events vary. The papers presented at the IFIP World Computer Congress and at open conferences are published as conference proceedings, while the results of the working conferences are often published as collections of selected and edited papers.

Any national society whose primary activity is in information may apply to become a full member of IFIP, although full membership is restricted to one society per country. Full members are entitled to vote at the annual General Assembly, National societies preferring a less committed involvement may apply for associate or corresponding membership. Associate members enjoy the same benefits as full members, but without voting rights. Corresponding members are not represented in IFIP bodies. Affiliated membership is open to non-national societies, and individual and honorary membership schemes are also offered.

Theo Dimitrakos   Rajat Moona
Dhiren Patel   D. Harrison McKnight (Eds.)

Trust
Management VI

6th IFIP WG 11.11
International Conference, IFIPTM 2012
Surat, India, May 21-25, 2012
Proceedings

 Springer

Volume Editors

Theo Dimitrakos
British Telecommunications, Security Futures Practice
PP13G Orion Building, Adastral Park, Ipswich, IP5 3RE, UK
E-mail: theo.dimitrakos@bt.com

Rajat Moona
Indian Institute of Technology Kanpur
Department of Computer Science and Engineering
Kalyanpur, 208 016 Kanpur, India
E-mail: moona@iitk.ac.in

Dhiren Patel
NIT Surat, Department of Computer Engineering
Ichchhanath, 395 007, Surat, India
E-mail: dhiren29p@gmail.com

D. Harrison McKnight
Michigan State University
Accounting and Information Systems Department
632 Bogue Street, East Lansing, MI 48824-1121, USA
E-mail: mcknight@bus.msu.edu

ISSN 1868-4238   e-ISSN 1868-422X
ISBN 978-3-642-42784-8   ISBN 978-3-642-29852-3 (eBook)
DOI 10.1007/978-3-642-29852-3
Springer Heidelberg Dordrecht London New York

CR Subject Classification (1998): K.6.5, C.2, E.3, D.4.6, H.4-5, J.1

Typesetting: Camera-ready by author, data conversion by Scientific Publishing Services, Chennai, India

Printed on acid-free paper

Springer is part of Springer Science+Business Media (www.springer.com)

Preface

This volume contains the proceedings of IFIPTM 2012, the 6th IFIP WG 11.11 International Conference on Trust Management, held in Surat, India, during May 21–25, 2012.

IFIPTM 2012 provided a truly global platform for the reporting of research, development, policy, and practice in the interdependent areas of privacy, security, and trust.

Building on the traditions inherited from the iTrust and previous IFIPTM conferences, IFIPTM 2012 was a multi-disciplinary conference focusing on areas such as: trust models, social, economic and behavioral aspects of trust, trust in networks, mobile systems and cloud computation, privacy, reputation systems, and identity management. Previous IFIPTM conferences have taken place in Denmark (2011), Japan (2010), USA (2009), Norway (2008), and Canada (2007).

IFIPTM 2012 was an open IFIP conference. The program of the conference featured both theoretical research papers and reports of real-world case studies from academia, business and government. IFIPTM 2012 received 51 submissions from 23 different countries, including: Australia, Canada, Denmark, Egypt, Finland, France, Germany, India, Ireland, Israel, Italy, Japan, Malaysia, The Netherlands, Norway, Pakistan, Poland, Singapore, Slovenia, Spain, Switzerland, the United Arab Emirates, the UK, and the USA. The Program Committee selected 12 full papers and 8 short papers for presentation and inclusion in the proceedings, which resulted in a highly competitive call with a 25%–30% acceptance rate for full technical papers.

We allocated submissions as full or short papers based on the opinions of the Program Committee. The full papers were unanimously deemed to be worthy of inclusion, while short papers were accepted if committee members believed them likely to introduce new concepts, report work in progress of likely high impact, or excite debate and discussion.

In addition, the program included presentations by academic and industry experts in the fields of trust management, privacy, and security:

- Audun Jøsang gave a keynote on "Robustness of Trust and Reputation Systems, Does it Matter?" as the trust management expert selected for the William Winsborough Commemorative Award and Address in 2012. Audun Jøsang is professor at the Department of Informatics at the University of Oslo. Prof. Jøsang has made a significant contribution to research and innovation for online trust management and for computational trust with the development of subjective logic.

– Rajat Moona, gave a keynote on "transCryptFS: A Trusted and Secure File
System." Rajat Moona is a Poonam and Prabhu Goel Chair Professor at
the Department of Computer Science and Engineering (CSE), IIT Kanpur,
and currently in-charge of C-DAC India as its Director General. He has
played a key role in defining standards for the Operating Systems for Smart
Cards for the Government of India, which are in use in applications such as
driving licenses, vehicle registration systems, Indian national ID, electronic
passports, and several other ID-related applications. He has also been in-
strumental in defining the strategy for smart card certification mechanisms
for the Government of India.
– Sundeep Oberoi presented a talk entitled "Operational Challenges in deploying Trust Management Systems—A Practical Perspective." Sundeep Oberoi
is the Global Head for Niche Technology Delivery Group in TCS (Tata Consultancy Services). He has authored the book *E-Security and You* explaining
the IT Act 2000 (India) and several other books as well as conference and
journal publications. He holds a PhD in Computer Science from IIT Bombay.
– Theo Dimitrakos presented an overview of the trust management discipline
and the evolution of the trust management community over the last 15 years.
Theo Dimitrakos is Chief Security Researcher in British Telecom and a co-
Founder of the iTrust Community in Europe in 2002, as well as a co-Founder
of the IFIP Trust Management working group in 2006. He served as the
Chair of the IFIP Trust Management Working Group (WG11.11) from 2009
to 2012 and was its Vice-Chair from 2007 to 2009.

The William Winsborough Commemorative Address and Award was inaugu-
rated to acknowledge the lasting effect that Professor Winsborough had on the
field of computational trust and trust management. The award will be given
annually from 2012 onward. The objective of the award is to publicly recognize
an individual, not a group or organization, who has significantly contributed to
the development of computational trust and/or trust management, especially
achievements with an international perspective and a lasting effect.

In the IFIPTM 2012 conference, as well as in previous IFIPTM conferences,
we had several accompanying workshops enabling the presentation of new ideas
and allowing the early exposure of ongoing research, particularly from PhD
students.

2012 was the first time that an international IFIP Trust Management conference took place in the Indian subcontinent and the second time that such a
conference took place in Asia (the first being IFIPTM 2010 in Japan) . We believe
the deep and wide profiles produced by all of the events will solidify IFIPTM as
an international, multidisciplinary trust conference with a truly global outreach.

Running an international conference requires an immense effort from all parties involved. We would like to thank the Program Committee members and external referees for having provided timely and in-depth reviews of the submitted

papers. We would also like to thank all members of the Organizing Committee and primarily Anirban Basu and Steve Marsh for having provided great help with organizing many technical aspects of the conference, the website and the implementation of its publicity and communications strategy. We also thank the EasyChair conference system, Springer, and the NIT Surat Computer Department team with Bhavesh Borisanya for the proceedings preparation. We hope you enjoy the proceedings.

May 2012

Theo Dimitrakos
Rajat Moona
Dhiren Patel
D. Harrison McKnight

Organization

General Chairs

Dhiren Patel   NIT Surat, India
D. Harrison McKnight   Michigan State University, USA

Program Chairs

Rajat Moona   IIT Kanpur, India
Theo Dimitrakos   BT Research and Technology, UK

Workshops and Tutorial Chairs

Bimal Roy   ISI Kolkata, India
Srijith Nair   BT Benelux

Panel / Special Session Chairs

S. Raghavan   IIT Madras, India
Steve Marsh   Communications Research Centre, Canada

Graduate Symposium Chairs

G. Sivakumar   IIT Mumbai, India
Yuko Murayama   Iwate Prefectural University, Japan

Postgraduate School Chairs

R.K. Shyamsunadar   TIFR Mumbai, India
Fabio Martinelli   IIT CNR, Italy

Publicity Chair

Anirban Basu   Tokai University, Japan

Program Committee

Adrea Zisman   City University London, UK
Andrew Jones   Kustar, UAE
Anirban Basu   Tokai University, Japan
Anish Mathuria   DAIICT Gandhinagar, India

Audun Jøsang	University of Oslo, Norway
Benjamin Stach	University of Kassel, Germany
Bimal Roy	ISI Kolkata, India
Christian Damsgaard Jensen	DTU, Denmark
D. Harrison McKnight	Michigan State University, USA
Daniele Quercia	University of Cambridge, UK
David Chadwick	University of Kent, UK
Dhiren Patel	NIT Surat, India
Ehud Gudes	Ben-Gurion University, Israel
Elena Ferrari	University of Insubria, Italy
Elisa Bertino	Purdue University, USA
Fabio Martinelli	IIT-CNR, Italy
Frederic Cuppens	Telecom Bretagne, France
G. Sivakumar	IIT Bombay, India
Ian Wakeman	University of Sussex, UK
Javier Lopez	University of Malaga, Spain
Jean-Marc Seigneur	University of Geneva, Switzerland
Kanta Matsuura	University of Tokyo, Japan
Ketil Stoelen	SINTEF, Norway
Licia Capra	University College of London, UK
Limin Jia	Carnegie Mellon University, USA
Mahesh Tripunitara	University of Waterloo, Canada
Masakatsu Nishigaki	Shizuoka University, Japan
Muttukrishnan Rajarajan	City University London, UK
Mogens Nielsen	Århus University, Denmark
Naranker Dulay	Imperial College London, UK
Nektarios Georgalas	BT UK
Nicola Dragoni	DTU, Denmark
Nurit Gal-Oz	Ben-Gurion University, Israel
Pandurangan Chandrasekaran	IIT Madras, India
Peter Herrmann	Norwegian University of Science and Technology, Norway
Pierangela Samarati	University of Milan, Italy
Pierre de Leuse	AGH, Poland
Pratyusa K. Manadhata	Symantec Research Labs, USA
R.K. Shyamasundar	TIFR Mumbai, India
Rajat Moona	IIT Kanpur, India
Rehab Alnemr	Hasso-Plattner Institute, Germany
Rino Falcone	CNR, Italy
Roslan Ismail	Universiti Tenaga Nasional (UNITEN), Malaysia
Srijith Nair	BT Benelux
Stephen Marsh	Communications Research Centre, Canada

Sponsored by

IFIP WG11.11
ISEAP NIT Surat India
TCS and C-DAC

Table of Contents

Full Papers

Short Papers

Invited Keynote Papers

Co-evolving Trust Mechanisms for Catering User Behavior

Tanja Ažderska

Laboratory for Open Systems and Networks, Jozef Stefan Institute, Jamova 39,
1000 Ljubljana, Slovenia
atanja@e5.ijs.si

Abstract. While most of the computational trust models devote to truthfully detecting trustworthy individuals, much less attention is paid to how these models are perceived by users, who are the core of the trust machinery. Understanding the relation between trust models and users' perception of those models may contribute for reducing their complexity, while improving the user-experience and the system performance. Our work recognizes reputation, recommendation and rating systems as online trust representatives and explores the biased behavior resulting from users' perception of those systems. Moreover, we investigate the relation and inter-dependencies between trust mechanisms and user behavior with respect to context, risk, dynamics and privacy. We perform experimental study and identify few types of cognitive biases that users exhibit. Based on the identified factors and the findings of the study, we propose a framework for addressing some of the issues attributed to users' biased behavior.

Keywords: trust, bias, context, reputation, recommendation, rating.

1   Introduction

Few decades ago, trust was a feeling and a reality. The curiosity of 'feelings often diverging from reality' made trust a major constituent of social studies. Person A may believe that B is trustworthy, although that is not the case, but A may also believe in the opposite (B being non-trustworthy), although it may not be the case. This led to the creation of social models of trust. Nowadays, trust has also come to represent people's beliefs in the entities met in the virtual world, leading to the design of many computational models of trust. However, the models that represent the relationship between A and B can easily fail to capture both sides of the story: how much A trusts B, and whether B is really trustworthy. In other words, how much the model resembles reality, how much it comes closer to human perceptions and actions, and how much the two differ. In this study, we take the stance that trust has its own representatives in the online environment. We recognize reputation, rating, and recommender systems (henceforth denoted as RRR systems) as the online representative of trust. We see the elements of the three (RRR) systems as ones that are different, but in often complement one another. However, the adequate combination of RRR depends on many factors, and the failure to recognize those factors leads to inconsistencies in the work of the RRR system as a whole. Moreover, user behavior is largely influenced by the work of those systems, and it largely influences the systems performance as well.

T. Dimitrakos et al. (Eds.): IFIPTM 2012, IFIP AICT 374, pp. 1–16, 2012.

The contribution of our work is in the following: we detect and analyze four factors that influence the work of RRR systems when they are required to co-evolve as a single solution for providing good user experience, system reliability and result accuracy. Those factors are context, risk, dynamics and privacy. We put users in the core of RRR systems, and investigate the inter-dependencies between RRR systems and user behavior with respect to the four identified factors. We analyze several types of cognitive biases that users exhibit in their online experiences with RRR systems. Then, we perform an experimental study that will allow us to identify several types of cognitive biases exhibited by the users, and that were not investigated in an RRR setting so far. Based on the identified factors and the findings of the experimental study, we propose a framework for addressing some of the issues attributed to users' biased behavior and explore the possibility of employing hidden signals in the RRR systems for the purpose of capturing some types of user behavior.

To provide a clear picture of our understating of social trust and its online representatives, in the following section we define the concepts. Then, we present related work in the area with the effort to move closer to each other the social and the technical aspect. Finally, we present the stated contributions throughout Sections 4 and 5. We conclude in Section 6.

2   The Notion of Trust and Its Online Representatives

2.1   Trust

From a social perspective, trust can be defined from two general aspects: cognitive and affective. The former is represented by concepts like rational choices, learning loops, institutional protocols, pattern detection, and imitation of established norms. Affective aspects, on the other hand, are mainly seen in the emotional side of trust interactions, and they account for the human feelings. As feelings are heavier on energy, whereas thoughts are heavier in information, affective properties often "take the blame" for contributing to cognitively biased decisions [1]. The 'social' literature on trust and reputation is exhaustive [1–3]. Clearly, when seeing trust as a purely social phenomenon, it can only be ascribed to living beings, and manifested through the property of trustworthiness of entities that are not necessarily living beings themselves. However, the ability to trust nowadays is disentangled from purely social contexts. A trusting entity can be any agent capable to resolve cognitive conflicts, or do preferential filtering, ranking, or sorting. This makes the definition and even the purpose of trust hard to grasp and determine. The blurred line of where the human factor starts or stops to influence trust and trustworthiness, usually leads to neglecting the affective side when defining the computational analog of trust. This, in turn, leads to the inability to predict the behavior of systems where trust models are deployed. These effects are caused by the highly non-linear nature of the trust phenomena, which do not allow a system to be designed according to the elegant principles of mathematical linearity and probabilistic averaging. Hence, knowing the composition of the system parts does not contribute a lot to inferring the properties of the system as a whole. It is critical to consider the interactions and dependencies between the entities that comprise the system, and capture the additional phenomena and properties that emerge from those interactions. Complementing this with the strong contextual dependence of trust explains why researchers have a hard time formalizing trust, and incorporating it into online scenarios analogous to those in the traditional social networks. Following Gambetta [4], we give the following initial definition:

Definition 1a. Trust is the belief, i.e., the subjective probability that an entity will perform in a way likely to bring the expected benefit, or not do an unexpected harm.

Considering trust only as a *subjective probability* leaves out an extremely important concept related to trust, that of *risk*. This fact has also been the catalyst of a vigorous debate between economists and social psychologists [3]. In circumstances where one entity *relies* on another, trust choices include a certain level of risk. Josang [5] defines two different types of trust, *Reliability* and *Decision trust*. The former covers the aspect of trust as stated by Definition 1a. The latter considers the risk brought about by the uncertainty of transactional outcomes and is used to extend our first definition:

Definition 1b. Trust is the extent to which one entity is willing to depend on others' decisions and actions, accepting the risk of a negative (undesired) outcome.

2.2 Online Representatives of Trust

Despite the relatively interchangeable use of trust and reputation in the research community, it is essential to understand the difference between the two.

Definition 2a. Reputation is the general standing of the community about an entity's trustworthiness, based on the past behavior, performance, or quality of service of that entity, in a specific context, i.e., a domain of interest.

Definition 2b. A system that facilitates the process of calculating and managing reputation is called a reputation system.

Hence, reputation is the amount of context-aware trust, i.e., a quantitative representation of the trust that the society places in an entity, bound by the domain of interest. In addition to reputation systems, we consider rating and recommendation systems to also be online representatives of trust. We define them as follows:

Definition 3. Rating systems manage the evaluation or assessment of something, in terms of quality, quantity, or a combination of both.

Definition 4. Recommender systems are a subclass of information filtering systems that seek to predict the rating or preference that a user would give to an item or a social element they had not yet considered, using a model built from the features of an item (content-based) or the user's social environment (collaborative filtering) [6].

We use the terms *trust mechanisms* and *RRR systems* interchangeably in this work.

3 Related Work

3.1 Social

Some of the work done in social and behavioral sciences that inspired computational trust research was discussed in the previous section [1–3]. Neuroscience has also revealed that emotions and cognition, present in different areas of the human brain, interfere with each other in decision making, often resulting in a primacy of emotions over reasoning [7]. A very similar, although deceptively simple idea stands behind the outstanding work in Perceptual Control Theory: our perceptions are the only reality we can know, and the purpose of all our actions is to control the state of this perceived world [8]. The psychology of making trust-related choices is directly related to how people think and feel, perceive and decide. The brain has developed complex mechanisms for dealing with threats and risks. Understanding how it works and when it fails is critical to understanding the causal loop between trust-related perceptions and trust-related choices. An area with remarkable results about the irrationality, bias, and unpredictability of human actions in various circumstances and mindsets is Behavioral Economy [9–11]. In the context of preferential reasoning, their analyses show that users are often unaware of their taste, even for experiences from previously felt outcomes. Not only this reveals that taste is much more subtle than preference, but it shows that preference itself is not a stable property of human reasoning [12]. Experiments on persistency of user preferences about identical items at different instances of time proved significant fluctuation in the repeated preferential choices [10][13]. In contract and utility theory, the potential of employing trust mechanisms for dealing with information asymmetry was recognized long ago. When the possibility of post-contractual opportunism creates a context of moral hazard, trust mechanisms are employed for sanctioning undesired behavior. Another context of information asymmetry is adverse selection, and arises when one is required to choose a transaction partner whose type (good or bad) is unknown. In his work, Akerlof analyzes the effect of social and trading reputation on transaction outcome and market maintenance [14]. The study demonstrates that goods with low quality can squeeze out those of high quality because of the information asymmetry present in the buyers' and sellers' knowledge about the products – the problem of so called "lemon markets". Reputation mechanisms would balance this asymmetry, helping buyers make better-informed decisions by signaling the behavioral types of sellers, and at the same time providing incentives for sellers to exchange high-quality goods. Thus, Akerlof makes an instructive distinction between the *signaling* and the *sanctioning* role of RMs, which was only recently considered in computer science.

3.2   Technological

Understanding the behavioral implications of users in the field of computational trust is crucial, as the user factor in the processes met in online trust mechanisms is omnipresent. As online representatives of trust, RRR systems are also assigned the role of "devices" that help decision-making under information asymmetry (reputation and rating systems), and information overload (recommendation systems). In the former case, they have sanctioning and signaling role, and in the later case – directing and filtering role. The goal of employing RRR systems is to reduce the complexity that arises from information overload, and to lower the uncertainty present in the contexts of information asymmetry. Depending on the general context, however, the combination of the three (reputation, recommendation, and rating) requires different structuring to achieve the desired goals. This is discussed further in the following section. RRR systems rely to a great extent on preference inputs from users. Bias in these inputs may have a cascading error effect on the performance of the applied algorithms. This does not only affect the accuracy of the results, but it also influences the perceived system reliability. Hence, user preferences are malleable and affect system performance, but they are also largely influenced by the information provided by RRR systems. Yet, biased behavior, its causes and effects, are relatively unexplored issues in the field. But the fact that only a narrow set of cognitive biases has been tackled by the research community does not imply there are no significant studies made in this regard. In [18] and [19], authors investigate the so called self-selection bias, whereby users only rate the items (movies) they like most, causing extremely high average rating for the rated items. Such ratings are representative only for a specific group of users, but do not truthfully depicture the item's general quality. Furthermore, self-selection bias was proved to not only be a transient phenomenon, but also a steady state in the system [15]. Although seemingly absurd, there is also one positive implication from this result of "self-selection bias" sustainability: if there was a strategy in the managerial principles of some company to cause inflated ratings for certain products by the "first-mover effect" [17], this effect would be flattened out on the long run. Such issues may appear to have purely economic nature, but they seriously compromise the reliability and performance of current RRR systems. The high impact of online reviews on product sales was demonstrated in [18], uncovering some of the motifs behind companies' efforts to appear competitive on the market. Positive rating bias was noted throughout systems of different nature. eBay is claimed to owe its success to its reputation/feedback system, yet out of the 57% of the users that decide to leave feedback, 99% issue positive feedback [19]. Moreover, large amount (41%) of users prefers to stay silent rather than to leave a negative feedback. A proposal to interpret silence as part of the user feedback was proposed in [20].

4 Cognitive Bias and Its Loops of Causality in RRR Systems

Cognitive bias describes a replicable pattern in perceptual distortion, inaccurate judgment, or illogical interpretation [10]. Clearly, bias can be noticed in both perceptions and actions, and the two are bound by the way people process their perceptions in order to take an action (including non-action). The paradox that arises in RRR systems is that, although user preferences are overly biased and affect the system performance and reliability, the preferences themselves are largely influenced by the ratings and the results provided by RRR systems. In this section, we explore the causes and effects related to cognitive bias in RRR systems, and we identify four major factors that influence these causal loops of biased behavior.

4.1 Context and Bias

Context is the set of circumstances or facts that surround a particular event or situation. Here, we analyze three general contexts in which an online interaction can take place: one with *pure collaborative* elements, one with *collaborative and competitive* elements, and one with *collaborative, competitive, and monetary* elements. Clearly, each subsequent context includes the elements of the previous, implying added system complexity. Therefore, it is crucial to understand which elements can be adequately combined in order to meet a system design-goal, without encumbering its performance and flexibility to the extent of edging users out.

Once a reputation score becomes part of users' profiles, the users themselves become identifiable by their reputation, as if it guards their 'online brand'. Hence, maintaining a stable identity is crucial for the joined reputation value to make sense. On the other hand, being equipped with an online identity as a synonym for one's reputation gives rise to some new dimensions in the context of impression management. Once reputation is used as a signal for the user behavioral type, pure collaborative context ceases to exist. The requirement for conducting a successful impression management adds a competitive component to the system, and makes the reputation explicitly recognized as part of a person's social capital. Coupling this with the presence of bias implies that inflated (overly positive) reputation values in a system devaluates the reputation itself, as if the presence of reputation value defeated its purpose. Such a situation creates the need for additional incentives that will shift the reference for a good behavior from impression management to another context. What is often done in this regard is applying monetary elements to provide incentives for a desired behavior, which brings its own issues. Mixing purely collaborative context with monetary elements was already proved to throw a shadow on both the social intentions and the opportunity for monetary gain [10]. In addition to these more subtle influences, there are more detrimental effects that arise from inadequately combining such context-elements. Including monetary elements drastically increases the complexity of the system, and introduces inter-locking dependencies between the trust mechanisms and the outside environment. From a systemic perspective, this implies that the boundaries of the system are open to additional disturbances [21]. As a result, claiming predictability of the users' reputation scores, or moreover, of user and system behavior, diminishes, and failing to recognize this leads to system degradation, and eventually, system failure. This is also the core idea behind the Tragedy of Commons [22].

The soundness of the matters elaborated above was also demonstrated in practice. By announcing its Partner's Program[1] in May 2007, YouTube explicitly offered its highest rated users to earn revenue from advertisements placed next to their videos. This instantly triggered series of events of users blaming each other for using automated programs to inflate their videos' ratings[2]. While the effect of these blames is related to the tragedy of commons [22], the effect of using programmed agents to inflate one's own rating is known as the Cobra effect [23]: the solution of a problem makes the problem worse. These effects are often result of systemic ignorance, and only retrospectively analyzed by many system designers.

Pure collaborative contexts exist when a reputation is used internally in the system (for e.g., to provide a reference or serve as a regulator for the flow of some system processes), also implying keeping users' reputation private, or if the acquiring of reputation is not bound to one's performance, i.e. it is not used for signaling purposes.

Clearly, when making the decision of which contextual elements to choose as part of a system, context is intimately related to risk. With the addition of each element, the complexity increases, and the perceived risk is hardened by additional factors. Furthermore, privacy appears worthy of consideration as an option for limiting the detrimental effects of added complexity. The goal of this study is to have a holistic look on RRR systems through the defined factors, rather than analyzing each of them independently. Therefore, the next section examines the link between risk and bias.

4.2   Risk and Bias

Risk is conceived as the possibility of triggering unexpected, unlikely, and detrimental consequences by means of a decision attributable to a decision maker [21].

---

[1]   http://www.youtube.com/creators/
[2]   http://gigaom.com/video/real-or-robot-the-lisanova-controversy/

Uncertainty is part of every online interaction. The extent of uncertainty, the expected utility, and the cost required for performing an action, influence the perceived risk a transaction brings. The field of prospect theory offers an incredible amount of experimental work demonstrating the myriad of cognitive biases that people exhibit when faced with risk and uncertainty [11]. A phenomenon that binds risk and uncertainty is the so called *pseudo-certainty effect*, which reflects the tendency of people to be risk-averse if the expected outcome is positive, but risk-seeking when they want to avoid negative outcomes. While it is a curiosity to inspect the properties of each bias independently, in reality biases are often coupled together, acting as both the cause and the effect of human perceptions and actions. The property of non-linearity we assigned to trust systems implies that complementing few biases together does not mean that their causes and effects will work in an additive fashion. Prospect theory has demonstrated that people underutilize consensus information, and when given descriptive facts about the quality of a person, they make choices regardless of the statistics offered about that person [11]. Josang et al. provide a formal proof of this phenomenon known as the *base-rate fallacy*, and give a formal framework for accounting for this fallacy in a computational setting [24]. Information offered in RRR systems is to a great extent a statistic produced by the collective efforts of the community members. This information can be represented in various ways - numerically, descriptively, as a single or multi-valued component, or as a combination of those. Therefore, it is important to explore how users perceive different types of information, and whether the descriptive and the numerical representation of an entity's quality can collide in users' perception. This is something we also investigate in our experimental study.

4.3   Dynamics and Bias

To some extent, we already touched on the issue of dynamics and bias when discussing the inconsistency of user preferences over time [10]. Here, we stay more in the context of trust and reputation, and connect the dynamics-factor with the previously defined – risk and context.

From the definitions of trust and reputation (Definitions 1and 2), it becomes clear that the dynamics of trust differs from the dynamics of reputation. This discrepancy cannot be captured by any model, as both trust and reputation are in reality intangible matters. Yet, the social models and protocols for detecting malice seem to be successful. In RRR systems, one way the dynamics of reputation is embedded in the models is through discounting the relevance of gathered information by some time-factor. However, such approach disregards the importance that some information had in the past in terms of its impact on the outcome. In other words, discounting by recency and frequency is not equal to discounting by impact. Doing the former may provide disincentives for the users who take important actions at a lower rate. Closely related to this issue is the bias of *rosy retrospection*, which is a tendency to rate past events more positively than they were actually rated when the event occurred [11]. This reflects the importance of accounting for the time-interval between item-consumption and provided feedback about that item. Unfortunately, our current experimental study does not tackle any of the concepts related to dynamics. However, as a disintegrable part of the bigger picture of online trust mechanisms, dynamics must be taken into consideration. Our future work will devote more attention to this factor.

4.4   Privacy and Bias

In [25], authors show that individual interpretations of trust and friendship vary, and the two concepts are correlated to other characteristics of a social tie and to each other in a non-symmetric way. Furthermore, they provide evidence that raters consider how a ratee's reputation might be affected by the feedback. This fear of bad-mouthing and reciprocation in the context of impression management is directly related to the fear of retaliation in e-commerce systems [19]. Together, these factors also help to explain patterns like higher reciprocity in public ratings, and the near absence of negative ratings. Given this reluctance to publicly leave negative feedback, the question arises: why offer multi-valued choice for item evaluation in the first place. Moreover, why showing it publicly if it affects the users' decisions to an extent that makes it useless.

Closely related to privacy and the context of impression management are the concepts of individual and group behavior, and similarly, individual and group bias. Whereas most of the biases we mentioned so far were characteristic for an individual, we would fall extremely short on a useful discussion if we do not touch upon group behavior as well. After all, building reputation is essentially a social process, regardless of the fact that trust individuals cherish for one another underlies this process.

In [26], authors study the anchoring effect that item ratings have on user preferences. They find that users' inclination towards providing positive feedback is additionally amplified if users see the current rating that an item got by the rest of the community members. That people imitate, or do what others do, especially when having no determined preferences, is nothing new. This is often the cause of what is known as group polarization, bandwagon effect, or herd behavior, depending on the field of study that identifies it [9]. In the context of RRR systems, a study on group polarization on Twitter showed that, like-minded individuals strengthen group identity [27]. In other words, when part of group situations, people make decisions and form opinions that are extreme than when they are in individual situations. For RRR systems, this implies that it is not only important to acquire a significant amount of user feedback, but to also investigate whether this amount of user opinions was inferred from sufficient number of independent sources. A formal apparatus for resolving such issues in a computational setting can be found in [28], where the author provides a framework for reasoning with competing hypothesis using Subjective Logic.

The following section describes the experimental study and analyzes the findings through the factors defined above. Moreover, it proposes some ways to address the revealed issues.

5   Experimental Work

Objectives: The major objective of this survey was to provide data that will help us investigate the compatibility between users' perceptions of the RRR system and its design objectives, but also reveal new directions for reasoning about the interrelations between users and systems. The main questions we aim to answer are:

— Which descriptive model resembles closest user perception of numerical feedback?
— How does a slight difference in the 'tone' of presented choices in the two descriptive models influence users' decision?

— How does the presence/absence of different contextual elements influence user choice, and is it related to the nature (numerical or descriptive) of the alternatives?

Design and Methodology: Two types of methods were used to gather the necessary data – an online survey method[3] was chosen for better geographical spread of respondents, speed of data collection and independence of participants' opinions; and direct (one-on-one) interviews were performed to capture some of the subtleties that are ungraspable by only observing the outcomes of the systems. Such subtleties are the discrepancy between preferences of the majority of individuals and the group preference, the huge difference in the choices made as new contextual elements are introduced or taken away, the difference and inter-dependence between trustworthiness and acquaintanceship, etc. Each survey contained the same two questions, but offered slightly different evaluation choices. The questions represented real reviews for HP Laptop taken from *Epinions*[4]. To not disturb the flow of the paper, they are given in the Appendix. All three groups were asked to rate the reviews for their usefulness. The first group (Survey 1) was asked to give a numerical rating on a scale 1 to 5 (1 = lowest and 5 = highest rating). The second and the third group were offered descriptive evaluation choices. However, among the possible answering choices for Survey 2, there were also such that stated explicit negative experience (Not useful at all), whereas the answering choices for Survey 3 varied from neutral to positive.

Table 1. Statistics about the experimental setting

Survey Info. Respond. Info.	Type of Survey			
	Survey 1	Survey 2	Survey 3	
	1-5 Num. Feedback	Neg.Descriptive	Neutral-Pos. Descriptive	Total
Answering choices	1	Not useful at all	Neutral	
	2	Hardly useful	Somewhat useful	
	3	Somewhat useful	Quite useful	
	4	Quite useful	Very useful	
	5	Extremely useful	Extremely useful	
Responded	22	22	22	66

Respondents: The experimental work is conducted over a population (both female and male) of 86 people, at the age of 20 – 50. Its completion required no special technical knowledge, and subjects had no difficulty understanding the assignment. Respondents were divided into 5 groups. Three groups of 22 people were formed for each survey type. Table 1 summarizes these statistics. 30 of the 66 survey respondents were also additionally interviewed. The results from these interviews are presented in the final subsection. In addition to the three groups, another 20 users were asked to independently evaluate each review (10 users per review). They expressed their evaluations both numerically, as in Survey 1, and descriptively, as in Survey 2.

Results: The following subsections show the major findings from this experimental study. Although the experiment was of relatively small scale, some interesting results were revealed with respect to the given objectives.

---

[3] www.surveymonkey.com
[4] www.epinions.com

5.1   Distinction Bias

As a first step in revealing the potential presence of cognitive bias in our experimental setting, we compare the results from the individually evaluated reviews with those obtained by the three surveys, where the two reviews were put together for evaluation. The goal is to reveal the potential presence of a *distinction bias*, manifested as a tendency to view two options as more dissimilar when evaluating them simultaneously than when evaluating them separately. This bias is often exploited in commerce scenarios, when sellers aim to sell a certain product (anchor) by placing it along with another - decoy product that appears as the worse option when put together with the anchor [10]. Fig.1 presents the results from the 20 independent evaluations of the two reviews. The horizontal axis shows the rating values, whereas the vertical – the number of users who provided the rating. As shown, both reviews were evaluated as equally useful, 2 on a 1 to 5 scale, and descriptively qualified as Somewhat Useful.

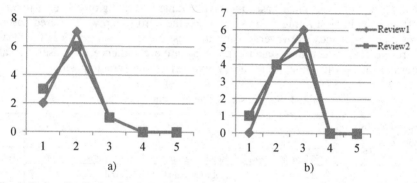

Fig. 1. Rating distribution for each review by offline users a) Numerically b) Descriptively

Fig.2 shows the difference in ratings between the two reviews for each of the surveys. Clearly, that they do not match with those shown in Fig1. In all three cases, Review 1 was evaluated as being better than Review 2. The mean values for the ratings of Review 1 and Review 2 for the three surveys are given in Table 2. Since preferences are often formed through distinction between given options, joint evaluation of recommendations may often result in a choice mismatch. The consequence is that the choice that appeared as the best option may not provide the best user experience, leading to dissatisfaction. Clearly, the issues of distinction bias and anchoring effect are important to account for in the design of RRR systems. The question is: what is the cause of those biases, what their effects are, and how to account for them in practice. The next section aims to provide the answer.

Table 2. Mean value for the ratings of the surveys

	1-5 Num. Feedback	Neg. Descriptive	Neutral/Pos. Descriptive
Review 1	3,727	3,545	3,636
Review 2	2,5	3,18	1,95

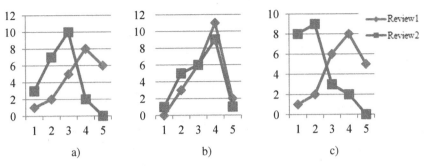

Fig. 2. Rating Distribution for the two reviews for a) Survey 1, b) Survey 2 and c) Survey 3

5.2 Numerical-Descriptive Discrepancy and Positive Bias

In order to address distinction bias and anchoring effect, we must first understand if and how the presented evaluation choices affect the user opinion. This section investigates which of the descriptive surveys comes closest to the one with numerical ratings. The practical implication is in exploring if the current RRR systems that offer numerical ratings really match the user understanding about the meaning of those ratings. For that purpose, we compare the rating distributions of the two reviews for Survey 1 to those of Survey 2 and Survey 3.

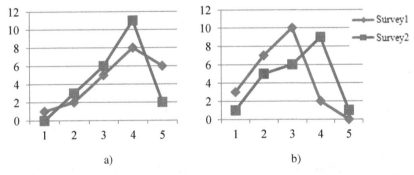

Fig. 3. Difference in Rating Distribution between Survey 1 and 2 for a) Review1 b) Review2

The results are shown in Fig.3 and Fig.4 respectively. It can be noticed that there is a good match for the distributions of Review 1 in both of the cases. However, compared to the distributions on Fig.1, there is still a great difference between the average rating value for Review 1 (1.9) provided by the independent user evaluations, and the average rating value for Review 1 in Survey 1 (3.727), Survey 2 (3.545) and Survey 3 (3.636). We identify the following causal link: distinction bias is caused when Review 1 and Review 2 are put together for evaluation, whereby Review 1 appears as the better option; moreover, Review 1 also appears as one of exceptional quality, leading to a positive bias and exaggerated positive rating.

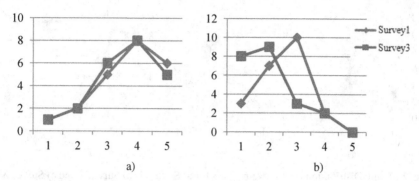

Fig. 4. Difference in Rating Distribution between Survey 1 and 3 for a) Review1 b) Review2

5.3 Positive Bias and the Framing Effect

In this section, we analyze the two surveys with descriptive evaluation choices. They differ slightly by the tone of positivism, although both offer five choices. Survey 2 contains more explicit negative statements, while the choices in Survey 3 vary from neutral to positive. The question we want to answer is *How does a difference in descriptive choices affect users evaluation?* To do that, we compare the rating distribution of the reviews for Survey 2 and Survey 3. The results are given in Fig.5a) and b).

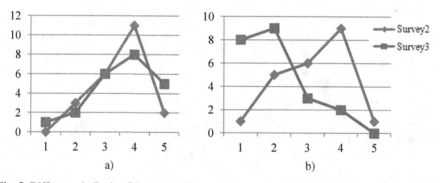

Fig. 5. Difference in Rating Distribution between Survey 2 and 3 for a) Review 1; b) Review 2

They reveal large difference in the evaluations of the reviews between the surveys, although the offered choices differ only slightly. This demonstrates that people tend to draw different conclusions from the same information, depending on how that information is presented, known as the *framing effect*. On Fig.5a), this effect is demonstrated as a slight smoothing of the exaggerated positives. Complementing these results with those shown on Fig.2b), we can conclude that for Survey 2, the ratings for the two reviews also come close to each other. One interesting result is the high mean rating value for Review 2 in Survey 2. Compared to the results on Fig.1, we see that the presence of a positive bias is higher when users are offered to chose between negative-positive evaluations, compared to a setting where they are required to choose between neutral-positive. In the next section, we use these findings to form our proposal on how to address some of the issues of the explored biased behavior.

5.4   Proposal: Hidden Signals and "Shades of Grades"

The remarkably higher number of neutral evaluations demonstrated by the experiment (Fig.5b)), which is even higher than the positive evaluations for Review 2 (Fig.5a)), not only confirms the reluctance of users to give negative ratings, but also points out the importance of neutral vote as a connector between negative and positive. In addition to introducing neutral as a "shade" between negative and slightly positive, another finding in our study is that introducing Very Useful as a shade between Quite Useful and Extremely Useful shifts the exaggerated positives towards lower ratings. Both of these effects smooth the effects from positive bias, but also better capture people's perception of the offered choices. This might also explain why the offline model of social reputation succeeds to detect untrustworthy individuals without requiring consensus on someone's trustworthiness. The offline world offers numerous opportunities to pick on the hidden clues behind people's intentions. We consider the idea of introducing such hidden signals in the online RRR systems worth exploring.

The framework we propose for addressing the presented issues of biased behavior can be summarized as follows: first, by accounting for the specific context elements, we propose disentangling the collaborative, competitive and the monetary elements when deciding on the RRR design. Second, by accounting for those context elements, a decision should be made about which of them are desirable as public features. Then, it is crucial to determine the right representation of publicly displayed features in a way that fits the users' perception of the feature's meaning. Finally, by introducing hidden signals and shades of grades about the qualitative types of the entities, a better and more truthful distribution of the results can be obtained.

5.5   Closing the Loop: The Market of Lemons on the Market of Opinions?

This section will close the loop of our study on cognitive bias by returning to the point where we started the discussion – context. The impact of context in the formation of cognitive bias required more interactive work with the respondents of the survey. Therefore, we additionally interviewed 30 people. The results are the following:

Q1. If you know that, depending on the ratings given for their reviews, reviewers will get proportionally higher/lower amount of money, would you give the same grade?

22 answered: *No, one or two grades lower.* **1** was *Not Sure*; **7** answered *Yes*;

Q2. What if you yourself were a reviewer and the amount of money you would get depended on the amount of money other reviewers for the same product get?

27 answered *Definitely a lower grade*; **3** answered *Still the same grade.*
The 3 who gave the 2b) answer were additionally asked:

Q3. If you see that the opinion you consider of low quality is the one that got the highest number of votes, would you reason the same the next time?

2 answered: *No*; **1** answered *Yes*.

The purpose of these questions was to investigate the reasoning of the respondents as they were required to switch between contexts. The interview is of very small scale, but still pointed to new directions for reasoning about user behavior through the elaborated contextual elements. There is, however, a deeper meaning of the obtained results: the exaggerated positives, the slight change in evaluation options followed by high difference in evaluations, and the rest of the biases we explored, may be merely the effects of user behavior in RRR systems. Different combination of particular contextual elements leads to different manifestation of the effects from those biases. Introducing monetary elements must be done with great caution, as it may cause information to be treated as a limited resource of monetary value, or as a trading resource in the process of acquiring social capital. This in turn leads to squeezing entities (items, agents, users) of potentially high quality out of the system, leading to what we refer here to as "the market of lemons on the market of opinions".

6   Concluding Remarks and the Way Forward

Trust is a feeling, a model, and a reality, with people in their core. Understanding how they work and how closely they resemble each other is essential for their design practices. Our work detected and analyzed context, risk, dynamics and privacy as factors that influence both the work of RRR systems and the users' understanding of that work. We explored the relation between RRR systems and user behavior with respect to those factors and analyzed few types of biases exhibited through the users' online experiences with RRR systems. In an experimental study that included 86 users, we found that users exhibit distinction bias, positive bias, anchoring effect, and framing effect. These have not been investigated in such a holistic manner for any of the current RRR systems. Based on the identified factors and the findings of the experimental study, we proposed a framework for tackling some of the issues attributed to users' biased behavior and address the possibility of employing hidden signals and shades of grades in the RRR systems for the purpose of capturing some of the detected biases.

Our future work will concentrate on investigating more the factor of dynamics. As we already referenced Perceptual control theory and Subjective Logic as an apparatus that provides formal reasoning with respect to human beliefs and perceptual behavior, the major part of our work will be directed towards joining the ideas of the two and employing them to formalize trust relationships under biased user behavior.

Acknowledgments. Authors wish to thank Tomaž Klobučar, Dušan Gabrijelčič and Borka Jerman Blažič for the devoted time and energy, their opinions, critiques, and immensely beneficial discussions regarding the topics of this work.

References

1. Zajonc, R.B.: Feeling and thinking: Preferences need no inferences. American Psychologist 35(2), 151–175 (1980)
2. Conlisk, J.: Why Bounded Rationality? Journal of Economic Literature 34(2), 669–700 (1996)
3. Castelfranchi, C., Falcone, R.: Trust is much more than subjective probability: Mental components and sources of trust. In: 32nd Hawaii International Conference on System Sciences - Mini-Track on Software Agents, Maui, vol. 6 (2000)
4. Gambetta, D.: Can We Trust Trust? In: Trust: Making and Breaking Cooperative Relations

5. Josang, A., Ismail, R., Boyd, C.: A survey of trust and reputation systems for online service provision. Decision Support Systems 43(2), 618–644 (2007)
6. Ricci, F., Rokach, L., Shapira, B.: Introduction to Recommender Systems Handbook. In: Ricci, F., Rokach, L., Shapira, B., Kantor, P.B. (eds.) Recommender Systems Handbook, pp. 1–35. Springer US, Boston (2011)
7. MacMullen, R.: Feelings in history, ancient and modern. Regina Books (2003)
8. Powers, W.T.: Behavior: The Control of Perception, 2nd edn. Benchmark Publications, Inc. (2005)
9. Kahneman, D.: Maps of Bounded Rationality: Psychology for Behavioral Economics. American Economic Review 93(5), 1449–1475 (2003)
10. Ariely, D.: Predictably Irrational: The Hidden Forces That Shape Our Decisions, 1st edn. HarperCollins (2008)
11. Kahneman, D., Tversky, A.: Subjective probability: A judgment of representativeness. Cognitive Psychology 3(3), 430–454 (1972)
12. Ariely, D., Loewenstein, G., Prelec, D.: Tom Sawyer and the construction of value. Journal of Economic Behavior & Organization 60(1), 1–10 (2006)
13. Cosley, D., Lam, S.K., Albert, I., Konstan, J.A., Riedl, J.: Is seeing believing?: how recommender system interfaces affect users' opinions. In: Proceedings of the SIGCHI Conference on Human Factors in Computing Systems, New York, NY, USA, pp. 585–592 (2003)
14. Akerlof, G.A.: The Market for "Lemons": Quality Uncertainty and the Market Mechanism. The Quarterly Journal of Economics 84(3), 488–500 (1970)
15. Kramer, M.: Self-Selection Bias in Reputation Systems. In: Trust Management, vol. 238, pp. 255–268. Springer, Boston (2007)
16. Li, X., Hitt, L.M.: Self-Selection and Information Role of Online Product Reviews. Information Systems Research 19(4), 456–474 (2008)
17. Lieberman, M.B., Montgomery, D.B.: First-mover advantages. Strategic Management Journal 9(S1), 41–58 (1988)
18. Chevalier, J.A., Mayzlin, D.: The Effect of Word of Mouth on Sales: Online Book Reviews. Journal of Marketing Research 43(3), 345–354 (2006)
19. Resnick, P., Zeckhauser, R.: Trust among strangers in internet transactions: Empirical analysis of eBay' s reputation system. Advances in Applied Microeconomics 11, Bingley: Emerald (MCB UP), 127–157
20. Dellarocas, C., Wood, C.A.: The Sound of Silence in Online Feedback: Estimating Trading Risks in the Presence of Reporting Bias. Management Science 54(3), 460–476 (2008)
21. Luhmann, N.: Risk: a sociological theory. Transaction Publishers (2005)
22. Hardin, G.: Tragedy of the Commons. Science 162(3859), 1243–1248 (1968)
23. Siebert, H.: DerKobra-Effekt :wie man Irrwege der Wirtschaftspolitik vermeidet:Piper (2003)
24. Josang, A., O'Hara, S.: The base rate fallacy in belief reasoning. In: 2010 13th Conference on Information Fusion (FUSION), pp. 1–8 (2010)
25. Adamic, L., Lauterbach, D., Teng, C.-Y., Ackerman, M.: Rating Friends Without Making Enemies. In: Proceedings of the Fifth International AAAI Conference on Weblogs and Social Media, pp. 1–8 (2011)
26. Zhang, J.: Anchoring effects of recommender systems. In: Proceedings of the Fifth ACM Conference on Recommender Systems, New York, NY, USA, pp. 375–378 (2011)
27. Yardi, S., Boyd, D.: Dynamic Debates: An Analysis of Group Polarization Over Time on Twitter. Bulletin of Science, Technology & Society 30(5), 316–327 (2010)
28. Pope, S.: Analysis of Competing Hypotheses using Subjective Logic. Systems Technology, 13–16 (June 2005)

Appendix: Survey Questions (Reviews)

Review 1:

User Rating: OK; Ease of Use: 2;Quality of Tech Support: 1

Pros:1)Intel core i3 processor;2)Finger Print Sensor;3)Battery life

Cons:1)Build material;2)Intel integrated graphics;3)320GB hard disk space

The Bottom Line: This laptop is not recommended to any one, because of poor support quality. The products of HP were good 3 years ago. People loved them for their looks, reliability, performance and budgeted price. But after 2008 the reliability ratio of HP as compared to its competitors is far below in almost all aspects including price, performance, looks and the most important reliability. I myself was a big fan of this company but after facing the failure of consecutively two the PCs' from this company, I changed my view. My wife had this laptop and I bought this laptop for her as her birthday present three months ago, but just after two months, the screen got dead spot (small black spots) and the hing connecting the screen with keyboard also got broken. Still the laptop was running fine but last week its keyboard also stopped working, which sucks. All the money I paid for it gone in vain. My experience about: PROCESSOR: Intel core i3 processor clocked at 2.1 GHZ works really very fine for multitasking but it is not designed to handle more tasks. This pc is fine for web-surfing, word-processing, office work, watching movies. GRAPHICS: Intel integrated graphics are not capable of running blue ray movies silky smooth. BUILD MATERIAL: This laptop is made of seriously very cheap plastic. Its glossy surface is just a fingerprint magnet and you have to clean up the laptop after every single use. The glossy screen also causes panic while watching movies in sunlight. LACK OF HDMI PORT: This laptop lacks some of the most important port which is included in the laptops of this price range, i-e; HDMI port. The sound quality is good, battery life is also impressive and last about 3 hours (6 cell) even when watching movies. The security feature like Finger Print Sensor works great. Its light weight makes it easier to carry this laptop everywhere but it can't be called ultraportable laptop. Over all this laptop isn't recommended to any one whether the person is student or house wife.

[Recommended: No]

Review 2:

User Rating: Excellent; Ease of Use: 5; Quality of Tech Support: 4

Pros: I would buy another computer from HP

Cons: multiple hardware faults. (i.e hard to type and sensitive mouse pad)

HP ProBook 4530s is a extremely good product. The computer is lightweight and rugged. It's able to be put in a backpack and stuffed wherever you need to go. When i bought and received the computer i liked how the computer didn't come with a lot of extra software junk. Next, i like having a numeric pad and i will continue to buy computers with them from now on. For just web browsing and playing light computer games this computer is extremely fast. The key pad is not sensitive enough and i have to hit the keys hard a lot. Also if you have multiple fingers close to the mouse pad, the mouse pad goes crazy due to its many settings. The speaker system is excellent the loudest system i have heard on any computer system. The software for the finger ID gets weird every now and then i have to input my fingers a couple of times to log in. The settings are easy to change on the computer. The battery life is average to other computers. The computer hardware is nicely laid out and easy to find. Computer is worth the price i paid for it.

[Recommended: Yes]

Perturbation Based Privacy Preserving Slope One Predictors for Collaborative Filtering

Anirban Basu[1], Jaideep Vaidya[2], and Hiroaki Kikuchi[1]

[1] Graduate School of Engineering, Tokai University,
2-3-23 Takanawa, Minato-ku, Tokyo 108-8619, Japan
abasu@cs.dm.u-tokai.ac.jp, kikn@tokai.ac.jp
[2] MSIS Department, Rutgers, The State University of New Jersey
1, Washington Park, Newark, New Jersey, 07102-1897, USA
jsvaidya@business.rutgers.edu

Abstract. The prediction of the rating that a user is likely to give to an item, can be derived from the ratings of other items given by other users, through collaborative filtering (CF). However, CF raises concerns about the privacy of the individual user's rating data. To deal with this, several privacy-preserving CF schemes have been proposed. However, they are all limited either in terms of efficiency or privacy when deployed on the cloud. Due to its simplicity, Lemire and MacLachlan's weighted Slope One predictor is very well suited to the cloud. Our key insight is that, the Slope One predictor, being an invertible affine transformation, is robust to certain types of noise. We exploit this fact to propose a random perturbation based privacy preserving collaborative filtering scheme. Our evaluation shows that the proposed scheme is both efficient and preserves privacy.

1 Introduction

Recommender systems have come to the rescue of individuals accosted with the problem of information overload [1] as a result of the numerous services being offered over the World Wide Web, e.g. social networks, e-commerce catalogs, amongst others. Most automated recommendation systems employ two techniques: *profile-based* and *collaborative filtering* (CF). The former puts to use the information that relate to users' tastes in order to match the items to be recommended to them. In contrast, prediction through CF results from the recorded preferences of the community. While profile-based recommendation for a user with rich profile information can be thorough, CF is fairly accurate, without the need for the user's preferential history. CF has, thus, positioned itself as one of the predominant means of generating recommendations.

Based on filtering techniques, CF is broadly classified into: *memory-based* or *neighbourhood-based* and *model-based*. In *memory-based* approaches, recommendations are developed from user or item neighbourhoods, based on some sort of proximity (or deviation) measures between opinions of the users, or the ratings of the items, e.g. cosine similarity, Euclidean distance and various

T. Dimitrakos et al. (Eds.): IFIPTM 2012, IFIP AICT 374, pp. 17–35, 2012.
© IFIP International Federation for Information Processing 2012

statistical correlation coefficients. Memory-based CF can also be distinguished into: *user-based* and *item-based*. In the former, CF is performed using neighbour-hood between users computed from the ratings provided by the different users. The latter is item-based where prediction is obtained using item neighbourhoods, i.e. proximity (or deviation) of ratings between various items.

Model-based approaches, in contrast, are sometimes more applicable on large datasets for which some memory-based approaches do not scale well. In model-based approaches, the original user-item ratings dataset is used to *train* a compact model, which is then used for prediction. Such a model can be developed by methods borrowed from artificial intelligence, such as Bayesian classification, latent classes and neural networks; or, from linear algebra, e.g. singular value decomposition (SVD), latent semantic indexing (LSI) and principal component analysis (PCA). Model-based algorithms are usually fast to query but relatively slow to update. There are also the fast-to-query, fast-to-update well-known Slope One CF predictors [2].

CF based approaches perform better with the availability of more data. Furthermore, it may be possible to perform cross domain recommendations, if the corresponding data can be utilised (e.g. a person with a strong interest in horror movies may also rate certain Halloween products highly). However, sharing user-item preferential data for use in CF poses significant privacy and security challenges. Competing organisations, e.g. Netflix and Blockbuster may not wish to share specific user information, even though both may benefit from such sharing. Users themselves might not want detailed information about their ratings and buying habits known to any single organisation.

Due to the privacy concerns, recently there has been significant research on privacy-preserving collaborative filtering (PPCF). The two main classes of solutions are: *encryption-based* and *randomisation-based*. In the encryption-based techniques, prior to sharing individual user-item ratings data are encrypted using cryptosystems that support homomorphic properties. In the randomisation-based privacy preserving techniques, the ratings data is randomised either through random data swapping or data perturbation or anonymisation. Given the large quantities of data, there has been a growing push to perform CF on the cloud[1]. Since CF is typically done at the application level, it is ideally suited to Software as a Service (SaaS) clouds, which are used to deploy applications scalably on the cloud. However, all of the existing PPCF solutions suffer from either scalability or security when deploying on SaaS clouds.

Our key insight is that Lemire and MacLachlan's weighted Slope One predictor is very well suited for SaaS clouds, and being an invertible affine transformation, is robust to certain types of noise. We exploit this fact to propose a random perturbation based privacy preserving collaborative filtering scheme. We now give a short illustrative example to demonstrate this.

---

[1] For example, Netflix uses Amazon Web Services for their computing needs (http://techblog.netflix.com/2010/12/
four-reasons-we-choose-amazons-cloud-as.html)

1.1   Illustrative Example

In (unweighted) Slope One, we usually have $f(x) = x + b$ where x is a rating given in the rating query while b is extracted from the deviation matrix[2]. Let us take a simple example with five ratings of two features X and Y.

```
X = [1 3 1 3 5]
Y = [5 2 4 3 4]
```

If we are to predict Y from X, we can use the basic Slope One predictor as $Y = X + \overline{(Y - X)}$ where the $\overline{(Y - X)}$ (i.e. the mean of the differences between Y and X) can be pre-computed. With the given data, we have $\overline{(Y - X)} = 1$, which gives us our Slope One predictor as a line $Y = X + 1$. If we now added random noise from a Gaussian distribution $\mathcal{N}(\mu = 0, \sigma = 5)$, we have a noisy data as follows.

```
pX = [-0.501160796 4.221286539 6.991751095 -7.917938198 10.47511263]
pY = [-1.388415841 8.382367701 12.66566552 1.829093784 -1.433503247]
```

Given this perturbed data, we have $\overline{(pY - pX)} = 1.357231329$, which gives us our Slope One predictor as a line $pY = pX + 1.357231329$. Thus, the lines

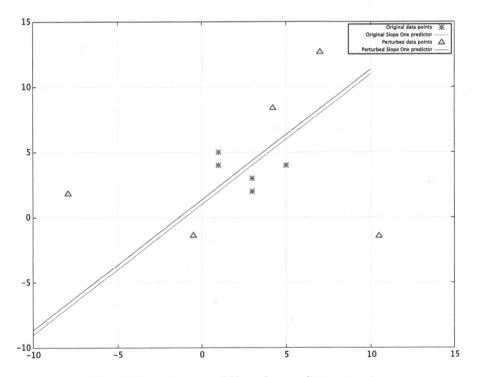

Fig. 1. The robustness of Slope One predictors to noise

---

[2] Please see the §2 for the basics of Slope One predictors.

represented by $Y = X + 1$ and $pY = pX + 1.357231329$ are parallel with a small offset between them.

In figure 1, we plot the scatter digram of the original data points, the perturbed data points and then the two Slope One predictor lines. From the figure, we can infer that despite the the perturbed data being significantly different from the original data, the basis for prediction – the Slope One lines – are very similar in both cases, identifying the robustness of Slope One to additive noise. Thus, the key insight of this paper is that the Slope One predictor is essentially a line on a 2D graph which is largely unaffected by data perturbation and is easy to compute. This lends itself as a robust perturbation based CF suitable for the cloud.

1.2   Our Contribution

In this paper, we demonstrate the effect of noise on the weighted Slope One predictor, and then, propose a privacy preserving collaborative filtering scheme. The specific contributions of this paper are: (i) ours is the first attempt, to our knowledge, to have proposed a PPCF scheme using random data perturbation on the weighted Slope One predictor; (ii) we present comparative performance analysis of more than one data perturbation methods alongside other related randomisation-based PPCF work; and (iii) we also take into account implementation concerns in real world cloud computing platforms particularly in terms of scalability.

The rest of the paper is organised as follows: we briefly present background of Slope One in §2 followed the key related work in this area and our previous work in §3. In §4, we examine the effects of random noise on the weighted Slope One predictor leading to the §5 which presents the problem statement in §4.1, proposals of PPCF schemes and a discussion on the level of privacy. In §6, we present implementation and evaluation results of our proposal followed by a conclusion and promising future directions in §7.

2   Slope One for Collaborative Filtering

2.1   The Weighted Slope One Predictor

Lemire and MacLachlan proposed [2] a CF scheme based on predictors of the form $f(x) = x + b$, hence the name "slope one". Before delving into PPCF, we present a brief overview of the Slope One predictors. In the following example, we will use the discrete integral range of ratings $[1 - 5]$ with "0" or "-" or "?" representing absence of ratings. Table 1 shows a simple user-item ratings matrix of users rating airlines companies.

The simplest Slope One prediction of rating for any user for an item i_1 given the user's rating for i_2 (i.e. r_{i_2}), is of the form $r_{i_1} = \overline{\delta_{i_1,i_2}} + r_{i_2}$ where $\overline{\delta_{i_1,i_2}}$ is the average deviation of the ratings of item i_1 from those of item i_2 while r_{i_2} is the rating the user has given to item i_2. The average deviation of ratings between a pair of items is calculated using only those ratings where both items have been rated by the same user.

Table 1. A simple three users, three items rating matrix

	British Airways	Emirates	Cathay Pacific
Alice	2	4	4
Bob	2	5	4
Tracy	1	?	4

Using the *unweighted* Slope One predictor, we derive the missing rating as:

$$? = \frac{(\frac{(4-2)+(5-2)}{2} + 1) + (\frac{(4-4)+(5-4)}{2} + 4)}{2} = 4.0$$

The unweighted scheme estimates a missing rating using the average deviation of ratings between pairs of items with respect to their *cardinalities*. Slope One CF has two stages: pre-computation (or update) and prediction of ratings. In the pre-computation stage, the average deviations of ratings from item a to item b is given as:

$$\overline{\delta_{a,b}} = \frac{\Delta_{a,b}}{\phi_{a,b}} = \frac{\sum_i \delta_{i,a,b}}{\phi_{a,b}} = \frac{\sum_i (r_{i,a} - r_{i,b})}{\phi_{a,b}} \tag{2.1}$$

where $\phi_{a,b}$ is the count of the users who have rated both items while $\delta_{i,a,b} = r_{i,a} - r_{i,b}$ is the deviation of the rating of item a from that of item b both given by user i.

In the prediction stage, the rating for user u and item x using the *weighted* Slope One is predicted as:

$$r_{u,x} = \frac{\sum_{a|a \neq x}(\overline{\delta_{x,a}} + r_{u,a})\phi_{x,a}}{\sum_{a|a \neq x} \phi_{x,a}} = \frac{\sum_{a|a \neq x}(\Delta_{x,a} + r_{u,a}\phi_{x,a})}{\sum_{a|a \neq x} \phi_{x,a}}. \tag{2.2}$$

Thus, we can pre-compute the *difference (or deviation) matrix*[3] $\Delta = \{\Delta_{a,b}\}$ and the *cardinality matrix* $\phi = \{\phi_{a,b}\}$, shown in figure 2. Note that for space efficiency, we only need to calculate the upper triangulars of those matrices because the lower triangulars can be easily derived from the upper ones, and the leading diagonals are irrelevant. The weighted Slope One has been found to be efficient, e.g. achieving a mean absolute error (MAE) rate close to 0.7 on the MovieLens 100K dataset[4], which is better than CF schemes using cosine similarity or another CF scheme using the Singular Value Decomposition, using a reference implementation in Apache Mahout[5].

In Slope One, the generalised form $f(x) = x + b$ where the constant b represents the deviation between an item pair makes this predictor particularly immune to additive random noise.

---

[3] Note that we do not need to compute average differences according to equation 2.2.
[4] http://www.grouplens.org/node/73
[5] http://mahout.apache.org/

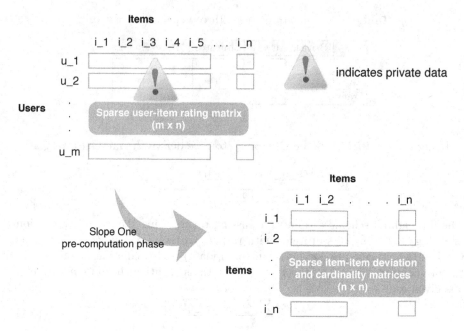

Fig. 2. The pre-computation phase of Slope One

3   Related Work

The problem of privacy preservation is compounded by the remarkable scales of real world datasets. Often, in PPCF, achieving efficiency or accuracy on one hand and preserving privacy of user-item preferential data on the other are orthogonal problems. While encryption-based solutions result in no loss of accuracy, homomorphic operations take toll on computational efficiency. In contrast, randomisation-based solutions are many orders of magnitude faster but only at the cost of accuracy. Servers these days are no longer just single units but clusters, or private and public clouds. The design of PPCF solutions ought to consider efficiency (both computational and storage) because of the immediate implications on costs.

There are a number of existing works on privacy-preserving collaborative filtering (PPCF). One of the earliest such efforts is due to [3] which uses a partial Singular Value Decomposition (SVD) model and homomorphic encryption to devise a multi-party PPCF scheme. In [4], the authors propose a naïve Bayesian classifier based CF over a P2P topology where the users protect the privacy of their data using masking, which is comparable to randomisation. Another homomorphic encryption based SVD scheme has been proposed in [5] but the authors also describe that their scheme does not scale well for realistic datasets; while a randomisation based SVD approach is described in [6]. A general survey of privacy preserving data mining in presented in [7].

In our recent works [8,9,10], we have proposed PPCF solutions based on the well-known weighted Slope One predictor [2]. Particularly, in [10] we also showed the applicability of our PPCF scheme on a real world public cloud computing platform.

One of the main differences between the existing works (including our own previous works) and the work presented in this paper is that the latter is more *efficient* than solutions using threshold homomorphic encryption while having an *accuracy* comparable to the more accurate encryption based PPCF schemes. Further to that, the model presented in this paper is applicable to a SaaS cloud, which most PPCF solutions are not.

3.1 Types of Privacy Threats to CF and Their Solutions

In general, whenever a CF scheme requires intermediate matrices (e.g. Slope One, SVD-based solutions) that do not contain private data, one can either opt for hiding (cryptographically or with perturbation) the values of ratings as they are submitted, or attempt to de-link such submissions from users by using some identity anonymisation mechanism. At query time, depending on how the intermediate matrices have been computed, the user's query vector can also be hidden using similar techniques. The cryptographic procedures ensures no change in accuracy from the original CF scheme but it comes at the cost of performance. The random perturbation methods ensure better performance at the cost of accuracy. In addition, a combination of both may also be usable depending on the CF scheme.

Notice that there is yet another scenario, which we do not cover in this paper. It is a multi-site scenario where user-item rating data is stored unencrypted, unperturbed in each site. The privacy of the data is considered a concern when it is shared amongst cites. This is particularly applicable in cross-domain collaborative filtering where users trust the sites that store their user-item rating data. In this paper, we assume the users do not trust any CF site and therefore the privacy of their data must be preserved throughout.

In figure 2, we observe that the user-item rating matrix poses a privacy risk for individual users but the item-item deviation and cardinality matrices do not. This privacy threat exists at the time of pre-computation or update of the deviation and cardinality matrices. There is also a privacy risk at the time of query in which the rating vector of the querying user may be exposed.

Preserving Privacy at the Time of Pre-computation. A number of measures can be taken to preserve the privacy at pre-computation time. One well-known procedure is to use a threshold homomorphic cryptosystem. Prior research works [5,9,10] have proposed that over other CF schemes as well as Slope One. Individual user's rating data are encrypted at the time of submission by a shared public key, thus leading to an encrypted deviation matrix. CF queries can then be responded to using the homomorphic property of the cryptosystem and decrypted by trusted third-party threshold decryption servers on behalf of the user. The main downside of this is the dependency on the trusted third party. In addition, the CF computation time is also increased due to the computational overhead of cryptographic operations.

Alternatives to the homomorphic encryption approach include anonymising as well as random perturbation of the data as they are recorded. Depending on the type of CF used, it may be necessary to get rid of the noise added through random perturbation. Techniques for noise removal include Bayesian filtering and spectral filtering amongst others. This is, however, not required in the weighted Slope One for certain types of noise distributions, as we will see in §4. In order to hide the number of ratings a particular user submits, some PPCF schemes normalise the user-item rating data, which essentially converts a sparse data problem into a dense one (e.g. [6]) contributing to significant costs in storage and computation.

Preserving Privacy at Query Time. At the time of query, the query vector (containing sensitive ratings) could be encrypted using a homomorphic cryptosystem, thus hiding the private ratings. The result of such queries ought to be decrypted by trusted third party servers. Alternatively, homomorphic public-key encryption may also be used in a different way (e.g. our earlier proposal [10]) whereby the querying user is solely in charge of decrypting the response, which helps eliminating the need for trusted third parties. On the other hand, the query may also contain randomly perturbed ratings such that the effects of the noise are removed from the noise after the prediction result is obtained. This technique, however, contributes to reduced accuracy.

4 Privacy-Preserving Slope One

4.1 Problem Statement

The problem can be formally defined in the following fashion:

Definition 1 (Privacy-Preserving weighted Slope One Predictor). *Given a set of m users $u_1, \ldots, u_m$ that may rate any number of n items $i_1, \ldots, i_n$, build the weighted Slope One predictor for each item satisfying the following two constraints:*

- *no submitted rating should be deterministically linked back to any user.*
- *any user should be able to obtain a prediction without leaking his/her private rating information.*

4.2 Additive Random Noise

In this section, we discuss the effects of various ways of including additive random noise: (1) random noise is added to the weighted Slope One deviation matrix only; (2) random noise is added to the user-item data for the weighted Slope One predictors; (3) in both cases, random noise is added to the query vector;

In our experiments, we also show the situation where random noise is not added to the query vector but the noisy deviations are rounded off to nearest integers to facilitate the use of a public-key cryptosystem in the query, as is the case in our earlier work [10].

Noise Added to Deviations Only. In the *pre-computation stage*, random noise (denoted by $\epsilon_{i,a,b}$), obtained from a known probability distribution, added to the deviation of a pair of items (a and b) by a user i generates a noisy deviation, given as:

$$\hat{\delta}_{i,a,b} = r_{i,a} - r_{i,b} + \epsilon_{i,a,b}. \tag{4.1}$$

where $\delta_{i,a,b} = r_{i,a} - r_{i,b}$ is the original deviation of the rating of item a from that of item b both given by user i. Therefore:

$$\hat{\Delta}_{a,b} = \sum_i \delta_{i,a,b} + \sum_i \epsilon_{i,a,b} = \Delta_{a,b} + \sum_i \epsilon_{i,a,b}, \tag{4.2}$$

In the *prediction stage*, adding another similar random noise (denoted as $\nu_{u,a}$) for every item a rated by the user u, the rating for the user u and item x using the *weighted* Slope One on the noisy deviations is predicted as:

$$\hat{r}_{u,x} = \frac{\sum_{a|a\neq x}(\hat{\Delta}_{x,a} + (r_{u,a} + \nu_{u,a})\phi_{x,a})}{\sum_{a|a\neq x}\phi_{x,a}} \tag{4.3}$$

$$\implies \hat{r}_{u,x} = \frac{\sum_{a|a\neq x}\Delta_{x,a} + r_{u,a}\phi_{x,a}}{\sum_{a|a\neq x}\phi_{x,a}} + \frac{\sum_{a|a\neq x}\sum_i \epsilon_{i,a,b}}{\sum_{a|a\neq x}\phi_{x,a}} + \frac{\sum_{a|a\neq x}\nu_{u,a}\phi_{x,a}}{\sum_{a|a\neq x}\phi_{x,a}} \tag{4.4}$$

$$\implies \hat{r}_{u,x} = r_{u,x} + \frac{\sum_{a|a\neq x}\sum_i \epsilon_{i,a,b}}{\sum_{a|a\neq x}\phi_{x,a}} + \frac{\sum_{a|a\neq x}\nu_{u,a}\phi_{x,a}}{\sum_{a|a\neq x}\phi_{x,a}}. \tag{4.5}$$

It is evident from equation 4.4 that the noisy prediction $\hat{r}_{u,x}$ contains small proportions of random noise. For example, if the noise data are drawn from a Gaussian distribution $\mathcal{N}(\mu = 0, \sigma = ubound(r))$ (where $ubound(r)$ denotes the maximum positive value of the ratings themselves) then the component

$$\frac{\sum_{a|a\neq x}\sum_i \epsilon_{i,a,b}}{\sum_{a|a\neq x}\phi_{x,a}}$$

nearly vanishes and the component

$$\frac{\sum_{a|a\neq x}\nu_{u,a}\phi_{x,a}}{\sum_{a|a\neq x}\phi_{x,a}}$$

is reasonably small for sufficiently large number of data points. This suggests that the prediction accuracy will be better if we added random noise only at the time of pre-computation. Results from our experiments confirm this analysis.

Noise Added to Ratings Only. In the *pre-computation stage*, random noise (denoted by $\kappa_{i,a}$ and $\lambda_{i,b}$), obtained from known probability distributions, added to the rating of each item respectively in a pair of items (a and b) by a user i generates a noisy deviation, given as:

$$\hat{\delta}_{i,a,b} = (r_{i,a} + \kappa_{i,a}) - (r_{i,b} + \lambda_{i,a,b}). \tag{4.6}$$

where $\delta_{i,a,b} = r_{i,a} - r_{i,b}$ is the original deviation of the rating of item a from that of item b both given by user i. Therefore:

$$\hat{\Delta}_{a,b} = \sum_i \delta_{i,a,b} + \sum_i (\kappa_{i,a} - \lambda_{i,a}) = \Delta_{a,b} + \sum_i (\kappa_{i,a} - \lambda_{i,a}). \qquad (4.7)$$

In the *prediction stage*, adding another similar random noise (denoted as $\iota_{u,a}$) for every item a rated by the user u, the rating for the user u and item x using the *weighted* Slope One on the noisy deviations is predicted as:

$$\hat{r}_{u,x} = \frac{\sum_{a|a\neq x}(\hat{\Delta}_{x,a} + (r_{u,a} + \iota_{u,a})\phi_{x,a})}{\sum_{a|a\neq x} \phi_{x,a}} \qquad (4.8)$$

$$\implies \hat{r}_{u,x} = \frac{\sum_{a|a\neq x} \Delta_{x,a} + r_{u,a}\phi_{x,a}}{\sum_{a|a\neq x} \phi_{x,a}} + \frac{\sum_{a|a\neq x}\sum_i(\kappa_{i,a} - \lambda_{i,a})}{\sum_{a|a\neq x} \phi_{x,a}} + \frac{\sum_{a|a\neq x} \iota_{u,a}\phi_{x,a}}{\sum_{a|a\neq x} \phi_{x,a}} \qquad (4.9)$$

$$\implies \hat{r}_{u,x} = r_{u,x} + \frac{\sum_{a|a\neq x}\sum_i(\kappa_{i,a} - \lambda_{i,a})}{\sum_{a|a\neq x} \phi_{x,a}} + \frac{\sum_{a|a\neq x} \iota_{u,a}\phi_{x,a}}{\sum_{a|a\neq x} \phi_{x,a}}. \qquad (4.10)$$

Similar to adding noise to deviations, we observe from equation 4.9 that the noisy prediction $\hat{r}_{u,x}$ contains small proportions of random noise. Again, if the noise data are drawn from a Gaussian distribution $\mathcal{N}(\mu = 0, \sigma = ubound(r))$ (where $ubound(r)$ denotes the upper bound of the range of rating values) then the component

$$\frac{\sum_{a|a\neq x}\sum_i(\kappa_{i,a} - \lambda_{i,a})}{\sum_{a|a\neq x} \phi_{x,a}}$$

nearly vanishes and the component

$$\frac{\sum_{a|a\neq x} \iota_{u,a}\phi_{x,a}}{\sum_{a|a\neq x} \phi_{x,a}}$$

is reasonably small for sufficiently large number of data points. Once again, this suggests that the prediction accuracy will be better if we added random noise only at the time of pre-computation. In fact, equation 4.9 is better in accuracy than equation 4.4 because the vanishing component

$$\frac{\sum_{a|a\neq x}\sum_i(\kappa_{i,a} - \lambda_{i,a})}{\sum_{a|a\neq x} \phi_{x,a}} < \frac{\sum_{a|a\neq x}\sum_i \epsilon_{i,a,b}}{\sum_{a|a\neq x} \phi_{x,a}}.$$

Do We Need Noise at the Time of the Query? Although in both of the above cases we used additive noise at the time of the query, it is possible to not use noise. As we will see in the experimental results, not using noise at the time of query increases accuracy. However, in order to preserve the privacy of the data in the rating query, we will have to use encrypted query with an additively homomorphic cryptosystem as we did in our earlier PPCF proposal in [10]. To facilitate the use of homomorphic encryption, we ought to round off fractional values of deviations before using them in the encrypted response of the query. In our experimental results, we show the effects of such rounding-off on accuracy.

4.3   Multiplicative Random Noise

Random noise multiplied to the deviation of a pair of items by a user i is given as:

$$\hat{\delta}_{i,a,b} = (r_{i,a} - r_{i,b})\epsilon_{i,a,b} = \delta_{i,a,b}\epsilon_{i,a,b}. \tag{4.11}$$

where $\delta_{i,a,b} = r_{i,a} - r_{i,b}$ is the deviation of the rating of item a from that of item b both given by user i, and $\epsilon_{i,a,b}$ is the noise multiplied to the deviation. Therefore:

$$\hat{\Delta}_{a,b} = \sum_i \delta_{i,a,b}\epsilon_{i,a,b}. \tag{4.12}$$

In the prediction stage, the rating for user u and item x using the *weighted* Slope One is predicted as:

$$\hat{r}_{u,x} = \frac{\sum_{a|a\neq x}(\hat{\Delta}_{x,a} + r_{u,a}\nu_{u,a}\phi_{x,a})}{\sum_{a|a\neq x}\phi_{x,a}} \tag{4.13}$$

We found that result of adding multiplicative noise is that the noise components are significant. Without further reconstruction methods, which are beyond the scope of this paper, the data with random multiplicative noise is unsuitable for use in prediction. Therefore, in the remainder of the paper, we present results only with additive noise.

5   Proposal for Privacy-Preserving Collaborative Filtering

5.1   Proposal A: Additive Noise to Ratings or Deviations

Having observed the theoretical effects of additive noise, we note that it is more efficient than adding multiplicative noise. One of our PPCF proposals is to have Gaussian noise added to either individual ratings or rating pair deviations as they are added by the users. This helps in masking the actual ratings at the time they are submitted. The CF site can use those submissions to update the deviation and cardinality matrices. At the time of query, once again, the user utilises Gaussian additive noise to hide the actual rating data in the query. The system architecture for PPCF utilising additive noise in this way is presented in the form of UML sequence in figure 3.

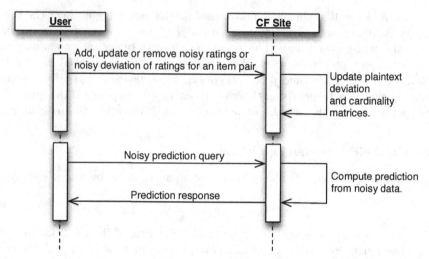

Fig. 3. UML sequence diagram of the proposed PPCF architecture utilising just noise

5.2   Proposal B: Combination of Additive Noise with Encrypted Query

In our second proposal, we suggest that while additive random noise can be used at the time of submitting the data to the CF site, the user can also combine that with encrypted queries using public-key encryption. Homomorphically encrypted queries are beyond the scope of this paper but can be found in our proposal on encrypted PPCF in [10]. The system architecture of this PPCF scheme supporting encrypted query is shown in figure 4.

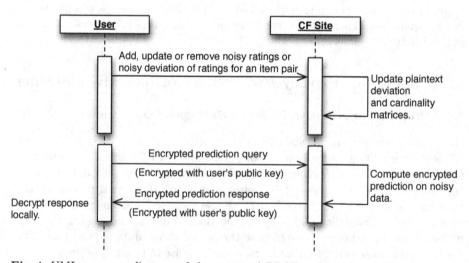

Fig. 4. UML sequence diagram of the proposed PPCF architecture utilising noise as well as encrypted queries

One important observation in terms of accuracy in this scheme is that the values of deviations are rounded off to nearest integers because we will need a specialised mechanism to encrypt IEEE floating point numbers with the Paillier cryptosystem. Such a mechanism may greatly reduce the usable length of the key space, which is why we round off the deviations to nearest integers. That will, however, have a small penalty on the accuracy of the prediction as we shall see in the results.

5.3 Level of Privacy

A number of methods [11,12,13] exist for quantification of the level of privacy preserved in a given data mining algorithm. Yet, it still an open question, beyond the scope of this paper, as to which one is the best [14]. Therefore, in this paper we qualitatively describe the level of privacy with the additive random noise, as shown in the aforementioned sections. Denoting the random noise variable by ϵ, the original rating variable by r, and the perturbed values by $\hat{r}$, we have $\hat{r} = r + \epsilon$. To an attacker, the distribution of ϵ is known and the distribution of $\hat{r}$ can be observed. The objective is to attempt to reconstruct the distribution of r.

Assuming that ϵ is derived from a Gaussian distribution $\mathcal{N}(\mu = 0, \sigma = k)$ where $k \geq ubound(r)$ ($ubound(r)$ is the upper bound of the range of rating values), we know that the distribution tapers off towards the positive and negative infinities, with majority of the values centered around the mean, i.e. 0 in our case. Now, let us use some concrete numbers. Let us say that $k = 5$ and that for any particular observation, we find $\hat{r} = -40$. Also, assume that the attacker is trying to determine if $r = 1$ for this case. If the attacker had another observation of $\hat{r} = 5$ then, in terms of conditional probability, we can tell $\Pr(\hat{r} = -40 \mid r = 1) < \Pr(\hat{r} = 5 \mid r = 1)$ simply because of the nature of the noise distribution, or even in general $\Pr(\hat{r} = -40 \mid r = 1)$ and in fact $\Pr(\epsilon = -41)$ is low. However, that statement does not imply that $\Pr(r = 1 \mid \hat{r} = -40)$ is equally low, or vice-versa, which is the inverse fallacy [15]. Therefore, the attacker cannot imply that $\Pr(r = 1 \mid \hat{r} = -40) < \Pr(r = 1 \mid \hat{r} = 5)$, because while $\Pr(r = 1 \mid \hat{r} = -40)$ could be low, that could be equal to $\Pr(r = 2, 3, 4, 5 \mid \hat{r} = -40)$ if r was following a uniform distribution. This leaves the attacker with little deterministic ability to infer the value of r. This observation is especially true because of the small bounded range of r and the large unbounded range of ϵ and therefore $\hat{r}$.

Now, from another angle for $\hat{r} = -40$ and $r = 1$, we know $\epsilon = -41$. If $r = 2, 3, 4, 5$ then $\epsilon = -42, -43, -44, -45$. We know that $\Pr(\epsilon = -41)$ is low and so are $\Pr(\epsilon = -41, -42, -43, -44, -45)$ and these probabilities are also very close to each other. Therefore, because of the bounded and small range of r, just looking at any value of $\hat{r}$, it is not possible to determine with the value of r with a high probability.

That proves that the unbounded range of the perturbed values makes it difficult to confidently determine the value of the original rating, without knowing the distribution of the original ratings. This is the scenario where noise is added to the ratings. If the noise is added to the deviation of ratings, the ability to determine the original ratings is decreased further. In addition, since the deviations also have a bounded small range, it is equally hard (as we discussed above) to determine even the value of the deviation from the value of the perturbed deviations when the noise, and therefore the perturbed deviations, have unbounded ranges.

6   Implementation and Evaluation

6.1   Implementation

Consideration: Reduce I/O Operations and Storage Volumes. With the intention to implement our proposals on a real world public cloud computing environment, we took the following considerations in mind. I/O with non-volatile storage is expensive both in terms of time and money on cloud computing platforms. Non-volatile storage on the cloud usually involves in a backend database, which is often replicated (e.g. high-replication datastore in Google App Engine). That implies that one database write operation could entail multiple write operations to database replicas, which in turn increases CPU and bandwidth usage, translating into direct costs to the cloud user. In addition to that, storage space is also charged per unit space per unit time, e.g. gigabytes per month. The larger the storage, the worse the costs. Therefore, it is essential to store as little data as possible.

Keeping this in mind, we have deliberately avoided a particular method of random perturbation: calculating the z-scores of rating data prior to introducing noise, in order to hide the number of items one user might have rated. This essentially transforms a sparse matrix problem into a dense matrix problem, which represents a huge performance hit. Both Amazon RDS and Google GAE/J cost significantly to store data. A dense matrix makes matters worse. For example, the MovieLens 100K dataset, when normalised to z-scores contains over 1.58 million data points compared to the sparse 100,000 in the original rating data. That is an over 1,500% increase in stored data translating directly into that much increase in storage costs in addition to the CPU costs for redundant storage. In fact, we do not store the user-item rating matrix at all but store the sparse deviation and cardinality matrices.

Implementation Environment and Data Structures. The results presented in this paper are obtained from a trial, non-cloud, single-machine implementation on Java. We used a 64-bit Mac OS X 10.7.2 and 64-bit Java 1.6.0_29 environment on an Apple Macbook Pro running a 64-bit 2.53GHz Intel Core i5 and 8GB RAM.

The storage of the following two matrices is an important factor in the efficiency of pre-computation as well as prediction: (1) the item-item deviation matrix, and (2) the item-item cardinality matrix. Note that we do not store the user-item ratings matrix at all.

There is significant level of sparseness in the stored data. Although the deviation and cardinality matrices are not as sparse as the user-item ratings matrix, only the upper triangulars of the deviation and cardinality matrices are stored. Using in-memory storage, the sparseness requirement informs us that a 2-dimensional array (e.g. `long[][]`) is an unsuitable storage data structure. While the simple 2-D array provides constant time, i.e. $O(1)$ lookup performance, it is an unjustifiable waste of storage space and makes resizing difficult. The resizable `ArrayList` implementation provides an $O(1)$ lookup performance but $O(n)$ time complexity for the addition operation.

If we access a 2-D matrix by either row-major order or column-major order but not both at the same time then it can be represented by a `Map<K1, Map<K2, V>>`. Java's `TreeMap` implementation provides $O(log\ n)$ lookup and storage performance while `Hashtable` and `HashMap` both provide constant time lookup and storage. Having tested Oracle (Sun) JVM's `HashMap` and `Hashtable` implementations, we found that `HashMap` is faster although there is no theoretical basis supporting this view and may be purely JVM implementation specific. Although mostly similar, one of the differences between `Hashtable` and `HashMap` is that the latter allows `null` values for keys and objects, which is irrelevant in our context. `HashMap` iterator is fail-safe, which means changes made to the map get reflected in its iterator.

Having chosen an efficient data structure, i.e. `HashMap`, we looked at the data types for `K1`, `K2` and `V` because that affects performance too. Both `K1` and `K2` are integers (perhaps `long`) while `V` could contain double precision floating point numbers (`double`) for deviations and `long` for cardinalities. Realistically, the value of the keys is well expressed by Java's primitive 32-bit `int` with a positive range of $[0\ (2^{31} - 1)]$. This is enough for indexing rows and columns: a $(2^{31} - 1)$ by $(2^{31} - 1)$ square matrix is extremely large! There is also another advantage of a `HashMap<Integer,V>` because `Integer` provides "a hash code value for this object, equal to the primitive int value represented by this Integer object"[6], which is faster to compute than that for a `Long`, i.e. "`(int)(this.longValue()^(this.longValue()>>>32))`"[7].

In this context, the semantics of an "empty" deviation-cardinality tuple must be understood in order to ensure that the deviation-cardinality matrix allows sparseness by not storing empty tuples. Since the deviation value of zero does not indicate an absence of deviation, "emptiness" is determined by the cardinality value of zero. There is also another point that aids the sparse nature of the matrix – the storage of the upper triangular of the matrix only, discarding the lower triangular and the leading diagonal. While this behaviour is controllable through the matrix access methods, the tuple itself in our implementation enables access to the not-stored lower triangular by inverting the stored value in the upper triangular. Note that the cardinality is not inverted but the deviation (Δ) is, i.e. $\Delta_{i,j} = -\Delta_{j,i}$.

---

[6] See: `http://download.oracle.com/javase/6/docs/api/java/lang/Integer.html`
[7] See: `http://download.oracle.com/javase/6/docs/api/java/lang/Long.html`

In the Context of the Cloud. Note that the choice of this local in-memory storage data structure somewhat corresponds to storage on the cloud too. For fast access to the deviation-cardinality data on the cloud, we have to use some kind of distributed cache (e.g. memcached) – both Google App Engine for Java and Amazon Web Services provide distributed cache services, which are somewhat similar to the basic `Hashtable<K,V>` structure. Beyond the cache, the distributed databases can also store individual sparse data points using matrix row-column based 2D indexing through database tables, i.e. to store the value at the ith row and the jth column, we simply add a row in the database table that contains the matrix row number (i.e. i), the column number (i.e. j) and any values associated with them. This is the way, we stored data in our earlier PPCF proposal [10].

6.2   Evaluation Results

All experiments have been run with the MovieLens 100K dataset. In table 2, we present different combinations of our PPCF proposals. We also cite the results of Polat and Du's paper [6], our own work on homomorphic encryption based

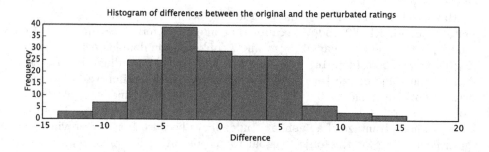

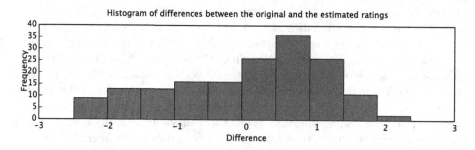

Fig. 5. Histograms showing the comparison of the difference between the original and perturbed ratings, and that between the original and the estimated ratings for a random user. In this histogram, we have only compared those values for which the original ratings were present.

Table 2. Comparison of results of this work with others using the MovieLens 100K dataset

	PPCF strategy	MAE	Prediction time	Stored data
Non-PPCF baseline	None	0.7019	0.22ms	Item-item deviation, cardinality matrices.
A1	Perturbation	0.8346	0.23ms	Item-item deviation, cardinality matrices.
A2	Perturbation	0.8307	0.234ms	Item-item deviation, cardinality matrices.
B1	Perturbation	0.7113	0.233ms	Item-item deviation, cardinality matrices.
B2	Perturbation	0.7081	0.231ms	Item-item deviation, cardinality matrices.
Basu et al. [9]	Encryption	0.7057	4500ms	Item-item deviation/cardinality matrices
Polat and Du [6]	Perturbation	0.7104[a]	Unknown	z-scored and randomised user-item rating matrix and its singular value decompositions.

[a] This data provides approximate comparability with our results because of the differences of samples over which the MAE calculations have been made as well as the level of noise added. For example, the noise added in Polat and Du's paper had a standard deviation of 1 whereas we used a standard deviation of 5.

PPCF [9] and the baseline Slope One for comparison. The different combinations of our PPCF proposals are listed as follows.

A1: This is where Gaussian random noise is added to ratings both at the time of submission and at the time of query.

A2: Here we add Gaussian random noise to deviations of rating pairs at the time of submission and similar noise to ratings at the time of query.

B1: We add random noise to the ratings at the time of submission but we round off deviations (for encryption) at the time of query.

B2: The Gaussian noise is added to deviations of rating pairs but the deviations are rounded off at the time of query.

In all the experiments, the random noise is drawn from a Gaussian distribution $\mathcal{N}(0,5)$.

In figure 5, we present a comparison of original ratings, perturbed and estimated ratings for a random user (amongst the 943 users in the MovieLens 100K dataset) using proposal B1. Notice how the majority of the difference between the original and the estimated ratings like lie between 0 and 1, while those between the original and perturbed ratings lie between 0 and -5.

Note that both B1 and B2 are supposed to be used with encrypted queries so the actual prediction time will include homomorphic encryptions and multiplications, hence will be perceptibly slower than what is shown in the results.

7   Conclusion and Future Work

Given that the Slope One predictor from Lemire and MacLachlan [2] is robust to additive noise, in this paper, we have proposed some privacy-preserving solutions for the problem of collaborative filtering using random perturbation. Our solution is based on the weighted Slope One predictor and unbounded additive random noise. We have discussed how it is difficult to determine original ratings from the perturbed data while the perturbed data is still good enough for fairly accurate predictions. We have also presented comparative results from a trial implementation and shown design considerations for cloud implementations.

In future, we will explore other randomisation techniques and the applicability of ϵ-differential privacy on the Slope One CF predictors. We will also port our trial implementation to cloud platforms such as Google App Engine for Java and the Amazon Elastic Beanstalk to facilitate practical experimentation at a larger scale.

Acknowledgments. Special thanks to Theo Dimitrakos from British Telecom for his valuable inputs on this paper. The work at Tokai University has been supported by the Japanese Ministry of Internal Affairs and Communications funded project "Research and Development of Security Technologies for Cloud Computing" involving Tokai University, Waseda University, NEC, Hitachi and KDDI. Jaideep Vaidya's work is supported in part by the United States National Science Foundation under Grant No. CNS-0746943 and by the Trustees Research Fellowship Program at Rutgers, The State University of New Jersey. Contributions by Theo Dimitrakos relate to research in British Telecommunications under the IST Framework Programme 7 integrated project OPTIMIS that is partly funded by the European Commission under contract number 257115.

We would also like to thank the anonymous reviewers for their constructive criticism.

References

1. Schafer, J.B., Konstan, J., Riedi, J.: Recommender systems in e-commerce. In: Proceedings of the 1st ACM Conference on Electronic Commerce, pp. 158–166. ACM Press, New York (1999)
2. Lemire, D., Maclachlan, A.: Slope one predictors for online rating-based collaborative filtering. Society for Industrial Mathematics (2005)
3. Canny, J.: Collaborative filtering with privacy. In: Proceedings 2002 IEEE Symposium on Security and Privacy, pp. 45–57 (2002)
4. Kaleli, C., Polat, H.: P2P collaborative filtering with privacy. Turkish Journal of Electric Electrical Engineering and Computer Sciences 8(1), 101–116 (2010)
5. Han, S., Ng, W.K., Yu, P.S.: Privacy-Preserving Singular Value Decomposition. In: IEEE 25th International Conference on Data Engineering, pp. 1267–1270 (2009)
6. Polat, H., Du, W.: SVD-based collaborative filtering with privacy. In: Proceedings of the 20th ACM Symposium on Applied Computing (2005)
7. Aggarwal, C.C., Yu, P.S.: A General Survey of Privacy-Preserving Data Mining Models and Algorithms. In: Privacy-Preserving Data Mining, ch. 2, pp. 11–52. Springer (2008), http://www.springerlink.com/index/u4419h332616un75.pdf

8. Basu, A., Kikuchi, H., Vaidya, J.: Privacy-preserving weighted slope one predictor for item-based collaborative filtering. In: Proceedings of the International Workshop on Trust and Privacy in Distributed Information Processing (workshop at the IFIPTM 2011), Copenhagen, Denmark (2011)
9. Basu, A., Vaidya, J., Kikuchi, H.: Efficient privacy-preserving collaborative filtering based on the weighted Slope One predictor. Journal of Internet Services and Information Security 1(4) (2011)
10. Basu, A., Vaidya, J., Kikuchi, H., Dimitrakos, T.: Privacy-preserving collaborative filtering for the cloud. In: Proceedings of the 3rd IEEE International Conference on Cloud Computing Technology and Science (Cloudcom), Athens, Greece (2011)
11. Agrawal, R., Srikant, R.: Privacy-preserving data mining. ACM Sigmod Record 29, 439–450 (2000)
12. Agrawal, D., Aggarwal, C.C.: On the design and quantification of privacy preserving data mining algorithms. In: Proceedings of the Twentieth ACM SIGMOD-SIGACT-SIGART Symposium on Principles of Database Systems, pp. 247–255. ACM (2001)
13. Evfimievski, A., Srikant, R., Agrawal, R., Gehrke, J.: Privacy preserving mining of association rules. Information Systems 29(4), 343–364 (2004)
14. Evfimievski, A.: Randomization in privacy preserving data mining. ACM SIGKDD Explorations Newsletter 4(2), 43–48 (2002)
15. Villejoubert, G., Mandel, D.: The inverse fallacy: An account of deviations from Bayes's theorem and the additivity principle. Memory & Cognition 30(2), 171–178 (2002)

Robustness of Trust Models and Combinations for Handling Unfair Ratings

Lizi Zhang, Siwei Jiang, Jie Zhang, and Wee Keong Ng

School of Computer Engineering
Nanyang Technological University, Singapore
{y080077,sjiang1,zhangj,awkng}@ntu.edu.sg

Abstract. In electronic marketplaces, after each transaction buyers will rate the products provided by the sellers. To decide the most trustworthy sellers to transact with, buyers rely on trust models to leverage these ratings to evaluate the reputation of sellers. Although the high effectiveness of different trust models for handling unfair ratings have been claimed by their designers, recently it is argued that these models are vulnerable to more intelligent attacks, and there is an urgent demand that the robustness of the existing trust models has to be evaluated in a more comprehensive way. In this work, we classify the existing trust models into two broad categories and propose an extendable e-marketplace testbed to evaluate their robustness against different unfair rating attacks comprehensively. On top of highlighting the robustness of the existing trust models for handling unfair ratings is far from what they were claimed to be, we further propose and validate a novel combination mechanism for the existing trust models, Discount-then-Filter, to notably enhance their robustness against the investigated attacks.

Keywords: Trust models, Unfair ratings, Robustness, Multi-agent system, Electronic marketplaces.

1 Introduction

Nowadays, electronic marketplaces (*e.g.*, eBay) have greatly facilitated the transaction processes among different people. However, unlike traditional face-to-face transaction experiences, it is hardly possible for buyers to evaluate the products provided by sellers before they decide whether to buy from a potential seller. Current e-commerce systems like eBay, allow buyers to rate their sellers according to the quality of their delivered products after each transaction is completed.

In the context of the multiagent-based e-marketplace, when a buyer agent evaluates the reputation of a potential seller agent, he may need to ask for other buyers' opinions (advisor[1] agents' ratings) towards that seller agent. We define the following terms discussed in the remaining paper:

---

[1] When a buyer evaluates a seller, other buyers are that buyer's advisors. The terms *advisor* and *buyer* are used interchangeably in this paper.

T. Dimitrakos et al. (Eds.): IFIPTM 2012, IFIP AICT 374, pp. 36–51, 2012.

- *Honest seller*: A seller that delivers his product as specified in the contract.
- *Dishonest seller*: A seller that does not deliver his product as specified in the contract.
- *Reputation*: A value calculated by trust models to indicate whether a seller will behave honestly in the future: the higher reputation, the higher probability that the seller will behave honestly.
- *Positive rating*: A rating given by a buyer/advisor to a seller indicating a seller is an honest seller.
- *Negative rating*: A rating given by a buyer/advisor to a seller indicating a seller is a dishonest seller.
- *Honest buyer/advisor*: A buyer that always provides positive ratings to honest sellers or negative ratings to dishonest sellers.
- *Dishonest buyer/advisor or Attacker*: A buyer that provides negative ratings to honest sellers or positive ratings to dishonest sellers. Exception: some special attacker (*e.g.* Camouflage Attacker) may strategically behave like an honest buyer.
- *Trust or Trustworthiness*[2]: A value calculated by trust models to indicate whether an advisor is honest or not: the higher trustworthiness, the higher probability that the advisor is honest.

Cheating behaviors from sellers, such as not performing the due obligations according to the transaction contract, are still possible to be sanctioned by law if trust models fail to take effect. However, advisors' cheating behaviors, especially providing *unfair ratings* to sellers, are more difficult to be dealt with. Dellarocas distinguished unfair ratings as unfairly high ratings ("ballot stuffing") and unfairly low ratings ("bad-mouthing") [1]. Advisors may collude with certain sellers to boost their reputation by providing unfairly positive ratings while bad-mouthing their competitors' reputation with unfairly negative ratings. An example is that three colluded men positively rated each other several times and later sold a fake painting for a very high price [10].

To address this challenge, researchers in the multiagent-based e-marketplace have designed various trust models to handle unfair ratings to assist buyers to evaluate the reputation of sellers more accurately. Recently it is argued that the robustness analysis of these trust models is mostly done through simple simulated scenarios implemented by the model designers themselves, and this cannot be considered as reliable evidence for how these systems would perform in a realistic environment [4]. If a trust model is not robust against, or vulnerable to, certain unfair rating attack, mostly it will inaccurately rate a dishonest seller's reputation higher than that of an honest seller; thus, it will suggest honest buyers to transact with a dishonest seller, and sellers can gain higher transaction volumes by behaving dishonestly. Therefore, there is an urgent demand to evaluate the robustness of the existing trust models under more comprehensive unfair rating attack environment before deploying them in the real market. The "Agent

---

[2] Generally, the terms *reputation, trust* and *trustworthiness* are used interchangeably in many works. To avoid confusion, in this work we use them to model behaviors of sellers and buyers/advisors separately.

Reputation and Trust Testbed (ART) [3] is an example of a testbed that has been specified and implemented by a group of researchers. However, it is currently not flexible enough for carrying out realistic simulations and robustness evaluations for many of the proposed trust models [4].

In this work, we select and investigate four well-known existing trust models (BRS, iCLUB, TRAVOS and Personalized) and six unfair rating attack strategies (Constant, Camouflage, Whitewashing, Sybil, Sybil Camouflage, and Sybil Whitewashing Attack). We classify these trust models into two broad categories: *Filtering-based* and *Discounting-based*, and propose an extendable e-marketplace testbed to evaluate their robustness against different attacks comprehensively and comparatively. To the best of our knowledge, we for the first time experimentally substantiate the presence of their multiple vulnerabilities under the investigated unfair rating attacks. On top of highlighting the robustness of the existing trust models is far from what they were claimed to be—none of the investigated single trust model is robust against all the six investigated attacks, we further propose and validate a novel combination approach, *Discount-then-Filter*, for the existing trust models. This combination notably enhances their robustness against all the attacks: our experiments show most of Discount-then-Filter combined trust models are robust against all the six attacks.

2   Related Work

2.1   Cheating Behavior from Advisors—Unfair Rating Attack

Typical cheating behaviors from sellers, such as *Reputation Lag*, *Value Imbalance*, *Re-entry*, *Initial Window*, and *Exit*, have been studied by Kerr and Cohen [6]. They assumed maximal cheating in their paper: a cheating seller does not ship out his product thus no cost is incurred, and the buyer will learn the results only after the lag has lapsed. Recent work by Jøsang and Golbeck identified more seller attack strategies and reduced all types of advisor cheating behaviors to Unfair Rating Attack [4]. Particularly, Kerr and Cohen found combined seller attacks are able to defeat every investigated trust model. Researchers, especially those models' designers, might be tempted to argue that, cheating behaviors from sellers are possible to be handled by law and their models are still robust against advisors' unfair rating attack rather than sellers' attack strategies.

We argue that even though cheating behaviors from sellers are possible to be sanctioned by law, advisors' cheating behaviors are still able to defeat the existing trust models; thus, improving the robustness of the existing trust models for handling unfair ratings is urgently demanded. To begin with, online transactions are essentially contracts: sellers are obliged to deliver products as specified by themselves and buyers are obliged to pay the specified amount of money. Therefore, most sellers' cheating behaviors can be considered as unlegal: in the real life, it is very common that buyers may sue their sellers if the delivered products are not as good as specified by the sellers according to the contract law. Although sellers' cheating behaviors can be sanctioned by law, advisors' unfair ratings can only be considered as unethical rather than unlegal [4], therefore there is an urgent demand to address the unfair rating problem. Our paper focuses on cheating behaviors from advisors and below are a list of typical unfair rating attacks[3] that may threaten the existing trust models in e-marketplaces.

Constant Attack. The simplest strategy from dishonest advisors is, constantly providing unfairly positive ratings to dishonest sellers while providing unfairly negative ratings to honest sellers. This simple attack is a baseline to test the basic effectiveness of different trust models in dealing with unfair ratings.

Camouflage Attack. Dishonest advisors may camouflage themselves as honest ones by providing fair ratings strategically. For example, advisors may provide fair ratings to build up their trustworthiness (according to certain trust models) at the early stage before providing unfair ratings. Intuitively, trust models assuming attackers' behaviors are constant and stable may be vulnerable to it.

Whitewashing Attack. In e-marketplaces, it is hard to establish buyers' identities: users can freely create a new account as a buyer. This presents an opportunity for a dishonest buyer to *whitewash* his low trustworthiness (according to certain trust models) by starting a new account with the default initial trustworthiness value (0.5 in our investigated trust models).

Sybil Attack. When evaluating the robustness of trust models, it is usually assumed that the majority of buyers are honest. In our experiments, the aforementioned three types of attackers are minority compared with the remaining honest buyers. However, it is possible that dishonest buyers (unfair rating attackers) may form the majority of all the buyers in e-marketplaces. In this paper, we use the term *Sybil Attack*, which was initially proposed by Douceur, to describe the scenario where dishonest buyers have obtained larger amount of resources (buyer accounts) than honest buyers to constantly provide unfair ratings to sellers [2]. This attack can be considered as, dishonest buyers are more than honest buyers and they perform Constant Attack together.

Sybil Camouflage Attack. As the name suggests, this attack combines both Camouflage Attack and Sybil Attack: dishonest buyers are more than honest buyers and perform Camouflage Attack together.

Sybil Whitewashing Attack. Similar to Sybil Camouflage Attack: dishonest buyers are more than honest buyers and perform Whitewashing Attack together.

Non-Sybil-Based and Sybil-Based Attack. Obviously, under the Constant, Camouflage and Whitewashing Attack, the number of dishonest buyers is less than half of all the buyers in the market (minority). We refer to them as the *Non-Sybil-based Attack*. On the contrary, the number of Sybil, Sybil Camouflage, and Sybil Whitewashing Attackers is greater than half of all the buyers (majority), and these attacks are referred to as the *Sybil-based Attack*.

---

[3] Some attack names are used interchangeably in both seller attacks and advisors' unfair rating attacks (*e.g.*, Sybil Attack), in this paper we refer to the latter.

2.2   Trust Models for Handling Unfair Rating—Defense Mechanisms

Various trust models have been proposed to deal with different attacks. In the interest of fairness, we select four representative models proposed during the year 2002—2011 that self-identified as applicable to e-marketplaces and robust against unfair rating attacks. In this section, we also classify them into two broad categories: *Filtering-based* and *Discounting-based*.

Beta Reputation System (BRS). The Beta Reputation system (BRS) was proposed by Jøsang and Ismail to predict a seller's behavior in the next transaction based on the number of honest and dishonest transactions (the two events in the beta distribution: $[p, n]$, where p and n denote the number of received positive and negative ratings) he has conducted in the past [5]. Whitby *et al.* further proposed an iterative approach to filter out unfair ratings based on the *majority rule* [9]. According to this approach, if the calculated reputation of a seller based on the set of honest buyers (initially all buyers) falls in the rejection area (q quantile or $1 - q$ quantile) of the beta distribution of a buyer's ratings to that seller, this buyer will be filtered out from the set of honest buyers and all his ratings will be considered as unfair ratings since his opinions (ratings) are not consistent with the majority of the other buyers' opinions (the majority rule). Then the seller's reputation will be re-calculated based on the updated set of honest buyers, and the filtering process continues until the set of honest buyers eventually remains unchanged. Obviously, the majority rule renders BRS vulnerable to Sybil-based Attack because the majority of buyers are dishonest and the other honest buyers' (the minority) ratings will be filtered out.

iCLUB. iCLUB is a recently proposed trust model in handling multi-nominal ratings [7]. It adopts the clustering approach and considers buyers' local and global knowledge about sellers to filter out unfair ratings. For local knowledge, the buyer compares his ratings with advisors' ratings (normalized rating vectors) towards the *target seller* (the seller under evaluation) by clustering. If an advisor's ratings are not in the cluster containing the buyer's ratings, they will be considered as not consistent with the buyer's opinions, and will be filtered out as unfair ratings. Obviously, comparing advisors' ratings with the buyer's own opinions is reliable since the buyer never lies to himself. If transactions between the buyer and the target seller are too few (few evidence), the buyer will not be confident to rely on his local knowledge, and global knowledge will be used. The buyer will compare his and the advisors' ratings towards all the sellers excluding the target seller by performing clustering. A set of advisors who always have similar ratings with the buyer (in the same cluster) towards every seller are identified. Eventually, these advisors are used to filtered out the other untrustworthy advisors' ratings when evaluating all advisors' ratings to the target seller. In general, buyers' local knowledge is more reliable than his global knowledge. This is because when the set of advisors whose opinions are always similar to the buyer's cannot be found, the global knowledge will use the majority rule to filter out unfair ratings; this may be vulnerable to Sybil-based Attack.

Filtering-Based Trust Models. BRS and iCLUB filter out unfair ratings before aggregating the remaining fair ratings in evaluating a seller's reputation, therefore, we classify them as **Filtering-based**. The reputation of the seller S, $\Gamma(S)$, is calculated as:

$$\Gamma(S) = \frac{\sum p_i + 1}{\sum p_i + \sum n_i + 2} \tag{1}$$

where p_i and n_i are the number of positive and negative ratings from each advisor i to the seller S after unfair ratings are filtered out. When S does not receive any ratings, his initial reputation is 0.5.

TRAVOS. Teacy *et al.* proposed TRAVOS to evaluate the trustworthiness of advisors, τ_i, and use τ_i to discount their ratings before aggregating these ratings to evaluate the target seller's reputation [8]. To evaluate an advisor's trustworthiness, first, a set of reference sellers are identified if these sellers' reputation are similar to the target seller's reputation as calculated by using this advisor's ratings towards them. Then the buyer will use the cumulative distribution function of beta distribution based on the total number of his positive and negative ratings to each reference seller to compute the trustworthiness of that advisor. Compared with BRS, TRAVOS incorporates a buyer's personal transaction experiences with the target seller in the process of evaluating his advisors' trustworthiness. However, TRAVOS assumes the advisors' behaviors are constant; thus, this model may be vulnerable if the attackers camouflage themselves by giving fair ratings strategically before providing unfair ratings.

Personalized. Zhang and Cohen proposed a personalized approach to evaluate an advisor's trustworthiness τ_i in two aspects: private and public trust [10]. To evaluate the private trust of an advisor, the buyer compares his ratings with the advisor's ratings to their commonly rated sellers. Greater disparity in the comparison indicates discounting of the advisor's trustworthiness to a larger extent. Similarly, the public trust of an advisor is estimated by comparing the advisor's ratings with the majority of the other advisors' ratings towards their commonly rated sellers. Obviously, public trust adopts the majority rule in evaluating an advisor's trustworthiness and therefore may be vulnerable to Sybil-based Attack. Since private trust is more reliable, when aggregating both private and public trust of an advisor, this model will allocate higher weightage to private trust if the buyer has more commonly rated sellers with the advisor (more evidence). When the number of such commonly rated sellers exceeds a certain threshold value (enough evidence), the buyer will only use the private trust to evaluate the advisor's trustworthiness more accurately.

Discounting-Based Trust Models. TRAVOS and Personalized calculate advisors' trustworthiness and use their trustworthiness to discount their ratings before aggregating them to evaluate a seller's reputation. Thus, we classify them as **Discounting-based**. The reputation of the seller S, $\Gamma(S)$, is calculated as:

$$\Gamma(S) = \frac{\sum \tau_i \times p_i + 1}{\sum \tau_i \times p_i + \sum \tau_i \times n_i + 2} \tag{2}$$

where p_i and n_i are the number of positive and negative ratings from each advisor i to the seller S, and τ_i is the trustworthiness of the advisor i. When S does not receive any ratings, his initial reputation is 0.5.

3 Evaluation Method

3.1 The E-Marketplace Testbed

Our experiments are performed by simulating the transaction activities in the e-marketplace. As mentioned in Section 1, the existing ART testbed is not suitable for carrying out experiments to compare robustness of trust models under different unfair rating attacks. In light of its limitations, we design and develop an e-marketplace testbed, which is extendable via incorporating new trust or attack models.

In our e-marketplace testbed, there are 10 dishonest sellers and 10 honest sellers. To make the comparison more obvious, we consider a "Duopoly Market": there are two sellers in the market that take up a large portion of the total transaction volume in the market. We assume a reasonable competition scenario: one duopoly seller (*dishonest duopoly seller*) tries to beat his competitor (*honest duopoly seller*) in the transaction volume by hiring or collaborating with dishonest buyers to perform unfair rating attacks. We refer to the remaining sellers (excluding the duopoly sellers) as *common sellers*. Typically, trust models are most effective when 30% of buyers are dishonest [9]. To ensure the best case for the trust models, we added 6 dishonest buyers (attackers) and 14 honest buyers in the market for Non-Sybil-based Attack, and switch their values for Sybil-based Attack. The entire simulation will last for 100 days. On each day, each buyer chooses to transact with one seller once. Since most trust models are more effective when every advisor has transaction experiences with many different sellers, we assume that there is a probability of 0.5 that buyers will transact with the duopoly sellers while there is another probability of 0.5 that buyers will transact with each common seller randomly. The value of 0.5 also implies the duopoly sellers take up half of all the transactions in the market. When deciding on which duopoly seller to transact with, honest buyers use trust models to calculate their reputation values and transact with the one with the higher value, while dishonest buyers choose sellers according to their attacking strategies. After each transaction, honest buyers provide fair ratings, whereas dishonest buyers provide ratings according to their attacking strategies.

The key parameters with their values in the e-marketplace testbed are summarized as follows:

- *Number of honest duopoly seller*: 1
- *Number of dishonest duopoly seller*: 1
- *Number of honest common seller*: 9

- *Number of dishonest common seller*: 9
- *Number of honest buyer/advisor* $(|B^H|)$: 14 (Non-Sybil-based Attack) or 6 (Sybil-based Attack)
- *Number of dishonest buyer/advisor or attacker* $(|B^D|)$: 6 (Non-Sybil-based Attack) or 14 (Sybil-based Attack)
- *Number of simulation days (L)*: 100
- *The ratio of duopoly sellers' transactions to all transactions (r)*: 0.5

3.2   The Trust Model Robustness Metric

To evaluate the robustness of different trust models, we compare the transaction volumes of the duopoly sellers. Obviously, the more robust the trust model, the larger the transaction volume difference between the honest and dishonest duopoly seller. The robustness of a trust model (defense, Def) against an attack model (Atk) is defined as:

$$\Re(Def, Atk) = \frac{|Tran(S^H)| - |Tran(S^D)|}{|B^H| \times L \times r} \tag{3}$$

where $|Tran(S^H)|$ and $|Tran(S^D)|$ denote the total transaction volume of the honest and dishonest duopoly seller, and the values of key parameters in the e-marketplace testbed $|B^H|$, L, and r are given in Section 3.1.

If a trust model Def is *completely robust* against a certain attack Atk, $\Re(Def, Atk) = 1$. It means the reputation of the honest duopoly seller is always higher than that of the dishonest duopoly seller as calculated by the trust model, so honest buyers will always transact with the honest duopoly seller. On the contrary, $\Re(Def, Atk) = -1$ indicates, the trust model always suggests honest buyers to transact with the dishonest duopoly seller, and Def is *completely vulnerable* to Atk. When $\Re(Def, Atk) > 0$, the greater the value is, the more robust Def is against Atk. When $\Re(Def, Atk) < 0$, the greater the absolute value is, the more vulnerable Def is to Atk[4].

In Eq. 3, the denominator denotes the transaction volume difference between the honest and dishonest duopoly seller when the trust model (Def) is completely robust against or vulnerable to a certain attack (Atk): all the honest buyers (B^H) always transact with the duopoly honest seller (S^H, when completely robust) or duopoly dishonest seller (S^D, when completely vulnerable) in the 100 days with a probability of 0.5 to transact with the duopoly sellers. In our experiment, the denominator is 700 ($14 \times 100 \times 0.5$) if Atk is Non-Sybil-based Attack, or 300 ($6 \times 100 \times 0.5$) if Atk is Sybil-based Attack.

4   Robustness of Single Trust Models

In this section, we evaluate the robustness of all the trust models against all the attack strategies covered in Section 2 with the e-marketplace testbed described

---

[4] When Def is completely robust against or vulnerable to Atk, in our experiments $\Re(Def, Atk)$ can be slightly around 1 or -1 because the probability to transact with the duopoly sellers may not be exactly 0.5 in the actual simulation process.

Table 1. Robustness of single trust models against attacks. Every entry denotes the mean and standard deviation of the robustness values of trust model against attack.

	Constant	Camouflage	Whitewashing	Sybil	Sybil Cam	Sybil WW
BRS	0.84±0.03	0.87±0.04	-0.48±0.08	-0.98±0.09	-0.63±0.08	-0.60±0.10
iCLUB	1.00±0.04	0.98±0.03	0.81±0.10	-0.09±0.33	0.95±0.11	-0.16±0.26
TRAVOS	0.96±0.04	0.88±0.04	0.98±0.04	0.66±0.10	-0.60±0.09	-1.00±0.08
Personalized	0.99±0.04	1.01±0.03	0.99±0.04	0.84±0.12	0.67±0.09	-1.00±0.11

*Sybil Cam: Sybil Camouflage Attack; Sybil WW: Sybil Whitewashing Attack

in Section 3. In our experiments, when models require parameters we have used values provided by the authors in their own works wherever possible. The experiments are performed 50 times, and the mean and standard deviation of the 50 results are shown in Table 1 in the form of $(mean \pm std)$. We discuss the robustness of all the single trust models against each attack.

Constant Attack. All the trust models are robust against this baseline attack. Consistent with Whitby *et al.*'s experimental results, our experiment also shows BRS is not completely robust against Constant Attack [9]. Fig. 1 and Fig. 2 depict under Constant Attack, how the transactions of the duopoly sellers grow day after day when BRS and iCLUB are used by honest buyers to decide which duopoly seller to transact with. The transaction volume difference between the honest and dishonest duopoly seller on Day 100 (around 700) indicates that iCLUB is completely robust against Constant Attack. Space prevents the inclusion of such figures for every trust model; throughout this paper, all key data are presented in Table 1—2 and we use charts where illustration is informative.

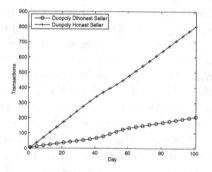
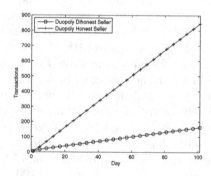

Fig. 1. BRS vs. Constant   **Fig. 2.** iCLUB vs. Constant

Camouflage Attack. In this experiment, Camouflage Attackers give fair ratings to all the common sellers to establish their trustworthiness before giving unfair ratings to all sellers (with a probability of 0.5 to transact with the duopoly sellers). From the results of Table 1, without enough attackers, Camouflage Attack does not threaten the trust models very much.

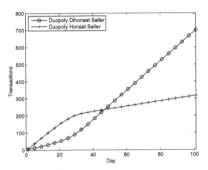

Fig. 3. BRS vs. Whitewashing

Whitewashing Attack. In our experiment, each Whitewashing Attacker provides one unfair rating on one day and starts with a new buyer account on the next day. The value $\Re(BRS, Whitewashing) = -0.48$ in Table 1 shows BRS is vulnerable to this attack. According to Fig. 3, the honest duopoly seller has more transactions than the dishonest one at the beginning. However, after some time (around Day 45) the dishonest duopoly seller's transaction volume exceeds his competitor. In fact, after some time the calculated reputation of a seller will more easily fall in the rejection area of the beta distribution of an honest buyer's single accumulated ratings (single $[p, 0]$ to an honest seller and single $[0, n]$ to a dishonest seller, where p and n become very large as transaction experiences accumulate) rather than Whitewashing Attackers' multiple one-transaction ratings (multiple $[0, 1]$ to an honest sellers and multiple $[1, 0]$ to a dishonest seller). The other trust models are robust against Whitewashing Attack.

Sybil Attack. As described in Section 2, BRS is completely vulnerable to Sybil Attack due to its employed majority-rule. The robustness of iCLUB is not stable as indicated by its standard deviation of 0.33. To explain, an honest buyer can rely on his local knowledge to always transact with one duopoly seller while using the global knowledge, which is wrong when majority of advisors are attackers, to evaluate the reputation of the other duopoly seller. The duopoly seller to always transact with can be either honest or dishonest as long as his reputation is always higher than that of his competitor, which is possible in either case. Besides, TRAVOS and Personalized are not completely robust against Sybil Attack. This is due to the lack of transactions among different buyers and sellers at the beginning. For TRAVOS, at the beginning it is hard to find common reference sellers for the buyer and the advisor so the discounting is not effective (we refer to this phenomenon as *soft punishment*). When majority are dishonest buyers, their aggregated ratings will overweigh honest buyers' opinions. For instance, if the trustworthiness of each dishonest and honest buyer are 0.4 and 0.6, and all buyers provides only one rating to a particular seller, according to Eq. 2, the reputation of an honest seller is $0.41 < 0.5$ ($0.41 = (0.6 \times 6 + 1)/(0.4 \times 14 + 0.6 \times 6 + 2)$) and that of a dishonest seller is $0.59 > 0.5$ ($0.59 = (0.4 \times 14 + 1)/(0.4 \times 14 + 0.6 \times 6 + 2)$);

both suggest inaccurate decisions. However, if a Discounting-based model is able to discount the trustworthiness of a dishonest buyer to a larger extent, say 0.1, while promote that of an honest buyer to a larger extent, say 0.9, the evaluation of sellers' reputation will become accurate. For Personalized, at the beginning the buyer will more rely on public trust to evaluate the trustworthiness of an advisor, which is inaccurate when majority of buyers are dishonest. Fig. 4 and Fig. 5 show that, as transactions among different buyers and sellers grow, TRAVOS becomes more effective in discounting advisors' trustworthiness and Personalized tends to use private trust to accurately evaluate advisors' trustworthiness.

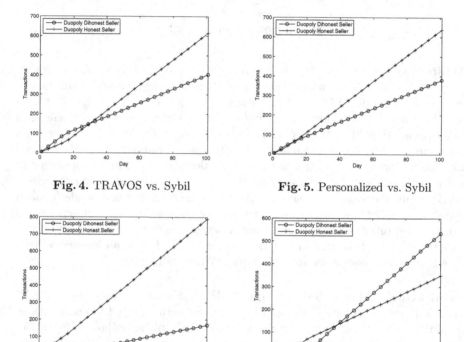

Fig. 4. TRAVOS vs. Sybil   **Fig. 5.** Personalized vs. Sybil

Fig. 6. TRAVOS vs. Camouflage   **Fig. 7.** TRAVOS vs. Sybil Camouflage

Sybil Camouflage Attack. Unlike Sybil Attack, Sybil Camouflage Attack is unable to render BRS completely vulnerable. This is because at the beginning attackers camouflage themselves as honest ones by providing fair ratings, where BRS is always effective. After attackers stop camouflaging, the duopoly dishonest seller's transaction volume will soon exceed his competitor. For iCLUB, during the camouflaging stage, the honest duopoly seller will only transact with honest buyers. After attackers stop camouflaging, only the reliable local knowledge will be used by honest buyers to evaluate the trustworthiness of the honest duopoly seller (of high value), and honest buyers will continue to transact with him. Compared with Camouflage and Sybil Attack, Personalized becomes less robust against Sybil Camouflage Attack. This is because the public and private trust of attackers have not been discounted to a large extent right after they complete the camouflaging stage (soft punishment). When the majority are attackers, their aggregated ratings will overweigh honest buyers' opinions. After attackers stop camouflaging, their private trust will continue to drop and Personalized will be effective. Compared with Camouflage Attack, TRAVOS becomes vulnerable to Sybil Camouflage Attack: although TRAVOS will inaccurately promote the trustworthiness of a Camouflage Attacker (most are slightly larger than 0.5), when majority are honest buyers, the aggregated ratings from attackers are still not able to overweigh honest buyers' opinions. However, under Sybil Camouflage Attack, when majority are dishonest buyers, these attackers' aggregated ratings will easily overweigh honest buyers' opinions and render TRAVOS vulnerable. Fig. 6 and Fig. 7 clearly show the difference of the robustness of TRAVOS against Camouflage Attack and Sybil Camouflage Attack.

Sybil Whitewashing Attack. This is the strongest attack: it can defeat every single trust model as observed from Table 1. Similar to Sybil Attack, the robustness of iCLUB against Sybil Whitewashing Attack is still not stable. Compared with Whitewashing Attack, BRS is still vulnerable to Sybil Whitewashing Attack while TRAVOS and Personalized change dramatically from completely robust to completely vulnerable. For TRAVOS, since every whitewashing attacker provides only one rating to a duopoly seller, buyer cannot find reference seller to effectively discount the trustworthiness of whitewashing attackers to a large extent. When majority are soft punished dishonest buyers, TRAVOS will always suggest honest buyers to transact with the dishonest duopoly seller. For Personalized, since every whitewashing attacker provides only one rating to a duopoly seller, the buyer cannot find enough commonly rated sellers and will heavily rely on public trust to evaluate the trustworthiness of an advisor, which is inaccurate when majority of buyers are dishonest. Therefore, similar to TRAVOS, the trustworthiness of whitewashing attacker cannot be discounted to a large extent and the soft punishment renders Personalized completely vulnerable.

It is also noted that although discounting-based TRAVOS and Personalized are robust against Whitewashing, Camouflage, and Sybil Attack, their robustness drops to different extents when facing Sybil Whitewashing and Sybil Camouflage Attack. Based on our results demonstrated in Table 1, we conclude that, none of our investigated single trust models is robust against all the six attacks. Therefore, there is a demand to address the threats from all these attacks.

5   Robustness of Combined Trust Models

5.1   Combining Trust Models

Based on the results of Table 1, Discounting-based trust models may change from vulnerable to robust if some attackers' ratings can be filtered out by Filtering-based models to reduce the effect of Sybil-based Attack to that of Non-Sybil-based Attack. On the other hand, based on analysis in Section 4, under most

Table 2. Robustness of combined trust models against attacks. Every entry denotes the mean and standard deviation of the robustness values of trust model against attack.

	Constant	Camouflage	Whitewashing	Sybil	Sybil Cam	Sybil WW
Filter-then-Discount						
BRS + TRAVOS	0.89±0.06	0.87±0.03	-0.55±0.10	-1.01±0.11	-0.55±0.09	-0.59±0.11
BRS + Personalized	0.89±0.06	0.88±0.03	-0.34±0.05	-0.96±0.07	-0.53±0.08	-0.58±0.08
iCLUB + TRAVOS	0.96±0.03	0.98±0.04	0.95±0.04	0.85±0.08	0.97±0.10	0.70±0.12
iCLUB + Personalized	0.98±0.03	0.99±0.03	0.92±0.06	0.88±0.13	0.98±0.09	0.67±0.13
Discount-then-Filter						
TRAVOS + BRS	0.95±0.03	0.86±0.06	0.98±0.04	0.91±0.06	-0.57±0.12	0.98±0.10
TRAVOS + iCLUB	0.95±0.04	0.92±0.03	0.93±0.03	0.91±0.12	0.91±0.10	0.94±0.12
Personalized + BRS	0.99±0.03	0.98±0.03	1.01±0.03	0.96±0.11	0.87±0.08	1.00±0.10
Personalized + iCLUB	0.97±0.04	0.95±0.02	0.98±0.04	0.92±0.09	0.94±0.09	0.93±0.07

*Sybil Cam: Sybil Camouflage Attack; Sybil WW: Sybil Whitewashing Attack

attacks Discounting-based models are still able to discount the trustworthiness of dishonest buyers to lower than 0.5 (although only slightly). Intuitively, filtering out ratings from advisors with lower trustworthiness may be a promising pre-filtering step before using Filtering-based models. Therefore, we combine trust models from different categories to evaluate their new robustness to the same set of attacks. Generally, there are two approaches for combination: **Filter-then-Discount** and **Discount-then-Filter**. Details are given below.

Approach 1—Filter-then-Discount:

1. Use a Filtering-based trust model to filter out unfair ratings;
2. Use a Discounting-based trust model to aggregate discounted ratings to calculate sellers' reputation.

Approach 2—Discount-then-Filter:

1. Use a Discounting-based trust model to calculate each advisor i's trustworthiness τ_i;
2. If $\tau_i < \epsilon$, remove i's all ratings ($\epsilon = 0.5$ in our experiment);
3. Use a Filtering-based trust model to filter out unfair ratings before aggregating the remaining ratings to calculate sellers' reputation.

5.2   Robustness Evaluation

Eight possible combinations of trust models are obtained and their robustness against all the attacks have been evaluated. Notice that the new model name follows the order of using the two different models. We will discuss the robustness enhancement of each combined model against all attacks based on the experimental results presented in Table 2.

BRS + TRAVOS and BRS + Personalized. Similar to BRS, they are still vulnerable to many attacks such as Whitewashing, Sybil, Sybil Whitewashing, and Sybil Camouflage Attack. The reason is, under these attacks BRS will inaccurately filter out some honest buyers' ratings and keep some dishonest buyers' ratings after the first step of Approach 1; the remaining unfair ratings will be used by Discounting-based trust models to inaccurately suggest honest buyers to transact with the dishonest duopoly seller.

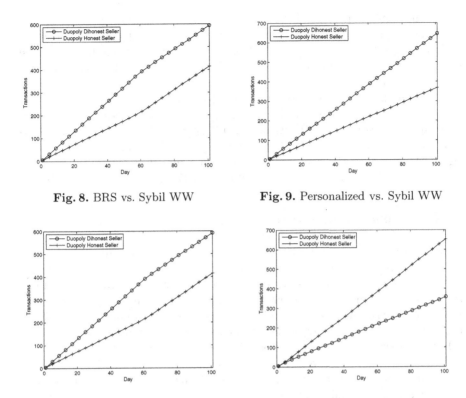

Fig. 8. BRS vs. Sybil WW   **Fig. 9.** Personalized vs. Sybil WW

Fig. 10. BRS + Personalized vs. Sybil WW   **Fig. 11.** Personalized + BRS vs. Sybil WW

iCLUB + TRAVOS and iCLUB + Personalized. Contrary to BRS, iCLUB is robust against Whitewashing and Sybil Camouflage Attack. Therefore, iCLUB + TRAVOS and iCLUB + Personalized are also able to effectively filter out unfair ratings at the first step of Approach 1, and are robust against these attacks. However, due to the instability of the robustness of iCLUB against Sybil and Sybil Whitewashing Attack, iCLUB + TRAVOS and iCLUB + Personalized are still not completely robust against these attacks.

Discount-then-Filter. The complete robustness of TRAVOS and Personalized against Whitewashing Attack ensures all the attackers' ratings will be filtered out at the first step of Approach 2. As described in Section 4, although TRAVOS and Personalized are unable to discount the trustworthiness of a Sybil, Sybil Whitewashing or Sybil Camouflage Attacker to a large extent (soft punishment: only slightly lower than 0.5), the threshold value we choose ($\epsilon = 0.5$) is able to filter out all these attackers' ratings at the second step of Approach 2. Therefore, Personalized + BRS and Personalized + iCLUB are completely robust against Sybil, Sybil Whitewashing and Sybil Camouflage Attack. Likewise, TRAVOS + BRS and TRAVOS + iCLUB are completely robust against most attacks. One exception is that, TRAVOS + BRS is still vulnerable to Sybil Camouflage Attack. This is because TRAVOS inaccurately promotes attackers' trustworthiness (most are slightly higher than 0.5) and their ratings are unable to be filtered out at the second step of Approach 2. Unlike iCLUB, which is robust against Sybil Camouflage Attack, BRS is vulnerable to it.

Based on the results in Table 1—2, we conclude that, robustness of single trust models can be enhanced by combining different categories, and Discount-then-Filter is most robust. Particularly, TRAVOS + iCLUB, Personalized + BRS, and Personalized + iCLUB are robust against all the investigated attacks. Fig. 8-11 show how the robustness of the trust models is enhanced with the Discount-then-Filter approach, while Filter-then-Discount is still vulnerable.

6   Conclusion and Future Work

Trust models can benefit us in choosing trustworthy sellers to transact with in the e-marketplace only when they are robust against external unfair rating attacks. Recently it is argued some trust models are vulnerable to certain attacks and they are not as robust as what their designers claimed to be. Therefore, robustness of trust models for handling unfair ratings have to be evaluated under a comprehensive attack environment to make the results more credible.

In this paper, we designed an extendable e-marketplace testbed to incorporate each existing trust model under a comprehensive set of attack models to evaluate the robustness of trust models. To the best of our knowledge, this is the first demonstration that multiple vulnerabilities of trust models for handling unfair ratings do exist. We conclude that, in our experiments there is no single trust model that is robust against all the investigated attacks. While we have selected a small number of trust models for this initial study, we can hardly believe that other trust model will not have these vulnerabilities. We argue that, in the future any newly proposed trust model at least has to demonstrate robustness (or even complete robustness) to these attacks before being claimed as effective in handling unfair ratings. To address the challenge of existing trust models' multiple vulnerabilities, we classified existing trust models into two categories: Filtering-based and Discounting-based, and further proposed two approaches to combining existing trust models from different categories: Filter-then-Discount and Discount-then-Filter. We for the first time proved that most of the Discount-then-Filter combinations are robust against all the investigated attacks.

Although our work focused on unfair rating attacks, we plan to combine sellers' cheating behaviors with advisors' unfair ratings, and evaluate their threats to the existing trust models. We are also interested in re-designing new trust models to be completely robust against all the investigated attacks without combining existing ones. Since Sybil-based unfair ratings attacks are more effective than Non-Sybil-based, we also want to design more effective unfair rating attacks with limited buyer account resources. We believe these directions inspired by this work will yield further important insights in the trust management area.

Acknowledgement. We wish to acknowledge the funding support for this project from Nanyang Technological University under the Undergraduate Research Experience on CAmpus (URECA) programme.

References

1. Dellarocas, C.: Immunizing online reputation reporting systems against unfair ratings and discriminatory behavior. In: Proceedings of the 2nd ACM Conference on Electroic Commerce, pp. 150–157. ACM (2000)
2. Douceur, J.R.: The Sybil Attack. In: Druschel, P., Kaashoek, M.F., Rowstron, A. (eds.) IPTPS 2002. LNCS, vol. 2429, pp. 251–260. Springer, Heidelberg (2002)
3. Fullam, K., Klos, T., Muller, G., Sabater, J., Schlosser, A., Topol, Z., Barber, K., Rosenschein, J., Vercouter, L., Voss, M.: A specification of the Agent Reputation and Trust (ART) testbed: experimentation and competition for trust in agent societies. In: Proceedings of the 4th International Joint Conference on Autonomous Agents and Multiagent Systems, pp. 512–518. ACM (2005)
4. Jøsang, A., Golbeck, J.: Challenges for robust of trust and reputation systems. In: Proceedings of the 5th International Workshop on Security and Trust Management (SMT 2009), Saint Malo, France (2009)
5. Jøsang, A., Ismail, R.: The beta reputation system. In: Proceedings of the 15th Bled Electronic Commerce Conference, pp. 41–55 (2002)
6. Kerr, R., Cohen, R.: Smart cheaters do prosper: Defeating trust and reputation systems. In: Proceedings of the 8th International Conference on Autonomous Agents and Multiagent Systems, vol. 2, pp. 993–1000 (2009)
7. Liu, S., Zhang, J., Miao, C., Theng, Y.L., Kot, A.C.: iclub: an integrated clustering-based approach to improve the robustness of reputation systems. In: The 10th International Conference on Autonomous Agents and Multiagent Systems, vol. 3, pp. 1151–1152 (2011)
8. Teacy, W., Patel, J., Jennings, N., Luck, M.: Travos: Trust and reputation in the context of inaccurate information sources. Autonomous Agents and Multi-Agent Systems 12(2), 183–198 (2006)
9. Whitby, A., Jøsang, A., Indulska, J.: Filtering out unfair ratings in bayesian reputation systems. In: Proc. 7th Int. Workshop on Trust in Agent Societies (2004)
10. Zhang, J., Cohen, R.: Evaluating the trustworthiness of advice about seller agents in e-marketplaces: A personalized approach. Electronic Commerce Research and Applications 7(3), 330–340 (2008)

A Provenance-Based Trust Model for Delay Tolerant Networks

Jin-Hee Cho[1], MoonJeong Chang[2], Ing-Ray Chen[2], and Ananthram Swami[1]

[1] Computational and Information Sciences Directorate, U.S. Army Research Laboratory,
{jinhee.cho,ananthram.swami}@us.army.mil
[2] Department of Computer Science, Virginia Tech
{mjjang,irchen}@vt.edu

Abstract. Managing trust efficiently and effectively is critical to facilitating cooperation or collaboration and decision making tasks in tactical networks while meeting system goals such as reliability, availability, or scalability. Delay tolerant networks are often encountered in military network environments where end-to-end connectivity is not guaranteed due to frequent disconnection or delay. This work proposes a provenance-based trust framework for efficiency in resource consumption as well as effectiveness in trust evaluation. Provenance refers to the history of ownership of a valued object or information. We adopt the concept of provenance in that trustworthiness of an information provider affects that of information, and vice-versa. The proposed trust framework takes a data-driven approach to reduce resource consumption in the presence of selfish or malicious nodes. This work adopts a model-based method to evaluate the proposed trust framework using Stochastic Petri Nets. The results show that the proposed trust framework achieves desirable accuracy of trust evaluation of nodes compared with an existing scheme while consuming significantly less communication overhead.

Keywords: delay tolerant network, provenance, store-and-forward, message carrier, trust, trustworthiness.

1 Introduction

Delay or disruption tolerant networks (DTNs) are often observed in emerging applications such as emergency response, special operations, smart environments, habitat monitoring, and vehicular ad hoc networks. The core characteristic of DTNs is that there is no guarantee of end-to-end connectivity, thus causing high delay or disruption due to various inherent characteristics (e.g., wireless medium, resource constraints, or high mobility) or intentionally misbehaving nodes (e.g., malicious or selfish) [13]. Due to the characteristics of DTNs, trust management techniques are vital for effectively and efficiently identifying untrustworthy nodes based on accurate trust evaluation and low network resource consumption. We propose a provenance-based trust model to achieve both goals.

The Institute for Information Infrastructure Protection (I3P) emphasized the importance of data provenance for secure, efficient, and trustworthy systems, as one

T. Dimitrakos et al. (Eds.): IFIPTM 2012, IFIP AICT 374, pp. 52–67, 2012.

of the top homeland security research challenges in the 2009 report to the US Senate [18]. Data provenance has been used to analyze scientific data in many applications. The Open Provenance Model (OPM) was introduced to represent data provenance, process documentation, data derivation, and data annotation [10]. Since then, OPM has been widely adopted and extended by various research groups [8]. Freire et al. [5] surveyed various models of provenance management but did not discuss the use of provenance for security. McDaniel [9] associated security with provenance in that good security leads to good provenance with accurate, timely, and detailed provenance information, resulting in good security decisions.

Provenance has been used to verify trust, trustworthiness, or correctness of information in various research areas. Rajbhandari et al. [12] examined how provenance information is associated with a workflow in a Bio-Diversity application. Dai et al. [4] proposed a data provenance trust model to evaluate trustworthiness of data and data providers. Yu et al. [17] presented an agent-based approach to managing information trustworthiness in network centric information sharing environments. Golbeck [6] used provenance information to infer trust in Semantic Web-based social networks. However, the above works [4, 6, 12, 17] focused on evaluating trustworthiness in information without considering particular network attack models that may maliciously change the original messages and disrupt system goals.

Several provenance-based trust models have been proposed to evaluate trustworthiness of both sensed information and information providers (sensors) in sensor networks. Alam and Fahmy [1] proposed an energy-efficient provenance transmission and construction scheme for trust frameworks for evaluating trustworthiness of a sensed data item. Sultana [15] exploited the watermarking characteristics of their provenance mechanism to identify packet-dropping nodes. Wang et al. [16] and Lim et al. [7] proposed a provenance-based trust model to evaluate trust in information and sensors assuming that all paths are known and nodes are stationary. All the above works [1, 7, 15, 16] assumed full knowledge of the network topology, and did not consider attackers. Srivatsa et al. [14] exploited provenance information to propose an efficient cache strategy in DTNs, but did not consider attack behaviors.

In this work, we extend the existing provenance techniques for trust evaluation in DTNs; the challenges are due to the attackers who may modify or drop messages including provenance information or disseminate fake information. Leveraging the interdependency of trust in information and sources based on provenance, this work aims to achieve two goals for effective mission execution: (1) conducting accurate trust evaluation; and (2) incurring low communication overhead for trust evaluation.

We propose a provenance-based trust model that has the following features. First, the proposed scheme significantly reduces communication overhead by not incurring extra communication overhead for trust evaluation purposes in addition to message delivery. We achieve this by using provenance information (i.e., identification and opinion towards a previous message carrier) tagged in delivered message. In our protocol, a trustor does not directly request recommendations from third parties because collecting recommendations requires extra overhead, and recommendations are often not available in a sparse DTN. In addition, collecting indirect evidences via message delivery enables trust update even for two nodes that have not encountered each other for a long time. Second, we use reward and penalty strategies (i.e., increasing or decreasing trust level) to encourage nodes to behave. Third, our proposed trust model uses a composite trust metric embracing three trust properties: availability, integrity, and competence. Based on the literature [3], most existing trust management schemes evaluate a single trust property of a node in order to derive its trustworthiness. Last, we use a model-based evaluation method based on Stochastic Petri Nets (SPN) to identify an optimal minimum trust threshold (in selecting the[1] next message carrier) that maximizes trust accuracy while introducing low communication overhead.

2 System Model

We propose a distributed provenance-based trust management protocol. Each node is assumed to have capability to monitor its neighboring nodes with known probabilities of false positives and negatives in detecting attack behaviors or energy level.

2.1 Key Management

A node encrypts the entire "packet" (consisting of the message and provenance information) using a symmetric key $K_{S,t}$ given to legitimate members. Several trusted authorities (TAs) exist in the operational area so that a node is allowed to access a TA to obtain a valid symmetric key. However, the node may not be able to obtain a valid symmetric key either because no TA is available due the node's physical location or because its trust level is too low, below the minimum required system trust threshold T_{min}. TAs rekeys the symmetric key $K_{S,t}$ periodically based on their pre-deployed hash functions. The symmetric keys issued at the same time t by multiple TAs are the same so that all legitimate nodes can communicate with the same key. The symmetric key is used to prevent outside attackers, not inside attackers. A node forwards a packet to a node whose trust is equal to or above T_{min}.

We define the *provenance information* (PI) generated by node i as the tuple $(i, k, O_{i,k}^{D-integrity}(t))$, where k is the identification (ID) of the previous message carrier (MC), and $O_{i,k}^{D-integrity}(t)$ is the direct trust opinion of node i towards the previous MC k about its integrity. We use three attack behaviors to form the trust opinion: no identity or fake identity, mission message modification, and good/bad mouthing. We call a message to be used for mission execution as a "mission message (MM)" for notational convenience hereafter. Equation 4 describes how $O_{i,k}^{D-integrity}(t)$ is computed from its three trust components.

We simply denote $(i, k, O_{i,k}^{D-integrity}(t))$ as $P_{(i,k)}$ meaning PI provided by node i with its direct trust opinion towards the previous MC k. For example, a destination node (DN) may receive a message such as:

---

[1] In a typical MANET, one talks about the next hop node or the downstream or upstream neighbor. In a DTN, a node may carry a message for a long time until it encounters a node to whom this message can be passed on. We call this "next-hop node" as the next message carrier.

$$\left[\text{MM}, \left(P_{(0,\emptyset)} \right)_{k_n}, \left(P_{(1,0)} \right)_{k_{n-1}}, \left(P_{(2,1)} \right)_{k_{n-2}}, \dots, \left(P_{(m,m-1)} \right)_{k_{n-m}} \right]_{K_{S,t}} \tag{1}$$

where MM denotes a mission message and $K_{S,t}$ is a symmetric key issued at time t. The source node's ID is 0, and other intermediate MCs' IDs are 1, 2, ... , m where m is the number of intermediate MCs. The message including both MM and PIs is encrypted by a symmetric key $K_{S,t}$. Note that the source only encloses its ID since there is no previous MC. The apparent redundancy in the carried ID information is crucial in identifying some attacks, as discussed later. Typically, the addition of meta data by each relay node could lead to the so-called meta-data explosion problem if the number of hops or relays, m, is too large. However, this work does not have this problem because the proposed protocol is applied in a sparse DTN and it uses a trust threshold to filter trustworthy MCs.

To prevent modification of PIs inserted by previous MCs, we adopt an encryption key mechanism based on micro-TESLA [11]. Source and destination nodes obtain a base PI encryption key and decryption key, (k_0, k_n), from the closest TA. We assume that TAs are able to issue the same pair of keys (i.e., (k_0, k_n)) to a pair of source and destination nodes. A source encrypts its PI using k_n and generates $k_{n-1} = F(k_n)$ to dictate the next MC to use k_{n-1}. Similarly, the next MC will encrypt its PI using k_{n-1} and pass k_{n-2} to its next MC. This process continues until the message arrives at a DN. A MC does not know the previous MC's PI encryption key, so it cannot decrypt the PI of the previous MC. When the DN receives the message, it can check with (k_0, k_n) if correct keys are being used on the path, and can properly decrypt all PIs by tracing back the key chains.

Unless attackers capture the source or destination node, PIs cannot be fully altered. Attackers may collude and exchange PI encryption keys but PI modifications may occur between attackers themselves which have little impact on overall attack behaviors. If a MC does not comply with using a given PI encryption key, the DN will fail to decrypt all PIs and discard the message. This will eventually lead to identifying malicious nodes. Thus, we assume that smart attacker might want to follow the key policy to gain trust. However, using PI encryption/decryption keys does not guarantee that each MC provides correct provenance information. We consider that a node may drop or modify its own PI.

Symmetric keys and PI encryption/decryption keys are distributed via a public/private key pair. Each node will use a TA's public key to request proper keys and a TA is preloaded with public keys of all nodes in the network. Each node will decrypt a message carrying the symmetric or PI encryption key using its private key. Thus, non-TA nodes do not need to store public keys of all nodes. TAs are involved only in key management, not in the trust evaluation process.

2.2   Attack Model

The use of a symmetric key prevents outside attackers, but not inside attackers. We consider the following insider attacks:

- **Fake identity or no identity:** Our protocol requires that a MC should insert its ID in the PI tuple. However, an attacker may not add its real ID or may insert a fake ID. If this attack is successful, this attacker's misbehavior may be interpreted as another node's misbehavior, leading to inaccurate trust evaluation.

- **Good or bad mouthing:** A node may perform a good or bad mouthing attack by giving a bad direct opinion towards a good node or by providing a good direct opinion towards a bad node. This hinders accurate trust evaluation.
- **Message modification:** A legitimate node with a symmetric key may modify MM. To prevent PI modification by other MCs, we use PI encryption keys as discussed in Section 2.1.
- **Packet dropping:** A node may drop packets based on its inherent selfish nature to lower service availability, leading to service unavailability and inaccurate trust evaluation.

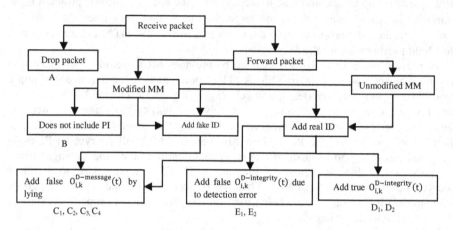

Fig. 1. Attack scenarios graph

Fig. 1 shows the attack scenarios considered in this work. Each node's behavior path is indicated with symbols such as A, B, C_1, C_2, C_3, C_4, D_1, D_2, E_1 and E_2. When a DN evaluates other nodes, if it does not see their ID in any received message and predicts energy depletion of the node, it will reduce a trust point for availability. If an attacker does not insert its ID or inserts a fake ID, it will be penalized by the decrease of the trust level. A smart attacker may want to reveal its real ID to avoid the penalty. If the attacker decides to insert a fake ID, it will provide false $O_{i,k}^{D-integrity}(t)$. Attacks can be performed with various combinations as shown in the paths described in Fig. 1.

2.3   Mobility Model and Node Deployment

We assume that nodes interact with each other not only to deliver messages, but also to exchange information for other purposes. A node is able to diagnose other nodes' attack behaviors based on its past direct experience. A given mission requires that each node, as a source, must send information to a list of destination nodes. Each node, as a DN, expects to receive information from a set of source nodes. For message delivery, nodes use the "store-and-forward" technique, meaning that a node carries messages until it encounters a MC.

Without loss of generality, we assume a square-shaped operational area consisting of m×m sub-grid areas with the width and height equal to wireless radio range (R). Initially nodes are randomly distributed over the operational area based on the uniform distribution. A node randomly moves to one of five locations (i.e., north, west, south, east, and current location) in accordance with its speed. The speed of node i, v_i, is chosen uniformly over $(0, v_{max}]$ m/s where v_{max} is the maximum possible speed, and v_i is then fixed during the node's lifetime. The boundary grid areas are wrapped around (i.e., a torus is assumed) to avoid end effects. For simplicity, we assume that each node is located in the center of its sub-grid. Nodes are modeled with heterogeneous characteristics with different speed, energy level, monitoring capability (i.e., detection error), group join and leave rate, and cooperation probabilities (i.e., packet dropping), and honesty probabilities (i.e., good/bad mouthing, fake identity, message modification).

- **Speed (v_i):** A node is assigned an average speed of its lifetime for analytical modeling, selecting from the range $(0, v_{max}]$ based on uniform distribution.
- **Energy level (E_j^{energy}):** A node is assigned an initial energy level selected from the range $[E_{min}, E_{max}]$ and its energy consumption is affected by its cooperativeness and membership status.
- **Detection error (P_i^{fp} / P_i^{fn}):** A node has monitoring capability with detection error probabilities of false positives and false negatives on integrity trust and predicting energy level for competence trust. Each node's detection error probabilities (P_i^{fp} and P_i^{fn}) are selected from the range $(0, P_{err}^{max}]$.
- **Group join and leave (λ / μ):** A node may leave or join a group where the inter-arrival time of the events is exponentially distributed with the rates λ and μ.
- **Cooperativeness (P_i^{coop}) and Integrity ($P_i^{integrity}$):** A node may drop a packet, or lie or modify a message based on the inherent characteristics of cooperativeness or integrity. We model these by assigning a seed probability for cooperativeness or integrity from the range $[GB_{min}, 1]$ based on uniform distribution.

2.4   Composite Trust Metric

The proposed trust metric consists of three trust properties: availability, integrity, and competence. First, *availability* property refers to service availability that is affected by system security and performance (e.g., quality-of-service). We mainly consider nodes' packet forwarding behavior to measure service availability. Loss of service availability may be caused by (1) a node's selfish or malicious behavior; (2) inherent network unreliability (i.e., link failure); (3) becoming a non-member by leaving the network; and (4) lack of access to a valid symmetric key. Second, *integrity* measures whether a node behaves without showing attacks described in Section 2.2. Third, *competence* property reflects the remaining battery lifetime of a node (a surrogate for resources available at the node) and the amount of positive experiences (PE).

Trust Aggregation: The trust value is formed with past evidence at time $(t - \Delta t)$ and new evidence, either direct or indirect, at time t. The trust value of node j evaluated by node i at time t is given by:

$$T_{i,j}(t) = T_{i,j}(t - \Delta t) + O_{i,j}^{new}(t), \quad T_{i,j}(t = 0) = \lceil (TV_{min} + TV_{max})/2 \rceil \qquad (2)$$

A trust value is a real number and clipped into the range $[TV_{min}, TV_{max}]$. The initial trust value $T_{i,j}(t = 0)$ is at the midpoint of the allowed range. Notice that the overall trust $T_{i,j}(t)$ is updated based on new direct or indirect observations on top of past experience at t-Δt.

Trust Formation: Newly observed (either directly or indirectly) trust evidence comprises three trust properties:

$$O_{i,j}^{new}(t) = O_{i,j}^{availability}(t) + O_{i,j}^{integrity}(t) + O_{i,j}^{competence}(t) \tag{3}$$

When nodes i and j encounter each other as 1-hop neighbors, node i will entirely rely on direct observations towards node j's behaviors to collect new evidence at time t. Direct trust evaluation can be assessed between any two encountering nodes based on their own assessment capability. Availability is measured by whether a node is available to serve requests. Integrity is evaluated based on three attack behaviors. Competence is assessed by energy level and positive experience. Thus, each trust component is evaluated with a single observation or multiple observations where each observation is counted as equal. We discuss details of the three trust components below in Direct Trust Evidences.

Note that node i is not necessarily a DN. However, indirect trust evaluation can be only conducted when node i is a DN. That is, node i (DN) will rely on received messages to evaluate trustworthiness of node j. In this case, time t represents the time that the DN evaluates trust towards node j based on the received information even if the trust evidences are collected by intermediate MCs on the way to deliver the message to the DN.

Direct Trust Evidences: When nodes i and j are 1-hop neighbors, a trust value is computed based only on direct new observations plus past experiences. Recall that nodes interact with each other for other purposes and are able to leverage the experience to assess direct trust towards 1-hop neighbors. We define α as a reward or penalty unit in trust level for each trust property.

- **Direct availability** ($O_{i,j}^{D-availability}(t)$): This is α if node i has received message(s) from its 1-hop neighbor node j during the last Δt period; -α otherwise. $O_{i,j}^{D-availability}(t)$ lies in $[-\alpha, \alpha]$.

- **Direct integrity** ($O_{i,j}^{D-integrity}(t)$): This consists of three trust components:

$$O_{i,j}^{D-integrity}(t) = O_{i,j}^{D-message}(t) + O_{i,j}^{D-honesty}(t) + O_{i,j}^{D-identity}(t) \tag{4}$$

$O_{i,j}^{D-message}(t)$ is α if node i believes node j did not modify MM; - α otherwise. $O_{i,j}^{D-honesty}(t)$ is α if node i believes node j did not lie about the integrity of the previous MC; - α otherwise. $O_{i,j}^{D-identity}(t)$ is α if node i believes node j inserted a real ID; - α otherwise. $O_{i,j}^{D-integrity}(t)$ lies in $[-3\alpha, 3\alpha]$.

- **Direct competence** ($O_{i,j}^{D-competence}(t)$): This is formed with two trust components, energy level and positive experience:

$$O_{i,j}^{D-competence}(t) = O_{i,j}^{D-energy}(t) + O_{i,j}^{D-PE}(t) \tag{5}$$

$O_{i,j}^{D-competence}(t)$ is 0 when $O_{i,j}^{D-availability}(t) < 0$. $O_{i,j}^{D-energy}(t)$ is α if $E_j^{energy}(t) > E^{th}$ where E^{th} is the minimum energy threshold required to execute a mission; - α

otherwise. $O_{i,j}^{D-PE}(t)$ is α if $O_{i,j}^{D-availability}(t) + O_{i,j}^{D-integrity}(t) == 4\alpha$, meaning that node j gains extra reward when it behaves perfectly in both availability and integrity; - α otherwise. $E_{j}^{energy}(t)$ is extrapolated based on the direct (prior knowledge on initial energy level) and indirect information (availability). Note that we consider probabilities of false positives and negatives (P_{i}^{fp} and P_{i}^{fn}) in the above direct trust evaluation for an imperfect monitoring mechanism installed in each node. Imperfect detection is applied for integrity trust and energy level. Availability trust depends upon a receipt of the packet. Positive experience in competence trust is evaluated through the three components of integrity trust evaluated by considering detection errors and availability trust. $O_{i,j}^{D-competence}(t)$ ranges over $[-2\alpha, 2\alpha]$.

Indirect Trust Evidences: When node j is more than 1-hop distant from node i, node i (DN) will rely on provenance information in a received message, if any, to evaluate node j. However, node i may not receive any messages enclosing node j's ID (even no-ID insertion attack is not caught). In this case, when the energy level of node j is predicted as depleted, the following penalty will be given:

$$O_{i,j}^{ID-availability}(t) = -\alpha, \quad O_{i,j}^{ID-integrity}(t) = O_{i,j}^{ID-competence}(t) = 0 \tag{6}$$

If the node is caught by a DN for no-ID insertion or no-PI insertion, then it will be penalized for unavailability in addition to the ID attack as well.

- **Indirect availability ($O_{i,j}^{ID-availability}(t)$):** When node i, as a DN, receives a message, it evaluates node j's availability as follows:

$$O_{i,j}^{ID-availability}(t) = \begin{cases} \alpha \text{ if } O_{i,j}^{ID-identity}(t) > 0; \\ 0 \text{ otherwise}; \end{cases} \tag{7}$$

When node j's ID is shown in the received message and proven to be authentic, node j's availability trust is incremented by α. If node j's ID is inserted by a fake identity attacker, node j will not be penalized. See Equation 9 for $O_{i,j}^{ID-identity}(t)$.

- **Indirect integrity ($O_{i,j}^{ID-integrity}(t)$):** Similar with direct integrity trust, this is formed with three components as follows:

$$O_{i,j}^{ID-integrity}(t) = O_{i,j}^{ID-message}(t) + O_{i,j}^{ID-honesty}(t) + O_{i,j}^{ID-identity}(t) \tag{8}$$

Indirect identity trust, $O_{i,j}^{ID-identity}(t)$, is computed by:

$$O_{i,j}^{ID-identity}(t) = \begin{cases} \alpha \text{ if } D(ID_j, preID(m(j))) == 0 \text{ and } O_{m(j),j}^{D-identity}(t) > 0; \\ 0 \text{ otherwise}; \end{cases} \tag{9}$$

$$O_{i,k}^{ID-identity}(t) = \begin{cases} -\alpha \text{ if } O_{i,j}^{ID-identity}(t) == 0; \\ 0 \text{ otherwise}; \end{cases}$$

Here m (j) indicates the next MC to node j and $O_{m(j),j}^{D-identity}(t)$ is only considered when $T_{i,m(j)}(t - \Delta t) \geq T_{min}$, implying only trustworthy nodes' information is evaluated. $D(ID_j, preID(m(j)))$ returns 0 when the two IDs are the same; 1 otherwise. ID_j is the

ID inserted by node j and preID(m(j)) is the previous MC's ID provided by node m(j). $O_{m(j),j}^{D-identity}(t)$ is the direct observation on identity trust towards node j by the next MC m(j). When node j's ID is proven to be true based on Equation 9, node j's identity trust is incremented by α. Otherwise, node j is not penalized since it is a victim due to a fake identity attack performed by another node. If caught, the fake identity attacker, node k, is penalized instead.

Indirect honesty trust, $O_{i,j}^{ID-honesty}(t)$, is obtained by:

$$O_{i,j}^{ID-honesty}(t) = \begin{cases} \alpha \text{ if } T_{i,j}(t-\Delta t) \geq T_{min} \text{ and } O_{m(j),j}^{D-honesty}(t) > 0; \\ -\alpha \text{ otherwise}; \end{cases} \quad (10)$$

Similarly, m(j) is the next MC to node j and $O_{m(j),j}^{D-honesty}$ is only evaluated when $T_{i,m(j)}(t-\Delta t) \geq T_{min}$. Note that direct evidences used are collected when a message travels through intermediate MCs. At time t, node i (DN) evaluates node j based on the direct evidence provided by node m(j), the next MC of node j.

$O_{i,j}^{ID-message}(t)$ is evaluated based on the other two integrity trust components (identity and honesty) and a direct opinion of the next MC m(j) towards the previous MC j on mission message modification, and computed by:

$$O_{i,j}^{ID-message}(t) = \begin{cases} \alpha \text{ if } O_{i,j}^{ID-identity}(t) > 0 \text{ and } O_{i,j}^{ID-honesty}(t) > 0 \text{ and } O_{m(j),j}^{D-message}(t) > 0; \\ -\alpha \text{ otherwise}; \end{cases} \quad (11)$$

$O_{m(j),j}^{D-message}(t)$ is a direct message trust opinion of the next MC m(j) towards the previous MC j where m(j) has the past trust level, $T_{i,m(j)}(t-\Delta t) \geq T_{min}$.

- **Indirect competence ($O_{i,j}^{ID-competence}(t)$):** This is measured similarly as direct competence, but based on indirect evidences. This is given by:

$$O_{i,j}^{ID-competence}(t) = O_{i,j}^{energy}(t) + O_{i,j}^{ID-PE}(t) \quad (12)$$

2.5   Metrics

Recall that our goal in developing the proposed provenance model was to estimate trust accurately and efficiently. We use two performance metrics to evaluate the proposed trust model as follows:

- **Trust Bias ($T_{i,j}^{bias}$):** This is the time-averaged difference between trust of node j evaluated by node i and objective trust of node j evaluated by all encountered nodes based on direct observations with no detection errors. This metric considers both false positives and negatives. $T_{i,j}(t)$ is the trust value of node j evaluated by node i at time t and $OT_j(t)$ is an objective trust value of node j based on aggregated direct observations of all encountered nodes at time t. Given the entire mission lifetime LT, $T_{i,j}^{bias}$ is obtained by:

$$T_{i,j}^{bias} = \frac{\int_0^{LT} T_{i,j}^{bias}(t)}{LT} \text{ where } T_{i,j}^{bias}(t) = |T_{i,j}(t) - OT_j(t)|/OT_j(t) \quad (13)$$

- **Communication Overhead (C_{total}):** This is the communication cost per time unit (sec.) for a node to deal with trust evaluation ($C_{TE}(t)$) and message delivery ($C_{MD}(t)$) during the entire mission lifetime, LT. C_{total} is computed by:

$$C_{total} = \frac{\int_0^{LT} (C_{TE}(t) + C_{MD}(t))}{LT} \qquad (14)$$

- **Mission Message Correctness (N_{CR}):** This refers to how many packets a DN receives correctly during the entire mission lifetime, LT. The trustworthiness of intermediate MCs significantly affects the correctness of received messages. This is computed by:

$$N_{CR} = \sum_{p \in P} \prod_{k \in L_p} P_k^{p-message}(t) \qquad (15)$$

$$P_k^{p-message}(t) = \begin{cases} 1 \text{ if a MC k did not modify message p;} \\ 0 \text{ otherwise;} \end{cases}$$

here P is the set of messages sent by a source node to a DN and the k nodes are intermediate MCs delivering message p. L_p is the set of all intermediate MCs involved in delivering each message p.

3   Hierarchical Modeling Using Stochastic Petri Nets

We use SPN because of its efficient representations of a large number of states where the underlying model is a continuous-time Markov or semi-Markov chain. We develop a hierarchical modeling technique based on SPN to avoid state explosion problems and to improve solution efficiency for realizing and describing the behaviors of each node and obtaining objective trust values.

We develop event subnets to describe a node's behavior and its actual trust value as shown in Fig. 2. A hierarchical SPN technique is used to derive interactions or trust relationships with other nodes in the system. We conduct this process by running the SPN subnet N times for the N nodes in the network. We use the information obtained from SPN for trust evaluation. In SPN, we call each oval shown in Fig. 2 a "place" where "mark (place name)" is the number of tokens in the place. The number of tokens in different places indicates the status (state) of a node. Each transition bar (i.e., T_NAME) is the rate at which the corresponding event is triggered.

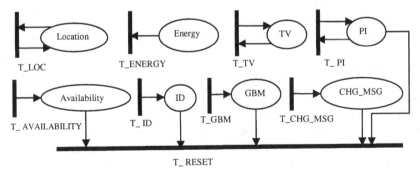

Fig. 2. Node SPN Subnet

Location Subnet: This subnet computes the probability that node i is in a particular grid area j at time t. This information along with the information of other nodes' locations at time t provides the information about when two nodes encounter as 1-hop neighbors at time t. Since node movements are assumed to be independent, the probability that two nodes are in a particular location at time t is given by the product of the two individual probabilities. Location probabilities are used to compute the probabilities that two nodes encounter or a node obtains a valid symmetric key based on the location of itself and TA's fixed location. The transition T_LOC rate is computed as v_i/R where v_i is node i's average speed given and R is radio range.

Energy Subnet: This subnet is used to obtain each node's energy lifetime. The number of tokens in place Energy indicates the battery life (hours) in energy. We approximately estimate energy consumption depending on a node's status: available vs. unavailable. We regard a node's availability as forwarding packets where a node may drop packets with any reason (See Availability Subnet below). When a node is not available, energy consumption is slowed down. The transition T_ENERGY is modeled by:

$$\text{if(mark(Availability)} == 0), \ \text{rate(T\_ENERGY)} = 1/(2T_{energy})$$

$$\text{else rate(T\_ENERGY)} = 1/T_{energy}$$

(16)

We assume that one token represents energy consumed for T_{energy} for normal activities. When a node is in sleep mode or does not serve any request (i.e., unavailable status), it is predicted as consuming one half of normal energy consumption.

Trust Value Subnet: The number of tokens in place TV represents a direct trust value observed by 1-hop neighbors. We assume that a node shows consistent behavior patterns to all nodes, so the views of 1-hop neighbors towards the same node are assumed synchronized. Thus, mark (TV) is computed based on the equations on direct trust evidences described in Section 2.4 without considering any detection error. This trust value is used as an objective trust to obtain a trust value at time t based on direct observations by all encountered nodes. Direct trust evaluation is performed per encounter interval with the transition T_TV rate being $1/T_{i,encounter}$, meaning that node i encounters another node with the average inter-arrival time of $T_{i,encounter}$. $T_{i,encounter}$ is computed by $\sum_{j \in N} R/[(P_i^{loc-1} \sum_{n \in S} P_j^{loc-n})(v_i + v_j)]$ where node j belongs to the set N including all nodes in the network, R is radio range, P_i^{loc-1} is the time-averaged probability that node i is located in area l, S is the set of adjacent locations of node i, and v_i is the speed of node i.

Availability Subnet: A token in place Availability indicates that node i is available and cooperative upon receiving a request; zero token otherwise. The rate for the transition T_AVAILABILITY is affected by: (1) join probability (i.e., $P^\lambda = \lambda/(\lambda + \mu)$ where λ and μ are join and leave rates); (2) whether node i is able to obtain a symmetric key from the closest TA (P_{sk}); (3) the probability that node i is cooperative to serve packet forwarding (P_i^{coop}); (4) link reliability based on network or node conditions (P_{link}); and (5) whether or not a node's trust is below T_{min} ($P_{untrustworthy}$). Upon the receipt of a newly arrived packet, a node may become available as determined by the following condition:

$$if\bigl(mark(Availability) == 0 \text{ and } P_{sk} > 0 \text{ and } P_{untrustworthy} > 0\bigr)$$

$$rate(T\_AVAILABILITY) = \bigl(P^\lambda P_i^{coop} P_{link}\bigr)/T_{i,encounter} \qquad (17)$$

$$else \qquad disable \; T\_AVAILABILITY$$

P_{sk} is computed based on node i's location and fixed locations of TAs. P_{sk} is 1 when a symmetric key is obtainable; 0 otherwise. $P_{untrustworthy}$ is 1 when a node has its trust value below T_{min}.

PI Subnet: A token in place PI means that node i decides to insert provenance information; no token otherwise. The rate for transition T_PI is given by $P_i^{coop}/T_{i,encounter}$.

ID, GBM and CHG_MSG Subnets: Identity, message, and honesty trust components in integrity are evaluated similarly. When place ID, GBM or CHG_MSG has a token, it means that a respective attack is performed; zero token otherwise. The rates for transitions T_ID, T_GBM and T_CHG_MSG are given by $(1 - P_i^{integrity})/T_{i,encounter}$. These attacks do not occur when no provenance information is inserted, i.e., mark(PI)==0. A good or bad mouthing attack occurs when a fake ID is inserted.

Transition T_RESET flushes all tokens from those places with output arcs into the transition upon encountering a new node with the rate of $1/T_{i,encounter}$.

4   Numerical Analysis and Results

This section compares the proposed provenance-based trust model (PT) with a baseline trust model (BT) in terms of the proposed metrics. We choose the model described in our prior work [2] as the existing BT that evaluates a node's trust based on direct observation or experience and recommendations. For fair comparison, we slightly modify BT that fits the trust metric considered in this work. BT uses the same trust metric as PT except the way it aggregates trust with direct and indirect trust evidences based on recommendations as follows:

$$T_{i,j}(t) = T_{i,j}(t - \Delta t) + \beta \, O_{i,j}^{direct-new}(t) + (1 - \beta) \, O_{i,j}^{indirect-new}(t) \qquad (18)$$

where $O_{i,j}^{direct-new}(t)$ is computed based on Equation 3 and β and $(1-\beta)$ are the weights applied to direct and indirect trust evidences. $O_{i,j}^{indirect-new}(t)$ is evaluated by recommendations from all encountered nodes. The encountered nodes pass recommendations only based on direct observation in order to avoid any security vulnerability by passing a derived trust.

Table 1. Default values used

Parameter	Value	Parameter	Value
v_{max}	15 m/sec.	β	0.8
GB_{min}	0.8	E^{th}	0
T_{min}	5, 10, 15, 20, 25	LT	100,000 sec.
α	1	P_{link}	0.99
R	100 m	$[TV_{min}, TV_{max}]$	[0, 30]
λ	Once per hour	μ	Once per 4 hours
P_{error}^{max}	0.01	$[E_{min}, E_{max}]$	[12, 24]

In this case study, 165 packets each with 2 copies (total 330 packets) are sent from a source to a destination. In each run, 20 different source-destination pairs are deployed. We pick one pair and show the results (source: node 3, destination: node 15). A total of 20 nodes are spread over the operational area divided into 6 × 6 regions. The results are shown with the average values computed over 100 runs of trust evaluation.

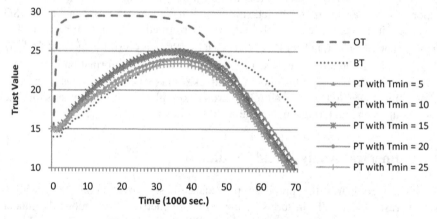

Fig. 3. Trust values over time: OT vs. BT vs. PT

Fig. 3 shows the average trust values of all nodes evaluated by a DN over time in OT, BT, and PT with various T_{min} based on Equation 13. OT ($OT_j(t)$ in Equation 13) is the objective trust value based on only direct trust evaluation by all encountered nodes. BT is not affected by using different T_{min} since trust evaluation is not dependent upon the selection of the next MC in the message delivery. Thus, we show only one curve under BT. However, PT is affected by various T_{min} used since provenance information tagged in the main message is used as indirect trust evidences for overall trust evaluation. BT underestimates trust values in the beginning half while overestimating trust values in the rest of the mission lifetime. Overall, PT performs better than BT without underestimating trust values in the beginning and showing relatively accurate trust assessment in the end. While BT only depends on the encounter event where nodes i and j can exchange information, PT can collect trust evidences indirectly based on the provenance information tagged with main messages, leading to better trust accuracy. As T_{min} increases, PT further underestimates trust values because using higher T_{min} in selecting the next MC only updates trust values of highly trustworthy nodes while decaying those of less trustworthy nodes due to their unavailability.

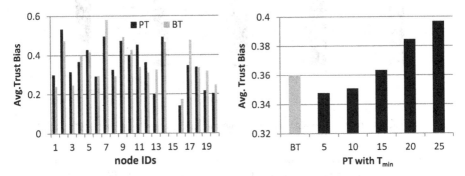

Fig. 4. Average trust bias per node: PT vs. BT **Fig. 5.** Average trust bias of all nodes: PT vs. BT

Figs. 4 and 5 (computed based on Equation 13) confirm the observation and conclusion derived from Fig. 3. Fig. 4 is the time-averaged trust bias per node with $T_{min}=10$. Fig. 5 is the overall time-averaged trust bias of all nodes. PT performs significantly better than BT in trust accuracy when a lower T_{min} is used.

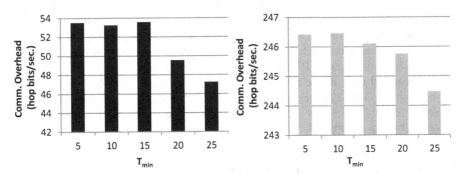

Fig. 6. Communication overhead in PT vs. **Fig. 7.** Communication overhead in BT vs. system trust threshold (T_{min})   system trust threshold (T_{min})

Figs. 6 and 7 show communication overhead (C_{total}) under PT and BT with respect to various T_{min} values based on Equation 14. When a higher T_{min} is used, a lower C_{total} results due to a smaller number of nodes with high enough trust values to do message delivery. The average C_{total} over different T_{min} in BT is 245.84 hop bits/sec. while that in PT is 51.39 hop bits/sec. This demonstrates that PT significantly reduces communication overhead compared to BT while achieving better performance in trust accuracy with low $T_{min} < 15$, as shown in Figs. 3, 4, and 5.

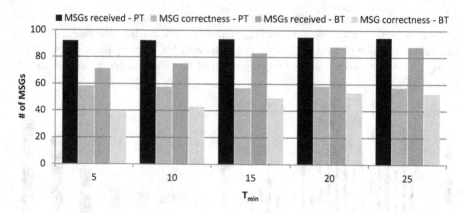

Fig. 8. The numbers of messages received and messages received correctly: PT vs. BT

Fig. 8 compares the two schemes in terms of the number of messages received and the number of correct messages among the received messages. In BT, as a higher T_{min} is used, more messages are received and more messages are correct among the received messages (computed based on Equation 15). That is, selecting a highly trustworthy node as the next MC positively affects message delivery ratio as well as message correctness. In PT, we do not observe much sensitivity over different T_{min} in terms of these two metrics. This is because trust update in PT is affected by whether a received message has provenance information about each node. This is determined by which node is selected as the next MC using T_{min}. When a higher T_{min} is used, only the trust values of nodes with higher trust values are updated while the trust values of other nodes with lower trust values decay over time due to unavailability, since they are not being selected as the next MC. Thus, the benefit of using a higher T_{min} is not prominent because nodes with the trust value above T_{min} may not be found easily with high T_{min}. In addition, since PT tends to underestimate trust values of nodes, it selects a more qualified node as the next MC than what is required, thus lowering risk. On the other hand, BT is more likely to overestimate especially towards the end of mission lifetime. This leads to a next MC with a less qualified node than what is expected, thus increasing risk. Therefore, overall PT performs better than BT.

5   Conclusions and Future Work

This paper proposed a provenance-based trust model that achieves better trust accuracy compared to an existing scheme while significantly reducing communication overhead for trust evaluation. The proposed scheme outperformed the existing scheme in three metrics: trust accuracy, communication overhead, and the number of messages received and message correctness.

We plan to extend this work by: conducting further sensitivity analysis; refining our attack model; and introducing dynamic minimum trust thresholds.

Acknowledgement. Dr. MoonJeong Chang was supported in part by the Army Research Office under Grant W911NF-12-1-0016.

References

1. Alam, S.M.I., Fahmy, S.: Energy-efficient provenance transmission in large-scale wireless sensor networks. In: IEEE Int'l Symposium on a World of Wireless, Mobile and Multimedia Networks, Lucca, Italy, June 20-23 (2011)
2. Chen, I.R., Bao, F., Chang, M., Cho, J.H.: Trust management for encounter-based touting in delay tolerant networks. In: IEEE Global Telecommunications Conf., Miami, FL, December 6-10, pp. 1–6 (2010)
3. Cho, J.H., Swami, A., Chen, I.R.: A survey of trust management in mobile ad hoc networks. IEEE Communications Surveys and Tutorials 13(4), 562–583 (2011)
4. Dai, C., Lin, D., Bertino, E., Kantarcioglu, M.: An Approach to Evaluate Data Trustworthiness Based on Data Provenance. In: Jonker, W., Petković, M. (eds.) SDM 2008. LNCS, vol. 5159, pp. 82–98. Springer, Heidelberg (2008)
5. Freire, J., Koop, D., Santos, E., Silva, C.T.: Provenance for computational tasks: A survey. IEEE Computing in Science and Engineering 10(3), 11–21 (2008)
6. Golbeck, J.: Combining Provenance with Trust in Social Networks for Semantic Web Content Filtering. In: Moreau, L., Foster, I. (eds.) IPAW 2006. LNCS, vol. 4145, pp. 101–108. Springer, Heidelberg (2006)
7. Lim, H.S., Moon, Y.-S., Bertino, E.: Provenance-based trustworthiness assessment in sensor networks. In: Proc. 7th Int'l Workshop on Data Management for Sensor Networks, Singapore, September 13 (2010)
8. Liu, Y., Futrelle, J., Myers, J., Rodriguez, A., Kooper, R.: A provenance-aware virtual sensor system using the open provenance model. In: Int'l Symposium on Collaborative Technologies and Systems, Chicago, IL, May 17-21, pp. 330–339 (2010)
9. McDaniel, P.: Data provenance and security. IEEE Security and Privacy 9(2), 83–85 (2011)
10. Moreau, L., Freire, J., Futrelle, J., McGrath, R.E., Myers, J., Paulson, P.: The Open Provenance Model: An Overview. In: Freire, J., Koop, D., Moreau, L. (eds.) IPAW 2008. LNCS, vol. 5272, pp. 323–326. Springer, Heidelberg (2008)
11. Perrig, A., Tygar, J.D.: Secure Broadcast Communication in Wired and Wireless Networks. Kluwer Academic Publishers (2002)
12. Rajbhandari, S., Wootten, I., Ali, A.S., Rana, O.F.: Evaluating provenance-based trust for scientific workflows. In: 6th IEEE Int'l Symposium on Cluster Computing and the Grid, Singapore, May 16-19, vol. 1, pp. 365–372 (2006)
13. Spyropoulos, T., Rais, R.N., Turletti, T., Obraczka, K., Vasilakos, A.: Routing for disruption tolerant networks: taxonomy and design. Wireless Networks 16(8), 2349–2370 (2010)
14. Srivatsa, M., Gao, W., Iyengar, A.: Provenance-driven data dissemination in disruption tolerant networks. In: Proc. 14th Int'l Conf. on Information Fusion, Chicago, IL, July 5-8 (2011)
15. Sultana, S., Bertino, E., Shehab, M.: A provenance based mechanism to identify malicious packet dropping adversaries in sensor networks. In: 31st Int'l Conf. on Distributed Computing Systems Workshops, Minneapolis, MN, June 20-24, pp. 332–338 (2011)
16. Wang, X., Govindan, K., Mohapatra, P.: Collusion-resilient quality of information evaluation based on information provenance. In: 8th Annual IEEE Communications Society Conf. on Sensor, Mesh and Ad Hoc Communications and Networks, Salt Lake City, Utah, June 27-30, pp. 395–403 (2011)
17. Yu, B., Kallurkar, S., Flo, R.: A Demspter-Shafer approach to provenance-aware trust assessment. In: Int'l Symposium on Collaborative Technologies and Systems, Irvine, CA, May 29-23, pp. 383–390 (2008)
18. National Cyber Security Research and Development Challenges: Related to Economics, Physical Infrastructure and Human Behavior, An Industry, Academic and Government Perspective (2009)

Trust Transitivity and Conditional Belief Reasoning

Audun Jøsang[1], Tanja Ažderska[2], and Stephen Marsh[3]

[1] University of Oslo, Norway
josang@mn.uio.no
[2] Jozef Stefan Institute, Slovenia
atanja@e5.ijs.si
[3] Communications Research Centre, Canada
steve.marsh@crc.gc.ca

Abstract. Trust transitivity is a common phenomenon embedded in human reasoning about trust. Given a specific context or purpose, trust transitivity is often manifested through the humans' intuition to rely on the recommendations of a trustworthy advisor about another entity that the advisor recommends. Although this simple principle has been formalised in various ways for many trust and reputation systems, there is no real or physical basis for trust transitivity to be directly translated into a mathematical model. In that sense, all mathematical operators for trust transitivity proposed in the literature must be considered *ad hoc*; they represent attempts to model a very complex human phenomenon as if it were lendable to analysis by the laws of physics. Considering this nature of human trust transitivity in reality, any simple mathematical model will essentially have rather poor predictive power. In this paper, we propose a new interpretation of trust transitivity that is radically different from those described in the literature so far. More specifically, we consider recommendations from an advisor as evidence that the relying party will use as input arguments in conditional reasoning models for assessing hypotheses about the trust target. The proposed model of conditional trust transitivity is based on the framework of subjective logic.

Keywords: Trust, Transitivity, Deduction, Abduction, Bayesian, Conditional.

1 Introduction

Trust transitivity based on recommendations is a concept that can have different meanings. It can, for example, mean that, if Alice trusts Bob, and Bob trusts Claire, then by transitivity, Alice will also trust Claire. This is expressed in Eq.(1).

$$\text{Indirect(Alice} \longrightarrow \text{Claire)} \quad := \quad \text{Direct(Alice} \longrightarrow \text{Bob} \longrightarrow \text{Claire)} \tag{1}$$

Alice is here the originator relying party, Bob is the recommender (i.e., the advisor), and Claire is the trust target that Alice indirectly trusts as a result of this process. This transitive process assumes that Bob recommends Claire to Alice, i.e., there must be some communication from Bob to Alice about Claire's trustworthiness. This kind of reasoning can also be observed among animals. For example, when bees signal to each other where to find pollen, the other bees can derive trust in a specific pollen harvesting area; when animals give warnings about danger, it can be interpreted as a recommendation

T. Dimitrakos et al. (Eds.): IFIPTM 2012, IFIP AICT 374, pp. 68–83, 2012.

about distrust, as in the case of a presence of potential predator. Trust is a phenomenon that emerges naturally among living species equipped with advanced cognitive faculties. When assuming that software agents can be equipped with capabilities to reason about trust and risk, and to make decisions based on that, one can talk about artificial trust, as described by rapidly growing growing literature [1,2,6,13].

It is also common, at least among humans, that the relying party receives recommendations about the same target entity from multiple recommenders whose recommendations express different and possibly conflicting trust. The relying party then needs to fuse the different trust recommendations and form a single trust opinion about the target entity. These are principles of analytical reasoning that people handle more or less unconsciously in everyday life. In the computational trust literature many formal models have been proposed for the same purpose, such as in [5,9]. A distinction can be made between interpreting trust as a belief about the reliability of the target, and as a decision to depend on the target [7]. In this paper, trust is interpreted in the former sense, i.e. as a belief about reliability of a target.

A fundamental problem about modelling trust transitivity is that there is no benchmark for comparison and validation in nature, since practical trust transitivity seems to be idiosyncratic for humans and animals, with no true analog among non-living forms (and in the physical world for that matter). The efficacy of long chains of transitive trust in these circumstances is debatable, but nonetheless chains of trust can be observed in human trust. Human subjective trust is in reality a state that results from the cognitive and affective predispositions of an entity to perceive and respond to external stimuli, and to combine them with the internal states and stimuli. However, it is the actual nature of trust that represents the relying party's subjective estimate of the reliability of the target entity for a purpose on which the relying party's welfare depends.

In contrast, when analysing the reliability of physical systems, there are mathematical models that can be easily validated through observation. For example, the correct operation of a serial system depends on the correct operation of each component, which translates into a conjunctive model where the system reliability can be predicted as the product of the reliabilities of each component in the series. The correct operation of a parallel system depends on the correct operation of at least one of its components, which translates into a disjunctive model where the system reliability can be predicted as the coproduct of the reliabilities of each component.

Let $p(x_i)$ express the reliability of component x_i, then the respective reliabilities of a serial system **Ser** and a parallel system **Par** are expressed as:

$$\text{Serial system reliability:} \quad p(\text{Ser}) = \prod p(x_i) \text{ , i.e. product of reliabilities}$$

$$(2)$$

$$\text{Parallel system reliability:} \quad p(\text{Par}) = \coprod p(x_i) \text{ , i.e. coproduct of reliabilities}$$

Addressing and computing trust based on chained recommendations, and on recommendations from multiple parties in parallel can not be modelled in the same manner as in Eq.(2), although some proposed trust models in the literature do precisely that. The product rule gives a very good estimate of serial system reliability, but is a very poor model for trust transitivity. To illustrate why this is so, assume a transitive trust path of n nodes where each node trusts the next with value p. The product rule dictates a derived trust $T = p^n$ which converges relatively quickly towards zero whenever $p < 1$, meaning that a trust value that is derived from a relatively long transitive trust path will be close to zero. Interpreting zero trust as distrust, as some models do, would clearly be wrong because there is no reason to think that an entity which is known only indirectly through a long transitive path should be distrusted for that reason. Interpreting zero trust as 'no information', as other models do, would be more intuitive in this case. Methods of computing trust transitivity that have been proposed for subjective logic [9] are analoguous to the latter interpretation, and we show that these methods are special cases of the conditional trust model for analysing trust transitivity proposed in this paper.

The contribution of this paper is to propose a new computational model for trust transitivity based on conditional belief reasoning using the formalism of subjective logic. The idea is to model trust transitivity in similar manner as analysing competing hypotheses. Such models are applied, e.g., in the area of intelligence analysis [14]. Modelling trust transitivity as a simple evidence analysis problem removes the mysticism of trust transitivity, i.e. it does not assume that trust transitivity exists as a separate natural process by itself. Our model assumes that trust transitivity implies weighing the obtained evidence in order to draw conclusions about the trust target. In this way, the principle of trust propagation becomes general and flexible, and thus applicable to the online communities of people, organisations and software agents. The higher purpose, however, is providing decision support based on collaborative interpretation of evidence by the community members. Consequently, this leads to enhancing the ability of online communities to support the emergent properties that result from transitive trust-relations among their members.

2   Subjective Logic Basics

2.1   General Opinions

A subjective opinion expresses belief about one or multiple propositions from a state space of mutually exclusive states called a *"frame of discernment"* or *"frame"* for short. Let X be a frame of cardinality k. Belief mass is distributed over the reduced powerset of the frame denoted as $\mathcal{R}(X)$. More precisely, the reduced powerset $\mathcal{R}(X)$ is defined as:

$$\mathcal{R}(X) = 2^X \setminus \{X, \emptyset\} = \{x_i \mid i = 1 \ldots k, \ x_i \subset X\}, \tag{3}$$

which means that all proper subsets of X are elements of $\mathcal{R}(X)$, but X itself is not in $\mathcal{R}(X)$. The emptyset $\emptyset$ is also not considered to be a proper element of $\mathcal{R}(X)$.

An opinion is a composite function that consists of a belief vector $\vec{b}$, an uncertainty parameter u and base rate vector $\vec{a}$. An opinion can also have as attributes the belief source/owner. Assigning belief mass to an element in the frame (i.e. to a singleton or a subset) is interpreted as positive belief that the proposition(s) represented by that element is/are true, and as negative belief in their complements. The belief vector can be additive (i.e. sum = 1) or sub-additive (i.e. sum < 1).

Uncertainty is expressed by not assigning the totality of belief mass, where the level of uncertainty is equal to the amount of unassigned belief. Uncertainty is here interpreted as the perceived imprecision of probability estimates. In case of total uncertainty, i.e. when $u = 1$, then the probability estimates of elements in the frame are equal to their base rate probabilities. The sub-additivity of the belief vector and the complement property of the uncertainty are expressed by Eq.(4) and Eq.(5) below:

$$\text{Belief sub-additivity:} \quad \sum_{x_i \in \mathcal{R}(X)} \vec{b}_X(x_i) \leq 1 , \quad \vec{b}_X(x_i) \in [0, 1] \tag{4}$$

$$\text{Belief and uncertainty additivity:} \quad u_X + \sum_{x_i \in \mathcal{R}(X)} \vec{b}_X(x_i) = 1 , \quad \vec{b}_X(x_i), u_X \in [0, 1] . \tag{5}$$

An element $x_i \in \mathcal{R}(X)$ is a *focal element* when its belief mass is non-zero, i.e. when $\vec{b}_X(x_i) > 0$. The frame X can not be a focal element, even when $u_X > 0$. The base rate vector, denoted as $\vec{a}(x_i)$, expresses the base rates of elements $x_i \in X$, and is formally defined below.

Definition 1 (Base Rate Function). Let X be a frame of cardinality k, and let $\vec{a}_X$ be the function from X to $[0, 1]^k$ satisfying:

$$\vec{a}_X(\emptyset) = 0, \quad \vec{a}_X(x_i) \in [0, 1] \quad \text{and} \quad \sum_{i=1}^{k} \vec{a}_X(x_i) = 1 . \tag{6}$$

Then $\vec{a}_X$ is a base rate distribution over X.

An opinion is normally denoted as $w_X^A = (\vec{b}, u, \vec{a})$ where A is the opinion owner, and X is the target frame to which the opinion applies [3].

Definition 2. General Opinion
Assume X to be a frame where $\mathcal{R}(X)$ denotes its reduced powerset. Let $\vec{b}_X$ be a belief vector over the elements of $\mathcal{R}(X)$, let u_X be the complementary uncertainty mass, and let $\vec{a}$ be a base rate vector over the frame X, all seen from the viewpoint of the opinion owner A. The composite function $w_X^A = (\vec{b}_X, u_X, \vec{a}_X)$ is then A's opinion over X.

The belief vector $\vec{b}_X$ has $(2^k - 2)$ parameters, whereas the base rate vector $\vec{a}_X$ only has k parameters. The uncertainty parameter u_X is a simple scalar. A general opinion thus contains $(2^k + k - 1)$ parameters. However, given Eq.(5) and Eq.(6), general opinions only have $(2^k + k - 3)$ degrees of freedom. The probability projection of hyper opinions is the vector $\vec{E}_X$ from $\mathcal{R}(X)$ to $[0, 1]^\kappa$ expressed as:

$$\vec{E}_X(x_i) = \sum_{x_j \in \mathcal{R}(X)} \vec{a}_X(x_i/x_j) \, \vec{b}_X(x_j) + \vec{a}_X(x_i) \, u_X , \quad \forall \, x_i \in \mathcal{R}(X) . \tag{7}$$

Table 1 lists the different classes of opinions [10], of which *hyper opinions* represent the general case. Equivalent probabilistic representations of opinions, e.g. as Beta pdf (probability density function) or a Dirichlet pdf, offer an alternative interpretation of subjective opinions in terms of traditional statistics.

Table 1. Opinion classes with equivalent probabilistic representations

	Binomial opinion Binary frame Focal element $x \in X$	**Multinomial opinion** n-ary frame Focal elements $x \in X$	**General (Hyper) opinion** n-ary frame Focal elements $x \in \mathcal{R}(X)$
Uncertain $(u > 0)$	**UB opinion**	**UM opinion**	**UH opinion**
Probabilistic repr.:	Beta pdf on x	Dirichlet pdf over X	Dirichlet pdf over $\mathcal{R}(X)$
Dogmatic $(u = 0)$	**DB opinion**	**DM opinion**	**DH opinion**
Probabilistic repr.:	Probability of x	Proba. distr. over X	Proba. distr. over $\mathcal{R}(X)$

Specific opinion types can be visualised as a point inside a barycentric coordinate systems in the form of a regular simplex. In particular, Fig.1.a visualises a binomial opinion as a point inside an equal sided triangle, and Fig.1.b visualises a trinomial opinion as a point inside a tetrahedron. Hyper opinions or multinomial opinions larger than trinomial can not be visualised in the same way, and are in general challenging to visualise.

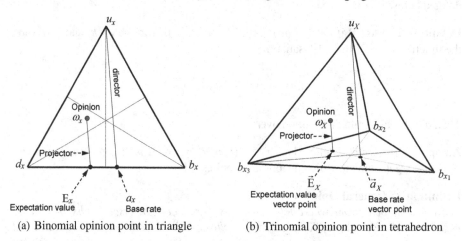

(a) Binomial opinion point in triangle   (b) Trinomial opinion point in tetrahedron

Fig. 1. Visualisation of opinions in barycentric coordinate systems

In the triangle on the left hand side, the belief, disbelief and uncertainty axes run from one edge to the opposite vertex indicated by b_x, d_x and u_x. The base rate a_x of a binomial opinion are shown on the base line, and the probability expectation value E_x is determined by projecting the opinion point to the base line parallel to the base rate director. In the tetrahedron on the right hand side the belief, and uncertainty-axes run from one triangular plane to the opposite vertex indicated by the labels b_{x_i} and by u_X. A *vacuous opinion* is when the opinion point is at the top of the simplex ($u = 1$), and a *dogmatic opinion* is when the opinion point is on the base line or plane ($u = 1$). The base rate vector $\vec{a}_X$ of the trinomial opinion is shown as a point on the base plane, and the probability expectation vector $\vec{E}_X$ is determined by projecting the opinion point onto the triangular base, parallel to the base rate director.

A special notation is used for representing binomial opinions over binary frames. A general n-ary frame X can be considered binary when seen as a binary partitioning consisting of one of its proper subsets x and the complement $\overline{x}$.

Definition 3 (Binomial Opinion). *Let* $X = \{x, \overline{x}\}$ *be either a binary frame or a binary partitioning of an n-ary frame. A binomial opinion about the truth of state x is the ordered quadruple* $\omega_x = (b, d, u, a)$ *where:*

   b, belief: *belief mass in support of x being true,*
   d, disbelief: *belief mass in support of $\overline{x}$ (i.e. NOT x),*
   u, uncertainty: *uncommitted belief, uncertainty of probability expectation of x,*
   a, base rate: *prior probability of x.*

We require $b + d + u = 1$ and $b, d, u, a \in [0, 1]$ as a special case of Eq.(5). The probability expectation value is computed with Eq.(8) as a special case of Eq.(7).

$$\mathrm{E}_x = b + au .\tag{8}$$

In case the point of a binomial opinion is located at the left or right base vertex in the triangle, i.e. with $d = 1$ or $b = 1$ and $u = 0$, the opinion is equivalent to boolean TRUE or FALSE, in which case subjective logic becomes equivalent with binary logic.

3   Previous Transitivity Operators of Subjective Logic

Several different trust transitivity operators for subjective logic have been proposed in the literature [9]. These are briefly described below.

Let A and B be two agents where A's trust in B's recommendations is expressed as $\omega_B^A = \{b_B^A, d_B^A, u_B^A, a_B^A\}$, and let C be an agent where B's trust in C is recommended to A with the opinion $\omega_C^B = \{b_C^B, d_C^B, u_C^B, a_C^B\}$. Let $\omega_C^{A:B} = \{b_C^{A:B}, d_C^{A:B}, u_C^{A:B}, a_C^{A:B}\}$ be A's derived trust in C as a result of the recommendation from B. Table 2 shows the derived opinion $\omega_C^{A:B}$ in case of uncertainty favouring transitivity, base rate sensitive transitivity, and opposite belief favouring transitivity.

Table 2. Trust transitivity operators of subjective logic proposed in the literature [9]

Uncertainty favouring $\omega_C^{A:B}$	Base rate sensitive $\omega_C^{A:B}$	Opposite belief favouring $\omega_C^{A:B}$
$b_C^{A:B} = b_B^A b_C^B$ $d_C^{A:B} = b_B^A d_C^B$ $u_C^{A:B} = d_B^A + u_B^A + b_B^A u_C^B$ $a_C^{A:B} = a_C^B$	$b_C^{A:B} = \mathrm{E}(\omega_B^A) b_C^B$ $d_C^{A:B} = \mathrm{E}(\omega_B^A) d_C^B$ $u_C^{A:B} = 1 - \mathrm{E}(\omega_B^A)(b_C^B + d_C^B)$ $a_C^{A:B} = a_C^B$ $\mathrm{E}(\omega_B^A) = b_B^A + a_B^A u_B^A$	$b_C^{A:B} = b_B^A b_C^B + d_B^A d_C^B$ $d_C^{A:B} = b_B^A d_C^B + d_B^A b_C^B$ $u_C^{A:B} = u_B^A + (b_B^A + d_B^A) u_C^B$ $a_C^{A:B} = a_C^B$

Uncertainty favouring transitivity means that A is uncertain about the trustworthiness of C not only to the extend that A is uncertain about the recommending agent B, but also to the extent that A distrusts B. *Base rate sensitive transitivity* means that that A's trust in C is a function of the expectation value of A's trust in the recommender B, which in turn is a function of the base rate. *Opposite belief favouring transitivity* means that *"the enemy of my enemy is my friend"*, i.e. that when A distrusts the recommending agent B, then A thinks that B consistently recommends the opposite of his real opinion, so that when C actually is trustworthy then B recommends distrust and vice versa.

While these three interpretations of trust transitivity provide relatively intuitive results in specific situations, none of them are suitable as a model for trust transitivity in general. The next section describes a general approach to modelling trust transitivity, where the three interpretations of Table 2 are special cases.

4   Conditional Belief Reasoning

Conditional reasoning with subjective logic is defined for binomial [8] and multinomial [4] opinions, and can also be extended to general opinions. For binomial deduction and abduction the following notation is used:

$\omega_{y|x}$: conditional opinion on y given that x is TRUE
$\omega_{y|\bar{x}}$: conditional opinion on y given that x is FALSE
ω_x : opinion on the antecedent state x
$\omega_{y\|x}$: deduced opinion on the consequent state y
$\omega_{y\|\hat{x}}$: hypothetically deduced opinion on y given vacuous $\omega_{\hat{x}}$

The image space of the deduced opinion $\omega_{y\|x}$ is a sub-triangle with base vertices defined by the two conditionals $\omega_{y|x}$ and $\omega_{y|\bar{x}}$, and the top vertex defined by the consequent opinion $\omega_{y\|\hat{x}}$ of the vacuous antecedent $\omega_{\hat{x}}$. This mapping determines the position of the consequent opinion $\omega_{y\|x}$ within the child sub-triangle, as illustrated in Fig.2.

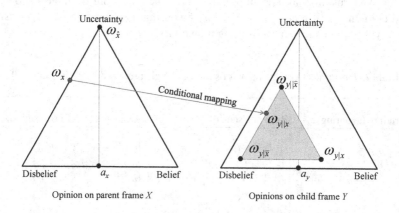

Fig. 2. Mapping from parent triangle to child subtriangle

It can be noticed that when $\omega_{y|x} = \omega_{y|\bar{x}}$, the child sub-triangle is reduced to a point, so that necessarily $\omega_{y\|x} = \omega_{y|x} = \omega_{y|\bar{x}} = \omega_{y\|\hat{x}}$ in this case. This means that there is no relevance relationship between antecedent and consequent.

In general, the child sub-triangle is not regular (equal-sided) as in the example of Fig.2. By setting base rates of x and y different from 0.5, and by defining conditionals with different uncertainty, the child image sub-triangle will be skewed (irregular), and it is even possible that the uncertainty of $\omega_{y\|\hat{x}}$ is less that that of $\omega_{x|y}$ or $\omega_{x|\overline{y}}$.

For multinomial opinions, let $X = \{x_i | i = 1 \ldots k\}$ be the parent frame and $Y = \{y_j | j = 1 \ldots l\}$ be the child frame. The general notation for conditionals is:

$\omega_{Y|X}$: set of conditional opinions on Y given that a specific state in X is TRUE

$\omega_{Y|\overline{X}}$: set of conditional opinions on Y given that a specific state in X is FALSE

ω_X : opinion on the antecedent (parent) frame X

$\omega_{Y\|X}$: deduced opinion on the consequent (child) frame Y

$\omega_{Y\|\hat{X}}$: hypothetically deduced opinion on Y given vacuous $\omega_{\hat{X}}$

Assume the antecedent opinion ω_X where $|X| = k$, and k conditional opinions $\omega_{Y|x_i}$. There is thus one conditional opinion for each element x_i, where a conditional opinion $\omega_{Y|x_i}$ expresses the subjective opinion on Y, given that x_i is TRUE. The subscript notation indicates not only the child frame Y it applies to, but also the element x_i in the parent frame it is conditioned on. The notation $\omega_{Y|X}$ expresses the set of $k = |X|$ different opinions conditioned on each $x_i \in X$ respectively.

Generalisation from the binomial case of Fig.2 to the multinomial case results in a parent regular simplex which is mapped to a sub-simplex inside the child simplex, defined by the set of conditional $\omega_{Y\|X}$. The ternary case is illustrated in Fig.3.

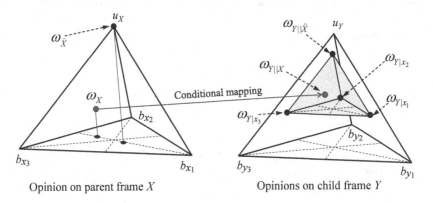

Fig. 3. Projection from parent opinion tetrahedron to child opinion sub-tetrahedron

The sub-simplex formed by the conditional projection of the parent simplex into the child simplex is shown as the shaded tetrahedron on the right hand side in Fig.3. The position of the derived opinion $\omega_{Y\|X}$ is geometrically determined by the point inside the sub-simplex that linearly corresponds to the opinion ω_X in the parent simplex.

In general, a sub-simplex will not be regular as in the example of Fig.3, and can be skewed in all possible ways. The dimensionality of the sub-simplex is equal to the smallest cardinality of X and Y. Visualising a simplex larger than ternary (tetrahedron) is difficult. Subjective logic conditional deduction is expressed as in Eq.(9).

$$\omega_{Y\|X} = \omega_X \odot \omega_{Y|X} \tag{9}$$

where $\odot$ is the general conditional deduction operator for subjective opinions.

Reasoning in the opposite direction is called derivative reasoning, or abduction. Let $\omega_{X|Y} = \{\omega_{X|y_j} | j = 1 \ldots l\}$ be a set of $l = |Y|$ different multinomial opinions conditioned on each $y_j \in Y$ respectively. Conditional abduction is expressed as:

$$\omega_{Y \overline{\|} X} = \omega_X \overline{\circledcirc} \, \omega_{X|Y} \tag{10}$$

where $\overline{\circledcirc}$ is the general conditional abduction operator. Detailed expressions for evaluating Eq.(9) and Eq.(10) are provided in [4,8,14].

5 Conditional Reasoning about Trust Transitivity

The basic idea of conditional trust transitivity is to express trust in the target entity in terms of conditional opinions. Assume the recommendation frame $X = \{x, \overline{x}\}$ interpreted as x: *"Positive"* and $\overline{x}$: *"Negative"*. Trust in the recommender can then be expressed as the conditional propositions $y|x$: *"Target is trusted in case of positive recommendation"* and $y|\overline{x}$: *"Target is trusted in case of negative recommendation"*, where the conditional opinions $\omega_{y|x}$ and $\omega_{y|\overline{x}}$ are the actual trust values. Note that $\omega_{y|\overline{x}}$ typically contains disbelief, meaning that the target is distrusted in case of negative recommendation. As an example, trust in the recommender B can be expressed as the conditional opinions $\omega_{y|x} = (0.9, 0.0, 0.1, a)$ and $\omega_{y|\overline{x}} = (0.0, 0.9, 0.1, a)$, illustrated in Fig.4.

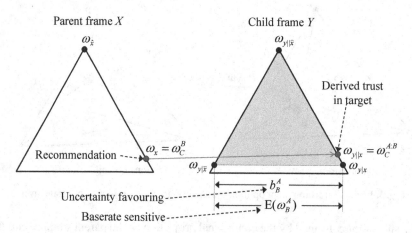

Fig. 4. Trusted recommender, derived transitive trust equals recommended trust

In case of absolute trust the child sub-triangle is equal to the child triangle itself. The consequence of this is that the recommendation opinion in the parent triangle on the left hand side will be mapped to the same position in the child triangle on the right hand side. In other words, the relying party will believe whatever the recommender says.

Strong distrust in the recommender can be specified by placing the conditional trust opinions at, or close to, the uncertainty vertex, e.g. as $\omega_{y|x} = (0.3, 0.0, 0.7, a)$ and $\omega_{y|\overline{x}} = (0.0, 0.3, 0.7, a)$. The result is a small sub-triangle, or a point in case of total distrust, at the top of the child triangle, as illustrated in Fig.5.

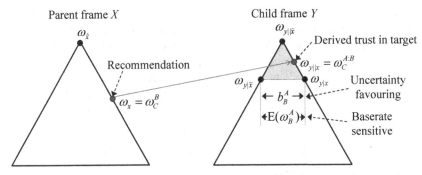

Fig. 5. Distrusted recommender, derived transitive conditional trust equals uncertainty

The examples of Fig.4 and Fig.5 are specific instances of conditional trust transitivity that is equivalent to both the uncertainty favouring and the base rate sensitive transitivity operators of Table 2. Conditional trust transitivity is equivalent to the uncertainty favouring and the baserate sensitive transitivity operators whenever 1) the child subtriangle is equal-sided, 2) the positive conditional $\omega_{y|x}$ is the rightmost conditional, and 3) the uncertainty of the sub-triangle is maximised. The latter requirement means that the child sub-triangle must be positioned as high as possible inside the child triangle, as in Fig.4 and Fig.5. In case of the uncertainty favouring transitivity operator the base of the sub-triangle equals b_B^A. In case of the baserate sensitive transitivity operator, the base of the sub-triangle equals $E(\omega_B^A)$.

The opposite belief favouring trust transitivity operator can be modelled by allowing the negative conditional $\omega_{y|\bar{x}}$ to be the rightmost trust opinion, e.g. expressed as $\omega_{y|x} = (0.2, 0.8, 0.0, a)$ (positive conditional trust opinion) and $\omega_{y|\bar{x}} = (0.8, 0.2, 0.0, a)$ (negative conditional trust opinion). The resulting sub-triangle is then flipped around, as illustrated with the check-pattern of Fig.6. However, the negative conditional is not necessarily the rightmost trust opinion, it can also be the leftmost trust opinion, as in the case of Fig.4. However, the situation where *"the enemy of my enemy is my friend"* and *"the friend of my enemy is also my enemy"* must be expressed with the negative conditional as the rightmost trust opinion, as in Fig.6 below.

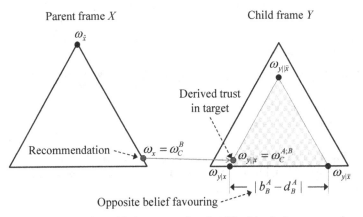

Fig. 6. Distrusted recommender, with the assumption that "the friend of my enemy is my enemy"

In case of opposite belief favouring trust transitivity it can be seen that the derived trust opinion inside the child sub-triangle is the opposite of the recommendation in the parent triangle. The opposite belief favouring operator is similar to the uncertainty favouring operator in the sense that it does not consider the base rate of w_B^A; the difference is that the sub-triangle produces minimal uncertainty, i.e. that it is located at the base of the child triangle. The criteria for the equivalence between the transitivity operators of Table.2 and conditional trust transitivity are expressed in Table (3).

Table 3. Equivalence criteria between transitivity operators [9] and conditional trust transitivity

Criteria for equivalence between conditional trust transitivity and $w_C^{A:B}$		
Uncertainty favouring $w_C^{A:B}$	Base rate sensitive $w_C^{A:B}$	Opposite belief favouring $w_C^{A:B}$
$b_{y\|x} - b_{y\|\bar{x}} = b_B^A$	$b_{y\|x} - b_{y\|\bar{x}} = \mathrm{E}(w_B^A)$	$\|b_{y\|x} - b_{y\|\bar{x}}\| = \|b_B^A - d_B^A\|$
$b_{y\|x} = d_{y\|\bar{x}}$	$b_{y\|x} = d_{y\|\bar{x}}$	$b_{y\|x} = b_B^A$
$d_{y\|x} = b_{y\|\bar{x}}$	$d_{y\|x} = b_{y\|\bar{x}}$	$b_{y\|\bar{x}} = d_B^A$
$u_{y\|x} = u_{y\|\bar{x}} = 1 - b_{y\|x} - d_{y\|x}$	$u_{y\|x} = u_{y\|\bar{x}} = 1 - b_{y\|x} - d_{y\|x}$	$u_{y\|x} = u_{y\|\bar{x}} = 0$

With the conditional transitivity model it is possible to specify any form of trust transitivity. As an example, assume a recommender whom the relying party finds unreliable in the sense that positive recommendations can only be relied upon by 50%, expressed as $w_{y\|x} = (0.5, 0.5, 0, a)$, and where negative recommendations are taken at face value, in order to be on the safe side, as expressed by $w_{y\|\bar{x}} = (0, 1, 0, a)$. The resulting child sub-triangle is then the triangle illustrated on Fig.7.

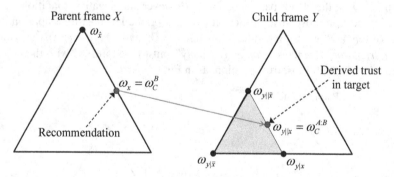

Fig. 7. Unreliable recommender, where positive recommendations are half trusted, and negative recommendations are fully trusted

The conditional trust transitivity model of Fig.7 is different from those specified in Table 2. In fact, conditional belief reasoning allows the specification of arbitrary trust transitivity models to suit any specific situation.

Table 3 demonstrates the formal side of the advantage of generalisation of conditional belief reasoning over the rest of the models in the current literature we stated at the beginning. Moreover, the provided example further clarifies the generalisation over the existing transitivity operators in Subjective Logic, showing the applicability of the approach in the context of trust modelling.

It is meaningful, however, to separate between the honesty and the ability to do something in the sense that an honest person will do their best to deliver a service, and the quality of the service then only depends on ability. A dishonest person who is able to deliver a quality service might on purpose deliver a low quality service.

In the previous examples it was implicitly assumed that trust in the recommender reflected the relying party's trust in honesty and ability simultaneously, except perhaps in case of the opposite belief favouring operator. When the relying party is able to assess honesty and ability of the recommender separately, it is possible to build a model which can express explicitly when a recommender does not provide their honest opinion. Trust in the presence of this assumption can be modelled as two separate conditional relationships, first between the recommendation and the recommender's internal trust opinion, and then between the recommender's internal trust opinion and the target trusted entity. The formal expression for trust transitivity from Eq.(1) can then be extended as in Eq.(11)

$$\text{Alice} \rightarrow \text{Claire} := \text{Alice} \rightarrow \text{Bob's recomm.} \rightarrow \text{Bob's opinion} \rightarrow \text{Claire} \qquad (11)$$

Assume, for example, that the recommender Bob is a financial advisor and that Alice asks him about an investment product called C. Bob's recommendations are represented as a ternary frame X consisting of x_1: *"Says C is good"*, x_2: *"Says C is bad"* and x_3: *"Says don't know"*. Let further Bob's genuine opinion be represented as the binary frame Y consisting of y: *"Bob judges C to be good"* and $\overline{y}$: *"Bob judges C to be bad"*. Alice makes the following assumptions about the advisor Bob: If the advice is x_1 (Says C is good) it is probably a product that he gets a commission on, but he does not necessarily judge it to be good, so for Alice it is uncertain what he really thinks is good, formally expressed as $\omega_{y|x_1} = (0, 0, 1, a)$. If the advice is x_2 (Says C is bad) the Bob probably judges it to be a bad product, formally expressed as $\omega_{y|x_2} = (0, 1, 0, a)$. If the advice is x_3 (Says don't know) then it is possible that he genuinely is uncertain about the quality, but it is also possible that he judges it to be good but because he does not get a commission he does not want to recommend it, but at the same time does not want to be caught lying about a product which objectively is good; hence, he does not want to give a recommendation against it either, leaving him the option of x_3 (Says don't know). It is therefore possible that Bob is either uncertain, or that he judges the product to be good i.c.o. x_3 (Says don't know), formally expressed as $\omega_{y|x_3} = (0.5, 0.0, 0.5, a)$.

Assume in addition that Alice does not have full trust in Bob's ability to objectively assess investment products. Let the possible qualities of the investment product C be represented as the binary frame $Z = \{z, \overline{z}\}$ expressed as z: *"Good product"* and $\overline{z}$: *"Bad product"*. Then, Alice's doubt in Bob's ability can be expressed as $\omega_{z|y} = (0.5, 0.0, 0.5, a)$ and $\omega_{z|\overline{y}} = (0.0, 0.5, 0.5, a)$. The conditional connection between Bob's recommendations and Alice's derived trust in the investment product *Claire* is visualised in Fig.8.

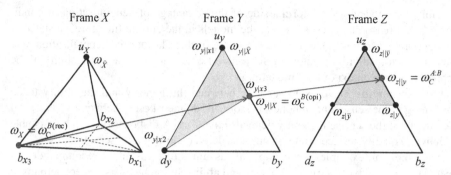

Fig. 8. Bayesian network for analysing recommendations from financial advisor

The visual analysis of Fig.8 can be done mathematically using the methods for conditional reasoning described in [8,4].

6   Determining Conditionals

So far we have not discussed methods for determining the actual trust conditionals, and for this purpose it is important to be aware of the base rate fallacy [11]. As implicitly assumed in the analysis of Sec.5, the relying party A could simply express its subjective trust in B as opinions on the following conditional hypotheses:

$$\omega^A_{C|(B:C)} : \text{"In case } B \text{ says } C \text{ has good quality, then } C \text{ has good quality"}$$
$$\omega^A_{C|(B:\overline{C})} : \text{"In case } B \text{ says } C \text{ has bad quality, then } C \text{ has good quality"} \tag{12}$$

These are called *derivative conditionals* because they are expressed in anti-causal form, meaning that the act of saying that C has good or bad quality does not cause C to have good or bad quality. In reality, the opposite is the case, i.e. the fact that C has good or bad quality causes B to get an opinion on C's quality and to express recommendations about it, which thereby can be expressed as causal conditionals. The important point is whether B's opinion correctly reflects C's quality. The values of $\omega^A_{C|(B:C)}$ and $\omega^A_{C|(B:\overline{C})}$ thus rely on B's capability to correctly detect C's quality, which must be expressed as opinions on the corresponding causal conditionals:

$$\omega^A_{(B:C)|C} : \text{"In case } C \text{ has good quality, then } B \text{ will say } C \text{ has good quality"}$$
$$\omega^A_{(B:C)|\overline{C}} : \text{"In case } C \text{ has bad quality, then } B \text{ will say } C \text{ has good quality"} \tag{13}$$

Trust in B is naturally expressed in terms of the causal conditionals of Eq.(13), because they express the reliability of B as a sensor for detecting C's quality. B's assessments can of course be wrong sometimes, which represent cases of false positive or false negative. When interpreting *"C has quality"* as the positive case, then Eq.(13) express the TPR (True Positive Rate) and FPR (False Positive Rate). However, the opposite conditionals are needed (i.e. those of Eq.(12)) for assessing C's quality.

The conditionals of Eq.(12) are influenced by the base rate of quality in the population of C. A problem can arise when the derivative conditionals, such as Eq.(12), have been determined in a population with a specific base rate, using the same conditionals in a population with a different base rate, producing untruthful conclusions. As an example, consider a medical test for a specific disease, where the test gives mostly true positive and true negative results in a population where the disease is common. When the same test gives a positive result for a person in a population where the disease is extremely rare, then it is most likely a false positive result. Ignoring this fact is called the base rate fallacy in medicine. In the context of trust systems, a well-known problem is the one of exaggerated positive evaluations in systems like Amazon and eBay [15,12], also known as positive bias. Failing to foresee the potential of base rate fallacy may lead to the conclusion that the system performs well just because of the low amount of false positives.

The base rate fallacy can be avoided by first determining the causal conditionals of Eq.(13), e.g. on a statistical or subjective basis, and subsequently inverting them into the form of Eq.(12) which takes into account the base rate of quality in target C's population. This is called derivative reasoning because of its nature, and can be done with the abduction operator of subjective logic, expressed in Eq.(10).

7 Discussion and Conclusion

Most of the current approaches that represent opinions of trust/distrust as a binary value of 1/0, without assigning any other attributes, dismiss all the shades of belief that exist between trust and distrust and capture only the two extremes of the state of trust met in the human perception and reasoning. Other approaches do account for the possibility to represent trust in a multi-valued manner, but assign maximum certainty to each of the values. Conditional belief reasoning, on the other hand, offers a framework for exploiting all the shades of trust-opinions that can be subject to the human perception and reasoning. By joining belief mass, uncertainty, and base rates into a single trust opinion, the model completely satisfies both the statistical and the subjective properties of trust inference and propagation that exist in the real world. It is reasonable to assume that, since trust in artificial systems is to an extent different, although derived from and modelled on, human subjective trust, the rules of transitivity can be more properly defined. Thus, when analysing trust transitivity through conditional belief reasoning, not only the frequentist nature of probability is captured (i.e., the count of positive and negative outcomes), but the ascribed subjectivity of trust also accounts for the impact of an entity's opinion on the outcome of a transaction.

The practical implications of employing conditional belief reasoning to address trust transitivity are much deeper than just providing the formal apparatus to reason about trust relationships in an intuitive way. One advantage of this approach is that the model easily accounts for situations where trust is not transitive, as well as situations where trust us transitive. Another advantage is that it successfully disentangles the notions of trust and reputation, in addition to acknowledging them as community values:

- it recognizes the influence of the subjective opinions of a single entity on the trust relationships established among community members – in this case, of a single recommender – on the perception of the relying entity about the target entity;

- it also implements the idea that the reputation, as a more general opinion about an entity's trustworthiness, results from the established trust relationships among all the community members.
- the introduction of conditionals in addition to the existing transitivity operators allows to capture the intuitive causality between trust and reputation that exists in the human reasoning, but is not always followed by rational decisions: e.g. "You are said to reputable, therefore i trust you", but also "You are said to be reputable, therefore i do not trust you";

Due to the formal framework for aggregating conflicting and non-independent opinions offered by subjective logic, a third advantage of the model is its power to reduce the complexity that arises from conflict resolution of differing (competing) trust-opinions. Moreover, by employing conditionals to infer an entity's trustworthiness based on presented evidence, the model accounts for the expectations of the relying party in the light of available evidence.

Although tacitly implied, it is worth pointing out the advantage of interoperability of conditional belief reasoning with subjective logic with the rest of the formal apparatus of statistics and probability theory used for modelling situations based on observed and statistical evidence. This makes conditional belief reasoning easily employable for the purpose of replacing, enhancing and adding functionality, or correcting some of the inefficiencies in the current models.

The main disadvantage of the model in its current state is that, although it accounts for the subjectivity of perceptions, the reasoning/inference phase still assigns a great deal of rationality on the side of the decision-maker. Despite of the fact that uncertainty is taken into consideration, its value results from a sound calculative model, rather than being an ad-hoc representation of the unpredictable nature of the transaction outcome. Further work will examine the potential for incorporating different aspects of this unpredictability, including via context, into the reasoning process, where changes in context (including, for instance, location or mobility) may change the subjective opinions of recommenders. This is interesting because, all other things being equal, changes in context may affect the final values even for the same recommenders.

References

1. Ding, L., Finin, T.: Weaving the Web of Belief into the Semantic Web. In: Proceedings of the 13th International World Wide Web Conference, New York (May 2004)
2. Fullam, K.K., et al.: The Agent Reputation and Trust (ART) Testbed Architecture. In: Proceedings of the 8th Int. Workshop on Trust in Agent Societies (at AAMAS 2005). ACM (2005)
3. Jøsang, A.: A Logic for Uncertain Probabilities. International Journal of Uncertainty, Fuzziness and Knowledge-Based Systems 9(3), 279–311 (2001)
4. Jøsang, A.: Conditional Reasoning with Subjective Logic. Journal of Multiple-Valued Logic and Soft Computing 15(1), 5–38 (2008)
5. Jøsang, A., Hayward, R., Pope, S.: Trust Network Analysis with Subjective Logic. In: Proceedings of the 29th Australasian Computer Science Conference (ACSC 2006), Hobart, Australia. CRPIT, vol. 48 (January 2006)

6. Jøsang, A., Ismail, R., Boyd, C.: A Survey of Trust and Reputation Systems for Online Service Provision. Decision Support Systems 43(2), 618–644 (2007)
7. Jøsang, A., Presti, S.L.: Analysing the Relationship between Risk and Trust. In: Jensen, C., Poslad, S., Dimitrakos, T. (eds.) iTrust 2004. LNCS, vol. 2995, pp. 135–145. Springer, Heidelberg (2004)
8. Jøsang, A., Pope, S., Daniel, M.: Conditional Deduction Under Uncertainty. In: Godo, L. (ed.) ECSQARU 2005. LNCS (LNAI), vol. 3571, pp. 824–835. Springer, Heidelberg (2005)
9. Jøsang, A., Marsh, S., Pope, S.: Exploring Different Types of Trust Propagation. In: Stølen, K., Winsborough, W.H., Martinelli, F., Massacci, F. (eds.) iTrust 2006. LNCS, vol. 3986, pp. 179–192. Springer, Heidelberg (2006)
10. Jøsang, A.: Multi-Agent Preference Combination using Subjective Logic. In: International Workshop on Preferences and Soft Constraints (Soft 2011), Perugia, Italy (2011)
11. Koehler, J.: The Base Rate Fallacy Reconsidered: Descriptive, Normative and Methodological Challenges. Behavioral and Brain Sciences 19 (1996)
12. Mackiewicz, J.: Reviewer Motivations, Bias, and Credibility in Online Reviews. In: Kelsey, S., Amant, K.S. (eds.) Handbook of Research on Computer Mediated Communication, pp. 252–266. IGI Global (2008)
13. Marsh, S.: Formalising Trust as a Computational Concept. PhD thesis, University of Stirling (1994)
14. Pope, S., Jøsang, A.: Analsysis of Competing Hypotheses using Subjective Logic. In: Proceedings of the 10th International Command and Control Research and Technology Symposium (ICCRTS). United States Department of Defense Command and Control Research Program (DoDCCRP) (2005)
15. Resnick, P., Zeckhauser, R., Swanson, J., Lockwood, K.: The Value of Reputation on eBay: A Controlled Experiment. Experimental Economics 9(2), 79–101 (2006),
http://www.si.umich.edu/ presnick/papers/
postcards/PostcardsFinalPrePub.pdf

Incorporating Honeypot for Intrusion Detection in Cloud Infrastructure

Bhavesh Borisaniya[1], Avi Patel[2], Dhiren R. Patel[1], and Hiren Patel[3]

[1] NIT Surat, India
{borisaniyabhavesh,dhiren29p}@gmail.com
[2] City University London, UK
avi2687@gmail.com
[3] SPCE Visnagar, India
hbpatel1976@gmail.com

Abstract. Cloud services delivered as utility computing over the Internet makes it an attractive target for cyber intruders. Protecting network accessible Cloud resources and services from ever increasing cyber threats is of great concern. Most of the Network based Intrusion Detection System (NIDS) being rule based and therefore only capable of identifying known attacks (through pattern matching). Traditional Anomaly Detection based IDS may generate more number of false positives.

In this paper, we attempt to amalgamate IDS with Cloud computing. Introducing Honeypot in Cloud IDS design can greatly help in detecting potential attacks with reduced number of false positives. This research work provides an impetus to strengthen network security aspects related to Cloud computing to make it more trustworthy.

Keywords: Cloud Computing, Intrusion Detection System, Honeypot, Eucalyptus IaaS framework.

1 Introduction

Cloud computing is a model for enabling convenient, on-demand network access to a shared pool of configurable computing resources (such as server, storage, applications, services etc.) that can be rapidly provisioned and released with minimal management effort or service provider interaction [1]. It is a major aid for start-ups offering online applications and services without investing much in storage, web, or computing infrastructure. Using known Internet protocols, standards and formats; Cloud computing exposes a set of consumable services delivered to end-users/consumers. These services range from computing utilities to platforms for application development.

1.1 Need for Security in Cloud

Cloud services are executed on the Cloud provider's site along with data. These require large amount of data to be transferred over the network. Cloud providers

T. Dimitrakos et al. (Eds.): IFIPTM 2012, IFIP AICT 374, pp. 84–96, 2012.

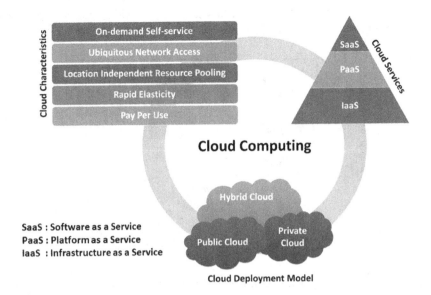

Fig. 1. Cloud computing

have to ensure about the quality of service, performance, reliability and basic security [2].

If an intruder gains unwanted access to Cloud services, he may also exploit the underlying architecture. In case of IaaS, the intruder may also be able to exploit the Virtual Machine Monitor (VMM) by using vulnerabilities in the implementation. Penetration to the hardware layer may allow an attacker to compromise any VM provided by the infrastructure.

Because of its provisioning through the Internet and vulnerabilities in involved (underlying) technologies; there are many issues related to security of Cloud infrastructure and its services. Major threats to Cloud computing includes insecure interface and APIs of shared technology, account and service hijacking [3] etc. Shared and distributed resources in the Cloud system make it difficult to develop a security model for detecting intrusion and ensuring the data security and privacy in Cloud. Because of transparency issue, no Cloud provider allows its customers to implement intrusion detection or security monitoring system extending into the management services layer providing back channel behind virtualized Cloud instances. IDS technology has been tested to be capable of working well in some large scale networks, however, its utilization and deployment in Cloud Computing is still a challenging task [2].

1.2 Intrusion Detection Systems (IDS)

Intrusion detection systems have proved to be a major tool for network administrators to protect their internal network from threats of cybercriminals and also of internal threats. A Common Intrusion Detection Framework (CIDF) which illustrates a general IDS architecture, based on the consideration of four types of functional modules as shown in Figure 2 [4].

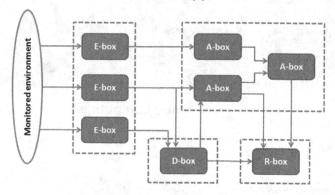

Fig. 2. Common Intrusion Detection Framework

The components of this IDS framework include the following:

E blocks (Event-boxes): These blocks contain sensor elements that monitor the target system and gather information events that can be analyzed by other blocks.

D blocks (Database-boxes): These are the blocks intended to store information from E blocks for subsequent processing by A and R boxes.

A blocks (Analysis-boxes): These are the processing modules which analyze the events and detect the potential hostile behaviour, so that some kind of alarm will be generated if necessary.

R blocks (Response-boxes): If any intrusion occurs, this block is responsible to provide a response to prevent the detected threat.

Network based IDS (NIDS) detects the intrusion by monitoring malicious activity in network traffic while Host based IDS (HIDS) inspects the unusual activity within the host by monitoring its file system.

Most of the NIDSs monitor network traffic and match it with the dataset of predefined attack patterns(signatures) to detect the attacks. For network intrusion detection, a signature can be as simple as a specific pattern that matches a portion of a network packet. However, signature-based technique fails to detect the unknown or new attacks whose signatures are not defined or not included in the dataset of signatures.

An anomaly based IDS establishes a baseline of normal usage patterns, and anything that widely deviates from it gets flagged as a possible intrusion [5]. A large number of false positives can limit this technique which can force it to sign even a genuine activity as an intrusion attempt.

The objective is to build efficient IDS which can work in Cloud environment with the capability of detecting known and unknown intrusions. The IDS must also prove to be a tool to the user to detect if the used-service or hosts are used to attack other victims.

The rest of the paper is organized as follows: In section 2, related work is reported. Section 3 discusses important design considerations for deploying IDS in Cloud. Section 4 discusses our approach to implement NIDS along with honeypot in Cloud framework. Section 5 describes implementation details using Eucalyptus Cloud framework and section 6 discusses experiments and results. We conclude in section 7 with references at the end.

2 Related Work

There has been relevant work done in the field about IDS for Cloud computing. The major approaches are listed as follows:

Sebastian Roschke et al. [2] points the need for deploying IDS in the Cloud by proposing extensible IDS architecture which can be used in a distributed Cloud infrastructure.

Noah Guilbault and Ratan Guha [6] shows a way for designing and implementing distributed grid based IDS using virtual servers deployed on Amazon's Elastic Compute Cloud service. Aman Bakshi et al. [7] proposed a framework for securing Cloud from DDoS attacks using an IDS in a virtual machine. This can be done by employing intrusion detection sensors installed in a virtual machine to sniff network traffic and to analyze packets over the Internet using Snort. Both these approaches incorporate IDS in each virtual machine, requires as many IDS as number of running virtual machine instances. Claudio Mazzariello et al. [8] has placed Snort as a NIDS on the virtual switch component of the physical machine. This physical machine hosts virtual machines of clients using open source Eucalyptus cloud computing framework. Virtual Switch enables the NIDS to monitor all in-bound and out-bound traffic from the entry-point. Chi-Chun Lo et al. [9] proposed a cooperative IDS framework for Cloud computing networks to reduce DDoS attacks. All these approaches use signature based technique, limited to detect only known attacks.

Kleber Vieira et al. [10] have described an intrusion detection based on Grid and Cloud computing system which can identify unknown as well as known attacks. However, this approach is only suitable for PaaS.

3 Design Considerations

Deploying IDS in the Cloud is a tricky issue. From the users' perspective, they need to make sure that the service they use is not subjected to any kind of attack. They should also know whether these services are being used to attack other hosts or not. On the other hand, Cloud providers need to ensure if its infrastructure is subjected to any attack or not. With knowledge of attacks and their behavior, the provider should be prompted to take appropriate actions.

In order to justify our approach and make it useful for a Cloud environment, we explored various Cloud frameworks for implementing IaaS as a service model and configure them for analysis in our lab environment. There are several open-source frameworks for Cloud computing viz; Eucalyptus [11], OpenNebula [12],

Globus Nimbus [13] etc. Amongst them, we have zeroed into Eucalyptus because it provides simpler interface, supports different virtual machine monitors (or hypervisors) and modular architecture, which provides us an easy alternative to incorporate honeypot with IDS.

Network based intrusion detection tools are usually deployed over a perimeter of an organization network in order to monitor inbound and outbound network traffic. We have looked at various intrusion detection tools chosen Snort[14], as it is configurable, widely used and constantly updated. We have augmented the simple honeypot to a dynamic honeypot and incorporated it into our proposed approach. For testing the proposed architecture, we have setup a configurable private Cloud using Eucalyptus framework. We have created and tested the installed machine images of different operating systems which can be delivered as virtual machine instances with different configurations (RAM and CPUs) to the Cloud users in context of private Cloud.

3.1   Eucalyptus Architecture

Figure 3 shows the Eucalyptus Cloud architecture containing various components [15,16]. Each high-level system component in the Eucalyptus design is implemented as a stand-alone Web service. These Web services expose a well defined language-agnostic API in the form of a WSDL (Web Service Descriptive Language) document, which contains operations that the service can perform and input/output data structures. It also support secure communications using WS-Security policies and rely upon industry-standard Web services software packages like Axis2, Apache and Rampart [15,16].

Basic Components of Eucalyptus Architecture and their functions are summarized in Table 1.

Table 1. Eucalyptus Components

No	Component	Function
1	Cloud Controller(CLC)	High level scheduling decisions
2	Node Controller(NC)	Management of virtual machine instances and its execution
3	Cluster Controller(CC)	Scheduling of virtual machine execution on specific hosts and virtual network management
4	Storage Controller(SC)	Storage of user data as well as storage service for virtual machine images

Eucalyptus provides a functionality called security groups which acts as a firewall for running machine instances. It is a named collection of network access rules, defining which incoming traffic is delivered to instances. A user can add or remove a security group to meet his security requirement. By using this, a user can open or close ports to control the inbound or outbound network traffic over it. By restricting the number of open ports in an instance; a user can only decrease the probability of an attack to some extent. If the services running on these ports are vulnerable, then its easy for an intruder to exploit it.

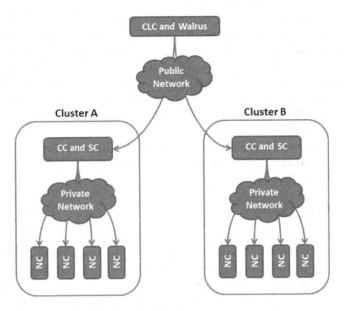

Fig. 3. Eucalyptus Cloud Architecture

3.2 Placement of a NIDS in Eucalyptus Based Private Cloud

Figure 4 shows the architecture of the system which comprises the NIDS. We have placed the NIDS in each Cluster Controller to monitor the network traffic

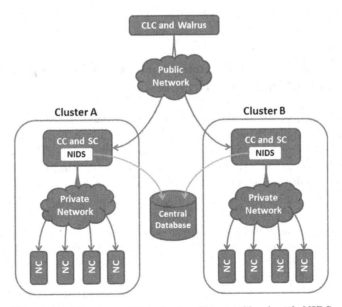

Fig. 4. Architecture of Eucalyptus Private Cloud with NIDS

of all the Node Controllers which report to the respective CC. NIDS will capture all the packets passing through the CC intended to the instances hosted by NCs and examine them for the malicious content. If malicious content is found, it generates alerts and logs that network activity into the central database. The Cloud administrator can view and analyze these logged alerts and network activities (i.e. packets) by accessing the database. Also, the owner of the instance can analyze the logged attack alerts related to it by querying the central database using interface through the instance.

This approach allows the Cloud administrator (Instance provider as well as instance owner) to monitor the type and source of the attack, which in turn can be used to prevent the similar future attacks.

3.3   Use of Honeypot

A honeypot is a deception system which allures the attackers. It has no production value and is intended to be compromised. All the traffic sent to a honeypot is almost certainly unauthorized meaning no false positives, false negatives or large data sets to analyze [17]. Any connection with honeypot can be considered as an attack and an attacker who breaks into a honeypot is comprehensively monitored. Honeypots are serving several purposes that include the following [17]:

1. They can distract attackers from more valuable machines on a network.
2. They can provide early warning about new attack and exploitation trends.
3. They allow in-depth examination of adversaries during and after exploitation of a honeypot.

In our approach, honeypot plays an important role. Any attempt to access honeypot is labeled as an attack.

4   Proposed Approach: Incorporating a Honeypot in Eucalyptus Based Private Cloud

Unknown attacks, for which signatures are not available, have to be dealt with caution and it requires a more efficient IDS mechanism. In our approach, we have incorporated a honeypot to enhance the working of a NIDS in a Cloud environment. The introduction of a honeypot allows identification of suspicious activities by monitoring those network packets which were previously marked as non-suspicious by a normal NIDS. In order to deploy a honeypot in a Cloud environment, we have considered a design in which the administrator launches instances through the honeypot manager. Honeypot manager is an administrative tool used for managing honeypot instances, which are made vulnerable and attractive for intruders to exploit (by running various services accessible through the Internet through open ports).

Figure 5 shows the NIDS incorporating a honeypot in a Cloud architecture. We have shown two such machine instances which work as honeypot. These instances have no production value and hence any inbound or outbound network activity with these instances is considered as malicious. Any packet passing through CC intended for honeypot machine instances will be captured by a packet sniffer and logged into the central database for later analysis.

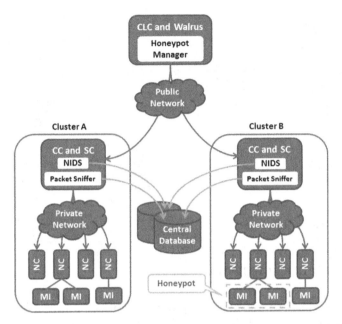

Fig. 5. Architecture of intrusion detection system using honeypot in Eucalyptus Cloud

Here, NIDS is placed in CC to listen the traffic intended for instances and generates (and logs) the alerts to the central database if any malicious activity is found. A packet sniffer sniffs and logs all network packets related to the honeypot instances in the central database.

All packets intended towards honeypot instances, also passes through NIDS. As cloud provider is not delivering honeypot instances to any client, any activity towards it can be considered as malicious. Hence, by querying the database for activities which are captured by honeypots and passed through NIDS, we are able to find such activities/attacks, which were not detected earlier. From these logged activities, we can find information like source (IP) of attack and services they are trying to access using destination and source port. Figure 6 depicts this intrusion detection process flow diagram.

The compromised honeypot instance image can also be used as a means to learn new ways, tools and methods to get into the system. It is also helpful to understand the motive of attacker, to avoid the future attacks and to make the existing NIDS more efficient.

The compromised honeypot instance image can also be used as a means to learn new ways, tools and methods to get into the system. It is also helpful to understand the motive of attacker, to avoid the future attacks and to make the existing NIDS more efficient.

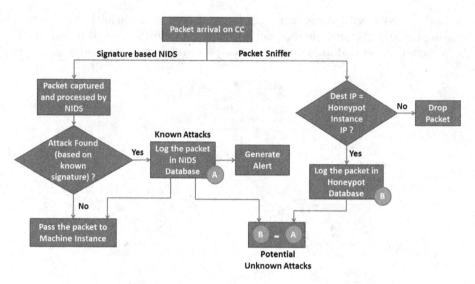

Fig. 6. Intrusion detection process in proposed framework

5   Implementation Issues

Figure 7 shows the experimental setup of a Eucalyptus private Cloud with the proposed framework of NIDS.

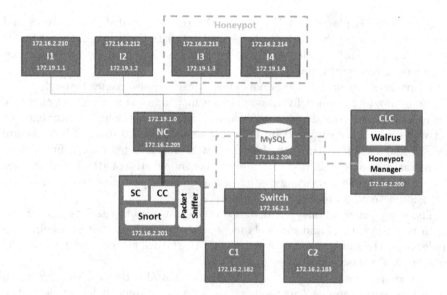

Fig. 7. Experimental Setup for NIDS using Honeypot in Cloud

Our setup consists of three machines, a Node Controller (NC), a Cloud Controller (CLC) and a machine consisting of both Storage Controller (SC) and Cluster Controller (CC). We have used a separate cluster controller (i.e. SC and CC) and database server (i.e MySQL) on different machines. They can also be placed on the same machine in which the CLC resides. I1, I2, I3 and I4 are four machine instances, made available over an external network as a Cloud service model i.e. IaaS, whereas C1 and C2 are clients utilizing these services from the Cloud.

Snort is configured in the CC machine along with a packet sniffer, while the Honeypot Manager is placed in the CLC. A set of machine images of different OS is used to create the honeypot in our environment. Under ideal circumstances, it should cover machine images of all the OS, whose instances are provided by the Cloud provider. These images are made in a way that can attract the attackers. In our experiments we have used machine images of Windows XP, Windows Server 2003 and Ubuntu 10.04. The central database contains the information of machine images that can be used to launch as honeypot instances. It also maintains the information of the fake Cloud users (for experimentation) like their username and credentials that can be used to run the honeypot instances with different instance ownership.

The honeypot manager is responsible for launching the honeypot instances. It gathers the information about the operating system and the state of open and closed ports for different services for all instances. Accordingly, the honeypot manager schedules the type of operating system to be used as a honeypot. The honeypot manager launches each machine instance of a different OS having the ownership of fake users. It also opens different ports for vulnerable services through a security group mechanism to make it more attractive. These machine instances are not delivered to normal users and also its owners credentials are only with the Cloud administrator (nobody can access these instances directly). Hence, any connectivity with these machine instances can be considered malicious.

A packet sniffer captures all the network packets which pass through the CC whose source or destination IP is one of the honeypot IPs. It logs all the captured packets into the central database. Snort examines those packets that are sniffed by the packet sniffer and generates alerts if it finds a known attack pattern within the packet content.

Controlled monitoring of vulnerable images can assist the behavioral analysis of an intruder. Vulnerable images are crafted to exploit with absolute zero or no security and placed in a DMZ. These images are monitored periodically for intrusion attempts. In case of an intrusion, an alert is reported on the primary basis. A local cache directory can be included on top of the Cloud architecture which saves copies of vulnerable images periodically on a version basis. Careful analysis can be done of these vulnerable images to record intruder activity and to enhance the security of the Cloud architecture there after using appropriate security measures.

6   Experiments and Results

We have used Snort as a NIDS and launched vulnerable machine instances to work as honeypots. In order to compare the vulnerability in both original as well as vulnerable copies of operating system images, we conducted a scan using Nessus by enabling all available plug-in modules. The statistics collected are shown in Table 2.

Table 2. Nessus vulnerability scan result of machine images

Operating System	Machine Instance	Total	High	Medium	Low	Open Port
Windows XP	Original	20	0	2	14	4
	Vulnerable	48	0	5	29	14
Windows 2003 Server	Original	11	0	1	8	2
	Vulnerable	32	5	1	18	8
Ubuntu 10.04	Original	21	0	0	17	4
	Vulnerable	64	1	2	43	18

We launched two instances of each operating system (i.e. Windows XP, Windows 2003 and Ubuntu 10.04) in the Cloud and opened the required ports for the services that run on different operating system instances using security group. Honeypot manager also launches instances of the vulnerable images relative to these operating systems.

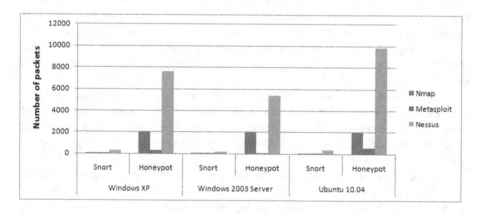

Fig. 8. Comparison of total number of packets logged by Snort and Honeypot in Cloud environment

We attacked all the nine machine instances (3 for each operating system - 2 normal and 1 launched by the honeypot manager) using Nmap, Nessus and Metasploit to test the designed system. Nmap scans all the open ports while Nessus and Metasploit send bad packets in order to find vulnerabilities and exploit them. Then we compared the alerts generated by Snort and honeypot in response to the attacks made by each tool.

Figure 8 shows the graphical representation for the comparison of the total number of logged packets by the honeypot and Snort.

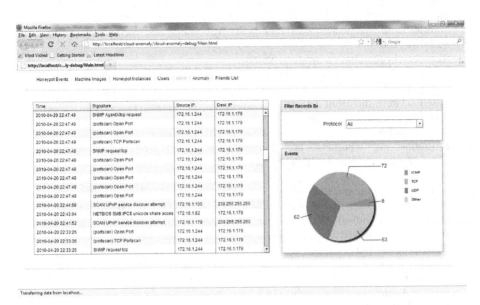

Fig. 9. Web application(screen shot) for analyzing proposed system

In order to verify the results, we formally developed a web application which gives the details of intrusion attempts logged by Snort as well as the honeypot. Screen shot of this web application is shown in Figure 9.

7   Conclusion

By incorporating honeypot, the proposed IDS for Cloud not only alerts the users (about possible network attacks) but also helps Cloud administrator to monitor unknown attacks to enhance its Intrusion Prevention Strategy. The proposed system can be implemented in a Cloud environment to make it more trustworthy by providing an intrusion alert mechanism for attacks against Cloud.

The core benefits of the proposed approach are:

1. It can detect known as well as potential unknown attacks.
2. Controlled use of honeypot generates less number of false alarms for unknown attacks making it an efficient solution for intrusion detection specific to private Cloud.

Though, the proposed scheme is implemented with a Eucalyptus framework, it may work well for other Cloud platforms. It can serve as model to study the behavior of NIDS for distributed environment.

References

1. Grance, T., Mell, P.: The nist definition of cloud computing. National Institute of Standards & Technology (NIST) (2009),
   http://www.nist.gov/itl/cloud/upload/cloud-def-v15.pdf
2. Roschke, S., Cheng, F., Meinel, C.: Intrusion detection in the cloud. In: IEEE International Symposium on Dependable, Autonomic and Secure Computing, pp. 729–734 (2009)
3. Top threats to cloud computing (2009),
   https://cloudsecurityalliance.org/topthreats/csathreats.v1.0.pdf
4. Garca-Teodoro, P., Daz-Verdejo, J., Maci-Fernndez, G., Vzquez, E.: Anomaly-based network intrusion detection: Techniques, systems and challenges. Computers and Security 28, 18–28 (2009)
5. Marinova-Boncheva, V.: A short survey of intrusion detection systems. Problems of Engineering Cybernetics and Robotics (2007),
   http://www.iit.bas.bg/PECR/58/23-30.pdf
6. Guilbault, N., Guha, R.: Experiment setup for temporal distributed intrusion detection system on amazon's elastic compute cloud. In: IEEE International Conference on Intelligence and Security Informatics, ISI 2009, pp. 300–302 (2009)
7. Bakshi, A., Dujodwala, Y.B.: Securing cloud from ddos attacks using intrusion detection system in virtual machine. In: International Conference on Communication Software and Networks, pp. 260–264 (2010)
8. Mazzariello, C., Bifulco, R., Canonico, R.: Integrating a network ids into an open source cloud computing environment. In: Sixth International Conference on Information Assurance and Security (IAS), pp. 265–270 (2010)
9. Lo, C.C., Huang, C.C., Ku, J.: A cooperative intrusion detection system framework for cloud computing networks. In: Proceedings of the 2010 39th International Conference on Parallel Processing Workshops, ICPPW 2010, pp. 280–284. IEEE Computer Society (2010)
10. Vieira, K., Schulter, A., Westphall, C., Westphall, C.: Intrusion detection for grid and cloud computing. It Professional 12(4), 38–43 (2010)
11. Eucalyptus, http://www.eucalyptus.com/
12. Opennebula, http://www.opennebula.org/
13. Nimbus, www.nimbusproject.org/
14. Snort, network intrusion detection and prevention system,
    http://www.snort.org/
15. Nurmi, D., Wolski, R., Grzegorczyk, C., Obertelli, G., Soman, S., Youseff, L., Zagorodnov, D.: The eucalyptus open-source cloud-computing system. In: Proceedings of the 2009 9th IEEE/ACM International Symposium on Cluster Computing and the Grid, CCGRID 2009, pp. 124–131. IEEE Computer Society (2009)
16. Nurmi, D., Wolski, R., Grzegorczyk, C., Obertelli, G., Soman, S., Youseff, L., Zagorodnov, D.: A technical report on an elastic utility computing architecture linking your programs to useful systems (2008), open.eucalyptus.com
17. Mokube, I., Adams, M.: Honeypots: concepts, approaches, and challenges. In: Proceedings of the 45th Annual Southeast Regional Conference, ACM-SE 45, pp. 321–326. ACM (2007)

Trust Model for Optimized Cloud Services

P.S. Pawar[1,2], M. Rajarajan[1], S. Krishnan Nair[2], and A. Zisman[1]

[1] City University London, London EC1V 0HB, United Kingdom
r.muttukrishnan@city.ac.uk, a.zisman@soi.city.ac.uk
[2] British Telecommunications, Security Practice, Adastral Park, Ipswich IP5 3RE, UK
{pramod.s.pawar,srijith.nair}@bt.com

Abstract. Cloud computing with its inherent advantages draws attention for business critical applications, but concurrently expects high level of trust in cloud service providers. Reputation-based trust is emerging as a good choice to model trust of cloud service providers based on available evidence. Many existing reputation based systems either ignore or give less importance to uncertainty linked with the evidence. In this paper, we propose an uncertainty model and define our approach to compute opinion for cloud service providers. Using subjective logic operators along with the computed opinion values, we propose mechanisms to calculate the reputation of cloud service providers. We evaluate and compare our proposed model with existing reputation models.

Keywords: Cloud, Trust, Reputation, SLA, Subjective logic.

1 Introduction

Cloud computing has been recognised as an important new paradigm to support small and medium size businesses and general IT applications. The advantages of Cloud computing are multifold including better use and sharing of IT resources, unlimited scalability and flexibility, high level of automation, reduction of computer and software costs, and access to several services. However, despite the advantages and rapid growth of Cloud computing, it brings several security, privacy and trust issues that need immediate action. Trust is an important concept for cloud computing given the need for consumers in the cloud to select cost effective, trustworthy, and less risky services [2]. The issue of trust is also important for service providers to decide on the infrastructure provider that can comply with their needs, and to verify if the infrastructure providers maintain their agreements during service deployment.

The work presented in this paper is being developed under the FP7 EU-funded project called OPTIMIS [5][13] to support organisations to externalise services and applications to trustworthy cloud providers. More specifically, the project focuses on service and infrastructure providers. One of the main goals of OPTIMIS is to develop a toolkit to assist cloud service providers to supply optimised services based on four different aspects, namely *trust, risk, eco-efficiency*, and *cost*. As part of the overall goal in OPTIMIS, this paper, describes a trust model to support service providers (SP) to verify trustworthiness of infrastructure providers (IP) during deployment and operational phases of the services supplied by the service providers.

T. Dimitrakos et al. (Eds.): IFIPTM 2012, IFIP AICT 374, pp. 97–112, 2012.
© IFIP International Federation for Information Processing 2012

The aim of the Service Provider (SP) is to offer efficient services to its customers using resources of the Infrastructure Provider (IP). The IP aims to maximize its profit by efficient use of its infrastructure resources ensuring that it provides good service to the SP and meeting all its requirements. The trust framework is active during the service deployment and service operation phases. The trustworthiness of the IP and the SP are monitored during these two phases of the service life cycle.

The scope and focus of this paper is mainly to evaluate the trustworthiness of the IP performed by the SP. During the *service deployment phase,* the objective of the SP is to select the most suitable IP for hosting its service based on the degree of trust expected from an IP. During the *service operation phase*, the SP monitors the IP's trust level and takes corrective actions. An example of an action is to select an alternative IP when the trust level of the IP is unacceptable, based on a negotiated level.

The trust model described in this paper calculates trust values based on three different parameters, namely (i) *compliance of SLA parameters* (e.g., when the IP fulfils the quality aspect specified in the SLA between an SP and the IP), (ii) *service and infrastructure providers satisfaction ratings* (e.g., when SP supplies a rating for the IP where the SP is being deployed), and (iii) *service and infrastructure provider behavior* (e.g., if the SP continues to choose the same IP independent of the rating that it has supplied for the IP). In the model, the satisfaction values can be either explicitly provided in terms of ranking measurements, or inferred based on relationships between the service and infrastructure providers, and behavior of the providers in terms of constant use of services, service providers, and infrastructure providers.

For each of the different parameters above, trust values are calculated based on an opinion model [8]. As in the case of [8][17], we have developed an opinion model that considers *belief, disbelief,* and *uncertainty* values. Our model is based on an extension of the Josang's opinion model [8], in which we consider uncertainty when calculating *belief* and *disbelief* values. In [8], uncertainty is considered based on the amount of evidence, in which uncertainty increases if the amount of evidence decreases. As in the case of [17], in our model uncertainty is considered based on the amount of evidence and on the dominance that exist between the positive and negative evidences. If the number of positive (belief) evidences is closer to the number of negative (disbelief) evidences, the uncertainty about the proposition increases. For example, if the number of times that an infrastructure provider (IP1) violates a quality property is the same as the number of times that IP1 does not violate the same property, the level of uncertainty of IP1 for that property increases.

In our model, as in the case of [17], but contrary to [8], the belief and disbelief values also consider uncertainty. The difference between our model and the model in [17] is with regards to uncertainty calculation. In [17], certainty is calculated as a *Probability Certainty Density Function (PCDF)* which is probability density function of the probability of positive experience. With no knowledge the uniform distribution has certainty of zero and as the knowledge increases the probability mass shifts, deviating from the uniform distribution, increasing the certainty towards one.

The remaining of this paper is structured as follows. Section 2 presents an example that will be used throughout the paper to illustrate the work. Section 3 describes the trust model used by the framework. Section 4 discusses the evaluation of the model. Section 5 provides an account of related work. Finally, Section 6 provides concluding remarks and future work.

2   Cloud Computing Example Scenario

In order to illustrate the work described in the paper, we present   a Cloud computing *education application* that is being deployed for Bristish Telecom customers such as Universities and other education institutions. The education application allows Universities and education institutions to have virtual laboratory environments for students, staff, and all other members of the institutions hosted over the cloud, providing access to the institution's applications,   desktops, and servers.

The key features of the application includes: i) flexibility to work from anywhere and anytime allowing the users to access the desktop and corporate applications from any PC, MAC, thin client or smartphone;   ii)   reduction of desktop management cost enabling the IT department to add, update, and remove applications in an easy way; iii) provision of good data security, good access control, and scalable storage platforms; iv) provision of scalability and elasticity for compute resources; v) comprehensive monitoring and management to support use and capacity planning and space usage;   and vi) backup and recovery functions. The application has several components, namley: web interface, active directory, desktop delivery controller (DDC), virtual machines, and storage. The web interface passes user credentials to DDC, which authenticates users against the active directory. The virtual machine is a virtual desktop accessed by end users after receiving the connection details.

For evaluating our proposed model we consider a scenario in the education application with five Service Providers (SPs) and five Infrastructure Providers (IPs). An SP hosts the application with its multiple components either at one IP or at multiple IPs.   The SP may also use a broker for the IP services. This example scenario considers that all the SPs host education applications. Fig. 1 shows the education application deployed by vairous SPs. As shown in the figure, each IP has multiple datacenter sites which may be geographically distributed. Each of these datacenters can have a large number of physical hosts/machines available with capabilities to execute multiple virtual machines.

The three datacenters of IP1 is composed of three, one, and one physical hosts, respectively. The IP1's datacenter with three physical hosts deploy five, three and one virtual machines, respectively. The figure shows that IP1 is in a federation with IP2 and IP3. In this case, IP1 is capable of leasing capacity from IP2 and IP3. Fig. 1 also shows a situation of a bursting scenario, in which organizations can scaleout their infrastructures and rent resources from third parties, as and when its is necessary. For example, as shown in Fig. 1, infrastructure provider IP1 may burst to infrastructure provider IP4 to meet the SLA requirements of any SP.   Fig. 1 also shows the brokers that are associated with the IPs and are capable of renting infrastructure resources from all the IP's. The figure indicates that the SPs have deployed the application in the cloud environment with different constraints (options), as described below.

Option 1: The application is deployed at a single IP, with a constraint of having all components of the application on the same host. SP1 in the figure have all its virtual machines (VM1.1, VM1.2, and VM1.3) running on   a single physical host of IP1.
Option 2: The application is deployed in a single datacenter of an IP. SP1 and SP2 have all its virtual machines running on the same datacenter of IP1.

Option 3: The application is deployed in a single IP's administration boundary (restrict usage of federation resources). SP1, SP2 and SP3 have all its virtual machines in the administration boundaries of IP1.

Option 4: The application is dployed in more than one IP. SP4 and SP5 deploy the application in IP1, IP4 and IP1, and IP5, respectively.

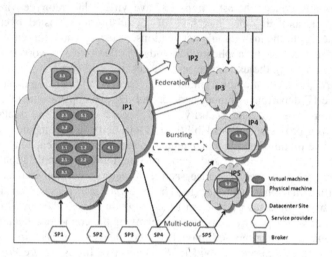

Fig. 1. Cloud computing educational application example

Several other deployment scenarios are possible, but for illustrative purpose we will concentrate on the above situations. Although Fig. 1 shows that SP1, SP2 and SP3 have currently deployed applications on only IP1, it is possible that they may have used other IPs (IP2, IP3, IP4 and IP5) in the past. Similarly, IP4 and IP5 have also used other IPs other than the current ones.

In the scenario, we assume that the institution that decides to use the education application above has SLAs with the SP describing expected quality of the services. The SLAs specify several indicators with which the SP is required to comply, and any violations may lead to penalty payments, as well as negative impact in the customer's satisfaction. Examples of SLA indicators are cpu, disk space, memory, and number of desktops. In order to meet the customer's requirements, the SP that uses the infrastructure services from the IPs also have SLAs with the IP. An SLA between an SP and an IP considers all the existing SLA's with the various customers and the possibility of growing the demand of the application. An SLA between an SP and IP represents elasticity requirements to support the SP to demand more resources dynamically based on the requirements. For example, when the application receives a request for a new desktop, it requests a virtual machine to be created in the infrastructure of the IP where the application is deployed. Similarly, the application can receive requests to increase memory, cpu, or disk space for the existing virtual desktops, which are forwarded to the IP to fulfil the requirements. If the IP, at any point of time fails to provide the requested resources, or is not able to maintain the resource requirements of existing virtual desktops, then this may lead to SLA violations for the corresponding indicators.

3   Trust Model

As described in Section 1, *Trustworthiness* of an IP is modelled using *opinion* obtained from three different computations, namely (i) *compliance of SLA parameters (SLA monitoring)*, (ii) *service provider satisfaction ratings (SP ratings)*, and (iii) *service provider behavior (SP behavior)*. The *opinion* is expressed in terms of *belief, disbelief, uncertainty* and *base rate* which is used in conjunction with the subjective logic [8].

The *opinion* of an entity (SP or IP) A for a proposition x is given as $W^A_x = (b^A_x, d^A_x, u^A_x, a^A_x)$, where b^A_x is the belief in the proposition, d^A_x is the disbelief in the proposition, u^A_x is the uncertainty of the proposition, a^A_x is base rate that provides the weight of uncertainty that contributes to the probability expectation. All b_x, d_x, u_x, a_x $\in$ [0.0, 1.0], and $b_x + d_x + u_x = 1$.

The *trustworthiness (T)* of an IP is modelled as the expectation of the combined opinion of all the three computations. The opinions are combined using the conjunction operator, consensus operator, and the discounting operator in the subjective logic [8], as defined below:

T=Expectation ($W_{(SPB \otimes SPR) \wedge SLA}$)	$W_{(SPB \otimes SPR) \wedge SLA} = (W_{SPB} \otimes W_{SPR}) \wedge W_{SLA}$

where $W_{SLA}, W_{SPR}, W_{SPB}$ are opinions obtained from the SLA monitoring (SLA), SP ratings (SPR), and SP behavior (SPB) values, respectively. The symbol $\wedge$ is the *conjunction operator* used to combine the opinions, and $\otimes$ is the *discounting operator* used as the recommendation operator. If $W_x = (b_x, d_x, u_x, a_x)$ and $W_y = (b_y, d_y, u_y, a_y)$, then $W_{x \wedge y} = (b_{x \wedge y}, d_{x \wedge y}, u_{x \wedge y}, a_{x \wedge y})$.

Consider A and B two agents, where $W^A_B = (b^A_B, d^A_B, u^A_B, a^A_B)$ is A's opinion about B's advice, and let x be the proposition where $W^B_x = (b^B_x, d^B_x, u^B_x, a^B_x)$ is B's opinion about x expressed as an advice to A. In this case, W^{AB}_x is called the discounting ($\otimes$) of W^B_x by W^A_B and is given as $W^{AB}_x = W^A_B \otimes W^B_x = (b^{AB}_x, d^{AB}_x, u^{AB}_x, a^{AB}_x)$.

Opinion Representation. For a proposition x, the opinion is given by

$$W_x = (b_x, d_x, u_x, a_x), \text{ with}$$

$b_x = c\,r/t$	$d_x = c\,s/t$	$u_x = t/(r\,s + f^2 + 1)$	$c = 1 - u_x$

where: r is the amount of positive evidence; s is the amount of negative evidence; t is the total evidence given as $t = r + s$; c or $c(t)$ *or* $c(r,s)$ is certainty that is a function of the total evidence; and f is the distance of focus to the centre of an ellipse.

The proposed opinion model considers two aspects of uncertainty due to the evidence at hand, namely: i) as the amount of evidence increases the uncertainty reduces; and ii) in a given total evidence, as the positive or negative evidence dominates, the uncertainty decreases, and as the positive and negative evidence equals, the uncertainty increases. These two aspects of uncertainty exhibit behavior similar to the properties of an ellipse, considering its size and shape, controlled by its axis and area.

In our model, uncertainty is defined as a function of an ellipse area and shape. More specifically, the uncertainty model is derived using the properties of an ellipse wherein the positive and negative evidence is mapped to the major and minor semi-axes of an ellipse. The first aspect of uncertainty (i.e. increases in evidence, decreases the uncertainty) is achieved by using the area of the ellipse given by the product of its two semi-axes. As the positive and negative evidence is being mapped to the major and minor semi-axes of ellipse, the increase in the major and minor semi-axes results in the increase of the area of ellipse and decrease of the uncertainty. The second aspect of uncertainty is due to dominance between positive and negative evidence, which is captured using the shape of an ellipse. The shape of an ellipse is a function of its two semi-axes. The positive and negative evidence being mapped to the semi-axes of an ellipse, as the major semi-axis continues to dominate, the distance of focus with the centre is a positive value and as the two semi-axes equals, this distance approaches to zero, transforming to a circle.

The change in major and minor semi-axes affects the distance of focus with the centre which is given as $f = sqrt (a^2 - b^2)$. If the total evidence is fixed to a constant, the variation of the positive and negative evidence affects the shape of the ellipse. If the positive and negative evidence equals, this makes $f = 0$, transforming the ellipse to a circle. This adds to a highest uncertainty in a given total evidence. As the positive and negative evidence continues to dominate, this leads to a positive value for f and this value is maximum when either positive or negative evidence in the total evidence is zero. This adds to a lowest uncertainty in a given total evidence. Both properties of uncertainty are captured in the uncertainty definition below:

$$u = t / (r\,s + f^2 + 1) \qquad \text{for } t \geq 1 \qquad \text{and} \qquad u = 1 \qquad \text{for } t < 1$$

where r is the amount of positive evidence; s is the amount of negative evidence; t is the total evidence given as $t = r + s$; and f is the distance of focus to the centre of an ellipse given as $f = sqrt (r^2 - s^2)$ considering $r > s$; The certainty in the opinion model and the expectation of the opinion about a proposition x is given as:

$$c(t) = 1 - u \qquad\qquad E(x) = b_x + a_x u_x$$

where $c(t)$ is the function of total evidence t and can also be represented as a function of positive and negative evidence given as $c(r,s)$. The opinion model uses certainty $c(t)$ to model the *belief*, *disbelief* and *uncertainty*.

SLA Monitoring. The SLA monitoring determines the opinion about an IP from the SLAs that the IP have established with the SPs for their services. The SP for each of its service has a single SLA that includes several indicators (e.g.; cpu, memory, disk space, number of virtual machines (vms)). For each indicator of an SLA, there is an associated monitor that evaluates the compliance/non-compliance of the indicator.

The SLA monitoring opinion about an IP is a two-step process. In the first step, a *consensus opinion* is created for an indicator type (e.g.; cpu) based on information from all the monitors verifying the compliance of the indicator. This opinion indicates the trust of an IP only based on the indicator used to create the *consensus opinion*. In the second step, a *conjunction opinion* is created about the IP for either a set of indicators or for all the indicators based on the requirement. The *conjunction opinion* indicates the trust of an IP for the set of indicators based on SLA monitoring.

Consider that there are m indicator types and n monitors associated with each indicator type. In this case, the opinion of the SLA monitoring is given as:

$$W_{SLA} = W_1^{(M1,1),\ldots,(M1,n)} \wedge W_2^{(M2,1),\ldots,(M2,n)} \wedge \ldots \wedge W_m^{(Mm,1),\ldots,(Mm,n)}$$

where, $W_1^{(M1,1),\,(M1,2),(M1,3),\ldots,(M1,n)}$ is the consensus opinion for the indicator type '1' given by monitors M1,1 to M1, n belonging to different SLAs. If $W_x^A = (b_x^A, d_x^A, u_x^A, a_x^A)$ and $W_x^B = (b_x^B, d_x^B, u_x^B, a_x^B)$ are the opinions given by agent A and agent B, respectively for the same proposition x, then the *consensus opinion* is given as in [8] by: $W_x^{A,B} = W_x^A \oplus W_x^B = (b_x^{A,B}, d_x^{A,B}, u_x^{A,B}, a_x^{A,B})$

Example. In order to illustrate, consider the education application described in Section 2. Consider a case wherein, at that end of academic year most university students need high computation resources such as large number of virtual machines, memory space, cpu and disk space for doing individual projects. For each of the Universities the requested resource to the SP is within the agreed SLA. The SP demands resources from the IP. As in the example scenario, since IP1 have all five SPs hosting the education application, the demand to increase the resources occurs almost in the same time frame. Given the constraint that IP1 cannot acquire resources from other IPs for these applications, there is a violation of the SLA after verifying that IP1 has no additional resource of its own to be provided.

In the scenario IP1 has five SLAs, with each of the SPs (SP1 to SP5) for four different indicator types (cpu, memory, disk, and virtual machine). Assume SLA1 with SP1, SLA2 with SP2, and so on. Consider the existence of monitors associated with each indicator of the SLAs. Assume four monitors (M1, M2, M3 and M4) to be associated with SLA1 for cpu, memory, disk space, and virtual machine, respectively. Similarly, monitors M5 to M8, M9 to M12, M13 to M16 and M17 to M20 are associated with SLA2, SLA3, SLA4 and SL5, for the various SLA indicators.

Each of the monitors associated with the indicators provides information about the compliance of the respective indicator for an IP. If we consider that monitors M1, M2, M3 and M4 indicated 150 compliances and 10 non-compliance (150 positive evidence and 10 negative evidence) for IP1. The opinions given by the monitors for SLA1 are calculated using the proposed opinion model as :

$$W_{CPU}^{M1} = (b_{CPU}^{M1}, d_{CPU}^{M1}, u_{CPU}^{M1}) = (0.93122, 0.062082, 0.006694)$$

$$W_{mem}^{M2} = W_{disk}^{M3} = W_{vm}^{M4} = (0.93122, 0.062082, 0.006694)$$

If we consider that all the other monitors M5-M20 associated with SLA2, SLA3, SLA4 and SLA5 also have 150 compliance and 10 non-compliance indicators, the opinion provided by these monitors are the same as the above ones.

The opinion for IP1 with respect to *cpu* is given as the *consensus opinion* of the five monitors M1, M5, M9, M13 and M17 as follows:

$$W_{CPU}^{M1,M5,M9,M13,M17} = (b_{CPU}^{M1,M5,M9,M13,M17}, d_{CPU}^{M1,M5,M9,M13,M17}, u_{CPU}^{M1,M5,M9,M13,M17}) = (0.936238, 0.062416, 0.001346)$$

Similarly, the opinion for IP1 based on memory, disk and virtual machine is:

$$W_{mem}^{M2,M6,M10,M14,M18} = W_{disk}^{M3,M7,M11,M15,M19} = W_{VM}^{M4,M8,M12,M16,M20} = (0.936238, 0.062416, 0.001346)$$

The overall opinion for IP1 based on all the indicators of the SLAs is given as the *conjunction opinion* of all *consensus opinions* for each of the indicator as follows:

$$W_{SLA} = W_{CPU}^{M1,M5,M9,M13,M17} \wedge W_{mem}^{M2,M6,M10,M14,M18} \wedge W_{disk}^{M3,M7,M11,M15,M19} \wedge$$
$$W_{VM}^{M4,M8,M12,M16,M20} = (0.768325, 0.227246, 0.004428)$$

SP Behavior. The SP behavior is defined in terms of the number of times the SP has used the infrastructure of an IP against the SPs total usage. An SP using a single IP for the majority of the times indicates the SPs good behavior towards an IP. The SP may use the infrastructure of an IP for one or more indicators specified in the SLA.

Consider that there are m indicator types that the IP has negotiated from all the 'q' SPs in the past. Let there be m monitors associated with each of the SPs to monitor how many times the SP used this IP for a given indicator, against its total usage for that indicator. Suppose that SP1 used IP1 five times, IP2 three times, and IP3 four times for cpu usage. This indicates that for cpu total usage of 12 times, SP1 has used IP1 five times. This information is used to model the opinion of SP1's behavior towards IP1 for cpu usage. Assume monitor M1,1 associated with the indicator of type '1' to monitor SP1's behavior towards IP1. In this case, the opinion is represented as $W_{SP1}^{M1,1}$. A single overall behavior of an SP towards an IP is given as a consensus opinion of all its indicators. The behavior of SP1 towards IP1 is given as:

$$(W_{SP1}^{M1,1} \oplus W_{SP1}^{M2,1} \oplus W_{SP1}^{M3,1} \oplus .... \oplus W_{SP1}^{Mm,1})$$

All 'q' behavior of SP towards an IP is given as the conjunction opinion as:

$$W_{SPB} = (W_{SP1}^{M1,1} \oplus .... \oplus W_{SP1}^{Mm,1}) \wedge ... \wedge (W_{SPq}^{M1,q} \oplus .... \oplus W_{SPq}^{Mm,q})$$

Example. In order to illustrate consider the education application described in Section 2 with monitors M1, M2, M3 and M4 verifying the compliance of the cpu, memory, disk and virtual machine usage, respectively, for SP1, and monitors M6-M8, M9-M12, M13-M16, and M17-M20 for SP2, SP3, SP4 and SP5. Suppose that monitor M1 associated with SP1, records that SP1 has opted to use IP1 for 200 times against SP1's 250 times total cpu usage. The opinion for the behavior of SP1 towards IP1 for cpu usage is calculated as:

$$W_{SP1}^{M1} = (b_{SP1}^{M1}, d_{SP1}^{M1}, u_{SP1}^{M1}) = (0.79579, 0.198947, 0.005263).$$

Similarly, assume that M2, M3 and M4 record the same usage as M1 for memory, disk space, and virtual machine, respectively. The opinions are calculated as:

$$W_{SP1}^{M2} = W_{SP1}^{M3} = W_{SP1}^{M4} = (0.79579, 0.198947, 0.005263)$$

Consider that SP2 and SP3 have the same evidence as in the case of SP1, with the associated monitors for these SPs providing evidences as monitors M1, M2, M3 and M4. Consider SP4 with monitors M13-M16 and SP5 with monitors M17-M20 using other IPs different from IP1 for its resources consumption. Assume the monitors for SP4 and SP5 provide 100 positive evidences and 150 negative evidences for each of its indicators. This evidence is transformed to the opinions below:

$$W_{SP4}^{M13} = W_{SP5}^{M17} = W_{SP4}^{M14} = W_{SP5}^{M18} = W_{SP4}^{M15} = W_{SP5}^{M19} = W_{SP4}^{M16} = W_{SP5}^{M20} = (0.39636, 0.594546, 0.009091)$$

The behavior of SP1 towards IP1 (and of SP2 and SP3) are calculated as:

$$W_{SP1}^{M1...M4} = W_{SP1}^{M1} \oplus W_{SP1}^{M2} \oplus W_{SP1}^{M3} \oplus W_{SP1}^{M4} = (0.798943, 0.199736, 0.001321)$$

The behavior of SP4 and SP5 towards IP1 based is given as:

$$W_{SP4}^{M13M14M15M16} = W_{SP5}^{M17M18M19M20} = (0.399085, 0.598627, 0.002288)$$

The total SPs behavior towards an IP is given as the *conjunction* opinion of all SPs towards a single IP, given as:

$$W_{SPB} = W_{SP1}^{M1...M4} \wedge W_{SP2}^{M5...M8} \wedge W_{SP3}^{M9...M12} \wedge W_{SP4}^{M13...M16} \wedge W_{SP5}^{M17...M20} = (0.081223, 0.917435, 0.001342)$$

SP Ratings. The service provider satisfaction rating is calculated based on the rates of the services given by an SP using an IP. The SP provides separate ratings for each SLA indicators of the IP's services. The ratings are used to form an opinion about an IP. Similar to the other cases, the computation of SP ratings to provide an opinion about an IP is based on consensus and conjunction ratings. Consider q SPs available and each of these SPs providing its opinion for one or more of the m indicator types that the IP supports. The service provider satisfaction rating is calculated as:

$$W_{SPR} = W_1^{SP1,SP2...,SPq} \wedge W_2^{SP1,SP2...,SPq} \wedge ... \wedge W_m^{SP1,SP2...,SPq}$$

where, $W_i^{SP1,SP2...,SPq}$ is the consensus opinion for indicator type 'i' from SP1 to SPq.

Example. As an example, suppose that SP1 has provided 100 excellent and 5 worst ratings for each of cpu, memory, disk, and virtual machine indicators. These ratings are transformed into 100 positive and 5 negative evidences for each of these indicators, as per the mapping described above. Based on the evidence of ratings for IP1, the opinion that SP1 has about IP1 for its indicators is given as:

$$W_{CPU}^{SP1} = (b_{CPU}^{SP1}, d_{CPU}^{SP1}, u_{CPU}^{SP1}) = (0.94284, 0.047142, 0.010023)$$

$$W_{mem}^{SP1} = W_{disk}^{SP1} = W_{vm}^{SP1} = (0.94284, 0.047142, 0.010023)$$

Suppose that SP2, SP3, SP4 and SP5 have provided (200 excellent, 5 worst), (200 excellent, 10 worst), (200 excellent, 20 worst), (200 excellent, 30 worst) ratings, respectively for IP1 for each of the four different indicators. These evidences provide the following opinions of SP2, SP3, SP4 and SP5 about IP1, calculated as:

$$W_{CPU}^{SP2} = W_{mem}^{SP2} = W_{disk}^{SP2} = W_{vm}^{SP2} = (0.97073, 0.024268, 0.005003)$$

$$W_{CPU}^{SP3} = W_{mem}^{SP3} = W_{disk}^{SP3} = W_{vm}^{SP3} = (0.94761, 0.04738, 0.005012)$$

$$W_{CPU}^{SP4} = W_{mem}^{SP4} = W_{disk}^{SP4} = W_{vm}^{SP4} = (0.90450, 0.09045, 0.005046)$$

$$W_{CPU}^{SP5} = W_{mem}^{SP5} = W_{disk}^{SP5} = W_{vm}^{SP5} = (0.86513, 0.12977, 0.0051)$$

The capability of IP1 for cpu, memory, disk, and virtual machine are given as the consensus of all SP's opinion by:

$$W_{CPU}^{SP1} \oplus W_{CPU}^{SP2} \oplus W_{CPU}^{SP3} \oplus W_{CPU}^{SP4} \oplus W_{CPU}^{SP5} = (0.928743, 0.070133, 0.001124)$$

$$W_{mem}^{\ SP1...SP5} = W_{disk}^{\ SP1...SP5} = W_{VM}^{\ SP1...SP5} = (0.928743, 0.070133, 0.001124)$$

The overall opinion formed for IP1 based on the ratings from the SPs is given as:

$$W_{SPR} = W_{CPU} \wedge W_{mem} \wedge W_{disk} \wedge W_{VM} = (0.744015, 0.252376, 0.003609)$$

SP Ratings Discounted by SP Behavior. The proposed trust model uses the behavior of the SP for discounting the opinion provided by the SP in SP ratings, for a particular indicator. More specifically, in the SP ratings, if SP1 is evaluating IP1 and is informed about the opinion of IP1 from SP2 regarding cpu indicator, this opinion of SP2 is discounted using SP2's behavior about cpu towards IP1.

In the case of SP behavior, if monitor M1,2 is associated with indicator type '1' to monitor SP2's behavior towards IP1, then this opinion is represented as $W_{SP2}^{M1,2}$. In the case of SP ratings, SP1 being informed about opinion from SP2 for IP1 based on indicator type '1' is represented as W_1^{SP2}. Based on the behavior of SP2 towards IP1 for cpu indicator, SP2's opinion for cpu is discounted. In other words, the opinion W_1^{SP2} is discounted by $W_{SP2}^{M1,2}$ value and is given as $W^{(M1,2)SP2}_1 = W^{M1,2}_{SP2} \otimes W_1^{SP2}$ $= (b^{(M1,2)SP2}_1, d^{(M1,2)SP2}_1, u^{(M1,2)SP2}_1, a^{(M1,2)SP2}_1)$

SP ratings after discounting opinions using the SP behavior for each of the indicator, also follows the two-step process of *consensus* and *conjunction* to get the combined opinion of SP rating and SP behavior which are given as follows:

$$W_{(SPR \otimes SPB)} = W_{SPB} \otimes W_{SPR} = (W^{M1,1}_{SP1} \otimes W_1^{SP1}) \oplus (W^{M1,2}_{SP2} \otimes W_1^{SP2}) \oplus ... \oplus (W^{M1,q}_{SPq} \otimes W_1^{SPq}) \wedge (W^{M2,1}_{SP1} \otimes W_2^{SP1}) \oplus (W^{M2,2}_{SP2} \otimes W_2^{SP2}) \oplus ... \oplus (W^{M2,q}_{SPq} \otimes W_2^{SPq}) \wedge ... \wedge (W^{Mm,1}_{SP1} \otimes W_m^{SP1}) \oplus (W^{Mm,2}_{SP2} \otimes W_m^{SP2}) \oplus ... \oplus (W^{Mm,q}_{SPq} \otimes W_m^{SPq})$$

4   Evaluation

In order to evaluate the proposed trust model, we have developed a prototype tool. We used this tool to evaluate the model in three different experiments. More specifically, in the first set of experiments we provide a comparison of the proposed opinion model with other existing models using data set from Amazon marketplace (www.amazon.co.uk). In the second and third sets of experiments, we use the example of the cloud computing scenario described in Section 2 to evaluate the use of the various parameters considered in our model. In the second set of experiments we analyze the proposed model for each individual parameter, namely (a) SLA monitoring, (b) SP ratings, and (c) SP behavior. In the third set of experiments, we analyze the model when considering combinations of the parameters in order to see if the use of more than one parameter provides better trust values.

4.1   Comparison of the Proposed Model

The dataset of Amazon marketplace used in this evaluation includes rating received by users for four sellers for a same music track CD. The seller1, seller2, seller3 and seller4 are rated by 618, 154, 422, and 314 unique users respectively. This data set contains ratings in the range of 1 to 5, for each seller, provided by the users. The rating is converted to the form <r:positive, s:negative> evidence such that r+s=1. More specifically, rating 1 maps to <0,1>, rating 2 maps to <0.25,0.75>, rating 3 maps to

<0.5,0.5>, rating 4 maps to <0.75, 0.25>, and rating 5 maps to <1,0>. A user performing the $(i+1)^{th}$ transaction has access to all the previous i ratings.

We compared the proposed model with Josang's [8] and Wang's [17] approaches. For all the three models, the experiment takes previous i ratings to predict the $(i+1)^{th}$ rating and calculates the expectation $E=b+au$ to predict the $(i+1)^{th}$ rating. The belief is calculated using the i previous ratings and the base rate is considered as 0.5. Fig. 2 shows the experimental results for a single seller. One time stamp on the x-axis represent 25 transactions and the y-axis represents errors that are computed as the average of 25 prediction errors based on the ratings. The results show that our model has lower prediction error when compared to Josang's [8] and Wang's [17] approaches. Table 1 summarizes the experiment performed for four sellers for the same music track CD.

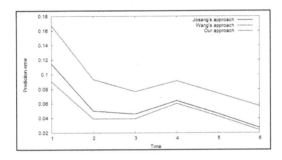

Fig. 2. Average prediction error for a Seller based on the ratings [1,5]

Table 1. Average prediction error for 4 sellers based on the ratings [1,5]

Approach	Seller1	Seller2	Seller3	Seller4
Josang's	0.10619	0.05736	0.06219	0.10809
Wang's	0.12753	0.09278	0.09415	0.14004
Our	0.10456	0.04878	0.05848	0.10449

4.2   Experiments Using Individual Parameters

SLA Monitoring. In this experiment, we consider only the SLA monitoring parameters with four resources (cpu, memory, disk, VM) associated with IP1 as fixed. We considered that the resource demand requests are sent by all SPs with incremental resources requirements. While IP1 is able to provide the demanded resources, IP1 is considered compliant with the SLA and this increases the positive evidence maintained by the SPs for IP1. At a certain point the requested resources exceed the capacity of the IP1 resulting in SLA violations. The SLA violations, add to the negative evidence maintained by the SPs for IP1. Fig. 3 shows that the reputation increases when each of the SPs have positive evidence; a maximum reputation is achieved by IP1 when each of the SPs had positive evidence of 150. After this point, the SLA violations accumulate negative evidences causing a reduction on the reputation.

SP Rating. In this experiment we considered that all the SPs used IP1 and rated IP1 for its performance based on cpu, memory, disk and virtual machine indicators. These ratings are preserved by the SPs for evaluating the IPs. The experiment starts with IP1 receiving positive ratings from each of the SPs. Each time the ratings are provided to IP1, SP1 calculates the reputation of IP1 taking into account its own ratings as well as the ratings of the other SP2 to SP5 providers. When a degraded performance is observed (i.e.; there are SLA violations), the SPs rate IP1 with negative ratings. In this experiment, the SP1's positive and negative evidence is fixed as 200 positive and 50 negative evidences. As shown in Fig. 3 the increase in the positive ratings received by SP1 from other SPs, increase the reputation until the positive evidence reaches 150. As SP1 starts receiving negative ratings from other SPs, the reputation reduces.

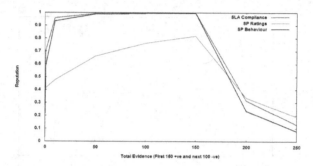

Fig. 3. Reputation based on   SLA monitoring, SP Ratings and SP Behavior only

SP Behavior. In this case, the experiment begins with all SPs using only IP1 for all its resources (cpu, memory, disk space, and virtual machine). The positive behavior of all SPs increases the positive evidence for all SPs, which increases the reputation of IP1 in terms of SPs behaving towards IP1. A degraded performance observed from IP1 may lead to SPs changing their infrastructure provider. This reduces the SPs positive behavior towards IP1 and increases the negative evidence for all SPs, reducing the reputation of IP1. Fig. 3 shows the results of this experiment.

In summary, the experiments with individual parameters considered show an increase in the reputation with SLA compliance evidence for SLA monitoring, and positive SP ratings and positive SP behavior towards an IP. Also violations of SLA, negative SP rating values, and negative behavior of an SP reduces the reputation of an IP.

4.3   Experiments Using Combination of Parameters

Combination of SP Rating and SP Behavior. In this experiment, we consider IP1 with positive ratings from all the SPs. SP1 calculates the reputation of IP1 considering its own ratings as well as ratings of SP2, SP3, SP4 and SP5. The ratings provided by SP2, SP3, SP4 and SP5 are first discounted using SPs behavior towards IP1. When maintaining constant SP ratings by all SPs, the SP behavior of SP2, SP3, SP4 and SP5 changes by increasing the positive behavior of these SPs for initially zero positive behavior to a very high value. Fig. 4 (a) shows that (i) as the SP behavior becomes more positive, the reputation of IP1 increases; (ii) when SP1 has less evidence, there is a large variation, which causes a bigger impact of the other SP behavior and as the SP1's amount of evidence increases, the reputation has less impact of SP behavior.

Combination of SP Rating and SLA Monitoring. In this experiment, to calculate the opinion of IP1 based on SP ratings, we consider all past provided SP ratings. We maintained constant opinions about IP1 and considered that the positive evidence of SLA compliance is varied from zero to a high amount of positive evidence for all SPs (SP1 to SP5). From Fig. 4 (b). it is observed that when the positive evidence from the SLA monitoring increases, the reputation of IP1 also increases.

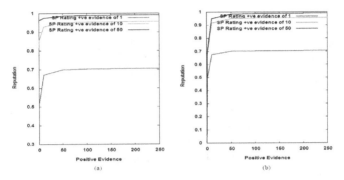

Fig. 4. Reputation based on (a) SP ratings and SP behavior, (b) SP ratings and SLA monitoring

Combination of SP Rating, Behavior and SLA Monitoring. In these experiments we calculated the reputation using all parameters. We considered the values of two of the parameters fixed and varied the third parameter, as explained below.

Effect of SP behavior. The SP rating is fixed at total of 10 positive evidences by each of the SPs. The SLA monitoring is fixed at 50 positive evidences as total evidence by each SP towards IP1. The SP behavior for SP1 to SP5 is varied from zero positive to a positive evidence of 250 in a total evidence of 250. Fig. 5 shows that with the increase in the positive evidence of SP behavior the reputation of IP1 increases.

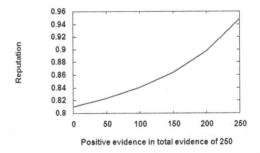

Fig. 5. Effect of SP behavior

Effect of SLA monitoring. The SP ratings provided by all SPs for IP1 and the SP be-havior for all SPs are fixed. The total evidence consists of only positive evidence obtained from SLA monitoring, which is varied from zero to 250. Fig. 6(a) shows that the reputation of IP1 increases with the increase in positive evidence obtained.

The effect of SLA monitoring information is important to evaluate reputation of an IP during the operational phase. In a cloud environment, when the SPs deploy their services on a particular IP, the services are retained for significantly longer duration. This results in less frequent updates of SP ratings and SP behavior. The provision of updates of compliance/non-compliance SLA monitoring information at regular inter-vals may have significant impact on the reputation of an IP, as shown in Fig. 6(a).

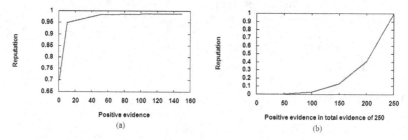

Fig. 6. (a) Effect of SLA compliance; (b) Effect of SP rating

Effect of SP ratings. The SP behavior of all SPs towards an IP and the SLA violation for an IP provided by all SPs are fixed. The positive evidence from all SPs for IP1 is varied from zero to 250 in a total evidence of 250. Fig. 6(b) shows that as the positive evidence increases and the negative evidence reduces, the reputation of IP1 increases.

5   Related Work

Trust and reputation have been the focus of research in several open systems such as e-commerce, peer-to-peer, and multi-agent systems [1] [7] [10][14]. Some trust and reputation approaches have been suggested for web-service systems [3] [4] [12][15][16]. In general, the web-services based approaches are limited [16]. For example, majority of these approaches rely on the use of a centralized repository to store and collect specific QoS feedback from consumers about a service. An excep-tion is found in [15] that uses different QoS registries organized in a P2P way for groups of service providers, but this approach is still limited to specific quality types of feedback and requires overhead of communication due to the use of complex struc-tures. The trust model for P2P systems in [18] considers transactions and shared experiences as recommendations and uses Bayesian estimation methods to compute trust values. The Beta reputation model in [9] is based on beta distribution that con-siders two parameters, positive evidence and negative evidence to estimates the repu-tation of an entity. Both models [18][9] are based on the belief theory, but in [18] the use of Bayesian estimation expects probabilities for each question of interest. The work in [9] has a mapping between opinion space and evidence space [8] and the opinion model allows operate with uncertain probabilities.

Trust is closely related to the concept of uncertainty. However, many of the existing reputation systems have not considered uncertainty in their work. Exceptions are found in the works described in [8][11][17]. The belief model in [8] uses metric called *opinion* to describe belief and disbelief about a proposition as well as the degree of uncertainty regarding probability of an event. The work on [17] proposes *opinion* metric as in [8] but giving importance to uncertainty due to the evidence that impacts the belief and disbelief about a proposition. In [8] the uncertainty is modeled only based on the amount of total evidence; i.e. as the total evidence increases the uncertainty decreases. In [17] the uncertainty also takes into account the amount of positive and negative evidence contained in the total evidence; i.e. given the total evidence the uncertainty is highest when the positive and negative evidence in the total evidence is equal, and the uncertainty reduces as the two evidences dominates.

In Cloud environment, trust based on reputation systems have been discussed in [5][6][2]. In [5], trust is one of the core component used by SP, along with risk, eco-efficiency and cost for evaluating the IP for their service. The work in [6] identifies several vulnerabilities in the existing cloud services provided by Google, IBM, Amazon and proposes an architecture to reinforce the security and privacy in the cloud applications. It suggests a hierarchy of P2P reputation system to protect cloud resources. However, there is no reputation model proposed [6]. Alhamad *et al.* [2] proposes a trust model for cloud computing based on the usage of SLA information. This work describes the requirements and benefits of using SLA for trust modeling in cloud environment, provides a high level architecture capturing major functionalities required, and provides a protocol for the trust model. As in [2] our model also includes SLA compliance information to model trust. We complement the trust model with SP ratings and SP behavior to assist modeling comprehensive trust aspects of an IP. Contrary to [2], we also provide a trust model to evaluate the trust of an IP.

The approach presented in this paper complements existing approaches for reputation of cloud computing environments. Different from existing works, our approach considers several parameters to calculate trustworthiness of infrastructure providers.

6   Conclusion and Final Remarks

This paper presents a trust model to support service providers to verify trustworthiness of infrastructure providers in cloud computing environments. The model calculates trust values based on different parameters, namely (i) SLA monitoring compliance, (ii) service provider ratings, and (ii) service provider behavior. The trust values are calculated based on an opinion model in terms of belief, disbelief, uncertainty and base rate. The work has been evaluated in different sets of experiments. We are currently extending the model to consider relationships that may exist between service providers and infrastructure providers, and use them as another parameter when calculating trust values. We are also performing some more experiments to evaluate the work in other scenarios.

Acknowledgement. This work has been partially supported by the EU within the 7th Framework Programme under contract ICT-257115 - Optimized Infrastructure Services (OPTIMIS). We also acknowledge Theo Dimitrakos, chief security researcher, BT, UK, for providing vital inputs towards the work in this paper.

References

1. Adler, B.T., de Alfaro, L.: A Content-driven Reputation System for Wikepedia. In: Proc. of World Wide Web Conference (2007)
2. Alhamad, M., Dillon, T., Chang, E.: SLA-Based Trust Model for Cloud Computing. In: 13th International Conference on Network-Based Information Systems (2010)
3. Artz, D., Gill, Y.: A Survey of Trust in Computer Science and the Semantic Web. Web Semantics 5(2) (2007)
4. Chang, E., Dillon, T.S., Hussain, F.K.: Trust and reputation for service-oriented environments: technologies for building business intelligence and consumer confidence. Wiley (2006)
5. Ferrer, A.J., Hernández, F., Tordsson, J., Elmroth, E., Ali-Eldin, A., Zsigri, C., Sirvent, R., Guitart, J., Badia, R.M., Djemame, K., Ziegler, W., Dimitrakos, T., Nair, S.K., Kousiouris, G., Konstanteli, K., Varvarigou, T., Hudzia, B., Kipp, A., Wesner, S., Corrales, M., Forgó, N., Sharif, T., Sheridan, C.: OPTIMIS: a Holistic Approach to Cloud Service Provisioning. Future Generation Computer Systems 28(1), 66–77 (2012)
6. Hwang, K., Kulkarni, S., Hu, Y.: Cloud Security with Virtualized Defense and Reputation-based Trust Management. In: Eighth IEEE International Conference on Dependable, Autonomic and Secure Computing (2009)
7. Josang, A., Ismail, R., Boyd, C.: A Survey of Trust and Reputation Systems for Online Service Provision. Decision Support Systems 43(2) (2007)
8. Josang, A.: A Logic for Uncertain Probabilities. International Journal of Uncertainty, Fuzziness and Knowledge-Based Systems 9(3), 279311 (2001)
9. Josang, A., Ismail, R.: The Beta Reputation System. In: Proceedings of the 15th Bled Electronic Commerce Conference e-Reality: Constructing the e-Economy (2002)
10. Kokash, N., van den Heuvel, W.J., D'Andrea V.: Leveraging Web Services Discovery with Customizable Hybrid Matching. In: Int. Conf. on Web Services (2006)
11. Li, F., Wu, J.: Uncertainty Modeling and Reduction in MANETs. IEEE Transactions on Mobile Computing 9(7) (2010)
12. Maximillen, E.M., Singh, M. P.: Reputation and Endorsement for Web Services. SIGecom Exchanges 3(1) (2002)
13. OPTIMIS. Optimized Infrastructure Services, http://www.optimis-project.eu
14. Pujol, J.M., Sanguesa, R., Delgado, J.: Extracting Reputation in Multi Agent Systems by Means of Social Network Topology. In: Proc. International Joint Conference Autonomous Agents and Multiagent Systems (2002)
15. Vu, L.-H., Hauswirth, M., Aberer, K.: QoS-Based Service Selection and Ranking with Trust and Reputation Management. In: Meersman, R. (ed.) OTM 2005, Part I. LNCS, vol. 3760, pp. 466–483. Springer, Heidelberg (2005)
16. Wang, Y., Vassileva, J.: Towards Trust and Reputation Based Web Service Selection: A Survey. International Transaction Systems Science and Applications 3(2) (2007)
17. Wang, Y., Singh, M.P.: Evidence-Based Trust: A Mathematical Model Geared for Multiagent Systems. ACM Transactions on Autonomous and Adaptive Systems 5(4), Article 14 (2010)
18. Wu, P., Wu, G.: A Reputation-Based Trust Model for P2P Systems. In: International Conference on Computational Intelligence and Security (2009)

Post-Session Authentication

Naveed Ahmed and Christian Damsgaard Jensen

Technical University of Denmark, Copenhagen
{naah,Christian.Jensen}@imm.dtu.dk

Abstract. Entity authentication provides confidence in the claimed identity of a peer entity, but the manner in which this goal is achieved results in different types of authentication. An important factor in this regard is the order between authentication and the execution of the associated session. In this paper, we consider the case of post-session authentication, where parties authenticate each other at the end of their interactive session. This use of authentication is different from session-less authentication (e.g., in RFID) and pre-session authentication (e.g., for access control.)

Post-session authentication, although a new term, is not a new concept; it is the basis of at least a few practical schemes. We, for the first time, systematically study it and present the underlying authentication model. Further, we show that an important class of problems is solvable using post-session authentication as the only setup assumption. We hope post-session authentication can be used to devise new strategies for building trust among strangers.

1 Introduction

Entity authentication is an important requirement for the security of interactive protocols, because if a party does not know with whom it is communicating then there is little left what one can achieve in terms of security. Whereas authentication may seem a simple concept, it is one of the most confusing goals in the security analysis [11]—even its operational definition[1] is not agreed upon.

Nevertheless, most security experts do agree that authentication does not correspond to one monolithic goal [8,14]. To us, the term refers to a set of fine level authentication goals (FLAGs) [16,9]. A few examples of FLAGs are identification, recognition, operativeness and willingness. For an entity A that authenticates a peer entity B, identification assures that A is able to compute the correct identity of B, while recognition makes sure that A is able to recognize B as the party with whom it has communicated before [23]. Similarly, the operativeness assures A that B is currently there at the far-end, and the willingness makes sure that B is aware that it is being authenticated. Since different protocols achieve different sets of these fine level goals, the interpretation of authentication varies.

---

[1] A conceptual definition is often in a natural language capturing the meaning and the use of a concept. An operational definition represents a computational procedure that provides *yes* or *no* answer corresponding to the presence or absence of the concept in a given system.

T. Dimitrakos et al. (Eds.): IFIPTM 2012, IFIP AICT 374, pp. 113–128, 2012.
© IFIP International Federation for Information Processing 2012

A party always uses authentication as a service in an application. In Lowe's words [8], "the appropriate authentication requirement will depend upon the use to which the protocol is put." We distinguish between the three classes of use-cases corresponding to the execution order of an authentication protocol and the authentication-dependent interactive session. The first class represents session-less authentication, e.g., RFID [20] and simple entity authentication [12]. In this class, the result of authentication is used by a system to update its state, e.g., a back-end database. Although the authentication result is not used for the other types of interaction, the result may influence how authentication is carried out subsequently, e.g., see the synchronization approach [20].

The second class represents pre-session authentication, which is the most common use of authentication. Here, the result of authentication is used in a subsequent session. For example, when a person logs in on a computer, the operating system uses the authentication result, the person's identity, to launch his session, and all access control decisions in the session essentially depend on it.

The third class, which is relatively less common, is post-session authentication, where authentication is carried out at the end of the associated session. Authenticating the parties when a session is already over may not seem so useful, but the following observations make this case worth considering. Firstly, if an instance of post-session authentication fails then parties can always reject the output of the session. Secondly, post-session authentication allows parties to anonymously interact in the session and build a trust level before authenticating each other, e.g., two spies may want to engage in such a session before revealing their identities. For online shoppers, this type of authentication could be attractive because it provides a kind of assurance that vendors are not using any user-dependent pricing strategy. Similarly, mutually distrustful parties can anonymously engage in an auction for a precious item, while keeping the thieves among the bidders at bay.

In a general model of post-session authentication, parties engage in an arbitrary distributed computation, and at the end they authenticate each other in the context of this computation. Clearly, an adversary can trivially take part in the computation, but, at the end, the adversary can not authenticate himself as a legitimate participant if the authentication protocol is secure.

Because the execution of a post-session authentication protocol is session-dependent, its requirements are clearly more stringent than a session-less authentication protocol. On the other hand, in the pre-session case, we may also need to protect the confidentiality of some protocol terms (e.g., a session key), in order to protect the integrity of the subsequent session. Sometimes a hybrid form of authentication is used, e.g., continuous authentication in Auth-SL [26], which may depend on a previous session, can be used for authorizing the access to a protected resource in a later session.

The rest of the paper is arranged as follows. A few motivating examples are presented in § 2. In § 3, we present our authentication model, and then in § 4 we demonstrate a plausibility result, namely session-less authentication, in principle, can be used to compute any multi-party function. In § 5, we briefly discuss some other interesting aspects of post-session authentication, followed by a summary of the related work in § 6 and concluding remarks in § 7.

2   Examples of Post-Session Authentication

In this section, we present four examples. The reader must note that a session does not necessarily include all of the messages exchanged between two parties. A session may represent a part of such interaction, such as the initial or middle part, depending on the interdependency of authentication and exchanged messages.

Probably, the first known application of post-session authentication is in PGP-fone [1], which uses the method of numeric comparison for authentication. As we know, against an active attacker, Diffie-Hellman key-agreement (DHKA) [21] can only provide confidentiality of the key if the man-in-middle scenario can be rejected. PGPfone use DHKA to establish a call. A hash value of the transcript of the key-agreement phase is computed and converted to numeric values at the both ends. Then, the two parties authenticate each other by simply reading off their respective numeric values.

The second example is of the Cocaine Auction (CA) protocol [3]. Its setup uses anonymous broadcast to carry out an English style auction among untrustworthy parties. The classic allegory for the protocol is as follows.

Consider a number of dealers gathered around a table. One of the dealers, the seller, offers his next shipment of cocaine to the the highest bidder, and he starts the auction by proposing an initial bid. It is required that the bidders remain anonymous to each other as well as to the seller. Also, the winner anonymously arranges a secret appointment with the seller, to receive the goods and to pay the bid. In the scenario described above, none of the parties completely trusts in any other party. There is no party that can act as a trusted arbitrator. For anonymity, even the seller should not able to find out the identity of the winner before committing the sale. The way the protocol achieves these goals is a good example of post-session authentication.

As the third example, we describe a secure communication protocol. Alice wishes to securely and anonymously communicate with her friend Bob over the Internet, but no public key infrastructure (PKI) is available to them, and neither they posses a common secret key. They can use the Diffie-Hellman protocol [21] to compute a common secret, but the protocol does not provide any authentication. Similarly, sending each other their public keys is of no use in absence of a common certification authority. Authenticating each other using biometrics, e.g., voice or video, is not good for anonymity, because a man-in-middle can then easily identify the two parties. In such a restrictive scenario, they can use the following post-session authentication protocol.

Alice and bob start an unauthenticated session, while also realizing the possibility of a man-in-middle attack. In this session, they present each other with a series of challenges, such that answering these challenges require the knowledge of their private interactions in the past. During the session they do not reveal the answers to these challenges. For robustness, we can rely on the challenges with *yes* (binary 1) or *no* (binary 0) answers. At the end of the session, the shared secret is computed by concatenating the answers of these challenges.

Once the shared secret is computed at the both ends, Alice and Bob can use this secret as a cryptographic key to authenticate each other using a suitable symmetric-key authentication protocol [12]. This particular configuration of the initial session and the authentication protocol clearly fits in the post-session authentication class, because the success of the protocol execution inevitably depends on the output of the preceding session.

The fourth example is the ordering system on an Amazon web store [22]. When a new user visits the web store, the Amazon web server stores a cookie containing a session ID in the user's machine. Although the user is completely anonymous to the web store, the web store maintains the temporary database record for the user's session, which is addressable by the session ID in the cookie. As a result, the user can conveniently explore the store, compare prices, select vendors, and manage the shopping basket allocated to the session.

When the user opts for the check out, the web server asks her to sign up with Amazon using her email address, which works as a pseudonym for the user, and then the user is asked to provide a shipping address and a valid payment option. In this way, the web store allows to complete all of the shopping activity except the actual payment without requiring any prior authentication.

As in the above example, the authentication is not necessary for the initial interaction, as long as a web store is willing to commit resources and allocate a unique shopping basket to every potential buyer. At the same time, it is also required that if the buyer proceeds to check-out then the result of her initial interaction—the basket—can some how be linked to the subsequent authentication during the store's check-out phase. On the other hand, note that this case of post-session authentication can well be implemented in the manner of pre-session authentication by forcing each potential buyer to sign up first, however, doing so may not be a good business strategy.

3   Model of Authentication

Authentication is what an authentication protocol does is a dangerous approach[2]. Many security models for protocols are not expressive enough to capture the authentication requirements (see § 6). Often, authentication properties are expressed in an indirect way, e.g., in terms of protocol messages [15] or runs [8]. We use our binding sequence based framework [9,17] to model post-session authentication.

Before going into the details of the actual model, we first motivate the reader by listing some of its advantages. The framework allows simple definitions of authentication goals, based on the notion of distinguishability. It is relatively straight forward to express all interesting authentication goals (which we refer to as FLAGs) in this framework. The framework allows to validate the security and the correctness goals of a protocol independently.

---

[2] By Dieter Gollmann in an invited talk.

The framework was originally used to model the session-less scenario [9], but the extension of that model to post-session authentication turns out to be quite straight forward and only requires the inclusion of one additional clause to the operational definitions of authentication goals.

Summary of Session-Less Authentication Model [9]

A set of FLAGs represents a possible set of correctness requirements for an authentication protocol. Two authentication protocols are functionally different for a calling routine (who may use an authentication protocol as a a service) if their sets of FLAGs are different. Of course, to achieve a certain FLAG, different protocols may employ different cryptographic techniques, e.g., public-key vs. symmetric-key ciphers, and nonces vs. time-stamps.

Let X_c represents the local entity for which a FLAG is being defined, and X_j and X_l are two other network entities, s.t. $c \neq j \neq l$. Let G be a variable on FLAGs.

$\text{RCOG}[X_c \rhd X_j] \stackrel{\text{def}}{=}$ If X_c verifies that X_j is the same entity that once existed then X_c is said to achieve the goal *recognition* for X_j.

$\text{IDNT}[X_c \rhd X_j] \stackrel{\text{def}}{=}$ If X_c verifies that X_j can be linked to a record in a pre-specified identification database then X_c is said to achieve the goal identification[3] for X_j.

$\text{OPER}[X_c \rhd X_j] \stackrel{\text{def}}{=}$ If X_c verifies that X_j currently exists on the network then X_c is said to achieve the goal operativeness for X_j.

$\text{WLNG}[X_c \rhd X_j] \stackrel{\text{def}}{=}$ If an entity X_c verifies that once X_j wanted to communicate to X_c then X_c is said to achieve willingness for X_j.

$\text{PSATH}[X_c \rhd X_j] \stackrel{\text{def}}{=}$ Pseudo single-sided authentication is achieved if an entity X_c verifies that a peer entity X_j, with a pseudonym $pid(X_j)$, is currently ready to communicate with X_c.

$\text{SATH}[X_c \rhd X_j] \stackrel{\text{def}}{=}$ Single-sided authentication is achieved if an entity X_c verifies that a peer entity X_j, with the identification j, is currently ready to communicate with X_c.

$\text{CNFM}[X_c \rhd X_j, G] \stackrel{\text{def}}{=}$ If an entity X_c verifies that the peer entity X_j knows that X_c has achieved a FLAG G for X_l then X_c is said to achieve the goal confirmation on G from X_j.

$\text{SSATH}[X_c \rhd X_j] \stackrel{\text{def}}{=}$ Strong single-sided authentication is achieved by X_c for X_j if X_c has the confirmation on the *single-sided authentication* for X_j from X_j.

$\text{MATH}[X_c \rhd X_j] \stackrel{\text{def}}{=}$ If an entity X_c verifies that both parties (X_c and the peer entity X_j) currently want to communicate with each other, then X_c is said to achieve mutual authentication.

---

[3] Further, if that record cannot be used to feasibly recover the identity j then it is qualified as anonymous identification. For brevity, we do not include the anonymity aspect in this exposition, but it is trivial to write the anonymous versions of FLAGs.

The above list of FLAGs is based on our experience. The FLAGs as presented above are independent of any protocol or any security model [5,14] and only capture the natural use of these terms. Now, we turn to the operational definitions of FLAGs, in order to provide computational procedures corresponding to whether or not certain FLAGs are achieved in the operational settings of an authentication protocol Π. A central concept in this regard is of a *binding sequence*.

Binding Sequence: A binding sequence β_{X_c} is a list of received messages in the protocol transcript of an entity X_c, such that the messages are guaranteed to be sent by honest parties.

A *binding sequence* can be replayed; only an unauthorized change in the list is not possible without being detected by X_c. For example, the list of received encrypted messages $[\{N_c\}_{K_c}, \{N_c + 1\}_{K_c}]$, where K_c is the public key of X_c, cannot be changed[4] by a man-in-middle without the possibility of being detected by X_c, although X_c may not know who is at the far-end and whether the list is being replayed. In the literature, sometimes such a property for an individual message is called the *message integrity*.

In the following, X_c can distinguish between two instances of a *binding sequence* if a distinguisher algorithm $\mathcal{D}(C_b, \lambda)$ (which runs in a polynomial time in the length of its input) can be constructed on X_c. Here, C_b is a challenge picked by X_c and is either C_0 or C_1; and λ is an auxiliary input, such as a decryption key. The distinguisher correctly outputs 0 or 1 corresponding to C_0 and C_1, with a high probability.

RCOG$(X_c \triangleright X_j, \beta_{X_c}(i)) \stackrel{\text{def}}{=}$ Let $\beta_{X_c}(i)$, $\beta_{X_c}(i')$ and $\beta_{X_c}(i'')$ be generated when X_c executes Π with X_j, X_l and X_j respectively, as shown in Fig. 1. Let the two challenges be $C_0 = (\beta_{X_c}(i), \beta_{X_c}(i'))$ and $C_1 = (\beta_{X_c}(i), \beta_{X_c}(i''))$. If there exists $\mathcal{D}^{rcog}(C_b, \lambda)$ on X_c for all choices of j and l then X_c is said to achieve the goal *recognition* of X_j from $\beta_{X_c}(i)$.

IDNT$(X_c \triangleright X_j, \beta_{X_c}(i)) \stackrel{\text{def}}{=}$ Same as RCOG$(X_c \triangleright X_j, \beta_{X_c}(i))$ except the distinguisher $\mathcal{D}^{idnt}(C_b, \lambda)$ gets a read-only access to an identification database containing the identification records of all network entities, as a part of its auxiliary input λ.

OPER$(X_c \triangleright X_j, \beta_{X_c}(i)) \stackrel{\text{def}}{=}$ Let $\beta_{X_c}(i)$ and $\beta_{X_c}(i')$ be generated when X_c executes Π twice with X_j, as shown in Fig. 1. Let the two challenges be $C_0 = \beta_{X_c}(i)$ and $C_1 = \beta_{X_c}(i')$. If there exists $\mathcal{D}^{oper}(C_b, \lambda)$ on X_c for all runs with X_j then X_c is said to achieve the goal *operativeness* for X_j.

WLNG$(X_c \triangleright X_j, \beta_{X_c}(i)) \stackrel{\text{def}}{=}$ If $\beta_{X_c}(i)$ is generated on X_c in a *run* involving X_c and X_j, as shown in Fig. 1, then IDNT$(X_j \triangleright X_c, \beta_{X_j}(i)) \Rightarrow$ WLNG$(X_c \triangleright X_j, \beta_{X_c}(i))$, where $\beta_{X_j}(i)$ consists of all those messages from $\beta_{X_c}(i)$ in which X_j is a peer entity.

---

[4] Standard assumptions apply: the public-key encryption scheme is secure, and the private key is only known to X_c.

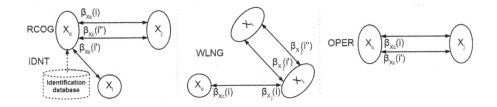

Fig. 1. Distinguishability Setups for FLAGs

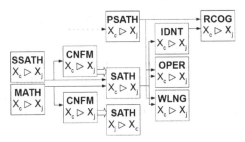

Fig. 2. Relations among FLAGs

$\text{PSATH}(X_c \triangleright X_j, \beta_{X_c}(i)) \stackrel{\text{def}}{=} \text{WLNG}(X_c \triangleright X_j, \beta_{X_c}(i)) \wedge \text{OPER}(X_c \triangleright X_j, \beta_{X_c}(i)) \wedge$
$\quad \text{RCOG}(X_c \triangleright X_j, \beta_{X_c}(i))$

$\text{SATH}(X_c \triangleright X_j, \beta_{X_c}(i)) \stackrel{\text{def}}{=}$
$\quad \text{WLNG}(X_c \triangleright X_j, \beta_{X_c}(i)) \wedge \text{OPER}(X_c \triangleright X_j, \beta_{X_c}(i)) \wedge \text{IDNT}(X_c \triangleright X_j, \beta_{X_c}(i))$

$\text{CNFM}(X_c \triangleright X_j, \beta_{X_c}(i), G) \stackrel{\text{def}}{=} \text{RCOG}(X_c \triangleright X_j, \beta_{X_c}''(i)) \wedge \text{OPER}(X_c \triangleright X_j, \beta_{X_c}''(i))$
$\quad \wedge G(X_c \triangleright X_j, \beta_{X_c}'(i)),$
$\quad \text{where } \beta_{X_c}(i) = \beta_{X_c}'(i) \| \beta_{X_c}''(i) \text{ (} \| \text{ stands for concatenation).}$

$\text{SSATH}(X_c \triangleright X_j, \beta_{X_c}(i)) \stackrel{\text{def}}{=} G \wedge \text{CNFM}(X_c \triangleright X_j, \beta_{X_c}(i), G),$
$\quad \text{where } G = \text{SATH}(X_c \triangleright X_j, \beta_{X_c}(i))$

$\text{MATH}(X_c \triangleright X_j, \beta_{X_c}(i)) \stackrel{\text{def}}{=} \text{SATH}(X_c \triangleright X_j, \beta_{X_c}(i)) \wedge \text{CNFM}(X_c \triangleright X_j, \beta_{X_c}(i), G),$
$\quad \text{where } G = \text{SATH}(X_j \triangleright X_c, \beta_{X_j}(i))$

The hierarchical relations between FLAGs that are valid (by definition) are shown in Fig. 2. *Identification, willingness* and *recognition* do not have any timeliness property. *Operativeness* and *willingness* do not require the knowledge of the identity (or pseudo identity) of a peer entity. The goal *confirmation* can be applied to any other goal, e.g., a confirmation on MATH may be regarded as a stronger form of *mutual authentication. Identification, operativeness,* and *single-sided authentication* are respectively comparable to *aliveness, recent aliveness* [8], and *strong entity authentication* [12].

Extension to Post-Session Class

For the post-session class, the definition of security—the binding sequence— remains the same. We extend the correctness requirements, by including a post-session clause in the operational definitions of FLAGs, to meet the requirement that authentication should only succeeds in the context of a session. Before introducing the new clause, we first elaborate the notion of a session itself.

In our model, a session only refers to the interactive part of a distributed computation, in which a number of parties interact with each other by passing messages over unreliable channels. Whether the computation is secure if some of the parties are dishonest [19], and whether the computation meets its functional requirements, are the concerns that are beyond the scope of our notion of (interactive) session[5]. Similarly, in the part of computation that is carried out locally by a party, all components and communication between the components are assumed to be trusted (cf. secure information flow.)

Next, we consider the specification of a session, so that it can be used in our computational model. On the one hand, one may need to specify a session at the level of primitive communication steps of interactive Turing machines. On the other hand, specifying a session by the end result of a computation may suffice. The right level of specification is certainly application dependent. We abstract away from this decision by defining the computational interpretation of a session in the following way.

Session: An i_{th} session $\Psi_i = f(\tau_i, .)$ is a set of terms computed by a party from the transcript of its interaction τ_i before the i_{th} execution of an authentication protocol, such that each Ψ_i is unique among all q sessions in the network, i.e., $\{\Psi_i : 1 \leq i \leq q\}$ is necessarily a q_{th} order set.

Depending on the required level of granularity, Ψ_i may well consists of a complete transcript of communication with the time-stamps (thus making each session trivially unique), a hash of the transcript, or a binary value distinguishing only between uncorrupted and corrupted sessions (modified by an adversary.) For our purpose, all sessions are in the set $\{\Psi_i : 1 \leq i \leq q\}$. This set will always be empty for session-less authentication.

Claim 1: An authentication protocol that achieves G is vulnerable to session hijacking if G does not depend on the session.

proof: Assuming G is not a valid post-session FLAG, a generic attack is possible. Let X_1 and X_2 be the two honest parties and $\mathcal{A}$ be an adversary. Now, $\mathcal{A}$ plays a man-in-middle role while executing Ψ_1 with X_1 and Ψ_2 with X_2. At the end of these sessions, $\mathcal{A}$ simply authenticate itself to X_1 and X_2. Consequently, X_1 and X_2 conclude that the prior session took place with $\mathcal{A}$. Hence, $\mathcal{A}$ is able to hijack (and claim the credit of) Ψ_1 and Ψ_2 □

To prevent session hijacking and similar problems, the distinction between *responsibility* and *credit* [27] is important. To summarize, in some applications a claimant of a session can be held responsible for the messages in the session, e.g., to make payment for an order in the last example of § 2, or the session may represent an access control policy that is to be enforced on the behalf of the

---

[5] This is why a seamless interaction with an MPC protocol is possible in § 4.

claimant. In the other applications, the claimant may expect credit for the session, e.g., winning bid in an auction, monetary reward for the session containing the solution to a puzzle, or an increase in the reputation score.

There is no incentive in hijacking a session if the hijacking only implies the responsibility at a later stage, however, making some honest party responsible for an adversary's generated session can be a real threat. On the other hand, if the claim on a session means some credit then certainly hijacking is well motivated.

Therefore, we further qualify the session computing function $f(\tau_i, .)$ in the definition of a session: if a session implies some credit (possibly in combination with responsibility) then we require that the inverse function $\tau_i = f^{-1}(\Psi_i, .)$ is a one-way function. There are several ways to meet this requirement, e.g., by employing a Diffie-Hellman type construction [1] or a nonce based commitment [3]. In the following, we assume that this requirement is always met. For a session that only leads to the responsibility, there is no such requirement.

Now, we extend the operational definitions of FLAGs to express the requirement of post-session authentication.

Post-Session Clause: G is a valid post-session FLAG *if* finding a pair of sessions Ψ_i and Ψ_j is infeasible such that, in a given run of authentication protocol, G can be validated in the run for both Ψ_i and Ψ_j.

Intuitively, if a party can derive a FLAG from its binding sequence after Ψ_i but the same FLAG can not be validated independent of Ψ_i, then this FLAG is a valid post-session FLAG for the party. To illustrate how the proposed extension works, let us once again consider the third example from § 2; the abstract narrations of the protocol are as follows.

1. Interactive Session:
   $X_{alice} \rightarrow X_{bob} : [c_i : 1 \leq i \leq |K|/2]$ (Alice sends her set of challenges.)
   $X_{bob} \rightarrow X_{alice} : [c_i : |K|/2 < i \leq |K|]$ (Bob sends his set of challenges.)
2. Computation of Session:
   $on\ X_{bob} : \Psi_{bob} = K_{bob} \leftarrow [c_i : 1 \leq i \leq |K|]$ (Compute Bob's version of key.)
   $on\ X_{alice} : \Psi_{alice} = K_{alice} \leftarrow [c_i : 1 \leq i \leq |K|]$ (Compute Alice's version of key.)
3. Authentication :
   $X_{alice} \rightarrow X_{bob} : N_{alice}$
   $X_{bob} \rightarrow X_{alice} : N_{bob}, \{N_{alice}, N_{bob}, Alice\}_{K_{bob}}$
   $X_{alice} \rightarrow X_{bob} : \{N_{bob}, N_{alice}\}_{K_{alice}}$

In this example, the authentication protocol (ISO/IEC 9798-2) can not succeed without the same session at both ends, i.e., the authentication succeeds only if Alice's key K_{alice} and Bob's key K_{bob} are equal. When the same session is used, Alice and Bob achieve a certain set of FLAGs; this set can be computed using the operational definitions of FLAGs.

Consider the operativeness of Bob: $OPER(X_{alice} \triangleright X_{bob}, \beta_{alice})$, where $\beta_{alice} = [\{N_{alice}, N_{bob}, Alice\}_{K_{bob}}]$. As per the operational definition, we need to consider two instances of the binding sequence in different runs of the protocol: $\beta_{alice}(0) = [\{N_{alice}^0, N_{bob}^0, Alice\}_{K_{bob}}]$ and $\beta_{alice}(1) = [\{N_{alice}^1, N_{bob}^1, Alice\}_{K_{bob}}]$.

Claim 2: Alice achieves a valid post-session FLAG for Bob:
$\mathrm{OPER}(X_{alice} \rhd X_{bob}, [\{N_{alice}, N_{bob}, Alice\}_{K_{bob}}])$.

proof: The two operativeness challenges on X_{alice} are $C_0 = \beta_{alice}(0)$ and $C_1 = \beta_{alice}(1)$. On X_{alice}, we use $\lambda = [K_{alice}, N^0_{alice}, N^1_{alice}]$ as the auxiliary input for the operativeness distinguisher $\mathcal{D}^{oper}$. We select a random bit b and invoke the distinguisher: $b' \leftarrow \mathcal{D}^{oper}(C_b, \lambda)$, where b' is the distinguisher's output. The distinguisher construction is as follows.

$\mathcal{D}^{oper}(C_{b'}, \lambda)$:

(1) Decrypt $C_{b'}$ using $\lambda[0]$ to compute $\{x, ..\}$.

(2) If $\lambda[2] = x$ then return $b' = 1$ else return $b' = 0$.

As per the operational requirement, if $b = b'$ then our distinguisher has done a good job. For a key of size $s = |K_{alice}|$ and a nonce of size $t = |N_{alice}|$, and assuming uniform distribution for the key and the nonce, an upper bound on the probability of failure for the distinguisher ($b \neq b'$) is $p.2^{-s} + p.2^{-t}$, where p is the number of protocol instances using the same key. Clearly, for sufficiently large s and t, the upper bound is negligible. Also, trivially, finding $\Psi_{bob} = K_{bob}$ and $\Psi_{alice} = K_{alice}$, such that $K_{alice} \neq K_{bob}$ and $\{N^0_{alice}, N^0_{bob}, Alice\}_{K_{bob}} = \{N^0_{alice}, N^0_{bob}, Alice\}_{K_{alice}}$ is infeasible. Hence, Alice can achieve the operativeness of Bob by running the protocol.

□

A similar, analysis can be done for Bob, which we leave out due to space constraints. Also the identification and willingness goals are trivially achieved because there are only two legitimate parties, e.g., for the identification case, the distinguisher can simply return the name of a far-end party after the successful decryption of the received messages.

About Security Analysis

As mentioned earlier, one advantage of the binding sequence based model is that the correctness analysis (for FLAGs) and the security analysis (for the binding sequence) are independent. In fact, the security analysis is no more than verifying the validity of the binding sequence of an authentication protocol. Since security analysis is not the main focus of this paper, we briefly discuss how the validation of a binding sequence can be done in complexity theoretic models [5] and in formal security models [24,25].

For the former case, let us consider the binding sequence of Bob corresponding to the last message he received: $\beta_{X_{bob}} = [\{N_{bob}, N_{alice}\}]$. There are three different ways in which this sequence can be modified: $[\{N_{bob}, N'_{alice}\}]$, $[\{N'_{bob}, N_{alice}\}]$ and $[\{N'_{bob}, N'_{alice}\}]$, where a primed term represents a modified message. Now, for each of these modified sequence, we calculate an upper bound of accepting the modified sequence by Bob. For a valid *binding sequence* these upper bounds should represent a negligible probability. Generalizing this method results in a security analysis that involves verifying $2^{|\beta_{X_c}|} - 1$ cases of modified sequences. Interested readers are referred to the appendixes of our technical report [17].

In an automated tool based on symbolic models, such as OFMC [24] or LYSA [25], one can easily verify the validity of a binding sequence by verifying the authenticity of each message in the binding sequence. Of course, this is an over-approximation of the actual requirements of the binding sequence, because a binding sequence can be replayed. We are currently investigating how to accurately specify the actual requirement that allows such a replay but forbids the replay of the individual messages in a binding sequence. For now, we can rely on an ad-hoc solution: ignore all those attack traces in which the whole binding sequence is being replayed.

4 Plausibility Result: Computable Class of Problems

In the classic problem of multi party computation (MPC) [19], a set of parties want to compute an arbitrary function, such that the computation preserves certain security properties, e.g., the correctness of the result and the privacy of the inputs. The set of MPC parties consists of both honest and dishonest parties. Most of the work on secure MPC, however, assumes the availability of authenticated communication channels between honest parties.

In reality, authenticated channels may not always available, and therefore it is interesting to consider the MPC security problem without this assumption. Clearly, if the channels are not authentic then an adversary can even disconnect the MPC parties and run the protocol with any one of them without the possibility of being detected. Therefore, one needs some weak assumption to achieve a useful security guarantee. For example, Barak et al. [10] introduce the assumption of *independent execution*: roughly speaking, if an adversary plays man-in-middle then he must engage in independent executions of a protocol with each of the protocol parties.

The post-session authentication is another such assumption, but this is strong enough that it suffices to realize any MPC functionality correctly, assuming that there exists an MPC protocol that computes this functionality on authenticated channels. Note that the privacy of the inputs may not be protected, but the correctness of the output is guaranteed. The reader may wonder that if the parties have the capability to authenticate each other after a session then why not they do so at the start and establish an authentic channel instead, however, this is not always possible; some of the possible factors are listed below.

- PKI may be off-line or only accessible for a short duration at regular intervals. In this situation, immediate authentication is not always possible.
- The honest parties of MPC may not necessarily trust each other. Therefore, their decision to reveal their identities should depend on the observed behaviour in the session.
- The authentication may require a long time, e.g., in using physical authentication or postal mail to deliver PIN codes. Therefore, instead of waiting, parties may decide to start a session based on a general trust level of their community.

Usually, the proof for a theoretical plausibility of MPC is based on the simulation paradigm [19], in which one shows the equivalence between an actual model and an appropriately constructed ideal model. For our post-session authentication problem, this means constructing an ideal model that is similar to the standard authenticated channel model ($\mathcal{F}_{auth}$ [10]) except it reveals all the inputs to an adversary; then, we need to show that the adversary gain is negligible in the post-session authentication case.

Instead of the simulation based approach, we employ an indirect and simpler method. We construct, which we call, the Tabular scheme that interacts with an arbitrary MPC protocol in a black-box manner to achieve the correct result, while running on unauthenticated channels. In this way, this scheme serves as a constructive proof of the correct computation of any MPC protocol.

Tabular Scheme: Consider n parties that take part in an MPC protocol, using unauthenticated channels. Each party P_i, where $1 \leq i \leq n$, maintains two tables: T_t and T_r, each having n rows[6]. In T_t, the j_{th} row, where $1 \leq j \leq n$, represents the list of messages sent to P_j. Similarly, in T_r, the j_{th} row represents the list of messages received supposedly (as the connections are not authentic) from P_j. When the MPC protocol terminates, we execute a post-session authentication protocol between each P_i and P_j pair, such that P_i authenticates P_j using the j_{th} row of T_t as its session, while P_j participate in the authentication using her i_{th} row of T_r as a session.

Claim 3: Consider a protocol Π_{MPC} between n parties communicating over authenticated channels to compute a probabilistic functionality $\mathcal{F}_{\mathrm{MPC}}$ within m interactions. If the inputs of n parties are not private then parties can also compute $\mathcal{F}_{\mathrm{MPC}}$ while communicating over unauthenticated channels and using an n-party post-session authentication protocol.

Proof: We augment each of the n parties of Π_{MPC} with our Tabular Scheme as specified above and use SATH (see § 3) as the definition of authentication in the scheme. For each party, the memory requirement of the tables is $|T_t| + |T_r| = 2 \times m \times n \times |M|$, where $|M|$ is the maximum size of any individual message in the protocol.

The authentication protocol in the Tabular Scheme succeeds between P_i and P_j only if j_{th} row of T_t (on P_i) and i_{th} row of P_r (on P_j) are exactly same and the two parties possess legitimate credentials. These two rows can be considered as the session footprint for the communication from P_i to P_j. On the other hand, if both of these rows are same then this guarantees that the adversary has not modified any message in these rows.

Next, we rerun the authentication protocol of the Tabular scheme to achieve SATH between every pair of the protocol parties, which requires running $n(n-1)$ instances[7] of two-party SATH protocol. If all these instances succeed then this guarantees that all parties agree on the messages that were exchanged in the session and the adversary has not fabricated, modified or

---

[6] Actually one needs $n - 1$ rows, but we use n to simplify the indexing.

[7] The number of permutation pairs on a set of order n.

deleted any message in the session. Hence, the output of the protocol Π_{MPC} is necessarily correct, i.e., $\mathcal{F}_{\mathrm{MPC}}$.   □

Clearly, the Tabular scheme interacts with Π_{MPC} in a black-box manner, which implies that we can deploy an arbitrary MPC protocol given that the protocol does not require input privacy. Also note that the overhead, in terms of memory ($2 \times n \times m \times |M|$ bits) and time ($n^2 - n$ instances of authentication), is polynomial in the size of a protocol.

We can optimize the Tabular scheme by using a hash function, i.e., instead of using a complete row we may use the hash value of the row as the representation of a session, which, in many cases, can be encoded as a single message in an authentication protocol. Depending on the requirements of an MPC protocol, the definition of authentication can be relaxed from SATH, e.g., if timeliness is not important then the operativeness goal (OPER) is not required.

5   Discussion and Future Directions

One may argue that the additional requirements in pre-session or post-session authentication are not the "real" authentication requirements. A good illustrative example is of a two-party secure communication protocol, in which a secret session key is computed to establish a secure channel between the parties. Here, the confidentiality of the key and authentication of the parties appear to be completely independent protocol goals.

This view, however, manifests its limitation as soon as we consider the goal of establishing two parallel secure channels between same two parties. Now, there are two authentication results and two secret session keys, and the associations between the keys (or the subsequent sessions) and the authentication results are indeed essential requirements. Such a situation is even more dangerous for post-session authentication, e.g., it will allow a session hijacking attack, in which an honest party does all the hard work in a session and then a dishonest party simply claims the ownership of the session at the end.[8]

The reader may have realized that not all the problems that are solvable using pre-session authentication can be solved using post-session authentication, partially because post-session authentication can not guarantee the confidentiality of the inputs. Another factor is that if the session involves some access to a protected resource, which only an authorized entity is allowed to do, then post-session authentication can not help, because an adversary can easily pretend to be an authorized party. Nevertheless, in many applications the effect of a session on a system can be reversed, e.g., cancelling the purchasing order (if the customer's credit card payment is later denied by the issuing bank) and redoing an auction.

The separation of correctness and security requirements as detailed in our earlier work [9] is not affected with the post-session extension. In particular, the

---

[8] The same attack is also described in the auction protocol [3].

validity of a binding sequence is the only required security property; all authentication properties of practical significance (FLAGs) can be derived from the binding sequence. We believe that the job of a security analyst (human/automated tool) would be less strenuous if security requirements are fewer and pure, considering the security analysis is an undecidable problem in general.

For the future work, an immediate challenge is to find a general method that can be used to specify the session computing function from a given set of application requirements. In this regard, the notions of credit and responsibility are critical and somehow needs to be specified formally. The notion of a session Ψ_i can be interpreted in a probabilistic sense to obtain precise security bounds especially when Ψ_i is a digest of a complete transcript. This will imply that the unique identification of sessions using their Ψ_i occurs with a certain (high) probability. More research on these issues will help to integrate post-session authentication into existing tools that automatically analyse authentication protocols or provide a provable security assurance.

6   Related Work on Authentication Models

We only cover some highlights in the area that concerns with the modelling aspect of authentication. Although the current models do not consider the post-session scenario, we believe they can be extended for this purpose.

Probably, the first attempt to model authentication is in BAN logic [4], which formalizes the authentication goals in terms of beliefs held by peer entities, however, this line of work has some limitations [13]. In cryptographic models, authentication in terms of matching conversation [5] is among the first, but still popular, approach. This requirement is too strong [12], but it can be extended to include a session to capture the post-session requirements.

Gollmann [7] presents an in-depth analysis of authentication. Roscoe [15] distinguishes between *intensional* and *extensional* style of authentication goals. Boyd and Mathuria [12] consider intensional specifications to be restrictive, and Gollman [11] even discourages such formal specifications. The underlying cause of this puzzle is that it is often not clear how an intensional property is related to an extensional property. In our model, this problem is resolved as FLAGs (extensional goals) are derived from the binding sequence (an intensional property).

Some other proposals for authentication goals [6,18,2] are not satisfactory [12]. Lowe [8] identifies four requirements of authentication with varying strength and formalize them using process algebra. Boyd and Mathuria [12] provide only two goals related to entity authentication. Cremer [14] introduces an hierarchy of authentication levels. In many formal methods of security analysis [25,24], the focus is on message authentication. Nevertheless, these tools enable an automatic validation of binding sequences, as indicated in § 3.

Gorrieri et al. [28] formalize the informal notions of credit and responsibility [27], which can be extended to formalize the session computation function. Squicciarini et al. [26] propose an authentication framework that supports an authentication decision based on the previous events that occurred in the system.

Such a framework can be used to support post-authentication, e.g., by defining an authentication policy that cryptographically connects a session to the success of a subsequent authentication event.

7 Conclusion

In this paper, we specify the requirements of post-session authentication and show that it can be used to solve any MPC problem that is solvable on authenticated channels and does not require the input privacy. Authenticating after a session, if possible, indeed offers some advantages, such as anonymity and less dependency on the availability of PKI. When the choice is available between post-session and pre-session authentication, relative pros and cons are normally application dependent. Although the use of post-session authentication is currently less common, we hope our work will be useful in recognizing its advantages, as well as its limitations, and building more innovative secure systems.

References

1. Zimmermann, P.R.: Pgpfone: Pretty good privacy phone owner's manual, version 1.0(5) (1996), http://web.mit.edu/network/pgpfone/manual/#PGP000057
2. ISO standard: Entity Authentication Mechanisms; Part 1: General Model. ISO/IEC 9798-1, 2nd edn. (September 1991)
3. Stajano, F., Anderson, R.: The Cocaine Auction Protocol: On the Power of Anonymous Broadcast. In: Pfitzmann, A. (ed.) IH 1999. LNCS, vol. 1768, pp. 434–447. Springer, Heidelberg (2000)
4. Burrows, M., Abadi, M., Needham, R.M.: A logic of Authentication. DEC System Research Center, Report 39 (revised February 22, 1990)
5. Bellare, M., Rogaway, P.: Entity Authentication and Key Distribution. In: Stinson, D.R. (ed.) CRYPTO 1993. LNCS, vol. 773, pp. 232–249. Springer, Heidelberg (1994)
6. Syverson, P.F., Van Oorschot, P.C.: On Unifying Some Cryptographic Protocol Logics. In: Proc.: S&P, pp. 1063–7109. IEEE (1994) ISSN:1063-7109
7. Gollmann, D.: What do we mean by entity authentication? In: Proc.: Symposium on Security and Privacy, pp. 46–54. IEEE (1996)
8. Lowe, G.: A Hierarchy of Authentication Specifications. In: Proc.: 10th Computer Security Foundations Workshop (CSFW 1997) (1997)
9. Ahmed, N., Jensen, C.D.: Demarcation of Security in Authentication Protocols. In: Proc.: 1st SysSec Workshop, pp. 43–50. IEEE Computer Society (2011)
10. Barak, B., Canetti, R., Lindell, Y., Pass, R., Rabin, T.: Secure Computation Without Authentication. In: Shoup, V. (ed.) CRYPTO 2005. LNCS, vol. 3621, pp. 361–377. Springer, Heidelberg (2005)
11. Gollmann, D.: Authentication—myths and misconception. In: Cryptography and Computational Number Theory, pp. 203–225. Birkhauser (2001)
12. Boyd, C., Mathuria, A.: Protocols for Authentication and Key Establishment. Springer (2003) ISBN: 978-3-540-43107-7
13. Kurkowski, M., Srebrny, M.: A Quantifier-free First-order Knowledge Logic of Authentication. Fundamenta Informaticae 72(1-3) (2006)

14. Cremers, C.J.F.: Scyther: Semantics and Verification of Security Protocols. IPA Dissertation Series 2006-20, Eindhoven (2006)
15. Roscoe, A.W.: Intensional specifications of security protocols. In: Proc.: Computer Security Foundations Workshop, pp. 28–38. IEEE (1996)
16. Ahmed, N., Jensen, C.D.: Definition of Entity Authentication. In: Proc.: 2nd IWSCN, pp. 1–7. IEEE (2010)
17. Ahmed, N., Jensen, C.D.: Adaptable Authentication Model: Exploring Security with Weaker Attacker Models. In: Erlingsson, Ú., Wieringa, R., Zannone, N. (eds.) ESSoS 2011. LNCS, vol. 6542, pp. 234–247. Springer, Heidelberg (2011); Technical Report: IMM-TR-2010-17
18. Menezes, A.J., Van Oorschot, P.C., Vanstone, S.A.: Handbook of Applied Cryptography. CRC Press (1997)
19. Goldreich, O.: Foundations of cryptography: Basic applications. Cambridge University Press (2004)
20. Juels, A.: RFID security and privacy: A research survey. Selected Areas in Communications 24(2), 381–394 (2006)
21. Diffie, W., Hellman, M.: New directions in cryptography. IEEE Transactions on Information Theory 22(6), 644–654 (1976)
22. Amazon UK web store, http://www.amazon.co.uk
23. Lucks, S., Zenner, E., Weimerskirch, A., Westhoff, D.: Concrete Security for Entity Recognition: The Jane Doe Protocol. In: Chowdhury, D.R., Rijmen, V., Das, A. (eds.) INDOCRYPT 2008. LNCS, vol. 5365, pp. 158–171. Springer, Heidelberg (2008)
24. Basin, D., Mödersheim, S., Vigano, L.: OFMC: A symbolic model checker for security protocols. International J. of Information Security, 181–208 (2005)
25. Bodei, C., Buchholtz, M., Degano, P., Nielson, F., Nielson, H.R.: Static validation of security protocols. Journal of Computer Security, 347–390 (2005)
26. Squicciarini, A.C., Bhargav-Spantzel, A., Bertino, E., Czeksis, A.B.: Auth-SL - A System for the Specification and Enforcement of Quality-Based Authentication Policies. In: Qing, S., Imai, H., Wang, G. (eds.) ICICS 2007. LNCS, vol. 4861, pp. 386–397. Springer, Heidelberg (2007)
27. Abadi, M.: Two facets of authentication. In: Proc.: Computer Security Foundations Workshop, pp. 27–32. IEEE (1998)
28. Gorrieri, R., Martinelli, F., Petrocchi, M.: A formalization of credit and responsibility within the gndc schema. ENTCS 157(3), 61–78 (2006)

An Efficient Approach for Privacy Preserving Distributed K-Means Clustering Based on Shamir's Secret Sharing Scheme

Sankita Patel, Sweta Garasia, and Devesh Jinwala

S.V. National Institute of Technology, Surat, Gujarat, India
{sjp,g.sweta,dcj}@coed.svnit.ac.in

Abstract. Privacy preserving data mining has gained considerable attention because of the increased concerns to ensure privacy of sensitive information. Amongst the two basic approaches for privacy preserving data mining, viz. Randomization based and Cryptography based, the later provides high level of privacy but incurs higher computational as well as communication overhead. Hence, it is necessary to explore alternative techniques that improve the overheads. In this work, we propose an efficient, collusion-resistant cryptography based approach for distributed K-Means clustering using Shamir's secret sharing scheme. As we show from theoretical and practical analysis, our approach is provably secure and does not require a trusted third party. In addition, it has negligible computational overhead as compared to the existing approaches.

Keywords: Privacy Preservation in Data Mining (PPDM), Secret sharing, Secure Multiparty Computation (SMC).

1 Introduction

Emerging knowledge based systems gather large amount of sensitive information from their customers. Availability of high speed Internet and sophisticated data mining tools has made sharing of this information across the organizations possible. These technologies when combined pose a threat to privacy concerns of individuals. Hence, there is a need to view data mining tools from different perspective i.e. adding privacy preserving mechanism yielding Privacy Preserving Data Mining (PPDM). Privacy preserving data mining aims to achieve data mining, while hiding sensitive data from disclosure or inference.

In general, for knowledge based systems, data is located at different sites and bringing data together at one place for analysis is not possible due to privacy laws or policies [1]. Hence incorporating privacy preserving mechanisms for distributed databases is necessary for such applications. For the distributed databases, data may be horizontally partitioned or vertical partitioned [1]. In horizontal partitioning, different sites collect the same feature set about different entities while in vertical partitioning, different sites collect different feature sets for the same set of entities. These partitioning models are formally defined in [2]. In this paper, we refer the horizontal partitioning model.

T. Dimitrakos et al. (Eds.): IFIPTM 2012, IFIP AICT 374, pp. 129–141, 2012.

Among the two main categories of PPDM approaches viz. *Randomization based* and *Cryptography based*, later provides higher level of privacy but poor scalability [3]. Amongst the two main Cryptography based approaches, the Secure Multiparty Computation (SMC) [4] provides higher level of privacy but incurs higher computational and communication overhead. As compared, homomorphic encryption based approach provides high level of privacy but incurs higher computational cost. This issue requires critical investigation when applied to data mining. This is so, since data mining requires huge databases as input; hence scalable techniques for privacy preserving data mining are needed to handle them. Therefore, in this paper, we mainly focus on reducing the computational cost of privacy preserving data mining algorithm. The secret sharing based approach is an attractive solution for PPDM which greatly reduces the computational and communication cost of SMC and provides high level of privacy [5].

In this paper, we focus on clustering application of data mining in distributed scenario. As discussed, Cryptography based approaches achieve high level of privacy but the resultant protocols are inefficient in terms of computation and communication overhead. As discussed further in section 2, the oblivious transfer based approaches proposed in [7-9] are not scalable due to their high computational and communicational overhead. Homomorphic encryption based approaches proposed in [9-11] are computationally expensive due to their complex public key operations. Hence, the scope of above two approaches is limited to small datasets and it is necessary to explore alternative technique that is scalable in terms of dataset size. Secret sharing based approaches proposed in [12] [13] aim to achieve this. However, approaches proposed in [12] [13] use either a dedicated server or Trusted Third Party (TTP) to achieve privacy. In practical scenario, the assumption about TTP cannot always be ensured and if ensured, compromise in TTP will jeopardize the privacy.

In this paper, we propose an algorithm for privacy preserving distributed clustering based on the paradigm of Shamir's secret sharing [14]. We modify the widely used K-means clustering algorithm [15-17] to run it in the distributed scenario and incorporate privacy preserving feature in it. We allow parties to collaboratively perform clustering and thus avoiding trusted third party. We compare our protocol with oblivious polynomial based and homomorphic encryption based protocols proposed in [11]. Our approach is more relevant in reducing computational cost as compared to communication cost (that does not constitute our major focus as of now, as mentioned earlier). It outperforms all the existing approaches in presence of very large datasets. Our theoretical and practical simulation supports the above argument. Further, our approach is collusion-resistant and avoids trusted third party.

2   Related Work

The review of state of the art methods for PPDM may be found in [3] [18-20]. Based on this review, PPDM approaches are classified into two categories: 1. *Randomization Based* and 2. *Cryptography Based*. The randomization based approach for privacy preserving clustering has been addressed in [6]. In this, the data being clustered is randomly modified first and then clustering is performed on the modified data. This results in approximately correct clusters. Approaches in the first category incur low computation and communication cost but compromise with the level of privacy.

The second category of approaches i.e. cryptography based approaches provide high level of privacy but at the cost of high computation and communication cost [5]. A broad overview of the intersection between the fields of cryptography and privacy-preserving data mining may be found in [21]. The Secure Multiparty Computation has been applied for clustering in [7-9]. The limitation of these approaches is that they are computationally expensive and hence their scope is limited to small datasets only.

The second category in cryptography based approach is the homomorphic encryption. A homomorphic encryption scheme allows certain algebraic operations to be carried out on the encrypted plaintext, by applying an efficient operation to the corresponding cipher text [22]. Privacy preserving clustering based on homomorphic encryption is proposed in [9-11]. Authors in [9] and [10] address privacy preserving clustering for arbitrarily-partitioned data for semi honest two party case models. However, the public key encryption schemes used in above techniques are computationally expensive and their scope is limited to small datasets. Authors in [11] address design and analysis of privacy-preserving k-means clustering algorithm for horizontally partitioned data using oblivious polynomial evaluation and homomorphic encryption. They only present the two party case for semi-honest model. Further, the scope of algorithms is limited to small datasets.

An attractive approach for privacy preserving data mining which is recently being introduced is based on the paradigm of secret sharing [14][23]. Detailed study of comparison of encryption-based techniques and secret sharing is given in [5]. According to [5], secret sharing for privacy preserving data mining achieves best of both worlds i.e. privacy at the level of SMC based approach and efficiency at the level of randomization based approach. Privacy preserving clustering based on secret sharing has been addressed in [12] [13]. Authors in [12] propose cloud computing based solution using Chinese remainder theorem based method of secret sharing. They rely on cloud computing servers to compute clusters. Authors in [13] propose solution based on additive secret sharing for vertically partitioned data using two non colluding third parties to compute cluster means. In this solution, collusion between two specific parties reveals each entity's distance to each cluster mean. This results in privacy violations.

In this paper, we use paradigm of secret sharing and specifically Shamir's secret sharing scheme [14] to achieve privacy preserving in K-means clustering. Our approach is similar to the one proposed in [24] for association rule mining. We give theoretical and practical analysis of our approach and show that our approach is collusion-resistant and suitable for large datasets due to its low computational overhead. Further it does not require any trusted third party/servers to compute results and does not reveal intermediate private information. To the best of our knowledge, ours is the first approach to privacy preserving clustering based on Shamir's secret sharing.

3   The Proposed Algorithm

We assume here the distributed database scenario in which the data is horizontally partitioned across n parties. We modify widely used K-means clustering algorithm to execute it for distributed scenario and then to incorporate privacy preserving feature in it. We utilize paradigm of Shamir's secret sharing to incorporate privacy preservation in K-means clustering.

3.1   Building Blocks

In this section, we review Shamir's secret sharing method [14] and distributed K-Means clustering approach without any privacy preserving mechanism [11].

Shamir's Secret Sharing
Shamir's secret sharing proposed in [14], is a form of secret sharing where a secret is divided into parts, giving each participant its own unique part, where some of the parts or all of them are needed in order to reconstruct the secret. The scheme is formally described as follows [14]:

The secret is some data D. The goal is to divide D into n pieces $D1 \ldots D_n$ in such a way that:

1. Knowledge of any k or more D_i pieces makes D easily computable;
2. Knowledge of any k-1 or fewer D_i pieces leaves D completely undetermined i.e. all its possible values are equally likely.

Such a scheme is called a (k, n) threshold scheme. The scheme is based on polynomial interpolation: Given k points in the 2-dimensional plane $(x_1, y_1) \ldots (x_k, y_k)$ with distinct x_i's, there is one and only one polynomial q(x) of degree $k - 1$ exists such that $q(x_i) = y_i$ for all i. Without loss of generality, we can assume that the data D is (or can be made) a number. To divide it into pieces D_i, we pick a random k-1 degree polynomial $q(x) = a_0 + a_1 x + \ldots a_{k-1} x^{k-1}$ in which $a_0 = D$, and evaluate:

$$D_1 = q(1) \ldots D_i = q(i) \ldots D_n = q(n)$$

Given any subset of k of these D_i values (together with their identifying indices), we can find the coefficients of q(x) by interpolation, and then evaluate D=q(0). Knowledge of just k- 1 of these values, on the other hand, does not suffice in order to calculate D. Pseudo code for the Shamir's scheme for n parties is shown in Figure 1.

In our approach, we use (n, n) threshold scheme. We require each party to participate in the protocol. Without the cooperation of all parties, it is not possible to recover the secret.

Distributed K-Means Clustering
The K-means clustering algorithm [15-17] is a well known unsupervised learning algorithm. It is the method of cluster analysis that aims to partition the objects into k nonempty subsets (clusters), in which each object belongs to the cluster with nearest mean. Given K initial clusters, the algorithm works in two phases: In the first phase, an object is assigned to the cluster to which it is the most similar, based on the distance between the object and the cluster mean. In the second phase, new mean is computed for each cluster. The algorithm is deemed to have converged when no more new assignment are found.

In the distributed scenario, where data are located at different sites, the algorithm for K-Means clustering differs slightly. In distributed scenario, it is desirable to compute cluster means using union of data located at different parties. We use distributed

---

Pseudo code 1. Shamir's secret sharing

D: Secret value
P: Set of parties $P_1, P_2,..., P_n$ to distribute the shares,
k: Number of shares required to reconstruct the secret.
Phase I: Generating and sending secret shares

1. Select a random polynomial $q(x) = a_{k-1}x_{k-1} +...+ a_1x_1+a_0$ where $a_{k-1}\neq0$ and $a_0 = D$
2. Choose n publicly known distinct random values $x_1, x_2, ... , x_n$ such that $x_i \neq 0$
3. Compute the share of each node p_i, where share(i)=$q(x_i)$
4. for i = 1 to n do
5.   Send share i to node P_i.
6. end for

Phase II: Reconstruction
Require: Every party is given a point (a pair of input to the polynomial and output).

7. Given subset of these pairs, find the coefficients of the polynomial using interpolation
8. The secret is the constant term (i.e. D)

Fig. 1. Shamir's secret sharing scheme [14]

K-Means clustering in our work to add privacy preserving feature in it. We adopt Weighted Average Problem proposed in [11] to compute intermediate cluster means. One way to perform distributed K-Means clustering for two parties, namely, A and B is to use Trusted Third Party as shown in Figure 2. Here, Trusted Third Party is used for intermediate computation of cluster means. The problem with this approach is that it discloses intermediate cluster means at various locations while computing $(a_i+d_i)/(b_i+e_i)$ resulting in privacy violations; where (a_i,d_i) and (b_i,e_i) are the sum of samples and no. of samples pair in each clusters for party 1 and party2 respectively. In our approach, we propose new and efficient privacy preserving computation of $(a_i+d_i)/(b_i+e_i)$ using Shamir's secret sharing method. We allow parties to collaboratively compute cluster means and thus totally eliminate trusted third party.

3.2   The Proposed Design

We use following settings in our design. Database DB is horizontally partitioned among n parties (namely $P_1, P_2... P_n$), where DB = $DB_1 \cup DB_2 ...\cup DB_n$. In this setting, all the parties have same set of attributes, and unlabeled samples. Now all parties want to conduct distributed k means clustering on their combined data sets, in which no party wants to disclose its raw data set to others because of the concern about their data privacy. We formulate privacy-preserving distributed k means clustering to preserve privacy of each party's data while performing clustering. We assume semi-honest model [22] here where each party correctly follows protocol run. Further, we assume that each party agrees in initial clusters before performing clustering. Now each party performs iteration locally. However, in each iteration, to find new cluster mean μi, all parties have to communicate with each other, as we are not using TTP.

Pseudo Code 2. Distributed K-means clustering [11]

---

n_A, n_B: no. of samples at party A and B
c: total no. of clusters
$u_1...u_c$: initial clusters

1.   do in parallel for each party $i \in \{A,B\}$
2.   begin initialize $n_A, n_B, c, \mu_1, ..., \mu_c$
3.   do classify n_A and n_B samples according to nearest μ
4.   for i := 1 to c step 1 do
5.   Let Ci_A and Ci_B be the i-th cluster for Party A and Party B
6.   Party A:Compute $a_i = \Sigma_{xj \in CiA}$ xj and $bi=|Ci_A|$
7.   Party B:Compute $di = \Sigma_{xj \in CiB}$ xj and $ei=|Ci_B|$
8.   Send (a_i, b_i) and (d_i, e_i) to TTP
9.   end for
10. end parallel
11. TTP recompute μ_i by (a_i+d_i/b_i+e_i)
12. Send u_i to each party $i \in \{A, B\}$
13. until no change in μ_i
14. return $\mu_1, ..., \mu_c$
15. end

Fig. 2. Distributed K-means clustering with Trusted Third Party[11]

Let the number of clusters is c. Each party finds two values (a_i,b_i) for cluster i using pseudo code shown in Figure 2, where a_i is the sum of samples in cluster i and b_i is the number of samples in cluster i. Now each party has to send pairs $((a_i,b_i),....,(.a_c,b_c))$ to each other to find new cluster mean u_i. If these pairs are sent in clear then there is threat to privacy violation of these data. Hence, we consider this pair (a_i,b_i) as a secret in our proposed algorithm. We share these values among the parties using the secure protocol of Shamir's secret sharing. The pseudo code of our approach for n party case is shown in Figure 3.

As shown in Figure 3, each party first decides a polynomial of degree k where k = n-1, and x publicly known distinct random values $x_1, x_2,..., x_n$. In the first phase, each party wants to send the value $v_s = (a_i,b_i)$ secretly. Each party selects a random polynomial $q(x) = a_{n-1}x_{n-1} + ... + a_1x_1 + v_s$, in which the constant term is the secret. Then it computes the shares for other parties such that the share of party P_r, is shr$(v_s,P_r) = q_i(x_r)$, where x_r is the rth element of X. During the second phase, each party adds all the shares received from other parties and then sends this result to all the other parties. That is, party P_i computes $S(x_i) = q_1(x_i) +q_2(x_i) +... + q_n(x_i)$ and sends to all other parties. At the third computation phase, each party P_i will have the n values of polynomial $S(x_i) = q_1(x_i) + q_2(x_i) +...+q_n(x_i)$ at X with the constant term equal to the sum of all secret values. The linear equation has a unique solution, and each party P_i can solve the set of equations and determine the value. It is the Vandermonde determinant, which gives the solution.

However it cannot determine the secret values of the other parties since the individual polynomial coefficients selected by other parties are not known to P_i.

Pseudo code 3. The proposed approach

P: Set of parties $P_1, P_2, ..., P_n$
$v_{is} = (a_i, b_i)$: Secret value of party P_i, where a_i is sum of samples and b_i is no. of samples in cluster
X: A set of n publicly known random values $x_1, x_2, ..., x_n$
k: Degree of the random polynomial, here $k = n - 1$
c: no. of clusters
1:   do in parallel for each party $P_i \in \{1...n\}$
          find $((a_i, b_i), ... , (a_c, b_c))$ using pseudo code described in Figure 2
2:        for each secret value $v_{is} \in \{a_i, b_i\}$
3:            Select a random polynomial $q_i(x) = a_{n-1}x_{n-1} + ... + a_1x_1 + v_{is}$
5:            for r = 1 to n do
6:                Compute share of party P_r, where $shr(v_{is}, P_r) = q_i(x_r)$
7:                send $shr(v_{is}, P_r)$ to party P_r
8:                receive the shares $shr(v_{rs}, P_i)$ from every party P_r.
9:            end for
10:           compute $S(x_i) = q_1(x_i) + q_2(x_i) + ... + q_n(x_i)$
11:           for r = 1 to n do
12:               Send $S(x_i)$ to party P_r
13:               Receive the results $S(x_i)$ from every party P_r
14:               end for
15:           Solve the set of equations using Lagrange's interpolation to find the
16:               sum of secret values
17:       end for
18: Recompute μ_i using sum of samples/no. of samples
19: until termination criteria met

Fig. 3. Privacy preserving distributed K-means clustering using Shamir's secret sharing

4   Theoretical Analysis

Several metrics for evaluating privacy preserving data mining techniques are discussed in [5] [8]. Based on this, we analyze our approach for privacy, correctness, computation cost and communication cost.

4.1   Privacy

In our proposed approach, the secret value v_i of a party P_i cannot be revealed even if all the remaining parties exchange their shares. Since each party P_i executes Shamir's secret sharing algorithm with a random polynomial of degree n-1, the value of that polynomial at n different points are needed in order to compute the coefficients of the corresponding polynomial, i.e., the secret value of party P_i. P_i computes the value of its polynomial at n points as shares, and then keeps one of these shares for itself and sends the remaining n-1 shares to other parties. Since all n shares are needed to reveal the secret, other parties cannot compute secret even if they combine their shares.

Further, no party learns anything more than its prescribed output. This is so, because as per the approach followed (explained in section 3.2), every party shares its local cluster means as the secret; for which it chooses different polynomial randomly. Hence, it is not possible for a party to determine the secret values of other parties, since the individual polynomial coefficient selected by each party is not known to other parties. In addition, disclosure of intermediate cluster means during the program execution is prevented as intermediate cluster means are calculated at each site and there is no need to communicate them.

4.2   Correctness

Each party is guaranteed that the output that it receives is correct. Assuming that party P_i has private vector A_i. According to method, they have to perform addition of all shares to get the secret value. The secret value is the constant term of the sum polynomial $S(x) = q_1(x) + q_2(x) + ... + q_n(x)$, so we need to solve the linear equations, noting there are n unknown coefficients and n equations.

$$D = \begin{vmatrix} x_1^{n-1} & x_1^{n-2} & ... & x_1 & 1 \\ x_2^{n-1} & x_2^{n-2} & ... & x_2 & 1 \\ & & \cdot & & \\ \cdot & & & \cdot & \\ \cdot & & & & \cdot \\ x_n^{n-1} & x_n^{n-2} & ... & x_n & 1 \end{vmatrix}$$

It is the Vandermonde determinant. When $D = \prod_{i,j=0,i<j}^{n}(xi - xj) = 0$, that is $x_i \neq x_j$, the equations has a unique solution, and each party P_i can solve the set of equations and determine the value of $\sum_{i=1}^{n} = Aij$. However it cannot determine the secret values of the other parties since the individual polynomial coefficients selected by other parties are not known to P_i.

4.3   Computation Cost

The computation cost depends on the initial clusters and the no. of iterations required for finding final clusters. We give here the computation cost for single iteration. Assume that for every party P_i, the cost of generating random polynomial $q_i(x)$, i = 1, 2,..., n is C. In proposed approach, we have two values as a secret so we have to generate random polynomial two times. So total computation cost is $O(n(C_1+C_2))$, where C_1= cost for generating random polynomial for sum of samples, C_2= cost for generating random polynomial for no. of samples and n= no of parties. The total number of 2n (n − 1) additions are calculated to find $s(x) = q_1(x) + q_2(x) + ,...,+ q_n(x)$.

Efficient $O(nlog^2n)$ algorithms for polynomial evaluation are available [14]. Hence the computation cost for our proposed approach is quadratic i.e. $O(n^2)$.

4.4   Communication Cost

Assuming there are r attributes in dataset and n parties and k clusters, for one iteration, the communication cost for each party is $kr(n-1)+2k(n-1)$ messages i.e. $O(krn)$. In comparison to Trusted Third Party based approach, our approach incurs more communication cost because for collaboratively computing cluster means, communication between every party is necessary.

5   Experimental Evaluation

We have implemented our algorithm in MATLAB. The experiments are conducted on Intel Core 2 Duo CPU with 4GB RAM and 2.93GHz speed. Our experiments are performed on Small, medium, large and very large data-sets as described below. We took two datasets similar to those used in [11] in order to perform fair comparison. We provide brief outline of datasets here, however interested readers may find details in [25-28]. Dataset1 is Mammal's Milk [25] with 2KB size, 25 samples and 6 attributes per sample. Dataset2 is the river dataset [26] with 25KB size, 84 samples and 15 attributes per sample. Dataset3 is a speech dataset [27] with 650KB size, 5687 samples and 12 attributes per sample. Dataset4 is taken mainly to show the feasibility of our approach for very large dataset. For this purpose, we have experimented with forest cover dataset [28] with 73MB size, 581012 samples and 54 attributes per sample. For our experiment, we select first two samples as initial cluster centers.

We model multiparty case where the number of parties is greater than two by randomly subdividing the samples into equal sized subsets and assigning them to each party. In real environments the size of the sets may be vastly different. We show feasibility of our approach by executing our algorithm on local machine with different processes for different parties. Therefore, the execution time for the algorithm does not include the actual communication time between different parties. We take two different settings to measure the performance of the proposed scheme:

1.   Executing our algorithm on four different size datasets.
2.   Executing our algorithm with different number of data holders.

To analyze the results, we find computation and communication cost of our algorithm. Computation cost is measured in terms of time required for execution and communication cost is measured in terms of the number of bytes exchanged during execution.

Our first observation is to show the effect of dataset size on computation cost, we run our algorithm for 3 parties and 6 parties and with dataset1, dataset2 and dataset3. The results are shown in Figure 4. As expected, there is a linear relationship between dataset size and computation cost. Further, we also measure execution time of our algorithm on very large forest cover dataset and show that it requires 668.8 seconds to perform clustering with 3 party setting. This observation shows the feasibility of our approach in practical scenario where large datasets exists.

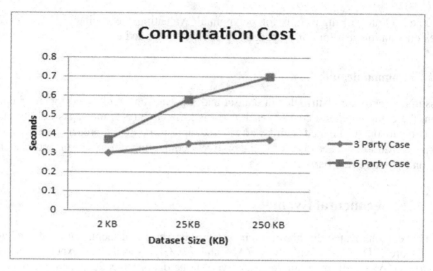

Fig. 4. Effect of dataset size on computation cost

Our next observation in Figure 5 is to show the effect of dataset size on communication cost. As discussed section 4, communication cost linearly depends on the number of attributes in dataset. We obtained similar results in our experimentation also. Dataset2 has more number of attributes as compared to dataset3; so the overall communication cost for dataset2 is more than dataset3. Further, results in Figure 5 show the effect of number of parties on communication cost. Increasing the number of parties has the effect of increasing the communication cost; simply because the number of messages required to be exchanged would be more.

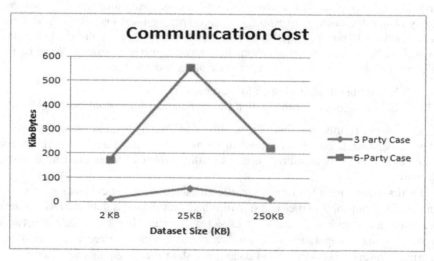

Fig. 5. Effect of dataset size on communication cost

We use results shown in [11] as a base for comparing our protocol against Oblivious Polynomial Transfer and Homomorphic encryption. In [11] authors have also taken dataset2 and dataset3 i.e. river and speech datasets respectively to conduct experiments. Experiments in [11] were conducted for a 2-party case, while here we experiment with a 3-party case. Selection of initials clusters may vary in our case and the one proposed in [11] and so is the overall cost for protocol execution. Hence, for fair comparison, we take attribute/iteration statistics i.e. cost of per attribute clustering in a single iteration of the K-Means algorithm and measure computation and communication cost for the same. We show, for our algorithm, percentage increase in resources with respect to distributed K-Means clustering algorithm without privacy preserving mechanism. Table 1 shows comparison of our protocol and the protocol proposed in [11].

In terms of computation overhead, our approach is about 200 times faster than the homomorphic encryption based approach for river dataset and about 85 times faster than the speech dataset. This is due to the fact that our approach uses only primitive

Table 1. Comparison of our approach with Oblivious Polynomial Evaluation and Homomorphic Encryption based approaches

Test	Communication Overhead	Computation Overhead
	* Percentage increase in bytes attributes/iteration	*Percentage increase in milliseconds attributes/iteration
River Dataset		
Distributed K-Means Clustering (without privacy preserving)	0%	0%
Oblivious Polynomial Evaluation [11]	40116.47%	22715.16%
Homomorphic Encryption [11]	314.35%	4915.67%
Our Protocol	533.33%	25.26%
Speech Dataset		
Distributed K-Means Clustering (without privacy preserving)	0%	0%
Oblivious Polynomial Evaluation [11]	34402.07%	6919.87%
Homomorphic Encryption [11]	268.08%	1474.58%
Our Protocol	533.33%	17.5%
*Percentage increase in resources is calculated with respect to Distributed K-Means Clustering approach without privacy preserving mechanism		

operations to perform clustering and eliminates costly public key operations that are required in homomorphic encryption based approach. Hence, our approach is more suitable for the practical scenario where organizations own large datasets.

In terms of communication overhead, our approach incurs slightly more overhead as compared to that in homomorphic encryption based approach. It is to be noted that results in [11] are for a two party case, whereas our results are for a 3 party case (the minimum parties required in our approach is two). We believe that our approach would be more efficient in terms of communication cost as compared to corresponding homomorphic encryption based approach in case of increased number of parties.

6   Conclusion

We presented an efficient algorithm for privacy preserving distributed K-Means clustering using Shamir's secret sharing scheme. Our approach collaboratively computes cluster means and hence avoid trusted third party. We compared our approach with the oblivious polynomial evaluation and homomorphic encryptions based approaches proposed in [11] and show that in terms of computation cost, our approach is hundreds of magnitude faster than the oblivious polynomial evaluation and homomorphic encryption based approaches and hence is more suitable for large datasets in practical scenario.

Currently our algorithm supports horizontal partitioning in presence of semi honest adversary model. As a future work, we intend to extend our algorithm in vertical partitioning in presence of malicious adversary model. In addition, we intend to show the results from a realistic distributed emulation.

References

1. Shaneck, M., Kim, Y., Kumar, V.: Privacy Preserving Nearest Neighbor Search. In: ICDM Workshops, pp. 541–545 (2006)
2. Aggarwal, C.C., Yu, P.S.: Privacy-Preserving Data Mining: A Survey. In: Michael, G., Sushil, J. (eds.) Handbook of Database Security, pp. 431–460. Springer (2007)
3. Wu., X., Chu, C.H., Wang, Y., Liu, F., Yue, D.: Privacy preserving data mining research: current status and key issues. In: 7th International Conference on Computational Science ICCS 2007, pp. 762–772 (2007)
4. Goldreich, O.: The Foundations of Cryptography, vol. 2. Cambridge Univ. Press, Cambridge (2004)
5. Pedersen, T.B., Saygin, Y., Savas, E.: Secret sharing vs. encryption-based techniques for privacy preserving data mining. In: UNECE/Eurostat Work Session on SDC (2007)
6. Oliveira, S.R.M.: Privacy preserving clustering by data transformation. In: 18th Brazilian Symposium on Databases, pp. 304–318 (2003)
7. Vaidya, J., Clifton, C.: Privacy-preserving k-means clustering over vertically partitioned data. In: 9th ACM SIGKDD International Conf. on Knowledge Discovery and Data Mining. ACM Press (2003)
8. Inan, A., Kaya, S.V., Saygin, Y., Savas, E., Hintoglu, A.A., Levi, A.: Privacy preserving clustering on horizontally partitioned data. Data Knowl. Eng., 646–666 (2007)

9. Jagannathan, G., Wright, R.N.: Privacy-preserving distributed k-means clustering over arbitrarily partitioned data. In: KDD, pp. 593–599 (2005)
10. Bunn, P., Ostrovsky, R.: Secure two-party k-means clustering. In: ACM Conference on Computer and Communications Security, pp. 486–497 (2007)
11. Jha, S., Kruger, L., McDaniel, P.: Privacy Preserving Clustering. In: di Vimercati, S.d.C., Syverson, P.F., Gollmann, D. (eds.) ESORICS 2005. LNCS, vol. 3679, pp. 397–417. Springer, Heidelberg (2005)
12. Upmanyu, M., Namboodiri, A.M., Srinathan, K., Jawahar, C.V.: Efficient Privacy Preserving K-Means Clustering. In: Chen, H., Chau, M., Li, S.-h., Urs, S., Srinivasa, S., Wang, G.A. (eds.) PAISI 2010. LNCS, vol. 6122, pp. 154–166. Springer, Heidelberg (2010)
13. Doganay, M.C., Pedersen, T.B., Saygin, Y., Savas, E., Levi, A.: Distributed privacy preserving k-means clustering with additive secret sharing. In: 2008 International Workshop on Privacy and Anonymity in Information Society, Nantes, France, pp. 3–11 (2008)
14. Shamir, A.: How to share a secret. Communications of the ACM 22(11), 612–613 (1979)
15. Forgey, E.: Cluster analysis of multivariate data: Efficiency vs. interpretability of classification. Biometrics 21(768) (1965)
16. Lloyd, S.P.: Least squares quantization in PCM. IEEE Transactions on Information Theory 28, 129–137 (1982)
17. MacQueen, J.: Some methods for classification and analysis of multivariate observations. In: Fifth Berkeley Symposium on Mathematical Statistics and Probability, vol. 1, pp. 281–296 (1967)
18. Kantarcioglu, M., Clifton, C.: Privacy-preserving Distributed Mining of Association Rules on Horizontally Partitioned Data. In: ACM SIGMOD Workshop on Research Issues in Data Mining and Knowledge Discovery (DMKD), pp. 639–644 (2002)
19. Verykios, S., Bertino, E., Fovino, I., Provenza, L., Saygin, Y., Theodoridis, Y.: Stateof-the-art in Privacy Preserving Data Mining. ACM SIGMOD Record 33(1), 50–57 (2004)
20. Bertino, E., Fovino, I., Provenza, L.: A Framework for Evaluating Privacy Preserving Data Mining Algorithms. Data Mining and Knowledge Discovery 11(2), 121–154 (2005)
21. Pinkas, B.: Cryptographic techniques for privacy-preserving data mining. SIGKDD Explor. Newslett. 4(2), 12–19 (2002),
http://doi.acm.org/10.1145/772862.772865, doi:10.1145/772862.772865
22. Lindell, Y., Pinkas, B.: Secure multiparty computation for privacy-preserving data mining. Journal of Privacy and Confidentiality 1(1), 59–98 (2009)
23. Ben-Or, M., Goldwasser, S., Wigderson, A.: Completeness theorems for non-cryptographic fault-tolerant distributed computation. In: 19th Annual ACM Conference on Theory of Computing (STOC), pp. 1–10. ACM Press (1988)
24. Ge, X., Yan, L., Zhu, J., Shi, W.: Privacy preserving distributed association rule mining based on a secret sharing technique. In: Second International Conference on Software Eng. and Data Mining, pp. 345–350 (2010)
25. http://www.uni-koeln.de/themen/statistik/data/cluster/milk.dat
26. Information and Computer Science. COIL 1999 Competition Data, The UCI KDD Archive. University of California Irvine (October 1999),
http://kdd.ics.uci.edu/databases/coil/coil.html
27. Information and Computer Science. Japanese Vowels. University of California Irvine (June 2000), http://kdd.ics.uci.edu/databases/JapaneseVowels/JapaneseVowels.html
28. http://archive.ics.uci.edu/ml/datasets/Covertype

From Subjective Reputation to Verifiable Experiences — Augmenting Peer-Control Mechanisms for Open Service Ecosystems

Sini Ruohomaa, Puneet Kaur, and Lea Kutvonen

University of Helsinki, Finland
sini.ruohomaa@cs.helsinki.fi
http://cinco.cs.helsinki.fi/

Abstract. In inter-enterprise collaborations, autonomous services from different organizations must independently determine which other services they can rely on. Reputation-based trust management in Pilarcos utilizes shared experience information on the actors' past behaviour in estimating the risks of a collaboration; these experiences are shared between members of the service ecosystem through a reputation system. As the reputation system becomes an essential peer-control mechanism for the open service ecosystem, it must be augmented with sanctions for misbehaviour and appropriate incentives for correct behaviour. A fair sanctioning system cannot be built on traditional subjective reports, as rebuttal of undeserved reports requires shared, objective measures. To make the shared experience information objective and verifiable, we associate it with whether the relevant collaboration contract was followed, backed up with evidence in the form of nonrepudiable receipts. In this way, we are able to protect automated reputation-based trust decisions from being skewed by misinformation.

1 Introduction

In inter-enterprise collaborations, services from different organizations and domains join together to fulfil a mutual goal. In the open service ecosystem, the services are autonomous, and there is no centralized control of the collaboration process. Each service must independently determine which other services it should collaborate with; a trust decision is made to determine this willingness to rely on another service. The Pilarcos inter-enterprise collaboration management infrastructure [9,8] contains a trust management system to automate these decisions in routine cases [17]; selected difficult or high-stake decisions are forwarded to a human user based on policy-defined rules [6].

A central element of the trust decisions is an estimation of the risk of collaborating with the given actor. The estimate is based on gathered experiences on the actor's past behaviour, which consists of both first-hand experiences from earlier collaborations with it, and shared experiences from third parties received through a reputation system.

T. Dimitrakos et al. (Eds.): IFIPTM 2012, IFIP AICT 374, pp. 142–157, 2012.

A reputation system has two tasks. First, from the enterprise perspective, it provides information to support trust decisions for each individual service; this helps the participants in the reputation system to find new partners and to steer clear of misbehaving services in order to limit their risk.

Second, from the ecosystem perspective, it introduces a form of peer control where misbehaviour towards other actors or the ecosystem infrastructure is punished through reputation loss. Sociological research indicates that direct first-order punishment for misbehaviour is not enough by itself to ensure that the ecosystem can scale up in size: it must be complemented with a second-order punishment to discourage unfair first-order punishments [3]. In other words, spreading false experiences must have a negative reputation impact on the source.

To contrast these requirements to current solutions, systems sharing reputation information are occasionally also considered as subjective recommender systems on other users; with such an approach, the aim is to promote commonly liked services rather than implement robust peer-based control. For a recommendation system, experiences are accepted as subjective reports on the fulfilment of expectations. As different expectations can lead to different reports even on identical behaviour, these reports do not objectively describe actual outcomes in the sense that reports on breaches of contract do. While they can still support individual decision-making as indicators of popularity, the subjectivity of the criteria in use makes recommender systems unsuitable for social control. Solutions have been proposed to promote similar understanding of the recommendation values [5,2]; however, shared semantics do not yet change the fact that the actors involved are stating their opinions, which cannot be used as a basis of judging whether a statement is unfair. As an extreme example, two honest actors may judge a musician's performance completely differently based on their tastes, due to a lack of objective measurement scale for what is "good music". To get around this ambiguity, we propose to monitor for and report objectively defined events: explicit breaches of collaboration contracts.

The core problems of unverifiability and subjectivity of experiences in current approaches hinder the use of reputation information in inter-enterprise collaborations, particularly for automated decision-making. Falsely accused actors must be able to rebut reports to clear their name, while honest reporters should be protected from retaliatory action, and the reciprocity of feedback [16] limited.

We advance a reputation system based on objective, verifiable experiences. It is designed to support automated trust decisions on inter-enterprise collaborations, and implements peer control in the service ecosystem by supporting second-order punishment: a successful rebuttal of a false experience causes reputation loss for the dishonest information source. This is achieved by introducing a nonrepudiable audit trail to collaborations, and defining reputation impacts of misbehaviour in collaboration contracts. Similarly, negative reputation impacts for misreporting are defined in a reputation network contract. The solution extends the existing Pilarcos collaboration management infrastructure [9,17].

The rest of the paper is structured as follows: Section 2 presents the Pilarcos ecosystem we build on, and related work. Section 3 maps evidence to reputation impacts through collaboration contracts to achieve objectivity, and specifies the process of creating new reputation information in which unverifiable experiences can be rebutted and removed from the system. Section 4 discusses the impact of the solution and compares it to the state of the art.

2   Background and Related Work

In the first subsection, we summarize the existing Pilarcos open service ecosystem, in which we utilize reputation for trust management. The second subsection presents related work on the topic of objective and verifiable experiences.

2.1   Reputation-Based Trust Management in Pilarcos

The Pilarcos collaboration management infrastructure provides support for partner discovery, interoperability management, contract negotiations, runtime monitoring, including contract breach detection and recovery, as well as local trust decisions evaluating the actors' willingness to collaborate with their potential partners [9,17]. The Pilarcos service ecosystem is collaboratively governed, rather than centrally controlled, to ensure its long-term viability and scalability [19].

We propose to strengthen the implemented reputation-based trust management system in Pilarcos [17] by providing it with a flow of objective and verifiable reputation information. The trust management system is modular, and can take advantage of different kinds of reputation systems as its information sources. It splits experience information into four dimensions: monetary, reputation, control and satisfaction. This allows risk evaluations to differentiate between e.g. misbehaviour that directly causes monetary loss, deterioration of own reputation caused by a partner spreading fraudulent reports afterwards, weakening of peer control due to an actor's misbehaviour as a recommender, and failures to satisfy the demands set in contracts, which may or may not have direct monetary consequences, respectively [17].

Collaboration contracts, or eContracts, are based on business network models that specify the structure and business processes of the collaboration, and relevant trust decision points [8,17]. These models are modular, reusable and public, and they are produced by domain experts in response to the needs of the ecosystem. During contract negotiations, open options in the models, such as particular quality of service requirements or the price of the service, can be further refined to form an agreement between the participants [7].

The trust management process can be divided into two parts: the trust decisions, and the evolution process of the reputation information. Both are governed by their own policies. A trust decision is triggered at specific points of the collaboration process, as further resources are committed and an up-to-date risk evaluation is needed. To evaluate the risk of proceeding with the collaboration, we predict the outcome it would have on different assets based on previous experiences, which are stored as reputation information; the details of the format are described in earlier work [17]. In this paper, we focus on the evolution of reputation information through sharing experiences in a reputation system.

2.2 Related Work to Support Objective and Verifiable Experiences

We distinguish three approaches for collecting experiences in a way that members in the service ecosystem can agree on their content: centrally orchestrated, fully distributed and a protocol-based approach utilizing third-party witnesses.

TrustCoM [22] represents the centrally orchestrated approach. In TrustCoM, performance monitors both internal and external to the actors collect information pertinent to fulfilling the Service Level Agreement (SLA), such as response times. The monitors send these raw observations to an SLA Evaluator, which is a third party trusted to pass a neutral judgement on the transacting parties. This result is, in turn, reported to a trusted third party reputation system, or used as a basis of removing a partner from the collaboration. The approach follows a tradition set by centralized workflow execution, such as implemented by CrossWork [12]. It involves a trusted infrastructure service or a hub member of the ecosystem running a distributed business process by using the other participants as components. This central operator can judge the performance of the other actors, and decide on sanctions directly. The main difference in operational environments is that in Pilarcos, control and monitoring are distributed among the autonomous and not fully trusted participants. As a result, there are no actors that are able to observe all collaborations in the ecosystem.

In the fully distributed approach (e.g. TrustGuard [20]), the transacting parties exchange nonrepudiable, i.e. cryptographically signed, receipts that act as evidence of their actions later. The main challenge in this approach is in the asymmetry of receipts: the party responsible for signing the last receipt can refuse to finish the protocol, which leaves a hole in the audit trail of evidence [13]. In TrustGuard, receipts document the intention to collaborate, which means that the service is not provided before the protocol has been completed. This scheme protects against submitting experiences of transactions that were never really started, but cannot stop unfair reports from being made after the transaction.

In the protocol-based approach (e.g. Li, Martin and Zhang [11]), a third party witness is included in transactions, observing them and implementing a fair, "atomic" exchange [13]. The proposal of Li et al. aims to secure an electronic marketplace, which can host a simple form of inter-enterprise collaboration where goods are exchanged in brief, fixed transactions. It involves an arbitrator, who acts as a witness and judge of a collaboration, and punishes misbehaviour through withdrawals on a monetary deposit that all participants have made beforehand in a trusted bank. In addition, the arbitrator can report experiences to a reputation system. When the arbitrator is not needed to resolve a disagreement, a central broker service reports a default positive experience once a specified time has passed since it matched the two actors [11].

Li et al. implement a centralized punishment system on top of the fair receipt exchange protocol, which is where they differ from Pilarcos. Our aim in this paper is to distribute punishment as peer-based control, while taking advantage of the third party witness approach to provide a stream of verifiable evidence on the outcomes of transactions in the collaborations.

To distinguish between a passive witness and the active arbitrator passing judgement, we denote the former as *notaries*: a notary's task is to verify with its own signature whether a protocol was followed according to the specification it has been given by the transacting partners. The notary must be trusted by the given partners to remain impartial on that exchange to eliminate asymmetry, and their agreement on a given notary must be nonrepudiable once the transaction begins. On the other hand, a specific notary does not necessarily need to be trusted by anyone else in the collaboration or the entire ecosystem, as each independent exchange can be observed by a different notary. This limits the power that any specific notary service can gain over the actors in the marketplace.

As a related branch, certification-based trust also relies on cryptographical verifiability, but should not be confused with the proposed approach of signed receipts. Certification-based trust is used in e.g. NICE [10]. Instead of being experience-based, the system relies on signed expressions of "I, Alice, trust Bob", and trust decisions are based on policies on whether a provided set of trust declarations, or certificates, are sufficient to make the decision-maker also trust the considered target. Other examples of certification-based trust used for access control include WS-TRUST [14] and KeyNote [1]. Misinformation is a relatively minor issue for these systems, as the group of accepted information sources is small, closed and managed offline: certificates document networks of pre-formed trust relationships between the sources rather than guiding their evolution.

In summary, related work shows that signed, nonrepudiable receipts provide a promising basis for the verifiability of experiences in open service ecosystems. We have found that third party witnesses, notaries, are needed to guarantee the fair exchange of receipts on the transaction, and that the concept has already been applied within electronic markets.

In the following section, we apply the solution to provide a basis for objective and verifiable reputation information in the open service ecosystem by first providing a mapping between the receipt evidence and the corresponding experience stored in a reputation system through contracts, then specifying a process for creation of new reputation information that allows experiences not backed by appropriate evidence to be rebutted and removed from the reputation system.

3   Sharing and Rebuttal of New Experiences

In order to make reputation information objective, it must be defined so that it has a measurable truth value, rather than as a subjective opinion. In this section, we define the basis for objective experiences, and specify the process for submitting them into the reputation system as well as for rebuting false experiences.

For inter-enterprise collaborations, objective experience sharing is made feasible by electronic contracts governing the collaborations: if the contract was followed, experiences should be positive; if it was violated, they should be negative. From the perspective of a single service, the impact of a specific outcome may vary from minor to major gain or loss [17], but in order to make the shared experience objective, the impact in the shared experience must be standardized through the contract as well. A natural source for this information is the business network model referenced by the contract. The business network model is a formal model for the collaboration and defines e.g. the communication protocols and compensation processes involved [9].

Determining the reputation effect of different outcomes becomes a part of the modelling process done by the domain expert, which makes the mapping reusable over multiple collaboration instances using the same model. The modelled values can be further fine-tuned in the contract negotiations, in case the same model can be used for collaborations dealing with very different stakes.

The collaboration contract, then, should specify a mapping of outcomes to experiences, for example that the event "goods received" should translate to an experience with major positive effect on the monetary and satisfaction assets, and no effect on the control and reputation assets [17]. In this example, the party receiving the goods (A) will submit this experience on the party who sent them (B). In order to support verifiability, it also produces a signed, non-repudiable receipt of the outcome of the step. The example communication protocol and the following experience submission process are depicted in Figure 1.

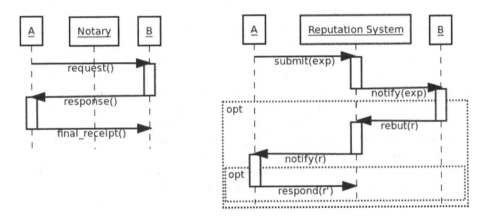

Fig. 1. An example collaboration protocol and submission of an experience report

The receipts, depicted in Figure 2, remain private unless they are used to rebut an experience, and they are stored by both collaborators. The source actor (A) is the provider of the receipt. The target actor (B) is the actor for whom the receipt is generated. The notary witnesses the transaction step when the protocol in the collaboration model so defines. In the optimistic fair exchange protocol [13], collaborators can choose to only involve the notary if one party fails to respond on time. This requires that the relevant exchange can be repeated with the notary listening in as needed, but it should significantly reduce the communication overhead: the threat of notary involvement removes the attractiveness of receipt omissions almost as effectively as the observation itself [13].

> - Source actor id, target actor id
> - Notary id
> - Business network model id, eContract id, task id
> - Task counter, receipt protocol step
> - Outcome of step (e.g. "goods received")
> - Signature of witness (source or notary)

Fig. 2. The contents of a receipt

The model and task information together provide a reference for determining the reputation impact represented by the receipt, and a unique identifier for the receipt (and corresponding experience) in case the same task is repeated multiple times. Each task can be expected to produce several receipts on relevant steps, most notably its start and end, and this is captured by the step identifier. The outcome of the step is the identifier of the given outcome as defined in the contract. The eventual signature of the witness depends on whether the exchange was notarized or not.

The notary only sends out receipts, and does not store them; it does not participate in the reputation system process afterwards.

Experience reports, depicted in Figure 3, are submitted to the reputation system by the source about the target, corresponding to the relevant receipts. The identifiers of the actors are as above. Although the main relevance of the notary is in the receipt phase, it is provided in the experience report in order to support credibility analysis: not all of the reputation system participants are required to consider all available notaries trustworthy. When identifying the transaction, the protocol step mentioned in the receipt is omitted here — the single task produces one experience per actor (possibly on both participants in the transaction), but there are multiple receipts that can be used as evidence on a single experience depending on how the transaction progressed. The signature of the source ensures that the experience report cannot be faked: this is required, as submitting a false report that is successfully rebutted has a reputation impact.

> - Source actor id, target actor id
> - Notary id, if applicable
> - Business network model id, eContract id, task id, task counter
> - Signature of the source
> - Timestamp (time of submission)

Fig. 3. The contents of an experience report

The timestamp here is set by the reputation system when it receives the report for dissemination. It is used to limit the time frame in which rebuttals must be made. Once the time has passed, the source and target are free to dispose of the receipts connected with the experience. In addition, the experience can then be incorporated into a permanent storage, e.g. transformed into counter increments or similar compound formats that are no longer individually processable.

A rebuttal, depicted in Figure 4, is typically made by the target of the experience to clear its name, as the source has produced the experience to submit. In the case of whitewashing, i.e. undeserved positive experiences, a third party can decide to rebut the experience as well.

- Source id, target id, rebutter id
- Business network model id, eContract id, task id, task counter
- Type of rebuttal: 1) Target rebuttal of false (negative) experience, 2) target noting a failure to report (positive) experience, or 3) target or third party rebuttal to (negative or positive) experience on a nonexistent transaction
- Evidence in form of signed receipts, as applicable
- Signature of the rebutter
- Timestamp (time of rebuttal)

Fig. 4. The contents of a rebuttal

The source and target id refer to their equivalents in the experience, while the rebutter id is either the target's or belongs to a third party whistleblower. The second line identifies the experience being rebutted. The type of rebuttal specifies which kind of response is expected:

For the first type, the target rebutting a (typically negative) experience, the rebutter (i.e. target) must provide any available reciepts proving it has followed the transaction according to contract. If the target's case is sufficient, the source suffers a reputation loss and the experience is removed. If its evidence does not fulfil the requirements of the rebuttal type and protocol, the rebuttal is ineffective. The verification of the evidence can be done centrally by the reputation system; in case the reputation system cannot be sufficiently trusted to follow this protocol fairly, the rebuttals and supporting evidence can be distributed to all the nodes to perform the rebuttal process locally. This choice ties to how information dissemination is organized in the reputation system in general, and is not forced either way by the model of how rebuttals work.

With the second type of rebuttal, the target notifies that the source should have reported a (typically positive) experience on it, but has not. The target, again, must provide the evidence to support its claim. This type forms a special case in defining the appropriate time for the rebuttal: the source should submit the experience without delay after it has provided the target with sufficient evidence, yet we cannot trust a timestamp in the receipt, as it can be set arbitrarily by the source. Instead, the fact that the target is able to present the evidence in the first place indicates that the experience should either be in the system or arriving simultaneously with the rebuttal. If this is not the case and the evidence from the receipts is sufficient, the source suffers negative reputation.

The third type of rebuttal demands a rebuttal response containing proof of the original experience. The target may rebut an experience, typically negative, of a transaction that never happened, or a third-party whistleblower may rebut it, suspecting an undeserved, typically positive experience. In both cases, the burden of proving that the transaction exists and ended as indicated by the experience lies with the source, and if it fails, it suffers a negative reputation impact. The relevant evidence consists of receipts signed by the target or a notary; receipts signed by the source alone are no more credible than the original signed experience report. In the case of the third party rebuttal, it is worth noting that the evidence may itself be a product of collusion between the source and target, in which case the rebuttal may have been appropriate but is still ineffective. The contents of the rebuttal response are depicted in Figure 5.

- Source id, target id, rebutter id
- Business network model id, eContract id, task id, task counter
- Evidence in form of signed receipts

Fig. 5. The contents of a rebuttal response

The rebuttal response can go unsigned, as the signatures of the receipts define its validity. It only needs to be identified as a continuation of the rebuttal before it, and provide the valid evidence. Its arrival time can be compared to the timestamp on the rebuttal, but it has no particular need for a timestamp itself: either it arrives on time to be accepted into the reputation system or it does not. A failure to respond adequately means the original rebuttal is accepted, while a successful response cancels out the rebuttal and the experience remains valid.

4   The Impact of Objective and Verifiable Experiences

We have defined an objective basis for experiences through associating them with contracts. This gives shared experiences the semantic clarity required to use them in automated decision-making. To ensure the verifiability of experiences, we enforce the fairness of the receipt exchange protocols through the use of notaries. Together, objectivity and verifiability provide a basis for using reputation information to implement social control in the open service ecosystems.

Obreiter discusses different types of nonrepudiable evidence and problems related to them [15]. Two issues in particular must be solved to ensure the acceptability of reputation systems for inter-enterprise collaborations:

- Actors have very limited incentive to provide any evidence of their own misbehaviour, while they may have an incentive to provide unfairly negative reports of their competitors to gain a competitive advantage.
- Two colluding actors can provide an unlimited amount of positive feedback on each other by faking transactions.

We first show how our proposal addresses the first issue by providing the participants appropriate incentives to ensure fair reporting of misbehaviour, and then focus on addressing the second issue through limiting the negative effects of ballot stuffing to other members of the ecosystem. In the third subsection, we compare our work to the state of the art to delineate our contribution.

4.1 Ensuring Fair Reporting on Existing Transactions

The protocol design for experience reporting and rebuttal aims to reduce the need for rebuttals, limit the incentive for false reporting and omissions by making inaccuracies easier to detect by interested parties, and to balance between giving incentive for third party whistleblowers to rebut likely inaccurate reports, but not to flood the system.

To limit fraudulent positive reports that do not result from collusion, we have chosen the source of a relevant receipt to be the one to submit the related experience to the reputation system. Positive experiences are assumed to be the norm. The target of an experience has motivation to ensure that any deserved positive experiences are reported, possibly also to produce false positive experiences and omit negative experiences. The source, in turn, has motivation to punish the target with honest negative experiences, possibly to report false negatives as well, and omit positive experiences, particularly if the target is a competitor. The target has an interest to report an omission of a positive experience or to clear its name after a false negative experience, and it will know to do this if the reputation system fails to send an expected kind of notification of a reported experience after a transaction. On the other hand, the production of positive experiences about nonexistent transactions with the claimed source requires the source to be around to react to them on time, or a third party whistleblower to take interest; our design sets the source as the reporter to eliminate this issue.

The three types of rebuttals have different motivations and effects. Our goal is to punish false experience reports. To achieve objectivity in this, the exact reputation effects of spreading misinformation are defined in a reputation network contract that must be signed before joining the reputation network. This contract specifies other relevant factors, such as the exact timeframes for rebuttals and their responses, as well. To make the punishment system effective, the rebutters must have an incentive to submit correct rebuttals, and to not submit ungrounded rebuttals.

Actors have a reputation-based incentive to rebut unfairly negative experiences towards themselves. In all cases, the correct or missing experience can be added into the reputation system as a result of a successful rebuttal, in addition to the incorrect experience being removed or marked as invalid. This new experience can be signed by the target, or the centralized reputation system that verifies the evidence, if the latter is available. The target rebutter, in other words, typically gains positive experience as a result, which creates an incentive for it to rebut an experience correctly. Unsuccessful target rebutters can be punished with a negative reputation effect, as they are in a good position to estimate whether they or the source have the evidence to back or counter a rebuttal.

Punishing or awarding third party whistleblowers for their rebuttals is more complicated, however, as their rebuttals at best rely on a guess on whether the experience was a result of a collusion or an attempt to get lucky. The number of third-party rebuttals processed from any actor at a given timeframe can be limited to control the load. A minor reward for a competing service provider is that the artificially inflated reputation of its competitor is reduced, increasing its own reputation in relation to it. A greater incentive can be created by providing a reputation reward for a successful third-party rebuttal, although this in turn must be combined with limitations on the frequency of such rebuttals in order to not create an incentive to flood the reputation system with random rebuttals. In addition, the reputation gains of third-party rebutters should not be as high as the reputation loss of the other actor, as this would create a market for moving reputation from the source to the rebutter. Finally, actors with very bad reputation cannot be reasonably incentivized to behave through threats of further reputation loss, and should therefore be eventually shut out of submitting new information or third-party rebuttals to the reputation system.

Even when a third-party rebuttal is ineffective in the objective sense, disseminating the rebuttal attempt allows reputation system participants trusting the whistleblower more than the source and target together to adjust their local credibility analysis accordingly. These kinds of side effects are an argument for distributing information about the rebuttals to the entire reputation system even if a centralized system could perform the analysis itself.

4.2   Addressing Collusion to Generate Positive Experiences

As collaborations in the open service ecosystem are impossible to externally observe by third parties unless the collaborating parties allow it, it is possible for two participants to collude to produce positive experiences on each other. To do this, they exchange nonrepudiable receipts according to a protocol, without actually committing concrete resources. They can include an honest notary to observe the exchange and gain further credibility, assuming that the business process does not require costly third-party services to be invoked. Limiting the attractiveness of collusion is a difficult problem. The victim of conducting fake business may also be unobvious: how can positive feedback be harmful?

Let us assume that in a competitive environment, having a higher number of positive experience reports stored on an actor directly influences their probability of being chosen into a collaboration. This, in turn, provides additional opportunities in gaining further positive reputation. The assumption implies that a relative loss of reputation in comparison to one's competitors translates to a monetary loss that is slowly growing over time. Punishment for unfairly causing reputation loss to a victim is intuitively important. When we also consider that within this assumption, a relative gain in reputation in comparison to one's competitors is similar to causing all of them reputation loss, the problem with ballot stuffing in reputation systems becomes acute.

Li et al. propose to solve the issue by assigning a cost to all transactions, which would increase the cost of collusion [11]. For the operational environment of Pilarcos, however, there is no clear single operator who could collect equal transaction-based fees from all members of the ecosystem, and allowing actors to choose the target of their payments would leave an opening for a more complex collusion that includes a dishonest operator service.

We must therefore resolve this issue within the domain of distributed peer control, and propose to do so by partially breaking the above assumption: positive experiences should not directly improve the probability of being chosen, but positive experiences that are locally found credible would have this effect. Negative experiences should generally have more weight in a decision than positive experiences, and they, in turn, must be backed by evidence.

By valuing local and possibly trusted partners' experiences above random shared experiences, the ecosystem members can limit the gains from collusion between isolated actors; we discuss a selection of different approaches to estimating the credibility of reputation information in earlier work [18,23]. Local credibility analysis based on e.g. social relations with the information source [4] or the relationship with local experiences [21] is subjective and therefore should only be used to select trustworthy and relevant information sources. It cannot form a basis for second-order punishment, as the reason for a disagreement between two experience sources can be caused by honestly reported discriminatory behaviour.

4.3   Comparison to the State of the Art

To demarcate our contribution to the state of the art, we compare our solution within Pilarcos to the protocol-based solution proposed by Li et al. [11] on five dimensions: application area, type of third party witness, target of observation, punishment method and implementation requirements. A summary of the comparison is provided in Table 1.

In *application area*, the proposals differ on two levels. Pilarcos operates in a governed open service ecosystem, where transactions are complex and may be long-lived, and varying communication protocols are defined through collaboration contracts. In the proposal of Li et al., the electronic marketplace supports exchanges of goods in simple transactions, and the same protocol suffices for all actors. A more complex environment also means that our view of misbehaviour must be broader, and as a result Li et al.'s theorem on removing actors' incentive to misbehave [11] does not generalize meaningfully into open service ecosystems.

Third party observation is implemented in Pilarcos through a notary who acts as a passive witness: it signs receipts, but does not act on them. In contrast, Li et al. have an active arbitrator who is also responsible for judging the outcome and punishing misbehaviour, which gives it more power. Despite this difference, the same impacts [11] and basic limitations of third party protocol-level monitoring apply to both solutions: only protocol-level misbehaviour can be detected through protocol-level monitoring, which means that e.g. compensation processes must be made visible on that level to have a reputation impact.

The *target of observation* in both proposals is the accurate completion of protocols; in Pilarcos they follow contract-defined business processes, while for Li et al. there is a fixed protocol for purchasing arbitrable and replicatable goods [11]. We therefore consider our solution to be a generalization of their work.

Table 1. Comparison of Pilarcos to the proposal of Li et al.

Dimension	Pilarcos	Proposal of Li et al.	Remarks
Application Area	Open service ecosystems: collaborators in complex transactions	Electronic multi-agent marketplace: service providers and consumers in simple transactions	Variation in participant roles; additional forms of misbehaviour; the same assumptions do not hold
Third Party Witness	Notary (passive witness)	Arbitrator (active resolver)	Impact & limitations of 3rd party witness apply to both
Target of Observation	Accurate completion of different contract-defined business processes	Completion of fixed protocol for purchasing arbitrable & replicatable (intangible) goods	Generalization; some requirements cannot be resolved globally, pushed to contract design instead
Punishment Method	Distributed: reputation-based peer control, contractual compensation	Centralized: fixed monetary and reputation gains and losses	Different focus and method, more complementary than contradictory
Implementation requirements	Notaries; protocol design; reputation systems with their own contracts, incl. the rebuttal protocol	Arbitrators; appropriate configurations of service fees collected globally; bank-controlled deposits	Global service fees not feasible; costs of witness protocols are comparable

Li et al. define arbitrability and replicatability, i.e. that the communication protocol can be repeated for the third-party witness, as requirements for arbitration be effective [11]. We expect that reasonable arbitrability can be reached through business process design for open service ecosystems as well; in some situations, additional third party mediators must be involved to control risks in the collaboration. For particularly trusted partners, these controls can be relaxed.

The *punishment methods* of the systems differ in focus and approach. The reputation-based punishment we propose in this paper is distributed and based on peer control. In addition to reputation-based punishment, Pilarcos contracts contain compensation clauses for misbehaviour, like any business agreements. Li et al. take a centralized point of view both in the arbitrator-based monetary punishment and optionally the broker selecting providers based on their reputation, which is also determined centrally. The approaches seem to be more complementary than contradictory; for example deposits can be applied in high-risk situations to ensure that contractual compensation can be enforced, and reputation-based service selection can be distributed to the actors themselves. We aim for a distributed solution to ensure the viability of the marketplace: as reputation information is worth money, granting a single central actor monopoly over all ecosystem members' reputation is equivalent to creating a new central bank in the ecosystem; this kind of power is disruptive and requires strong control mechanisms to balance for it.

The *implementation requirements* of the two solutions are different in nature. In the proposal of Li et al., the availability of the trusted arbitrator as well as deposit bank and broker is required, and the service fees must be configured globally to minimize incentives to misbehave while maintaining an incentive to use the system. In addition, all actors are required to make bank-controlled deposits which are held as collateral. The trusted third parties form a single point of failure to the marketplace, which Li et al. aim to distribute more in future work [11].

For Pilarcos, we require the existence of trusted notaries, and push the requirement for designing appropriate arbitrable protocols to specialist business network model designers. In addition, we demand that users of the proposed reputation system, where shared experience information is stored, agree to the reputation network contract. Other costs and impacts of the encompassing Pilarcos system and its trust management system have been discussed in earlier work [17]; we draw additional benefits from the infrastructure for the goal at hand. In contrast to the proposal by Li et al., we estimate that centrally collected global service fees for all transactions are unrealistic in the open service ecosystem, which means that they cannot be generally applied to solve the ballot stuffing problem. Instead, we propose the use of local credibility estimation to reduce the gains from such collusion. This credibility analysis can take into consideration the cost of faking the transaction as well, for example if there is an equivalent of service fees designed into the specific business process.

For implementation cost, the increased messaging for applying third party witnesses to problem situations is not a major cost when optimistic fair exchange protocols are used [13]. The runtime overhead of either system is dominated by cryptographic signing, and we estimate it is not remarkable, considering that the systems involved are capable of running full-blown business protocols.

In summary, our proposed solution is designed for a complex environment; we find that some of the impact of third party witnesses discussed by Li et al. hold for Pilarcos and give implications for collaboration protocol design, while other assumptions made in their game-theoretic analysis [11] cannot hold due to differences in collaboration types. Some aspects of the bank-based punishment proposed by Li et al. are best compared to contractual compensation in the Pilarcos context, and a system for contractually-agreed, deposit-based punishment could well coexist with reputation-based punishment for misbehaviour. Our proposal is distributed and reduces the amount of trust that must be placed on the third party witness or other involved actors.

5   Conclusion

We advance a reputation system for inter-enterprise collaborations that is based on objective, verifiable reputation: shared experiences denote whether the collaboration contract was followed or not. To standardize the semantics of experiences in order to make them shareable, we define the reputation effects of different kinds of collaborations in the collaboration contracts. To ensure that false experiences are caught and their submitters punished, an audit trail of the collaboration is produced by signed, nonrepudiable receipts. These receipts can be used to verify whether an experience report is truthful. Objectivity and verifiability go hand in hand: alone, the impact of either remains limited.

The major benefit from this combined approach is the implementation of a two-level sanctioning system, punishing both malicious behaviour and unfair punishments. In the absence of a strong centralized control mechanism, this is necessary to ensure that the service ecosystem does not deteriorate from rampant misbehaviour. In other words, we implement a distributed form of social control in the open service ecosystem.

Trust issues are not entirely solvable by technology alone; in our approach, as well, the final recourse involves lawsuits for contract breaches, and similar infrastructure for ensuring that notaries, i.e. trusted third parties, have an incentive to fulfil their duties. In contrast to the default assumption that trusted third parties are universally trusted, we have strongly limited the amount of trust necessary to place on the proposed notary services.

Objective and verifiable experiences make it possible to punish the spreading of misinformation in the reputation system; due to factors such as collusion to produce positive experiences with little invested effort, they do not remove the need to analyse reputation information locally. Local credibility analysis of all incoming experiences remains a central technical recourse against misinformation: it is not necessary nor prudent to accept all experiences as equal, be they subjective or objective.

References

1. Blaze, M., Feigenbaum, J., Keromytis, A.D.: KeyNote: Trust Management for Public-Key Infrastructures (position paper). In: Christianson, B., Crispo, B., Harbison, W.S., Roe, M. (eds.) Security Protocols 1998. LNCS, vol. 1550, pp. 59–63. Springer, Heidelberg (1999)
2. Dondio, P., Longo, L., Barrett, S.: A Translation Mechanism for Recommendations. In: Karabulut, Y., Mitchell, J., Herrmann, P., Jensen, C.D. (eds.) Trust Management II. IFIP, vol. 263, pp. 87–102. Springer, Boston (2008)
3. Fehr, E., Fischbacher, U.: The nature of human altruism. Nature 425 (October 2003)
4. Gal-Oz, N., Gudes, E., Hendler, D.: A Robust and Knot-Aware Trust-Based Reputation Model. In: Karabulut, Y., Mitchell, J., Herrmann, P., Jensen, C.D. (eds.) Trust Management II. IFIP, vol. 263, pp. 167–182. Springer, Boston (2008)
5. Hasan, O., Brunie, L., Pierson, J.-M., Bertino, E.: Elimination of Subjectivity from Trust Recommendation. In: Ferrari, E., Li, N., Bertino, E., Karabulut, Y. (eds.) TM 2009. IFIP AICT, vol. 300, pp. 65–80. Springer, Heidelberg (2009)
6. Kaur, P., Ruohomaa, S., Kutvonen, L.: User interface for trust decision making in inter-enterprise collaborations. In: Proceedings of the Fifth International Conference on Advances in Computer-Human Interactions (ACHI 2012), pp. 122–127. IARIA, Valencia (2012)
7. Kutvonen, L., Metso, J., Ruohomaa, S.: From trading to eCommunity management: Responding to social and contractual challenges. Information Systems Frontiers (ISF) - Special Issue on Enterprise Services Computing: Evolution and Challenges 9(2-3), 181–194 (2007)
8. Kutvonen, L., Ruokolainen, T., Metso, J.: Interoperability middleware for federated business services in web-Pilarcos. International Journal of Enterprise Information Systems, Special issue on Interoperability of Enterprise Systems and Applications 3(1), 1–21 (2007)

9. Kutvonen, L., Ruokolainen, T., Ruohomaa, S., Metso, J.: Service-oriented middleware for managing inter-enterprise collaborations. In: Global Implications of Modern Enterprise Information Systems: Technologies and Applications. Advances in Enterprise Information Systems (AEIS), pp. 209–241. IGI Global (December 2008)

10. Lee, S., Sherwood, R., Bhattacharjee, B.: Cooperative peer groups in NICE. In: Twenty-Second Annual Joint Conference of the IEEE Computer and Communications Societies (INFOCOM 2003), vol. 2, pp. 1272–1282. IEEE (April 2003)

11. Li, Q., Martin, K.M., Zhang, J.: Design of a multiagent-based e-marketplace to secure service trading on the Internet. In: Proceedings of the 13th International Conference on Electronic Commerce, Liverpool, UK (2011)

12. Mehandiev, N., Grefen, P. (eds.): Dynamic Business Process Formation for Instant Virtual Enterprises. Advanced Information and Knowledge Processing. Springer (June 2010)

13. Micali, S.: Simple and fast optimistic protocols for fair electronic exchange. In: Proceedings of the Twenty-Second Annual Symposium on Principles of Distributed Computing (PODC 2003), pp. 12–19. ACM (2003)

14. OASIS Web Service Secure Exchange TC: WS-Trust 1.3 OASIS Standard. OASIS (March 2007)

15. Obreiter, P.: A Case for Evidence-Aware Distributed Reputation Systems Overcoming the Limitations of Plausibility Considerations. In: Jensen, C., Poslad, S., Dimitrakos, T. (eds.) iTrust 2004. LNCS, vol. 2995, pp. 33–47. Springer, Heidelberg (2004)

16. Resnick, P., Zeckhauser, R.: Trust among strangers in internet transactions: Empirical analysis of eBay's reputation system. In: The Economics of the Internet and E-Commerce. Advances in Applied Microeconomics, vol. 11, pp. 127–157. Elsevier Science, Amsterdam (2002)

17. Ruohomaa, S., Kutvonen, L.: Trust and distrust in adaptive inter-enterprise collaboration management. Journal of Theoretical and Applied Electronic Commerce Research 5(2), 118–136 (2010)

18. Ruohomaa, S., Kutvonen, L., Koutrouli, E.: Reputation management survey. In: Proceedings of the 2nd International Conference on Availability, Reliability and Security (ARES 2007), pp. 103–111. IEEE Computer Society, Vienna (2007)

19. Ruokolainen, T., Ruohomaa, S., Kutvonen, L.: Solving service ecosystem governance. In: Proceedings of the 15th IEEE International EDOC Conference Workshops, pp. 18–25. IEEE Computer Society, Helsinki (2011)

20. Srivatsa, M., Xiong, L., Liu, L.: TrustGuard: countering vulnerabilities in reputation management for decentralized overlay networks. In: WWW 2005: Proceedings of the 14th International Conference on the World Wide Web, pp. 422–431. ACM Press, New York (2005)

21. Teacy, W.T.L., Patel, J., Jennings, N.R., Luck, M.: TRAVOS: Trust and reputation in the context of inaccurate reputation sources. Autonomous Agents and Multiagent Systems 12(2), 183–198 (2006)

22. Wilson, M.D., Arenas, A., Schubert, L., et al.: Trustcom framework V2, Deliverable D29, D35, D36. Tech. rep., TrustCoM WP27 (January 2006)

23. Yao, Y., Ruohomaa, S., Xu, F.: Addressing common vulnerabilities of reputation systems for electronic commerce. Journal of Theoretical and Applied Electronic Commerce Research 7, 1–15 (2012)

Integrating Indicators of Trustworthiness into Reputation-Based Trust Models

Insurance, Certification, and Coalitions

Sascha Hauke, Florian Volk, Sheikh Mahbub Habib, and Max Mühlhäuser

Technische Universität Darmstadt/CASED,
Telekooperation, Hochschulstraße 10, 64283 Darmstadt
{sascha.hauke,florian.volk,sheikh.habib}@cased.de,
max@informatik.tu-darmstadt.de

Abstract. Reputation-based trust models are essentially reinforcement learning mechanisms reliant on feedback. As such, they face a cold start problem when attempting to assess an unknown service partner. State-of-the-art models address this by incorporating dispositional knowledge, the derivation of which is not described regularly. We propose three mechanisms for integrating knowledge readily available in cyber-physical services (e.g., online ordering) to determine the trust disposition of consumers towards unknown services (and their providers). These reputation-building indicators of trustworthiness can serve as cues for trust-based decision making in eCommerce scenarios and drive the evolution of reputation-based trust models towards trust management systems.

1 Introduction

Internet-based and mediated services have managed to capture considerable market shares in what used to be primarily real-world markets. The further amalgamation of online and real-world service provisioning, such as online ordering of physical goods, e.g., books, or provisioning of services, be they hotel bookings or cloud compute services, promise additional convenience for consumers and business opportunities for providers. Personal and institutional procedures for evaluating whom to trust in this new environment are still in the process of being established. The relative ease of setting up an online business, as compared to brick-and-mortar enterprises, leads to more transience in a market.

In order to overcome these challenges and build trust in unregulated online markets, such as the present and future internet, two distinct schools of thought have emerged. On the one hand, the "hard" approach to trust dictates rigorous certification and provable chains of credentials between a (presumably) entirely trusted root and a node. This is used, for instance, in trusted computing applications. On the other hand, the "soft" way of thinking about trust relegates trust to the domain of probabilities, conventionally stating that trust is a *subjective probability* [4] of somebody else acting as expected. This probability is typically derived from feedback histories using (probabilistic) trust models, such as [11].

T. Dimitrakos et al. (Eds.): IFIPTM 2012, IFIP AICT 374, pp. 158–173, 2012.

In its current form, neither is entirely satisfactory when addressing the needs of (future) internet-based markets. While hard trust might be sufficient to provide information on the identity of another entity, possibly its persistence and even some of its capabilities, its shortcomings are in describing the behavior of that other entity. Soft trust, with its reliance on feedback and reputation, expressed as community standing, is prone to particular attacks. It also faces shortcomings such as those related to reinforcement learning.

In this paper, we present an extension to the established CertainTrust trust model [22]. The concepts of insuring, certifying, and coalition forming are adapted to be used as an extension to the model. By explicitly modeling cues that are already well-established in real-world interactions for use in a reputation-based trust model, the approach contributes to mitigating the cold start/market entry problem. Additionally, by allowing providers to represent their trustworthiness, the modeling of these approaches forms a first step of evolving CertainTrust into a trust management system (following the definition of such a system by Jøsang et al. [12]). By integrating certification processes with reputation-based trust, an integration of hard and soft trust approaches is potentially enabled.

The impacts on trust and reliance are discussed in the context of a cyber-physical service provision context. They are, furthermore, briefly presented in a qualitative agent-based simulation. Insurance and certification models were chosen, because for both there exist functioning real-world markets with highly-reputable service providers. These providers can serve as persistent trust anchors for more transient online services, such as cloud-based offerings by small and medium enterprises.

The contribution can, of course, be adapted to other reputation-based trust models and is not limited to the given use case by any means.

The remaining document is structured as follows: section 2 presents a use case for the proposed approach presented in section 3. Section 4 discusses the application of the indicators to the use case and presents the results of an agent-based simulation qualitatively showing the effect of the individual operators. Section 5 surveys related work. In section 6, some conclusions are drawn.

2   Use Case

For the use case, consider a customer trying to establish trust on a cyber-physical service. Furthermore, suppose that the customer does not have any prior experience with that particular service. It is therefore not immediately possible to derive the trustworthiness of the service provider from direct experience. In order to derive the reliability of the service, the conventional approach for reputation-based trust models (cf. e.g., [9,11,22]) is to query trusted witnesses for information. However, even in the absence of reliable witnesses, both initial reliability and decision trust [13] can be established from other cues.

In cyber-physical services, that involve both digital and real-world processes, such as online ordering and physical shipping of goods, service delivery is generally not monolithic. Rather, the service provisioning processes can be sub-divided into sub-components, some of which are visible to the customer and may be associated with distinct entities on which trust can be established individually.

Figure 1 outlines a general scenario in which a customer establishes trust on an unknown (foreign) composite service. By necessity, several components of the service are visible to the customer, such as payment/billing and shipping agents used by the service provider. We assume that the billing process is handled through an intermediary, specifically a credit card company. For the core service provisioning process, we further assume that the composite service provider chooses not

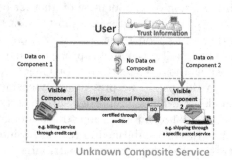

Fig. 1. Use Case: Cyber-Physical Service Composition

to reveal its internal processes to the customer directly. It may, however, use an external auditing and certification provider (e.g., ISO) to certify its internal processes. In this paper, we abstract from the multi-dimensionality of trust. Thus, a certification is considered to be representative for the reliability of the internal service provisioning process.

3   Approach

Meanings and definitions of trust have been discussed at some length in the literature (cf. e.g., [4,19,18]). Within the scope of this paper, we will follow [12] in differentiating reliability trust and decision trust. We will define reliability trust according to Gambetta [4,12]:

Definition 1. *Trust is the subjective probability by which an individual expects that another individual performs a given action on which its welfare depends.*

In particular, we consider trust to be an adequate approximator of trustworthiness. The expectation value E computed by the CertainTrust trust model represents such a trust score. When having to make a decision, however, further considerations are involved, beyond the supposed reliability expressed by the trust score. This is reflected in decision trust [12]:

Definition 2. *Trust is the extent to which a given party is willing to depend on something or somebody in a given situation with a feeling of relative security, even though negative consequences are possible.*

Reliability trust can be said to *inform* decision trust. However, risk, gain, loss and reliance [20] are also contributing to the decision-making process. Consequently, decision trust will be modeled using expected utility theory [13,17]. The probabilities, denoted as p, used in the computation of the expected utility will be derived from reliability trust. In particular, the values of various instances of p, e.g., used in equations 2 and 4, are approximated by the reliability trust score from CertainTrust.

Let G be a benefit expected from an interaction, i.e., the positive gain, and L the corresponding loss, or negative gain. Furthermore, let $p \in [0,1]$ be the probability of a beneficial outcome. Then, the expected utility EU of an interaction can be defined as [13,17]:

$$EU := p \cdot G - (1-p) \cdot L \qquad (1)$$

3.1   Using CertainTrust to Measure Reliability Trust

To model experiences as trust information, the CertainTrust model and the Human Trust Interface (HTI) from [22] are applied. CertainTrust models trust as opinions based on positive evidences r_i and negative evidences s_i. Using collected evidence (e.g., feedback), it allows to calculate an expectation value $E_{f,w,N}(t,c) = t \cdot c + (1-c) \cdot f$. The certainty c depicts on how much evidence the trust value t is based. A low amount of evidence (low certainty c) is compensated by using the (dispositional) initial trust value f. The parameter w allows to express the weight of dispositional trust, while N denotes the maximal amount of expected evidence, in this paper's case: the amount of single experiences.

The true value of the probability p can be considered an inherent quality of an entity that cannot be measured directly. It is assumed that $E_{f,w,N}$ is an appropriate approximator for p. In the following, various variables – e.g., c_{issuer}, t_{issuer}, $c_{candidate}$, $t_{candidate}$, and f – are derived using CertainTrust. In particular, they do not have to be determined manually.

3.2   Using Expected Utility to Model Decision Trust

Consumers selecting a service will generally try to maximize their utility. Thus, they will tend to select the service with the highest expected utility EU. The expected utility function is subject to uncertainty, because $E_{f,w,N}$ is used instead of the true value for p. Most variables here are either direct results of applying the trust model, are derived through the delegation mechanisms discussed in the following or are explicitly available from the context of an interaction (e.g., the premium a service provider charges for the use of a credit card, which offers an insurance option, would cover $L_{insurer}^{fix}$).

Prior experiences by consumers and indicators of trustworthiness are bound to service providers' identities. Therefore, persistent identities are desirable. Otherwise, bad reputation could easily be "whitewashed" by re-entering the market with a new identity [2]. An upfront monetary investment bound to an identity shows the dedication of a service provider to this identity and therefore reflects an incentive to act trustworthy [3]. Unlike the basic approach [3], that requires a trusted third party or a managed marketplace to bind an investment to an identity, our approach solely relies on "trust-building" services, e.g., insurance services and certification services.

3.3   Reliance through Insurance

The insurance case relies on three entities: The *consumer* trying to identify the most appropriate service provider to select, the *service provider* under evaluation, and an *insurance provider* insuring the transaction if the consumer decides to interact with the service provider. The relations between the entities are outlined in figure 2. Insurance provides reliance [20], and thus affects decision trust, by reducing the risk of asset loss attendant with an interaction. It therefore should contribute to *"[...] a feeling of relative security [...]"* (cf. definition 2).

Let $p_{candidate}$ be the probability of a successful interaction with a candidate service provider, and $p_{insurer}$ the probability of a successful interaction with an insurance provider that vouches or guarantees the interaction between consumer (acting as the initiator [22]) and the service provider (acting as the candidate). Furthermore, let the cost, or negative gain, the consumer experiences in case of an unsuccessful interaction with the service provider, be denoted $L_{candidate}$.

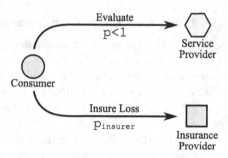

Fig. 2. Trust Delegation with Insurance

Analogously, $L_{insurer}^{fix}$ is the cost (if any) of the insurance contract to the consumer. Additionally, $L_{insurer}^{var}$ indicates the expenses incurred by the consumer when making an insurance claim against a failed interaction. In this case, the expected utility of the interaction for the consumer is:

$$
\begin{aligned}
EU := \ & p_{candidate} \cdot G \\
& - (1 - p_{candidate})(1 - p_{insurer}) \cdot (L_{candidate} + L_{insurer}^{var}) \\
& - (1 - p_{candidate})(p_{insurer}) \cdot L_{insurer}^{var} \\
& - L_{insurer}^{fix}
\end{aligned} \tag{2}
$$

Table 1. Reputation Updates with Insurance

Interaction		Update	
Provider	Insurer	Provider	Insurer
success	–	positive	–
failure	success	negative	positive
failure	failure	negative	negative

After an insured interaction between a consumer and the selected candidate took place, the consumer updates its trust values according to table 1. In case the interaction with the provider succeeded, additional positive evidence regarding the provider is created, e.g., by increasing the value of $r_{provider}$ by 1. In this successful case, action from the insurer is not demanded and no further evidence regarding the insurer is collected. However, if the interaction with the selected candidate fails, there are two possible cases. If the insurer is called upon and reimburses $L_{candidate}$ to the consumer, therefore compensating the negative gain for the consumer, new positive evidence for the insurer is collected. If the insurer fails in compensating the negative gain, new negative evidence regarding the insurer is collected, e.g., by increasing the value of $s_{insurer}$. In both cases, new negative evidence regarding the selected provider is created analogously.

3.4   Assessing Reliability through Certification

Similar to the insurance case from the previous section, this case consists of three interacting entities. The consumer is evaluating a service provider for selection. This service provider is certified by a certification provider the consumer has prior knowledge about but does not interact directly with (see figure 3).

For this paper, we assume a certification provider certifies service quality for an entire service or service component. We abstract from the multi-dimensionality of trust at this point. Certification of partial aspects of a service (component) can be combined into an overall rating, for instance using the propositional logic operators of CertainLogic [23]. Formally, a certification describes a specific minimum level of quality as $q_{cert} \in [0, 1]$ that a certification provider awards to the certified party, ideally after completing an audit.

This kind of limited trust delegation, employing a "probabilistic" certificate value and a certification provider that is not necessarily a completely trusted third party, influences the reliability trust for the candidate. In particular, in order to preserve the importance of direct experience over other kinds of information, we propose to include certification information in

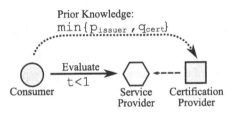

Fig. 3. Trust Delegation with Certification

the initial expectation value f of CertainTrust. In its simplest form, it thus follows:

$$p_{issuer} = E(t_{issuer}, c_{issuer})$$
$$= c_{issuer} \cdot t_{issuer} + (1 - c_{issuer}) \cdot f$$
$$f_{cert} = max(f, min(p_{issuer}, q_{cert})) \qquad (3)$$
$$E^{cert}(t_{candidate}, c_{candidate}) = c_{candidate} \cdot t_{candidate} + (1 - c_{candidate}) \cdot f_{cert}$$

The variables c_{issuer}, t_{issuer}, $c_{candidate}$, $t_{candidate}$, and f are derived using CertainTrust. In particular, they do not have to be determined manually.

The modified reliability trust score $E^{cert}(t_{candidate}, c_{candidate})$ informs the decision trust. Let $p^{cert}_{candidate} = E^{cert}(t_{candidate}, c_{candidate})$ be the probability of a successful interaction with a candidate service provider, given a certification from a certification provider. Then, the expected utility of the interaction between a consumer and a certified service provider can simply be described as:

$$EU := p^{cert}_{candidate} \cdot G - (1 - p^{cert}_{candidate}) \cdot L \qquad (4)$$

Table 2. Reputation Updates with Certification

Interaction		Update	
Provider	Certifier	Provider	Certifier
success	–	positive	positive
failure	–	negative	negative

Trust evidence updates after an interaction (as per [22]) are created according to table 2, taking into account only the performance of the selected provider. However, new trust evidence is created for both the selected provider and the certifier. Thus, while trust is delegated from the certification provider to the candidate service provider, trust updates are delegated from the service provider to the certification provider. In case of a negative outcome, the new evidence regarding the certifier is justified because the certification was incorrect for at least this interaction. While being unable to determine if this incorrect certification holds for all cases, it is perceived by the consumer as an incorrect certification for the selected provider. Thus, the certifier might also fail to certify other providers correctly, e.g., due to shortcomings in the certification or auditing process.

3.5 Joint Reliability through Coalitions

Another way for service providers to represent their trustworthiness is the formation of coalitions with other service providers. The motivation behind the introduction of this mechanism is the underlying assumption that a mutual association with another trustworthy provider serves as an indicator of trustworthiness. Lack of experience with one service provider, i.e., the candidate, can thus be compensated by the consumer, i.e., the initiator, via the delegation of trust from associated service providers, i.e., its associates, that might be known to the consumer.

While a coalition is different from an upfront monetary investment as insurance or certification, it is unlikely that established providers form coalitions with service providers that are unknown to them. Sybil attacks from malicious service providers that spawn many identities and create coalitions between them are unlikely – because they are ineffective: coalitions influence the probability of being selected by increasing the visibility of a service provider. Being associated with a *well-known and trusted* party becomes an implicit certification. A mutual coalition of unknown service providers does not increase the visibility of the participants.

Assume a consumer wishes to evaluate a candidate service provider. It lacks, however, past direct experiences and recommendations to form a reliable opinion. This lack of knowledge might lead the consumer to choose another, better known service provider or forgo the interaction altogether. In order to alleviate the problem and be able to realize a profit from the interaction, it is in the candidate's best interest to increase the consumer's perception of its trustworthiness. To this end, the candidate presents a list of other service providers it is associated with in a coalition to the consumer. As shown in figure 4, this is done under the expectation that the consumer has prior experiences with at least some of those. In this case, the experience the consumer has in the service provider's associates is transferred to the candidate.

Realizing Mutual Coalition. In composed services, coalitions are already in place. By taking into account the nature of the cooperation of service composition sub-components and their respective providers, trust delegation through the proposed coalition mechanism is a feasible method of establishing trust. Whether or not such a delegation is appropriate is dependent on the direction of the trust delegation with regard to the order of the

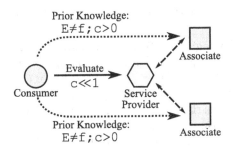

Prior Knowledge:
E≠f; c>0

Evaluate
c≪1

Consumer

Service
Provider

Associate

Prior Knowledge:
E≠f; c>0

Associate

Fig. 4. Trust Delegation with Associates

sub-components within the process, as well as on power symmetries and enforcement possibilities among the providers associated within a service composition. For instance, considering the use case in section 2, it can be argued that the credit card provider (i.e., visible component 1 in figure 1) is strongly connected to the grey box internal process. This is due to strong obligations and enforcement mechanisms (e.g., binding legal agreements and litigation possibilities) integrating the respective service providers.

If not explicitly cooperating in the service composition under evaluation, service providers that otherwise cooperate can enable coalition-based trust delegation through the following mechanism by advertising their cooperation to the customer. The customer, acting as initiator, can consequently verify the coalitions and transfer trust accordingly.

Mutual coalitions are realized through the exchange and mutual acknowledgment of cooperation messages. A process for this is depicted in figure 5.

1. Service provider A creates a message
   $m_{A,B} = < UID_A, UID_B, data >$ consisting of
   − a unique identifier representing provider A, e.g., an X.509 certificate.
   − a unique identifier representing associate B, e.g., an X.509 certificate.
2. Service provider A forwards $m_{A,B}$ to service provider B.
3. B acknowledges its coalition with A by signing $m_{A,B}$.
4. B returns the signed cooperation message $\{m_{A,B}\}_{sigB}$.
5. A forwards its signed counterpart cooperation message $\{m_{A,B}\}_{sigA}$.

These cooperation messages can then be presented to potential consumers, in order to facilitate the coalition-based trust delegation.

6. A potential consumer C evaluating service provider A requests indicators of trustworthiness from A.
7. A supplies C with a list of cooperation messages.
8. C may validate the coalition between A and B by requesting B to verify the signed cooperation message $\{m_{A,B}\}_{sigB}$.

9. Service provider B, as an associate of A, either confirms or denies the coalition with A, in particular regarding both the validity of the signature and currentness of the coalition.
10. The consumer C delegates the trustworthiness of B to A.

Delegating Trust in Coalitions.
Let $E_{f,w,N}(t_{candidate}, c_{candidate}) \approx f$ with certainty $c_{candidate} \approx 0$ be an estimate for $p_{candidate}$. $f \in [0,1]$ represents the initial trust disposition of the consumer [22], which is conventionally chosen conservatively low. Thus, for a trustworthy candidate, it should typically hold that if $c_{candidate} \to 1$, then $p_{candidate} \to t_{candidate} \gg f$. $t_{candidate}$ is the average of prior experiences the consumer had with the candidate, each of which can be either positive or negative. Let $r_{candidate}$ and $s_{candidate}$ be the sum of positive and negative experiences, respectively [22]. Then, $t_{candidate} = \frac{r}{r+s}$.

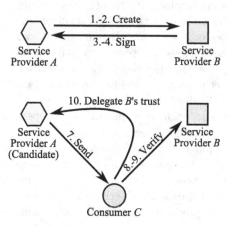

Fig. 5. Coalition Forming and Verification of Cooperation Messages

The condition that $c_{candidate} \approx 0$ implies that $r_{candidate} + s_{candidate} \ll N$, where N is a constant denoting the minimum number of experiences required to reach a certainty $c_{candidate}$ of 1, as per [22]. In the proposed coalition scheme, the gap between $r_{candidate} + s_{candidate}$ and N is to be filled with experiences on associated service providers.

Let associates $A_1, \ldots, A_m$ be service providers associated with the candidate provider. Furthermore, let $(r_{A_i}, s_{A_i}), i \in 1, 2, \ldots, m$ be the positive and negative experiences the consumer has made with service provider A_i. In order to minimize inequality effects regarding the number of experiences that influence trust delegation, we apply a normalization in the same manner as [22]:

$$norm_N(r,s) = \begin{cases} 1 & \text{if } r+s \leq N \\ \frac{N}{r+s} & \text{else} \end{cases}$$

$$\tilde{r} = r_{candidate} + \delta \cdot \alpha \sum_{i=1}^{m} norm_N(r_{A_i}, s_{A_i}) \cdot r_{A_i}$$

$$\tilde{s} = s_{candidate} + \delta \cdot \alpha \sum_{i=1}^{m} norm_N(r_{A_i}, s_{A_i}) \cdot s_{A_i}$$

The user-specified delegation factor α defines how much base weight an experience with an associated service provider has in relation to an experience made with the candidate provider itself. δ is a scaling factor that limits the influence of delegated information as certainty increases.

$$\delta = \frac{N - (r_{candidate} + s_{candidate})}{N}$$

Specifically, under total uncertainty $(r_{candidate} + s_{candidate} = 0)$ $\delta = 1$, under complete certainty $(r_{candidate} + s_{candidate} = N)$ $\delta = 0$.

$c_{candidate}$ and $t_{candidate}$ are computed based on $\tilde{r}, \tilde{s}$ instead of $r_{candidate}$, $s_{candidate}$.

$$c_{candidate} = \frac{N(\tilde{r} + \tilde{s})}{2(N - (\tilde{r} + \tilde{s})) + N(\tilde{r} + \tilde{s})}$$

$$t_{candidate} = \frac{\tilde{r}}{\tilde{r} + \tilde{s}}$$

Additionally, only experiences of those A_i with a certainty higher than a specific threshold might be taken into account. This would increase the impact of reputable and generally well-known coalition partners.

Thus, the expected utility for the consumer is $EU := p_{candidate} \cdot G - (1 - p_{candidate}) \cdot L$. $p_{candidate}$ is approximated as $p_{candidate} \approx E_{f,w,N}(t_{candidate}, c_{candidate}) = c_{candidate} \cdot t_{candidate} + (1 - c_{candidate}) \cdot f$.

Table 3. Reputation Updates with Coalitions

Interaction		Update	
Provider	Associates	Provider	Associates
success	–	positive	see text
failure	–	negative	see text

The trust updates after an interaction can be found in table 3: only new evidence for the selected service provider is collected regarding its performance. The selected provider alone is responsible for its performance as the only influence of the associates is the association itself. The future performance of the associates is independent from the selected provider. If the service provider and the associate are not part of same service composition, new evidence for the associates is collected only in the context of their ability to reliably form association. If they are, however, part of the same composite service (cf. section 2), the reputation is updated for all service components.

4   Evaluation

4.1   Evaluation within Use Case

The use case presented in section 2 introduces a composite cyber-physical process, in which some service components/providers are visible to the users, while others are contained in a grey box internal process. We deem this use case to be typical of an online goods ordering process. The payment functionality for the service is provided through a credit card company, while the delivery is handled by an independent parcel service. The grey box process is certified by a certification provider.

Assumptions. It can reasonably be assumed that the credit card company is well-known to and trusted by the customer. This stems both from past experiences, as well as (and possibly more importantly) from strong contractual obligations between a customer and his credit card company. Similar obligations exist between the credit card company and the provider of the composite service. Thus, social and legal assurances are in place to enforce the dependability of the partners in this setting. Furthermore, because a large number of internet services use a small number of credit card companies, experience with the credit card provider generally increases more rapidly than experience with any particular composite cyber-physical service. Additionally, a credit card company within a service composition offers insurance services to its customers.

Within the use case, the grey box internal process is certified by a certification provider (ideally following a thorough and transparent audit), for instance ISO (e.g., for quality management) or TRUSTe (for privacy, however cf. [1]). We abstract from the multi-dimensionality of trust within the scope of this paper. Certification providers are less strongly coupled with a service than the aforementioned credit card company. We assume that a limited number of certification providers is used by a considerable number of services, thus easing trust establishment on certification provider. Paying for a certification by a reputable certification provider indicates a service provider's initial commitment to remaining in a market (i.e., an incentive not to defect) [3].

Both insurance and certification depend heavily on reliance [20] on a third party. Trust in the insurance and certification providers to enforce user interests in case of service provider defection has to be established. If a certification provider is incapable or unwilling to enforce its certification rigorously, a certification can actually be interpreted as a sign of untrustworthiness [1]. It is therefore assumed that the user can reliably establish trust on insurance and certification providers using a trust model.

The shipping service represents the physical interface of the composite service to the customer. While the reliability of the shipping provider is essential to a successful overall service provisioning, it is not strongly coupled to the grey box internal process of the use case.

Component Integration. Modeling overall reliability trust in the unknown service composition requires combining the information on its components. Due to the highly regulated relationship between the the credit card provider and the grey box internal component of the service composition, the providers of these two components are considered to be in a coalition (cf. section 3.5). Therefore, the well-established trust the users has in its credit card provider is delegated to the internal component. As the shipping service is essential to the success of an interaction between customer and the service composition, but is only relatively loosely coupled to it, we propose the use of the CertainLogic AND operator ($\wedge_{CL}$) [23]. Including a certification provider to certify the grey box internal process (for which no prior experience has been recorded), the overall computed reliability trust in the unknown composite $c_{composite} = 0$ thus becomes:

$$p_{composite} \approx (t_{credit} \cdot \alpha \cdot c_{credit} + (1 - c_{credit} \cdot (f_{cert})))\wedge_{CL}E(t_{shipping}, c_{shipping})$$

Under a complete lack of information on *any* part of the composite service, the reliability trust value of the indicator-augmented trust computation corresponds to the CertainTrust value without indicators. The return value for $p_{composite}$ in this case is the user's initial expectation f. The same condition holds for complete certainty, i.e., $c_{composite} = 1$, in which case $p_{composite}$ is approximated as $t_{composite}$.

Figure 6 shows the behavior of trust evaluation of CertainTrust with and without indicators over 10 interactions (for $N = 10$ and $f = 0.5$). The trustworthiness of the credit card company and the certification provider were assumed to be high ($p = 0.95$) and known to the user at this level with certainty ($c = 1$). In this way, coalition and certification was essentially used to dynamically alter the initial trust in the unknown composite service, from $f = 0.5$ for the base CertainTrust case without indicators, to 0.95. The com-

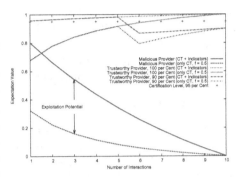

Fig. 6. Reliability Trust Expectation, for $N = 10$ and $f = 0.5$

posite cyber-physical service from our use case was therefore initially evaluated by the user at $p_{composite} \approx 0.95$. While trustworthy service providers can thereby overcome cold start issues effectively, it theoretically offers malicious service providers a considerably bigger potential to exploit this positive reputation.

The increase of the initial trust expectation from 0.5 to 0.95, however, was not arbitrary. Increasing the reliability trust in the unknown service was based on two criteria. The weaker one, certification, that the certification provider (e.g., ISO) would audit the service provider and possible revoke the certification in case of a complaint against the service. This certification provider backs this with its own behavior. The second, stronger criterion from a customer perspective, is the stronger reliance the credit card payment process offers. Because the credit card company does not stake its reputation, but also direct monetary values through an insurance service, it has a strong incentive to actually enforce the contractual obligations between itself and the core component of the unkown service composition (the grey box).

The reliance introduced through the credit card payment process does not only justify adjusting the initial expectation value of the reliability trust upwards, but also directly influences the customer's decision criterion, as per equation 2. This equation reflects the level of protection the credit card provider offers for an interaction with a possibly fraudulent service. For our use case, we assume that the cost of the ordered good (this includes additional costs such as shipping & handling) is paid upfront through a credit card. This money is potentially lost in the interaction, it therefore represents $L_{candidate}$. The gain G is at least as high as $L_{candidate}$, otherwise it would be unreasonable to begin the transaction. The cost of claiming a credit card insurance is assumed to be negligible compared to the cost of the product, while the fixed costs of the insurance ($L_{insurer}^{fix}$) are covered via a sur-charge on shipping and handling levied by the service provider. Due to strong con-tractual agreements between the customer and the credit card company, the trust-worthiness of the credit card provider (expressed as $p_{insurer}$) can be practically assured. Assuming that $L_{candidate} = G$ and $p_{insurer} \approx 1$, the decision criterion for the use case thus becomes $EU := p_{composite} \cdot G - (1 - p_{composite}) \cdot (1 - p_{insurer}) \cdot G - L_{insurer}^{fix}$. For $p_{composite} \ll 1$, as would be the case when facing an unknown service, the expected utility is considerably higher for the insurance through credit card case than it would be without the insurance option. Thus, even under the risk of increasing the exploitation potential w.r.t. malicious service providers, reliance mechanisms still allow the customer to feel safe.

4.2   Simulation

In order to show the feasibility of the proposed mechanisms in a qualitative way, each was implemented in the agent-based simulation framework used in [7]. The basic CertainTrust trust model [22] was used for evaluating providers, using $E_{f=0.5,w=1,N=10}$. The decision criterion was expected utility, as outlined in the previous chapters, with *softmax* and a decaying temperature parameter. A consumer population of 250 agents was arrayed in a clustered social network (generated according to [10]), to serve as recommenders. The same basic configu-ration was used to test all mechanisms against a base case, solely using experience and witness recommendation to select providers. The market was started with 15 providers (5 with $0.8 < p_{candidate} \le 0.95$, 5 with $0.5 < p_{candidate} \le 0.8$ and 5 with $0 < p_{candidate} \le 0.5$) and ran for 800 rounds. At round 300, a new provider with $p_{candidate} = 0.95$ is added, in order to test the market entry performance of the different mechanisms. The objective is for the consumers to select the best provider by learning their trustworthiness.

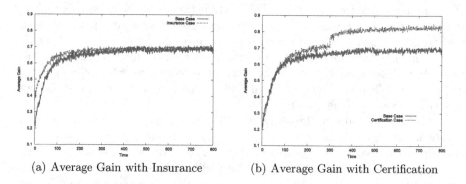

(a) Average Gain with Insurance   (b) Average Gain with Certification

Fig. 7. Agent-based Simulation Results for Insurance and Certification

Insurance. As figure 7(a) shows, over the entire simulation run, the perfor-mance of the insurance mechanism (measured as the averaged gain over all consumers) approaches the base case. Significantly better performance, as de-termined by a Wilcoxon rank-sum test (95 % confidence), was attained in the initial phase of the learning process, i.e., between timesteps 0 and 250. In this early phase, the *softmax* algorithm causes a higher exploration rate, thus leading to a higher proportion of untrustworthy providers with $p_{candidate} \leq 0.5$. Losses incurred are compensated by insurance providers, represented as randomly assigned agents with $0.5 < p_{insurer} \leq 0.95$.

Certification. The effects of certification (figure 7(b)) are complementary to the insurance case. While showing no improvement over the base case in the early rounds, it facilitates easier market entry for new providers with a high trustworthiness. The certification providers are assumed to be honest and certify conservatively ($q_{cert} = p_{candidate} - 0.1$). Certifier performance was learned using the CertainTrust trust model independently. The considerable improvement at timestep 300 is caused by the addition of the new, trustworthy provider, which is selected based on its certification, despite *softmax* already being highly exploitative.

Coalitions. Coalitions outperform the base case (figure 8) after initial exploration significantly. This is caused by trustworthy providers dissolving coalitions with less trustworthy ones, leading to highly selected coalitions of good providers. For this simulation, coalitions are formed with up to 2 other providers. Each provider in a coalition operates non-competitively from its associates, i.e., the simulation was run with three different provider populations of 15 providers each. Only one such market is plotted.

5 Related Work

Reputation and trust for eCommerce, as well as other fields, such as wireless routing, p2p networks or agentsystems, has been receiving considerable attention. An increasing number of survey articles attests to this ongoing interest, e.g., [6,11,24,25]. Typically, reputation-based trust models are driven by direct experience and witness recommendations [5,8,22]. In [12], the authors argue that comprehensive (reputation-based) trust management systems have to enable users

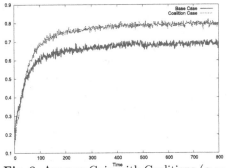

Fig. 8. Average Gain with Coalitions ($\alpha = 0.5$) Compared to Base Case

to assess providers reliably *and* that providers have to be given the chance to represent their trustworthiness. While the former has been the focus of much of the cited work, the latter still requires considerable efforts. Some trust models, such as FIRE [9], are modular to enable the integration of additional components, beyond experience and recommendations.

In [8], the authors address the exploration-vs-exploitation dilemma in trust-based service selection explicitly. This is, however, not done by incorporating additional information, but by analyzing temporal changes in provider behavior and adjusting random exploration accordingly.

Influences of reputation to the providers' amount of interactions have been shown in [21], exemplarily for eBay. The impact of reputation on revenue increases the attractiveness for attacks on reputation systems, leading to ongoing research in the design of robust reputation systems [14]. Incentivizing honest behavior has been directly linked to the ease with which providers can enter and leave a market [2,3,15].

Trust-based decision-making for eCommerce from a more user-centric perspective is formalized by [16]. They propose a conceptual framework to put trust, risk and their antecedents into context, lack however a computational integration.

6   Conclusions

We proposed three mechanism as indicators of trustworthiness for reputation-based trust metrics that influence the initial expectation of a customer towards a service. Each indicator has a distinct impact on the overall provider selection by consumer populations, allowing consumers to reduce their risk (insurance) and providers to represent their capabilities (certification and coalitions). By investing resources and staking reputation, service providers represent their commitment to a market, easing the service selection problem for the consumers. Future work will test the proposed and further indicators in a more comprehensive and quantitative manner, as well as investigating machine learning methods to predict trustworthy behavior based on (further) indicators. Empirical work on the positive and negative impact of certifications (e.g., [1]) is to be integrated into adapting initial expectations in the used trust model. Furthermore, specific trust-based exploration-vs-exploitation strategies will be integrated with indicators of trustworthiness.

Acknowledgments. The work presented in this paper was performed in the context of the Software-Cluster projects EMERGENT and InDiNet (www.software-cluster.org) and funded by the German Federal Ministry of Education and Research (BMBF) under grants no. "01IC10S01" and "01IC10S04". The authors assume responsibility for the content.

References

1. Edelman, B.: Adverse selection in online trust certifications. In: Proceedings of the 11th International Conference on Electronic Commerce, pp. 205–212. ACM (2009)
2. Feldman, M., Papadimitriou, C., Chuang, J., Stoica, I.: Free-riding and whitewashing in peer-to-peer systems. In: Proceedings of the ACM SIGCOMM Workshop on Practice and Theory of Incentives in Networked Systems, PINS 2004, pp. 228–236. ACM, New York (2004)
3. Friedman, E., Resnick, P.: The social cost of cheap pseudonyms. Ann Arbor 1001(2), 48109–1092 (1999)
4. Gambetta, D.: Can We Trust Trust? In: Gambetta, D. (ed.) Trust: Making and Breaking Cooperative Relations, pp. 213–237. Basil Blackwell, Oxford (1988)
5. Golbeck, J.: Computing and applying trust in web-based social networks. Doctoral thesis, University of Maryland (2005)
6. Grandison, T., Sloman, M.: A Survey of Trust in Internet Applications. IEEE Communications and Survey 3(4), 2–16 (2000)

7. Hauke, S., Pyka, M., Heider, D.: Towards Improved Trust Diffusion Through Active Recommender Propagation. In: 4th International Conference on Complex Distributed Systems (2010)
8. Hoogendoorn, M., Jaffry, S.W., Treur, J.: Incorporating Interdependency of Trust Values in Existing Trust Models for Trust Dynamics. In: Nishigaki, M., Jøsang, A., Murayama, Y., Marsh, S. (eds.) IFIPTM 2010. IFIP AICT, vol. 321, pp. 263–276. Springer, Heidelberg (2010)
9. Huynh, T.D.: Trust and Reputation in Open Multi-Agent Systems. PhD thesis, University of Southampton (2006)
10. Jin, E.M., Girvan, M., Newman, M.E.J.: Structure of growing social networks. Phys. Rev. E 64(4), 46132 (2001)
11. Jøsang, A., Ismail, R., Boyd, C.: A survey of Trust and Reputation Systems for Online Service Provision. Decision Support Systems 43(2), 618–644 (2007)
12. Jøsang, A., Keser, C., Dimitrakos, T.: Can We Manage Trust? In: Herrmann, P., Issarny, V., Shiu, S.C.K. (eds.) iTrust 2005. LNCS, vol. 3477, pp. 93–107. Springer, Heidelberg (2005)
13. Jøsang, A., Lo Presti, S.: Analysing the Relationship between Risk and Trust. In: Jensen, C., Poslad, S., Dimitrakos, T. (eds.) iTrust 2004. LNCS, vol. 2995, pp. 135–145. Springer, Heidelberg (2004)
14. Kerr, R., Cohen, R.: An Experimental Testbed for Evaluation of Trust and Reputation Systems. In: Ferrari, E., Li, N., Bertino, E., Karabulut, Y. (eds.) IFIPTM 2009. IFIP AICT, vol. 300, pp. 252–266. Springer, Heidelberg (2009)
15. Kerr, R., Cohen, R.: Trust as a Tradable Commodity: A Foundation for Safe Electronic Marketplaces. Computational Intelligence 26(2), 160–182 (2010)
16. Kim, D., Ferrin, D., Rao, H.: A trust-based consumer decision-making model in electronic commerce: The role of trust, perceived risk, and their antecedents. Decision Support Systems 44(2), 544–564 (2008)
17. Luce, R.D.: Utility of gains and losses: Measurement-theoretical and experimental approaches. Lawrence Erlbaum Associates Publishers, Mahwah (2000)
18. Marsh, S., Dibben, M.R.: Trust, Untrust, Distrust and Mistrust – An Exploration of the Dark(er) Side. In: Herrmann, P., Issarny, V., Shiu, S. (eds.) iTrust 2005. LNCS, vol. 3477, pp. 17–33. Springer, Heidelberg (2005)
19. McKnight, D.H., Chervany, N.L.: Trust and Distrust Definitions: One Bite at a Time. In: Falcone, R., Singh, M., Tan, Y.-H. (eds.) Trust in Cyber-societies. LNCS (LNAI), vol. 2246, pp. 27–54. Springer, Heidelberg (2001)
20. Pichler, R.: Trust and Reliance - Enforcement and Compliance: Enhancing Consumer Confidence in the Electronic Marketplace. Juridical sciences master, Stanford University (2000)
21. Resnick, P., Zeckhauser, R., Swanson, J., Lockwood, K.: The value of reputation on ebay: A controlled experiment. Experimental Economics 9, 79–101 (2003)
22. Ries, S.: Trust in Ubiquitous Computing. Doctoral thesis, TU Darmstadt (2009)
23. Ries, S., Habib, S.M., Mühlhäuser, M., Varadharajan, V.: CertainLogic: A Logic for Modeling Trust and Uncertainty (short paper). In: McCune, J.M., Balacheff, B., Perrig, A., Sadeghi, A.-R., Sasse, A., Beres, Y. (eds.) Trust 2011. LNCS, vol. 6740, pp. 254–261. Springer, Heidelberg (2011)
24. Sabater, J., Sierra, C.: Review on Computational Trust and Reputation Models. Artificial Intelligence Review 24, 33–60 (2005)
25. Wang, Y., Vassileva, J.: Toward trust and reputation based web service selection: A survey. International Transactions on Systems Science and Applications 3(2), 118–132 (2007)

Finding Trusted Publish/Subscribe Trees

Stephen Naicken, Ian Wakeman, and Dan Chalmers

Department of Informatics,
University of Sussex,
Brighton, UK
Initial.Lastname@sussex.ac.uk

Abstract. Publish/Subscribe systems assume that clients and brokers abide by the matching and forwarding protocols. Such an assumption implies implicit trust between all components of the system and has led to security issues being largely ignored. As publish/subscribe is increasingly used in applications where implicit trust can not be assumed, an approach is required to mitigate misbehaviour. We propose the construction and reconfiguration of the event forwarding topology, the publish/subscribe tree (PST), with respect to the trust requirements of the clients. The principal contribution of this paper is a trust metric for PSTs, which aggregates each client's trust evaluation of a PST to give a socially acceptable trust evaluation and allows for the ordering of PSTs. Additionally, we define the PST trust maximisation problem with overhead budget, which is solved by the PST that maximises trust within an overhead budget for a given advertisement. A tabu search based algorithm for this problem is presented and is shown to scale to large problem instances and give good approximations of the optimal solutions.

1 Introduction

Publish/Subscribe systems assume that brokers are implicitly trusted to correctly implement the matching and routing functions that are essential for the delivery of events from publishers to subscribers. Trust between clients (publishers and subscribers) and brokers is ensured by the presence of trusted administrative entities responsible for the event notification service (ENS) – the network of brokers responsible for propagation of events from publishers to subscribers – and external contracts between clients and administrative entities. Typically, publish/subscribe is used in application contexts where these mechanisms exist, for example news distribution services that are restricted to fee paying customers, but increasingly publish/subscribe is being utilised for applications where administrative entities and external contracts may not be present. In publish/subscribe based inter-networking, the scale and dynamicity of the network prohibit the use of external contracts, while mobile ad-hoc network publish/subscribe has the additional issue of the absence of an ENS under the aegis of trusted entities. These applications are vulnerable to misbehaviour that can disrupt communications, as mechanisms to ensure trust are absent.

T. Dimitrakos et al. (Eds.): IFIPTM 2012, IFIP AICT 374, pp. 174–190, 2012.

Motivated by research on the use of trust and reputation systems to safeguard Peer-to-Peer networks, this paper proposes a mechanism by which the publish subscribe tree (PST) that is used to distribute events from publishers and subscribers can be constructed and reconfigured to maximise the clients' trust of the PST. A trust metric for PSTs is defined that aggregates each and every client's trust evaluation of a PST in an equitable manner. Following from Rawls' difference principle, given a set of PSTs, the metric deems the most trusted PST to be the one that maximises the lowest trust opinion held by any client. The PST trust metric is used to define the PST Trust Maximisation problem with overhead budgets, which is solved by the PST that maximises trust within a prescribed overhead budget. An exhaustive search and tabu search algorithm to solve this problem are presented and evaluated. By maintaining, a PST that maximises trust given the clients' trust opinions, the PST is less vulnerable to misbehaviour and consequently service disruption. Brokers that are deemed by clients to be untrustworthy will be not be included in the initial PST construction or will be likely ejected upon PST reconfiguration.

The remainder of this paper is structured as follows. In section 2, the PST is defined and a PST overhead metric is presented. Section 3 details the trust metric for PSTs. The aggregation is underpinned by Rawls' difference principle to ensure that the aggregation is equitable to all clients. The definition of the PST trust maximisation problem with overhead budget (MTPSTO) is given in section 4. In section 5, an algorithm using the tabu search metaheuristic to solve the MTPSTO problem is presented. Finally, section 6 describes the evaluation of the tabu search algorithm with particular emphasis on the comparison of the results with those of an exhaustive search algorithm.

2   Publish/Subscribe Trees

2.1   Definition of Publish/Subscribe Trees

In publish/subscribe systems, publishers issue advertisements to the ENS that express their intent to publish events consisting of particular content (e.g. Java tutorial books for sale that are less than ten pounds). Subscribers submit subscriptions (e.g. Java tutorial books for sale) that express their interest to receive specific events to the ENS. Should a subscription match an advertisement owned by a given publisher, the ENS must ensure that matching events issued by this publisher are delivered to the interested subscriber.

As the ENS is a network of interconnected brokers, a forwarding topology is required that allows for the dissemination of events from publishers to subscribers. The topology is typically an acyclic graph, so it can be modelled as a tree. Definition 1 defines this tree as a publish/subscribe tree (PST). It exists in the context of an advertisement. For each advertisement, there is a PST that is rooted at publisher of the advertisement and spans a subset of brokers and all interested subscribers.

PSTs can also be used to model ad-hoc network publish/subscribe where there is no ENS and both brokers and subscribers may be responsible for the matching and forwarding of events. In this context, the set of internal nodes of a PST can include subscribers.

Definition 1 (Publish Subscribe Tree (PST)). *Given an undirected connected connectivity graph $G = (V, E)$, a publisher p such that $p \in V$, an advertisement A_p held by publisher p, a set of subscribers $S_{A_p} = \{s \mid sf_s(A_p) = true \wedge s \in V \setminus \{p\}\}$ where sf_s is the subscription function of s, and a set of routers $R_{A_p} = V \setminus (S_{A_p} \cap \{p\})$ is the set of candidate router nodes. A PST T_{A_p} for the advertisement A_p is a tree routed at p that spans all subscribers in S_{A_p} and a subset of R_{a_p} nodes where all $r \in R_{a_p}$ can not be a terminal node of the PST and for all $s \in S_{a_p}$, s may be either a branch node or a terminal node of the PST.*

2.2   Publish/Subscribe Overheads

PST construction with respect to overhead costs was first considered by Huang and Garcia-Molina in the context of publish/subscribe in wireless ad-hoc networks [8]. They define three types of subscription: inherent subscription; effective subscription; proxied subscription. The inherent subscription s_i of a subscriber i is given by its subscription function sf_i. The effective subscription S_i of a subscriber i is given by the disjunction of its inherent subscription s_i and its proxied subscription s_i', $S_i = s_i \vee s_i'$. The proxied subscription s_i' of a subscriber i is given by $s_i' = \bigcup_{j=1,\dots,n} S_j$ for each child $1, \dots, n$ of i. The overhead metric is defined with respect to these subscription types in definition 2.

Definition 2 (Publish/Subscribe Tree Overhead). *The overhead of a PST T, $C_T(E)$ is $O_T(E) = \sum_i O_{T_i}(E)$ where E is the set of events to be published and $O_{T_i}(E)$ is the overhead of receiving, processing and forwarding the events in E at node i of T. The overhead O_{T_i} at a node i, is given by $O_{T_i}(E) = (r + f) \cdot \Phi E(\neg s_i \wedge s_i') + f \cdot \Phi E(s_i \wedge s_i')$ where s_i is the subscription function at node i, s_i' is the proxied subscription of i, and $\Phi E(\alpha)$ gives the number of events from the set E that match the subscription function α.*

3   Theory

The aim of this section is to show how PSTs can be compared in terms of the trust imbued in the tree by different participants. A generalised trust metric that combines trust values of the nodes on a path, and allows for discrimination of the trust of two disparate paths, is given. Subsequently, the relationships between the participants in a PST are identified, leading to a natural formulation of the problem as an analysis of the trust within and between different paths for a given individual participant. Having defined a means for participants to order their preferences for different PSTs, the problem of how to aggregate these orderings is addressed by the use of social choice theory, albeit with a caveat about the comparability of trust functions.

3.1   Definition of Trust

Trust is "the firm belief in the competence of an entity to act dependably, securely and reliably within a specified context" [7]. The competence of a trustee is dependent upon a variety of trust sources with their importance to trust evaluation dependent upon the trustor. Vector-based trust models have been proposed that aggregate a vector of trust sources to give a single trust opinion of an entity [19]. A generalisation of this model is defined as follows and is used in this work.

Definition 3. *(Trust Vector) A trust vector is a d-dimensional real-valued vector $\Lambda_{i,j}^{\eta} = [\lambda_{i,j_1}^{\eta}, \lambda_{i,j_2}^{\eta}, \ldots, \lambda_{i,j_d}^{\eta}]$ such that for each λ_{i,j_n}^{η} is a real value, each representing a different property of trust, such as reputation, within some context η. $\Lambda_{i,j}^{\eta}$ is the trust vector representing i's trust opinion of j within some context η.*

Definition 4. *(Individual Trust Function) For each individual $i \in N$, i has a trust function $\tau_i : \mathbb{R}^d \to \mathbb{R}$ which is a mapping of trust vectors to trust values. Given a pair of individuals i and j, a trust vector $\Lambda_{i,j}^{\eta}$, $\tau_i(\Lambda_{i,j}^{\eta})$ is a real value representing i's trust in j within the context η.*

3.2   Trustworthiness of Paths

Using previous work on semiring-based trust models [23], we define our trust algebra as the set S, with two binary operators, $\oplus$ and $\otimes$. S contains the individual entities, with the level of trust. The $\otimes$ operator combines the entities into a path and returns the level of trust of that path, whilst the $\oplus$ operator compares paths and picks out the path with the maximum trust. We assume that $\oplus$ is commutative, and that $\otimes$ is distributive over $\oplus$, and further that there is a partial order over the operators such that $a \leq a' \wedge b \leq b' \Rightarrow a \oplus b \leq a' \oplus b' \wedge a \otimes b \leq a' \otimes b'$.

Mathematically inclined readers may note that we have defined an ordered semiring. An example of such an algebra is the trusted path definitions adopted by Marti and Garcia-Molina in [12], an instantiation of which is given in definition 5. We will be using this instantiation, but results remain valid for any other valid instantiation.

Definition 5. *(Trusted Path Semiring) The trusted path semiring is a semiring, $(S, \oplus, \otimes)$ where $S = [0, 1]$ and $\oplus$ and $\otimes$ are defined as:*

$$\text{for all } s_1, s_2 \in S, \; s_1 \oplus s_2 = max(s_1, s_2)$$
$$\text{for all } s_1, s_2 \in S, \; s_1 \otimes s_2 = s_1 s_2$$

Example 1. (**Example Use of Trusted Path Semiring**) Let σ_1 be a simple path, $\sigma_1 = (v_1, v_2), (v_2, v_3), \ldots, (v_{n-1}, v_n)$, where v_1 and v_{n+1} are the start and end vertex of the path, respectively. The trust v_1 has in σ_1 is given by $\tau(v_1, v_2) \otimes \tau(v_1, v_3) \otimes \ldots \otimes \tau(v_1, v_{n+1})$ where $\tau : V \times V \to S$ and gives the trust that one vertex has in another, represented by values from the set S of the semiring. Additionally, given p alternative simple paths from v_0 to v_{n+1}, the most trusted one is given by $\tau_{\sigma_1} \oplus \tau_{\sigma_2} \oplus \ldots \oplus \tau_{\sigma_p} = max(\tau_{\sigma_1}, \tau_{\sigma_2}, \ldots, \tau_{\sigma_p})$.

3.3   Individual Trust Evaluation Functions for PSTs

Using the individual trust function (def. 4) and the trusted path semiring (def. 5), the clients' trustworthiness of a PST can be defined. The relationships between publishers, internal subscribers and terminal subscribers are identified and evaluated using the aforementioned methods to give individual trust functions for these types of clients. The definitions below define how the trustworthiness of a PST is evaluated by the publisher, the internal subscribers and the terminal subscribers.

Publisher PST Trust Evaluation Function. The publisher has a contract to send events to each subscriber in the PST and has no preference over these subscribers. To ensure delivery of these events, the trust function should maximise the trustworthiness of each path to the subscribers. The publisher trust function aggregates the trust of each path to each subscriber in the PST. Where the publisher is adjacent to a subscriber, the trust value of the path is 1, as all notifications are sent directly to the subscriber.

Definition 6. *(Publisher PST Trust) Let $T = (V, E)$ be a PST, where $V = S \cup R \cup \{p\}$ for a publisher p, set of subscribers S and set of routers R, and let α be some aggregation function, $\alpha : \mathbb{R}^{|S|} \longrightarrow \mathbb{R}$. For each $s \in S$, there is a path $\sigma_{p,s} = \{p, \ldots, s\}$, a vertex sequence with initial vertex p, final vertex s and if $|\sigma_{p,s}| > 2$, it has intermediate vertices $\{v_1, v_2, \ldots, v_{|\sigma_{p,s}|-2}\}$, and whose trustworthiness is given by:*

$$\tau_p(\sigma_{p,s}) = \tau_p(\Lambda^\eta_{p,v_1}) \otimes \tau_p(\Lambda^\eta_{p,v_2}) \otimes \cdots \otimes \tau_p(\Lambda^\eta_{p,v_{|\sigma|-1}}) \tag{1}$$

The trust of T for p is a function of the trust of the paths to each subscriber and is given by:

$$\tau_p(T) = \alpha(\tau_p(\sigma_{p,s_1}), \tau_p(\sigma_{p,s_2}), \ldots, \tau_p(\sigma_{p,s_{|S|}})) \tag{2}$$

Terminal Subscriber PST Evaluation Function. Terminal subscribers receive events forwarded on the path from the publisher. Their trust in the PST is determined exclusively by the trust of this path. If the subscriber is adjacent to the publisher, its trust value of the path is 1, as it trusts the publisher to receive its events.

Definition 7. *(Terminal Subscriber PST Trust) Let $T = (V, E)$ be a PST, where $V = S \cup R \cup \{p\}$ for a publisher p, set of subscribers S and set of routers R. For each subscriber $s \in S$ such that s is a terminal of T and $\sigma_{s,p} = \{s, \ldots, p\}$ is a path in T with initial vertex s to terminal vertex p and if $|\sigma_{s,p}| > 2$ with intermediate vertices $\{v_1, v_2, \ldots, v_{|\sigma_{s,p}|-2}\}$, then the the trust of s in T is given by:*

$$\tau_s(T) = \tau_s(\Lambda^\eta_{s,v_1}) \otimes \tau_s(\Lambda^\eta_{s,v_2}) \otimes \cdots \otimes \tau_s(\Lambda^\eta_{s,v_{|\sigma_{s,p}|-1}}) \tag{3}$$

Internal Subscriber PST Evaluation Function. An internal subscriber receives events on the path from the publisher and forwards them to subscribers in the sub-tree of which it is the root. The node holds both the roles of terminal subscriber and publisher, so its trust function is a function of the trust to the publisher and the trustworthiness of the paths to each subscribers in its sub-tree.

Definition 8. *(Internal Subscriber PST Trust) Let $T = (V, E)$ be a PST, where $V = S \cup R \cup \{p\}$ for a publisher p, set of subscribers S and set of routers R. For each subscriber $s \in S$ such that s is an internal node, there is a path $\sigma_{s,p} = s, \ldots, p$ where s is the initial vertex, p is the final vertex and with intermediate vertices $\{v_1, v_2, \ldots, v_{|\sigma_{s,p}|-2}\}$ if $|\sigma_{s,p}| > 2$. The trust of the $\sigma_{s,p}$ is given by:*

$$\tau_s(\sigma_{s,p}) = \tau_s(\Lambda^\eta_{s,v_1}) \otimes \tau_s(\Lambda^\eta_{s,v_2}) \otimes \cdots \otimes \tau_s(\Lambda^\eta_{s,v_{|\sigma|-1}}) \tag{4}$$

Additionally, for each $s \in S$ such that s is an internal node, let $T_s = (V_s, E_s)$ be the sub-tree rooted at s. For each $s' \in (S \setminus s) \cap V_s$, there is a path $\sigma_{s,s'} = \{s, \ldots, s'\}$ that has initial vertex s, final vertex s', and intermediate vertices $\{v_1, v_2, \ldots, v_{|\sigma_{s,s'}|-2}\}$. The trust of the path $\sigma_{s,s'}$ is given by:

$$\tau_s(\sigma_{s,s'}) = \tau_s(\Lambda^\eta_{s,v_1}) \otimes \tau_s(\Lambda^\eta_{s,v_{|\sigma|-1}}) \otimes \tau_s(\Lambda^\eta_{s,s'}) \tag{5}$$

For each internal subscribe node s in a PST T, the trust of s in T is given by:

$$\tau_s(T) = \beta(\tau_s(\sigma_{s,p}), \tau_s(\sigma_{s,s'_1}), \ldots, \tau_s(\sigma_{s,s'_{d-1}})) \tag{6}$$

where $\beta : \mathbb{R}^d \longrightarrow \mathbb{R}$ is some aggregation function of trust values, and $d = |V_s \cap S| + 1$.

3.4   PST Trust Evaluation Function

Social Choice and Welfare Preliminaries. Social choice theory is the study of the specification of preferences, their motivating utilities, and the aggregation mechanisms of individual preferences to a socially acceptable preference. Here it is used to address the following problems: the aggregation of the trust evaluation of paths to give a client's trust evaluation of a PST; and the aggregation of the clients' PST trust evaluation functions to give the trustworthiness of a PST.

Sen [21] shows that if we can assign utility values to the preferences, and that the utilities are comparable between individuals, then a choice function is usable. As in nearly all other work building on trust preferences, we must assume that the utility of our trust preferences can be compared, both in deciding which individual is worse off (*ordinal level comparability*), and how much one gains when another loses (*cardinal level comparability*).

Rather than adopt a utilitarian approach to determining the most trusted PST, the PST that maximises the trustworthiness of the least well-off node is dominates the trust metric. This is motivated by Rawls' difference principle [18], which states that social and economic inequalities satisfy the condition that they are to be to the greatest benefit of the least advantaged members of society.

Definition 9. *(Individual Evaluation Function) An individual utility function is a real-valued function to the set of alternatives C for an individual i, $u_i : C \to \mathbb{R}$.*

Definition 10. *(Leximin Social Welfare Functional) Let $i(x)$ be the ith worst-off individual under the alternative x, that is there is a subset $M \subset N$ where $|C| = i - 1$ individuals such that for all $c \in C$, $u_i(x) \geq u_c(x)$. For any given pair of alternatives $x, y \in C$, xPy if and only if there is an $i \in N$ such that:*

1. *$u_{i(x)}(x) > u_{i(y)}(y)$; and*
2. *$u_{c(x)}(x) = u_{c(y)}(y)$ where $c \in \{n : n \in N \land u_i(x) \geq u_n(x)\}$.*

If $\forall i \in N. u_{i(x)}(x) = u_{i(x)}(x)$ then xIy.

Aggregation of Path Trust Evaluations in Individual PST Trust Functions. The aggregation functions α and β in definitions 6 and 8, are the leximin aggregation function given in definition 11 and the minimum aggregation function, respectively. As d - the number of paths - is variable across PSTs, for internal subscribers, β can not make use of analytical leximin aggregation (definition 11). The motivation for the choice of these aggregations is to allow a client's trust in a PST to be dominated by the least trustworthy path. Consider an internal subscriber in a PST with paths of very high trust, except for a path of low trust to a terminal subscriber. There is more risk of malicious behaviour on this path and the terminal is undeservedly punished in favour of others, as all subscribers should be treated equitably. This is a scenario our metric attempts to avoid.

PST Trust Evaluation Function. The social ordering of PSTs must improve the well-being of the least well-off with respect to trust, so it follows that the leximin social welfare functional is used, since it is assumed that all nodes are to be treated equally. Rather than implement the leximin social welfare function as one of pairwise comparisons, an analytical leximin function (def. 11) is used. This allows PSTs to be ordered by their trust values and a combinatorial optimisation problem that maximises the trust value of the PST for a given advertisement to be defined. Unfortunately, its use is not without issue, as it requires cardinal full comparability and it is, at the least, questionable if trust functions comply with this property.

Definition 11. *(Analytical Leximin Aggregation) The analytical leximin aggregation operator, $F_{leximin}$, is an ordered weighted average where each $a_i \in [0, 1]$ and the weight vector $W = [w_1, \ldots, w_{n-2}, w_{n-1}, w_n]$ is defined as follows:*

$$w_1 = \frac{\Delta^{n-1}}{(1 + \Delta)^{n-1}},$$

$$w_j = \frac{\Delta^{n-j}}{(1 + \Delta)^{n+1-j}} \text{ for all } 2 \leq j \leq n.$$

If $|a - b| < \Delta$ then $a = b$. If $a > b$ then $|a - b| > \Delta$.

Definition 12. *(Socially Trusted PST Aggregation)* Let $t = (V_t, E_t)$ be a PST where $V_t = S \cup R \cup \{p\}$. For each $i \in S \cup \{p\}$, there is a real-value $\tau_i(T)$ representing i's trust value of t. The social trust value of t is given by $F_{leximin}(\tau_{i_1}(T), \tau_{i_2}(T), \ldots, \tau_{i_{|S \cup \{p\}|}}(T))$.

4   The Problem

4.1   The PST Trust Maximisation Problem with Overhead Budget

Given this definition of aggregated social trust, we are now in a position to formally define the problem of maximising the trust of a Publish/Subscribe Tree that meets an overhead budget in terms of the cost of its links - the PST Trust Maximisation Problem with Overhead Budget (MTPSTO):

Problem 1 (The MTPSTO problem). Given an overhead budget $B > 0$, an event distribution E, an undirected connectivity graph $G_c = (V_c, E_c)$, a publisher p that holds an advertisement A_p, a set of subscribers $S = \{s \mid sf_s(A_p) = true\}$ where sf_s is the subscription function of s, a set of routers $R = V_c \setminus C$ where $C = \{p\} \cup S$, find a PST T that is rooted at p, spans C and maximises the trust value $\tau(T) = F_{leximin}(\tau_{c_1}(T), \ldots, \tau_{c_{|C|}}(T))$ where $\tau_{c_i}(T)$ is the trust evaluation of ith node in C, subject to $O_T(Ev) \leq B$.

The MTPSTO decision problem is shown to be in NP-hard by a polynomial time reduction from the Minimum Overhead PST Problem [2] and in NP by a polynomial time verification algorithm. We omit the proof due to space constraints.

5   The Algorithm

To solve the MTPSTO problem, an exhaustive search algorithm of all possible PSTs is presented. The algorithm must calculate the trust value and the overhead value of every PST in the connectivity graph $G_c = (V_c, E_c)$ that is rooted at the publisher p and spans all subscribers S, for an advertisement A_p. The set of all PSTs for A_p is a subset of the set of all Steiner trees in G_c that span p and S. Using this property and the fact that the set of all Steiner trees in G_c is given by the enumeration of all spanning trees in G_c and all its sub-graphs, the algorithm must find all the spanning trees in G_c and all its sub-graphs that are also feasible PSTs. Note that graphs and sub-graphs with router vertices with only one adjacent edge are ignored, as all spanning trees found will not be PSTs. The router will be a terminal node in every PST that spans the graph and this contradicts the definition of a PST.

5.1   Spanning Tree Enumeration

A number of algorithms have been proposed to solve the problem of enumerating all spanning trees of a graph. Backtracking-based techniques have $\mathcal{O}(m+n+mt)$

[14] and $\mathcal{O}(m+n+nt)$ [5] complexity for undirected graphs, where t is the number of spanning trees. Prior to the these techniques, Char [3] proposed an algorithm that lexicographically tests sub-graphs to determine if each is a spanning tree, and although a complexity analysis was not given, it was later shown to be of $\mathcal{O}(m + n + n(t + t_0))$ complexity where t_0 is the number of sub-graphs found that are not spanning trees [9]. Char's algorithm is shown to be more suitable for enumerating PSTs, as the spanning tree test of a sub-graph can be modified to determine if it is a PST.

5.2   Approximation through Tabu Search

A number of approaches to the Steiner problem in graphs that use the tabu search metaheuristic have been proposed [20] [6]. The Ribeiro and De Souza [20] approach finds solutions that are better than the Takahashi-Matsuyama heuristic [22] and F-tabu [6]. Given the relationship between Steiner trees and PSTs, and the successful use of tabu search to solve the Steiner problem, this metaheuristic is explored as means to solve the MTPSTO problem.

PST Tabu Move Selection and Evaluation. Similar to the move structure defined in [20], a tabu search move is defined as the addition or removal of a broker node from the PST. As is the case with Steiner trees, there is a subset of nodes that must always be included in the vertex set of the tree, these are the publisher node and the subscriber nodes. It follows that only the combination of broker nodes is variable, hence the choice of move structure. For insertion moves, a broker node and its edges (from the connectivity graph), which are adjacent to nodes in the PST, are added to the PST. For removal moves, a broker is removed from the PST and every edge in the connectivity graph between pairs of nodes in the PST are added to the PST.

In tabu search, the application of a move to an current PST solution gives a new solution, however the application of a move to a PST gives a sub-graph of the connectivity graph. To address this, the modified spanning tree algorithm (section 5.1) is used to find all PST in the sub-graph. Each PST is evaluated for its trust and overhead value. The PST that maximises trust and is below budget is then selected as the tree that is derived as a result of the application of the move to the current PST solution. If no tree is under budget, the one with the highest trust value is chosen.

Penalty Function. Tabu search is designed for minimisation and maximisation combinatorial problems without constraints, however the MTPSTO problem has an overhead budget constraint within which trust is maximised. Although a Near Feasibility Threshold (NFT) technique [11] was investigated, superior results were obtained with a static penalty function. In this approach, all over-budget PSTs are penalised by increasing the trust value by 50%.

Diversification Strategy. Takahashi and Matsuyama [22] present a Steiner tree heuristic that can easily be modified to find a Steiner tree that is a PST.

The modifications required is to stipulate that the subscribers and the publisher are the Steiner nodes. After every n iterations of the tabu search algorithm or when there are no moves for the tabu search to exploit, the diversification method is invoked.

Surrogate Objective Function. Each move when applied to a PST gives a number new solutions that must be evaluated for their trust and overhead values (objective values). Evaluation of each move can become costly as the size of the problem instance increases. To address this, the use of a surrogate evaluation function is proposed that estimates the trust value of solutions derived from a move. Moves that are likely to not result in an improvement over the current solution are discarded. The solutions derived from the smaller moves set are then fully evaluated for exact objective values.

A greedy approach is adopted for the surrogate objective function, as it attempts to maximise the improvement to the least well-off node. Given the subgraph G_{mod} that is induced by the application of a move m to the current PST solution, T_{PST}, the surrogate objective value is given by the most trusted path between the node with the least trust in T_{PST} and the publisher, p. Due to the fact that a semiring-based trust model for path trust is used, it is possible to to use the generic shortest distance algorithm algorithm defined in [23] to find the most trusted path between two nodes.

Tabu Search Algorithm for MTPSTO. The tabu search algorithm for the MTPSTO begins by using the diversification method to find the initial PST solution and setting to the current solution. Its objective value is evaluated and the tabu search iterates until the maximum number of iterations without an improvement in the objective value is met. During each iteration, first the set of moves is established by determining the routers that can be added and removed from the PST. Moves that are in the tabu list are discarded. Using the surrogate objective function, the move set is further reduced to the best estimated insertion and removal moves. The modified Char spanning tree algorithm is used to enumerate all PSTs resulting from the application of the moves in the move set to the current solution. These PSTs are then evaluated for their trust and overhead values. The PST with the highest trust value and lowest overheads is selected as the new current solution. If it is also better than the existing best solution found by the algorithm so far, then it is set as the new best solution. The move that yields the new current solution is marked is places in the tabu list and will not be available for selection for a given number of iterations.

6   Evaluation

In this section, an evaluation of the exhaustive search and the tabu search algorithms for the MTPSTO problem are presented. The evaluation is concerned with two properties, the quality of the solutions found and the running times of the algorithm. Solution quality is given by the relative error of the trust and overhead values with respect to the optimal solution.

The algorithms were implemented using Java and are dependent upon two third-party libraries, the Java Universal Network/Graph Framework (JUNG) (ver. 2.01) and the OpenTS library (ver. 1.0-exp10). JUNG is a framework for the modelling, analysis and manipulation of graphs. The OpenTS library provides a tabu search framework that is used as the basis of the implementations of the tabu search algorithms.

Each experiment was executed five times and the running times given in the results tables are averages over these executions unless stated otherwise. Experiments were performed on Amazon EC2 using a High-Memory Extra Large instance (m2.xlarge). The instance has 17.1 Gb of RAM, two virtual cores with 3.25 EC2 Compute Units reported as two 2.67 GHz Intel Xeon X5550 CPUs by cat /proc/cpuinfo, and 420 Gb of instance storage. Amazon Linux AMI 64-bit with Linux kernel 2.6.35.11 was the chosen operating system and the Java runtime environment used was IcedTea6 1.9.1. The only option passed to the Java virtual machine was to set the maximum heap size to 16 Gb, -Xmx16G. The choice of this evaluation environment was motivated by the high memory requirements of the exhaustive search algorithm. To ensure fair comparability of the running times, the same instance type was used for the tabu search algorithm, despite its lower memory usage.

6.1   Evaluation Test Data Sets

The test data sets are comprised of problem instances varying in $|R|$, as the primary objective is to analyse the proposed algorithms with respect to connectivity graphs of increasing sizes in both V and E_c. The graph density of all problem instances is approximately equal to 0.5. By increasing the number of routers in each problem and maintaining constant graph density, the test data sets allow for the evaluation of algorithms with respect to problems of increasing complexity, as both the number of possible moves at each iteration of the tabu search and the dominant factor of the PST enumeration algorithm $n(t + t_1)$ increase. For all problems, the cardinality of the set of subscribers, S, is 5.

Test data sets are made of subsets of five problems, each problem sharing identical parameters other than the value of the overhead budget, B. Each problem is identified by an identifier in the following format, <Problem Data set><Subset Number>-<Problem Number> where <Problem Data set> is the data set identifier (A and B), <Subset Number> indicates the value of $|R|$ for all problem instances in the subset, and <Problem Number> is the problem identifier where $1 \implies B = 2000, 2 \implies B = 3000, 3 \implies B = 4000, 4 \implies B = 5000$ and $5 \implies B = 2^{31} - 1$ (Java's largest maximum integer). The values chosen for B exclude 1000 as there is no optimal PST solution with an overhead value that is less than or equal to 1000 for problems where the optimal solution is known. No budgets are considered where $5000 < B < 2^{31} - 1$, as all optimal solutions found where $B = 2^{31} - 1$ are identical to those where $B = 5000$. The choice of $B = 2^{31} - 1$ is so that the algorithms can find the most trusted PST within the largest permitted integer overhead budget.

Problem set A consists of problems where $1 \leq |R| \leq 9$. Set A is the only problem set where optimal solutions are available for comparison to those found by the tabu search algorithms, as for larger problems, the running times of the exhaustive search are excessive. Problem set B consists of problems where $20 \leq |R| \leq 100$. Although no exact solutions known for these problems, the results are useful for evaluating the scalability of the tabu search algorithm.

6.2   Results

Table 1 shows the execution times of the exhaustive search for each subset of problems in problem set A. The average times given are those of the five algorithm runs for each subset of problems, except for A9 where this was impractical. Each experiment run finds the solutions where the overhead budget is 2000, 3000, 4000, 5000, and $2^{31} - 1$. For problem subsets A0 to A4, the exhaustive search executes quickly, however, there is an order of magnitude difference in the execution time with the addition of an additional router to problems subsets A5 and A8. The timings exhibit non-linear growth, which is to be expected, as the problem under consideration is in NP-Complete. Given the execution time of the exhaustive search for problem A9, attempts to solve larger problems were not attempted.

Table 1. Execution Times of Exhaustive Search Results for Problem Set A

Pr.	Min. (s)	Max. (s)	Avg. (s)
A0	0.0153	0.0871	0.0339
A1	0.0239	0.1522	0.058
A2	0.1238	0.3774	0.1852
A3	0.8051	1.2791	0.9304
A4	1.7682	2.4166	1.9041
A5	19.5833	20.212	19.7224
A6	285.8669	287.4492	286.3381
A7	945.8277	949.9657	947.4963
A8	6149.868	6164.197	6158.712
A9	97672.93	97672.93	N/A

Tables 2 and 3 give the results for the tabu search algorithms for problem sets A and B, respectively. The running times for problem subsets A1 to A4 are inferior to those of the exhaustive search. For problem subset A5 and above, the tabu search outperforms the exhaustive search algorithm with respect to execution time. For only seven problems in problem set A, the tabu search does not find the exact solution. Of these, four have negligible error to the optimal solution in the trust value of the PST. The average relative error in the overhead costs is 0.1148.

For problem set B, no exact solutions are available due to these problem instances being of too large for an exhaustive search. However, the results show that even for large problem instances, the tabu search algorithm is capable of finding solutions in running times that are considerably faster than those of the exhaustive search. The slowest time, 88.44s for problem B30-4, is some three times faster than that of an exhaustive search for problem instance consisting of six routers.

In conclusion, it has been shown that the tabu search scales to large problem instances with running times comparable to those of the exhaustive search algorithm for significantly smaller instances. The results for problem set A have demonstrated that the tabu search is capable of finding good approximation solutions.

7   Discussion

For a PST to form, the subscribers and routers must trust the publisher, so it is natural to devolve responsibility for the creation and selection of the PST to the publisher. Our protocol thus degenerates to the collection of trust vectors by the publisher for the candidate nodes in the tree, the execution of the tabu search algorithm, and finally the notification of the selected nodes of their roles and routing tables.

We have provided a formal definition of how trust can be used to evaluate the worth of a PST, dependent upon position, and under the assumption of full cardinal comparability of the trust metrics. Using this metric and existing work on PST overheads, we have shown how to derive optimal and near-optimal trees which maximise trust and meet a link cost budget. Under what circumstances does this assumption hold?

Trust can be formed using a number of trust sources, but typically in the literature, it is a function of reputation. In a given application context, such as a P2P file sharing system, users may have different perceptions of identical behaviour. Some may tolerate corrupted file downloads more than others, and in this scenario may rate identical transactions differently. For example, in Eigentrust [10], a given user i downloads a corrupted file from a user k and rates the transaction as -1, but a user j may download the same file from k and rates the transaction as 0, perhaps due to having a higher tolerance of malicious behaviour. When calculating trust values, it is therefore not possible to state that nodes i and j holding trust values of 0.7 in some entities are comparable, as their perceptions and understanding of trust and consequently their trust ratings of others differ.

Even when two entities have the same understanding of trust, they may assign different values to to trustees. This also applies to the trust valuations of alternatives under consideration. If the trust continuum is the unit interval, ordinal level comparability feasible, as an alternative can be rated as trusted, untrusted and indifferent or uncertain (a distinction can not be made), but the presence of an origin alone does not imply cardinal full comparability, a scale is required too. Trust can not, when represented using quantitatively, be inter-personally

Table 2. Solutions for Problem Set A using the Tabu Search algorithm

Pr	PST		Rel. Error		Sec
	τ_T	O_T	η_τ	η_O	
A1-2	0.0181	2398	-	-	3.01
A1-3	0.0181	2398	-	-	3.02
A1-4	0.0181	2398	-	-	3.01
A1-5	0.0181	2398	-	-	3.00
A2-1	0.0931	1850	-	-	8.44
A2-2	0.0931	1850	-	-	8.49
A2-3	0.0931	1850	-	-	8.40
A2-4	0.0931	1850	-	-	8.37
A2-5	0.0931	1850	-	-	8.36
A3-2	0.0224	2917	-	-	11.12
A3-3	0.0224	2917	-	-	11.12
A3-4	0.0224	2917	-	-	11.03
A3-5	0.0224	2917	-	-	11.06
A4-2	0.1855	2224	-	-	7.28
A4-3	0.1855	2224	-	-	7.21
A4-4	0.1855	2224	-	-	7.20
A4-5	0.1855	2224	-	-	7.21
A5-2	0.0542	2262	-	-	13.63
A5-3	0.0812	3580	-	0.1202	8.26
A5-4	0.0812	3580	-	0.1202	8.24
A5-5	0.0812	3580	-	0.1202	8.22
A6-3	0.0360	3846	-	-	139.19
A6-4	0.0360	3846	5×10^{-7}	0.1287	138.96
A6-5	0.0360	3846	5×10^{-7}	0.1287	127.22
A7-2	0.0692	3570	-	-	70.95
A7-3	0.0692	3570	-	-	72.92
A7-4	0.0692	3570	-	-	78.38
A8-3	0.0031	3657	-	-	9.77
A8-4	0.0031	3657	1×10^{-6}	0.0928	9.77
A8-5	0.0031	3657	1×10^{-6}	0.0928	9.82
A9-1	0.2184	1885	-	-	20.39
A9-2	0.2184	1885	-	-	14.69
A9-3	0.2184	1885	-	-	20.55
A9-4	0.2184	1885	-	-	20.49
A9-5	0.2184	1885	-	-	20.51

Table 3. Solutions for Problem Set B using the Tabu Search algorithm

Pr	τ_T	PST O_T	Sec	Pr	τ_T	PST O_T	Sec
B20-1	0.1210	2948	42.00	B30-1	0.1329	2234	57.19
B20-2	0.1210	2948	41.97	B30-2	0.1329	2234	61.82
B20-3	0.1210	3254	36.33	B30-3	0.1329	2234	72.58
B20-4	0.1210	3254	33.76	B30-4	0.1329	2234	88.44
B20-5	0.1210	3254	33.73	B30-5	0.1329	2234	84.46
B40-1	0.0245	2564	56.52	B50-1	0.0124	2224	18.96
B40-2	0.0245	2564	60.04	B50-2	0.0124	2224	18.87
B40-3	0.0245	2564	50.73	B50-3	0.0124	2224	18.70
B40-4	0.0245	2564	50.77	B50-4	0.0124	2224	19.70
B40-5	0.0245	2564	50.81	B50-5	0.0124	2224	19.96
B60-1	0.0661	1630	9.86	B70-1	0.0381	2838	30.00
B60-2	0.0661	1630	9.98	B70-2	0.0381	2838	29.99
B60-3	0.0661	1630	9.82	B70-3	0.0381	2838	46.44
B60-4	0.0661	1630	9.89	B70-4	0.0381	2838	46.77
B60-5	0.0661	1630	9.91	B70-5	0.0381	2838	45.85
B80-1	0.1320	1962	17.84	B90-1	0.0354	1282	11.56
B80-2	0.1320	1962	13.54	B90-2	0.0354	1282	11.59
B80-3	0.1320	1962	13.56	B90-3	0.0354	1282	11.59
B80-4	0.1320	1962	13.55	B90-4	0.0354	1282	11.57
B80-5	0.1320	1962	13.57	B90-5	0.0354	1282	11.57

comparable, unless there is agreement about the meaning of the scale of trust metrics, i.e. is there must be an accepted definition of a unit of trust.

But we do not form a single PST. Instead we will repeat the collection of trust vectors and the evaluation of trees *ad infinitum*, as the publishers and subscribers in the network change. We postulate that the dominant strategy within this repeated game is to converge to a common understanding of the range of trust values, and to be truthful about the levels of trust, allowing for full cardinal comparability. We hope to demonstrate this to be true in future work.

8   Related Work

Wang [24] produced one of the earliest descriptions of the security issues in publish/subscribe networks, which was then built upon by Raicu in [17] to provide a formal definition of confidentiality in content based publish/subscribe. Miklós describes a method to define access control policies on clients' advertisement and subscription filters [13], which assumes that the infra-structure is trusted. Fiege et al. [4] attempted to address the level of trust between publishers, subscribers and infra-structure through the development of scopes of visibility. An implementation on the REBECA [15] shows how such a scoping approach might work. An alternative approach using Role Based Access Control (RBAC) is demonstrated by Belokosztolski et al. [1], building on the HERMES middleware [16]. Policies have been used to control the tree construction by Wun [25].

9   Conclusion

We have presented an algorithm for evaluating trust in publish / subscribe trees, where assumptions about the participants are weaker than in prior work. This algorithm is based on our own trust metric combined with an overhead metric from [8] in order to maximise the trust in the tree with respect to both producers and consumers with respect to a given budget. In addition we present a Tabu-based approximation which is significantly more efficient.

References

1. Belokosztolszki, A., Eyers, D., Pietzuch, P., Bacon, J., Moody, K.: Role-based access control for publish/subscribe middleware architectures. In: Proc. 2nd Intl. Workshop on Distributed Event-Based Systems, pp. 1–8. ACM (2003)
2. Cao, X., Shen, C.: Subscription-aware publish/subscribe tree construction in mobile ad hoc networks. In: Intl. Conf. on Parallel and Distributed Systems, vol. 2, pp. 1–9. IEEE (2009)
3. Char, J.: Generation of trees, two-trees, and storage of master forests. IEEE Transactions on Circuit Theory 15(3), 228–238 (1968)
4. Fiege, L., Zeidler, A., Buchmann, A., Kilian-Kehr, R., Mühl, G.: Security aspects in publish/subscribe systems. In: 3rd Intl. Workshop on Distributed Event-Based Systems (DEBS 2004), pp. 44–49. Citeseer (2004)
5. Gabow, H.N., Myers, E.W.: Finding All Spanning Trees of Directed and Undirected Graphs. SIAM Journal on Computing 7(3), 280 (1978)
6. Gendreau, M., Larochelle, J., Sanso, B.: A tabu search heuristic for the Steiner tree problem. Networks 34(2), 162–172 (1999)
7. Grandison, T., Sloman, M.: A survey of trust in internet applications. IEEE Communications Surveys & Tutorials 3(4), 2–16 (2000)
8. Huang, Y., Garcia-Molina, H.: Publish/Subscribe Tree Construction in Wireless Ad-Hoc Networks. In: Chen, M.-S., Chrysanthis, P.K., Sloman, M., Zaslavsky, A. (eds.) MDM 2003. LNCS, vol. 2574, pp. 122–140. Springer, Heidelberg (2003)
9. Jayakumar, R., Thulasiraman, K., Swamy, M.: Complexity of computation of a spanning tree enumeration algorithm. IEEE Transactions on Circuits and Systems 31(10), 853–860 (1984)
10. Kamvar, S., Schlosser, M., Garcia-Molina, H.: The eigentrust algorithm for reputation management in P2P networks. In: Proc. of the 12th Intl. Conf. on World Wide Web, pp. 640–651. ACM (2003)
11. Kulturel-Konak, S., Norman, B., Coit, D.W., Smith, A.E.: Exploiting Tabu Search Memory in Constrained Problems. INFORMS Journal on Computing 16(3), 241–254 (2004)

12. Marti, S., Ganesan, P., Garcia-Molina, H.: SPROUT: P2P Routing with Social Networks. In: Lindner, W., Fischer, F., Türker, C., Tzitzikas, Y., Vakali, A.I. (eds.) EDBT 2004. LNCS, vol. 3268, pp. 425–435. Springer, Heidelberg (2004)
13. Miklós, Z.: Towards an access control mechanism for wide-area publish/subscribe systems. In: Proc. 22nd Intl. Conf. on Distributed Computing Systems Workshops, pp. 516–521. IEEE (2002)
14. Minty, G.: A Simple Algorithm for Listing All the Trees of a Graph. IEEE Transactions on Circuit Theory 12(1), 120–120 (1965)
15. Mühl, G.: Large-Scale Content-Based Publish/Subscribe Systems. Ph.D. thesis, Berlin Institute of Technology (2002)
16. Pietzuch, P., Bacon, J.: Hermes: a distributed event-based middleware architecture. In: Proc. 22nd Intl. Conf. on Distributed Computing Systems Workshops, pp. 611–618 (2002)
17. Raiciu, C., Rosenblum, D.S.: Enabling Confidentiality in Content-Based Publish/Subscribe Infrastructures. In: 2006 Securecomm and Workshops, pp. 1–11. IEEE (August 2006)
18. Rawls, J.: A theory of justice, 2nd edn. Oxford University Press (1971)
19. Ray, I., Chakraborty, S.: A Vector Model of Trust for Developing Trustworthy Systems. In: Samarati, P., Ryan, P.Y.A., Gollmann, D., Molva, R. (eds.) ESORICS 2004. LNCS, vol. 3193, pp. 260–275. Springer, Heidelberg (2004)
20. Ribeiro, C.C., De Souza, M.C.: Tabu search for the steiner tree problem in graphs. Networks 36, 138–146 (2000)
21. Sen, A.: Interpersonal aggregation and partial comparability. Econometrica: Journal of the Econometric Society 38(3), 393–409 (1970), http://www.jstor.org/stable/1909546
22. Takahashi, H., Matsuyama, A.: An approximate solution for the Steiner problem in graphs. Math. Japonica 24(6), 573–577 (1980)
23. Theodorakopoulos, G., Baras, J.: On trust models and trust evaluation metrics for ad hoc networks. IEEE Journal on Selected Areas in Communications 24(2), 318–328 (2006)
24. Wang, C., Carzaniga, A., Evans, D., Wolf, A.: Security issues and requirements for Internet-scale publish-subscribe systems. In: Proc. of the 35th Annual Hawaii Intl. Conf. on System Sciences (HICSS), pp. 3940–3947. IEEE (2002)
25. Wun, A., Jacobsen, H.A.: A Policy Management Framework for Content-Based Publish/Subscribe Middleware. In: Cerqueira, R., Pasquale, F. (eds.) Middleware 2007. LNCS, vol. 4834, pp. 368–388. Springer, Heidelberg (2007)

Rendering unto Cæsar the Things That Are Cæsar's: Complex Trust Models and Human Understanding

Stephen Marsh[1], Anirban Basu[2], and Natasha Dwyer[3]

[1] Communications Research Centre,
3701 Carling Avenue, P.O. Box 11490, Stn. H. Ottawa, ON K2H 8S2, Canada
`steve.marsh@crc.gc.ca`
[2] Tokai University, 2-3-23 Takanawa, Minato-ku, Tokyo 108-8619, Japan
and School of Informatics, University of Sussex, Brighton BN1 9QJ, UK
`abasu@cs.dm.u-tokai.ac.jp, a.basu@sussex.ac.uk`
[3] Victoria University, Footscray Park Campus,
Ballarat Road, Footscray, 3011, Australia
`natasha.dwyer@vu.edu.au`

Abstract. In this position paper we examine some of the aspects of trust models, deployment, use and 'misuse,' and present a manifesto for the application of computational trust in sociotechnical systems. Computational Trust formalizes the trust processes in humans in order to allow artificial systems to better make decisions or give better advice. This is because trust is flexible, readily understood, and relatively robust. Since its introduction in the early '90s, it has gained in popularity because of these characteristics. However, what it has oftentimes lost is understandability. We argue that one of the original purposes of computational trust reasoning was the human element – the involvement of humans in the process of decision making for tools, importantly at the basic level of understanding why the tools made the decisions they did. The proliferation of ever more complex models may serve to increase the robustness of trust management in the face of attack, but does little to help mere humans either understand or, if necessary, intervene when the trust models fail or cannot arrive at a sensible decision.

1 Introduction

Computational Trust is the study, formalization and implementation of human trust in computational settings [1]. It was intended to be used by autonomous systems of all types in their missions to perform their duties with humans in mind. This qualification is both interesting and important – there is an implicit, at least, expectation that the systems in question are working for humans, perhaps where humans co-exist with the systems themselves. Thus, we can imagine autonomous agents or devices in eCommerce scenarios [2,3], Smart Cities [4,5], Information Systems [6] and ubiquitous computing in general [7,8]. We have seen trust explored for example in user interfaces [9,10] and 'real world' marketplaces

T. Dimitrakos et al. (Eds.): IFIPTM 2012, IFIP AICT 374, pp. 191–200, 2012.
© IFIP International Federation for Information Processing 2012

[11]. A recent paper [12] tellingly did not build any trust model, noting that current trust models are inappropriate. Trust, of course, is everywhere people are, and if the people are using technology, then it makes sense, at some level, to allow trust to be used there too.

Trust has unquestionable utility – it has been used by humans for millennia to manage risk. Of course, humans have issues estimating and handling risk [13], a subject beyond the scope of this paper, but we could argue that this is another reason for trust being so important to people. People make trusting decisions, for better or worse, almost in the blink of an eye, and adapt these decisions over the lifetime of a relationship [14]. We should mention that, of course, they make mistakes all the time, but one of the strengths of trust is the implicit acknowledgment of the potential for mistakes in the face of incomplete information, and the fact that it is used anyway and still manages to work both at an individual and a societal level [15]. Perhaps one triumph of irrationality over rationality.

We are faced with something of a dilemma in the user of trust in technology, however. There is a noticeable trend to more and more complex models, using deeper mathematical techniques and constructs. Complex models (involving trust or related reasoning) have been applied in places as diverse as eCommerce [2,16] and Mobile Ad-Hoc Networking [17], through to financial systems (for instance in algorithmic trading). The use of such complex models in systems where time is of the essence, or even where attacks are both prevalent and can have far-reaching effects, is *potentially* both sensible and timely, but the failures can be interesting, to say the least – witness the Flash Crash of May 6th, 2010 for instance.[1] The use of 'trust' models in these instances is troubling to us because they explicitly preclude the human element, and it is the human element that makes trust trust.

This paper examines the purposes of computational trust, its human element, and the fact that, without the human element, there is a lost link. It goes on to argue that with increasing complexity the human element is ever-more difficult to enlist, even in circumstances where, as almost certainly must happen, the trust model cannot accomplish its task. We argue that the use of the term 'trust' in such systems is misleading, and as such potentially dangerous, and that the increasing complexity of the models does not advance the field or its understanding or applicability in systems where it can be at its best.

2   The Need for Models

Trust has long been seen as a tool for the reduction of complexity [18]. It allows people to exist in complex societies, where there are far too many considerations of what *might* go wrong, by taking certain things 'on trust' and not considering them. We can extend this to computational infrastructures in various interesting ways. Developers and creators of ICT systems are encouraged to engage trust, and solve the trust 'problem,' quickly because trust, in this mode reduces uncertainty.

---

[1] See, e.g. http://www.iosco.org/library/pubdocs/pdf/IOSCOPD354.pdf

This in turn can speed up transactions and 'grease the wheels' of e-commerce [19]. The complexity-reduction nature of trust is important here because, if trust is not resolved, a user can stay in a cycle of exploring possibilities [20]. Since trust results in the foreclosure of some future possibilities [21], this can remove the need to consider them, and results in a more satisfying, or at least more quickly engaging, experience. This is why trust is often viewed as a type of confidence, even when the confidence is not well placed. Distrust is at least as important in this respect also. Often seen as a negative attribute, distrust can in fact holds benefits for similar reasons. Distrust can also resolve a complex scenario, closing down possible paths for the individual to balance [22]. For this reason, an understanding of both trust, distrust, and everything inbetween is needed [23,24]. Perhaps ironically, whilst trust models can help create systems that more accurately follow humans, ostensibly the topic of this paper, they can also, properly executed, help in developing a greater understanding of the phenomenon *in* humans [1].

That said, we arrive at a juxtaposition where models in the technical setting have become increasingly complex, and as has in fact generally been the case, overly contextual and applicable in narrow domains. We see these as problems. The latter problem, perhaps, feeds the former, and is in a cycle fed by it. One reason that they are problems is that they are incomprehensible to the very humans that they, in *all* cases, must inevitably serve [25], but another is that they are not, in the final analysis, approximations of trust at all.

Models of any type, be it trust or anything else, helps us simplify our understanding of a phenomenon in natural sciences or social sciences. Empirical models are expected to be built on actual observations of large samples of data. We argue that models of a 'real' phenomenon (in this case, trust) should be, as close as possible, a fit to that real phenomenon. This is, perhaps obviously, because we would wish to use those models so as to confidently explain (and in some instances predict with some accuracy) future occurrences of the same phenomenon. We can happily accept that models of complex phenomena must in themselves be inherently complex, but we do not accept that models should be so complex as to be beyond the understanding of their creators, or, most tellingly in the case of models used to interact with humans in sensible ways, beyond the understanding of the very people that are intended to use them.

3   Where the Models Work, and Where They Don't

Trust models perform best when a general and abstract understanding of a context and associated trustworthiness of others is required, rather than detailed advice about a specific situation. For instance, the reputation system of Ebay can provide an adequate picture of whom the most trustworthy parties are – who deliver goods on time, who do not overcharge, whose goods are as described and of consistent expected quality, for instance. However, the model cannot say whether a user should definitely trust a particularly seller in a specific situation, particularly if the parties in question do not meet the measurement standards of the system. Consider for example a buyer who has found a rare item. The buyer may greatly desire the item, but the seller has a low rating. In this instance, the buyer can override caution and 'trust despite the low reputation' – Ebay gives reputation values that the buyer can use to ascertain their own trust levels. Since here the trade off for the reward is great, the trust calculation is weighed by the rarity of the item. Thus, Ebay can only guide to a certain point, and we have to be aware that trustworthiness (or reputation as calculated by Ebay) is no more than a guide in this respect.

Models also work when the users concern is a predictable one shared by the majority of others and does not stray far from the objectives others have. Models are not good at handling nuance. For instance, the movie recommender system Netflix can only work to a certain extent. For instance, over time and with experience, a user's taste changes [26]. Models encourage conformity, which in turn, creates conditions for the model to work, creating a self supporting system. Ahn and Esarey [27] explain that systems that provide some sort of information about what is expected as trustworthy behaviour (for instance, Wikipedia), actually foster trustworthy behaviour because users can learn from the system.

We find ourselves here in danger of a cardinal sin for trust and reputation systems – a conflation of trust and reputation – and this is an ideal example for us to approach and consider from the point of view of this paper – that an adequate understanding of what the model is trying to do is absolutely necessary for its successful use. Bearing in mind that trust decisions are based on two questions – how much do you have, and how much do you need (cf [1]) – the next steps should be clear in any evidence-gathering approach. Consider embedded reputation systems. In all instances of such systems the system is informing its user of the *reputation* of the person or thing they are considering. Reputation is a societal judgment of the past behaviour (hopefully in context) of the thing being considered. It is not an indication of the amount that the potential trustee can trust the other. For example, building from Allman et al. and others [28,29], [30] suggested the formulation of a reputation framework for network clients based on their behavioural histories in order to inform service providers to make decisions about future service provision. Although, on a continuous numeric scale $[-1 \quad 1]$ for the sake of comparability, the contextual reputations developed therein did not equate to or imply *trust* at the level of human connotation. Rather, the reputation was only an indicator. What service providers would do with such reputation would be policy specific, and outside the remits of the reputation framework.

In this context, we should also look at inherent challenges with numerical comparability. While during most part of our daily lives, we deal with numbers, we also do so with agreed upon (within some "community") standard units. These units are nothing but enforcements of connotations of numerical values. For example, a 500ml. bottle of water anywhere in the world will contain very close to 500ml. of water (excluding the minor measurement errors) because milliliters is an already agreed upon standard measurement unit. This is good because that helps our society to function. But, assigning numbers to anything without units takes away the very essence of comparability for which we resort to using numbers in the first place. Even if we suggest that such numerical values are only indicators that people should use to inform their trust decisions, the indications carry little meaning in the absence of comparability. Since, numbers are really hard to assign and units are even harder to define in such cases, perhaps, we should call on the use of more qualitative comparators, e.g. partial order. For example, the reputation of A is higher than B and the reputation of C is also higher than B gives us a reasonable (at least to human mind) qualitative indicator and stops us from making the mistake that reputation of A is equal to C. Humans will, inevitably, tend to make that mistake of comparison if they are presented with concrete numbers. Then the point about trust with humans is that we can safely ignore the internal workings of the human mind when it comes to making a trust based decision, and infer those workings based only on observation. On top of that, we also envisage that if we were to ask about such trust decisions from artificial agents, we should be able to get understandable explanations.

The reason for considering this is the following: models work best when they are best understood. Part of the responsibility for that understanding is the responsibility of the person using the system, that is clear. However, part of it must rest with the system itself, and how it is represented to the person. If reputation is shown as a 'trust' value, it is of little surprise when the sinful conflation occurs and mistakes are subsequently made. On the other hand, it is equally unsurprising to find that overly complex models for trust-reasoning technologies result in diminished, or zero, understanding by their target users, with, we suggest, a corresponding lack of engagement. In the next section we explore this problem further, and look at the concept of 'foreground trust' [31,25], which aims to bring trust right into the user interface by encouraging users to make their own decisions based on the evidence.

4   Putting People First

Trust and reputation models are there for people in much the same way as technologies are there for people – they make certain things more straightforward, or more easy. The implicit assumption that we are making is that all technologies are deployed in order to help, in some way, at least a subset of people. Thus, there is always a human in the loop [32] of technological advancement and deployment. It is indeed difficult to find instances of technology where this is not in some sense, the case – and anything that might be found begs a question, we conjecture, as to its worth. That said, we acknowledge the fact that some systems may have people so far from the immediate consideration that they are effectively ignored. That said, we propose that any system that uses trust or reputation must explicitly acknowledge and make room for the human element. If this is the case, it follows that the models must have not only predictive power, but explanatory power also.

4.1   The User Interface

User interfaces are important. They convey system states, valuable information, environmental states, history and predictions to users. In the case of trust (and reputation) systems, they convey recommendations, perspectives, decisions (or, better, suggestions) evidence and requirements. They might also ask for information in order to better do their jobs. They should also ask for help when necessary. Their design is vitally important. The terminology they use, as discussed in the previous section, has power to enlighten or confuse. Most especially, if complex models are used in the background for whatever reason, the user interface has a role to make the model understandable without losing any of its predictive power. Thus, if we consider models of the weather, an interface showing movement of air masses, and associated weather patterns, is infinitely more accessible to anyone than a mass of numbers on a screen, or the output of some set of algorithms. The same must be true for trust models.

4.2 When Systems Fail, People Pick Up the Pieces

Trust models and their operationalized reputation and trust management systems are ideal targets for attacks and misunderstandings. Whilst the attacks possible on reputation systems are relatively well understood, we would argue that spotting these attacks autonomously is difficult. There are nuances to attacks (hence their efficacy) that computerized systems are not good at spotting. Humans, however, are much better at spotting anomalies in trust reasoning and reputation. And it is to people that we must always turn when at the edges of trust – which include boundaries close to thresholds, cold-start problems, and possible ongoing attacks as well as less stress-laden situations (see e.g. [33]).

Designing trust systems that hide the way in which they work must result in misunderstandings, misinterpretations, and mistakes by the very people that the systems are serving. This is guaranteed to result in dissatisfaction and disengagement.

5 Is It Trust?

There are countless ways of defining trust, but most definitions engage with the notion of confidence and risk and there is an acknowledgement that there is a sense of the unknown embedded in the concept of trust. Möllering [34] goes as far to argue that there is something magical about trust, otherwise a concept is not trust. Thus models that claim to have removed uncertainty as much as possible are removing trust. If a situation is clear and the future outcome known, then trust is no longer the issue and the relevant ways of understanding a scenario is better described with notions such as control and security.

Making a trust model more complex does not solve the problem when a model interfaces with human reality. A trust model could dictate how much information a user is safe to reveal to others. In reality, humans are swayed by other factors. For instance, most people are aware that a birth date is information required to verify ones identity and most people are aware of identity theft. Even though there is this awareness, a large number of people put their birth date on their social networking profile presumably so that others can wish them a happy birthday. Vanity wins over sensible behaviour. And who can say that what people do in reality is wrong? To do so is to make a value judgment that prejudices rationality. So any trust model that tries to dismiss how humans actually work is not engaging with human reality. A trust model that can function without humans needs to be able to compute ambiguity; unpredictable irrationality, a continual state of uncertainty and lack of clarity, without any claims on what is a correct position. Ambiguity is different to complexity. Complexity is when a model can process a large amount of variables and conditions.

There are some human phenomena that cannot be short-cut [35], and we argue that trust is one these concepts. In the context of on-line dating, Stainer et al. [12] demonstrate how a machine can calculate a trust interaction, but when it comes to two people interacting, that calculation can mean very little. While not claiming that humans have a monopoly on trust, we argue that machines are not able to solely process trust without the input of humans. This is because trust is both a rational and irrational phenomena. Trust is a grey concept rather than a black and white, binary position. Computers are renowned for dealing with calculations quickly. Humans are schooled at dealing with ambiguity. Trust models that can incorporate the best of both human and machine work will excel.

6   Render unto Cæsar: A Manifesto

Trust models are approximations of human trust, and as such should be used sensibly and designed so that, whenever possible, humans can be involved. Our basic premise throughout this paper is that any system deployed in the 'real world' in fact influences, is influenced by, and/or works on behalf of humans (whether they like it or not!). When we consider this, we can examine a set of requirements for any trust model that may be designed and deployed in this world. We do not expect this is a complete list, and would expect it to evolve as our understanding of computational trust evolves.

(1) The model is for people.
(2) The model should be understandable, not just by mathematics professors, but by the people who are expected to use and make decisions with or from it.
(3) Allow for monitoring and intervention. Understand that a human's conception of trust and risk is difficult to conceptualise. Many mathematical and economic models of trust assume (or hope for) a 'rational man' who makes judgments based on self-interest. However, in reality, humans weigh trust and risk in ways that cannot be fully predicted. A human needs to be able to make the judgment.
(4) The model should not fail silently, but should prompt for and expect input on 'failure' or uncertainty.
(5) The model should allow for a deep level of configuration. Trust models should not assume what is 'best' for the user. Often design tends to guide users towards what the owner or developer of the site thinks what people should be doing [36]. However, only the user can make that call.

(6) The model should allow for querying: a user may want to know more about a system or a context. A trust interface working in the interest of the user should gather and present data the user regards as relevant. Some of the questions will be difficult for a system to predict and a developer to pre-prepare, so a level of dynamic information exchange is necessary.

(7) The model should cater for different time priorities. In some cases, a trust decision does need to be made quickly. But in other cases, a speedy response is not necessary, and it is possible to take advantage of new information as it comes to hand. A trust model working for humans needs to be able to respond to different timelines and not always seek a short-cut.

(8) The model should allow for incompleteness. Many models aim to provide a definitive answer. Human life is rarely like that. A more appropriate ap-proach is to keep the case open; allowing for new developments, users to change their minds, and for situations to be re-visited.

7   Conclusions

Trust models are becoming more prevalent, applied to many places in many different contexts. Models can be applied in narrow contexts or be much more generic and descriptive (see for example [37]), but we suggest in this paper that models of trust, pure or applied, are, as part of sociotechnical systems deployed in the world at a concrete level, human-oriented. If this is the case, computational trust models are only useful in situations where the people who interact with them *understand* them in a reasonable way. It is unsatisfactory to have eCommerce models, for instance, that use mathematical tools that are indecipherable to people who use eCommerce systems (and agents) because the ultimate endpoint is then a shift of trust from the other person to the model (I will do what it says because I can't figure out why, and it's smarter than I am) – this is not what computational trust in its origin was intended to achieve. Without human understanding and focus, trust models are not trust, but a mere statistical, probabilistic or other mathematical approach to uncertainty. We have provided a small manifesto for computational trust models that we hope can be of some service to the community – as a discussion point, as the start of a set of requirements above and beyond 'does it work in this instance, or against this attack?' and as a reminder that, (to paraphrase Einstein) in all of our considerations, humans are the root.

References

1. Marsh, S.: Formalising trust as a computational concept. PhD thesis, University of Stirling, Department of Computing Science and Mathematics (1994)
2. Ping, W., Jing, Q.: A mathematical trust model in e-commerce. In: 2007 Interna-tional Conference on Multimedia and Ubiquitous Engineering, MUE 2007 (2007)
3. Noorian, Z., Marsh, S., Fleming, M.: Multi-layer cognitive filtering by behavioural modeling. In: Tumer, Yolum, S., Stone (eds.) Proc. of 10th Int. Conf. on Au-tonomous Agents and Multiagent Systems, AAMAS 2011 (2011)

4. Mahizhnan, A.: Smart cities: The singapore case. Cities 16(1), 13–18 (1999)
5. Shapiro, J.: Smart cities: Quality of life, productivity, and the growth effects of human capital. Technical report, National Bureau of Economic Research (2005)
6. Li, X., Valacich, J.S., Hess, T.J.: Predicting user trust in information systems: A comparison of competing trust models. In: Proceedings of the 37th Annual Hawaii International Conference on System Sciences (HICSS 2004) - Track 8, vol. 8. IEEE Computer Society, Washington, DC (2004)
7. Shankar, N., Arbaugh, W.A.: On trust for ubiquitous computing. In: Workshop on Security in Ubiquitous Computing, UBICOMP 2002, pp. 44–54. IEEE Computer Society (2002)
8. Sillence, E., Briggs, P.: Ubiquitous computing: Trust issues for a "healthy" society. Social Science Computer Review 26(1), 6–12 (2008)
9. Riegelsberger, J., Sasse, A., McCarthy, J.D.: Shiny happy people building trust?: photos on e-commerce websites and consumer trust. In: Proceedings of the 2003 Conference on Human Factors in Computing Systems, pp. 121–128 (2003)
10. Riegelsberger, J.: Trust in Mediated Interactions. PhD thesis, University College London (2005)
11. Wakeman, I., Light, A., Robinson, J., Chalmers, D., Basu, A.: Bringing the Virtual to the Farmers' Market: Designing for Trust in Pervasive Computing Systems. In: Nishigaki, M., Jøsang, A., Murayama, Y., Marsh, S. (eds.) IFIPTM 2010. IFIP AICT, vol. 321, pp. 248–262. Springer, Heidelberg (2010)
12. Stanier, J., Naicken, S., Basu, A., Li, J., Wakeman, I.: Can We Use Trust in Online Dating? In: Proceedings of the International Workshop on Trusted Communications in Decentralised Computing (Workshop in IFIPTM 2010), Morioka, Japan (2010)
13. Zeckhauser, R.J., Viscusi, W.K.: Risk within reason. Science 248, 559–564 (1990)
14. Boon, S.D., Holmes, J.G.: The dynamics of interpersonal trust: resolving uncertainty in the face of risk. In: Hinde, R.A., Groebel, J. (eds.) Cooperation and Prosocial Behaviour, pp. 190–211. Cambridge University Press (1991)
15. Bok, S.: Lying: Moral Choice in Public and Private Life. Pantheon Books, New York (1978)
16. Zhang, Z., Zhou, M., Wang, P.: An improved trust model in agent-mediated ecommerce. Int. J. Intell. Syst. Technol. Appl. 4(3.4), 271–284 (2008)
17. Sun, K., Xu, R., Deng, J., Haynes, L., Li, J.H., Gruenwald, L., Sanchez, C., Weber, G., Mayhew, M.J.: Securing manet databases using metadata and context information. In: Proceeedings of MILCOM 2008: Military Comunications Conference, pp. 1–6 (2008)
18. Luhmann, N.: Trust and Power. Wiley, Chichester (1979)
19. Fukuyama, F.: Trust: The social virtues and the creation of prosperity. Free Press, New York (1995)
20. Cofta, P.: Trust, Complexity and Control, vol. 829528313. John Wilcy and Sons, New Jersey (2007)
21. Goffman, E.: Frame analysis. Harvard University Press, Cambridge (1974)
22. Cofta, P.: Distrust. In: Proceedings of Eight International Conference on Electronic Commerce (2006)
23. Marsh, S., Dibben, M.R.: Trust, Untrust, Distrust and Mistrust – An Exploration of the Dark(er) Side. In: Herrmann, P., Issarny, V., Shiu, S. (eds.) iTrust 2005. LNCS, vol. 3477, pp. 17–33. Springer, Heidelberg (2005)
24. McKnight, D.H., Chervany, N.L.: Trust and Distrust Definitions: One Bite at a Time. In: Falcone, R., Singh, M., Tan, Y.-H. (eds.) Trust in Cyber-societies. LNCS (LNAI), vol. 2246, pp. 27–54. Springer, Heidelberg (2001)

25. Marsh, S., Noël, S., Storer, T., Wang, Y., Briggs, P., Robart, L., Stewart, J., Esfandiari, B., El-Khatib, K., Bicakci, M.V., Dao, M.C., Cohen, M., Silva, D.D.: Non-standards for trust: Foreground trust and second thoughts for mobile security. In: Proceedings STM 2011. Springer (2012)

26. Lathia, N.: Evaluating collaborative filtering over time. PhD thesis, University College London (2010)

27. Ahn, T., Esarey, J.: A dynamic model of generalized social trust. Journal of Theoretical Politics 20(2), 151–180 (2008)

28. Allman, M., Blanton, E., Paxson, V.: An Architecture for Developing Behavioral History. In: Proceedings of the Workshop on Steps to Reducing Unwanted Traffic on the Internet (2005)

29. Wei, S., Mirkovic, J.: Building Reputations for Internet Clients. Electronic Notes Theoretical Computer Science 179, 17–30 (2007)

30. Basu, A.: A Reputation Framework for Behavioural History. PhD thesis, University of Sussex, UK (January 2010)

31. Dwyer, N.: Traces of Digital Trust: An Interactive Design Perspective. PhD thesis, School of Communication and the Arts, Faculty of Arts, Education and Human Development, Victoria University (2011)

32. Dautenhahn, K., Alan, H.B., Canamero, L., Edmonds, B. (eds.): Socially Intelligent Agents: Creating Relationships with Computers and Robots. Kluwer Academic Publishers (2002)

33. Kaur, P., Ruohomaa, S., Kutvonen, L.: User interface for trust decision making in inter-enterprise collaborations. In: ACHI 2012: The Fifth International Conference on Advances in Computer-Human Interactions (2012)

34. Möllering, G.: Trust, institutions, agency: towards a neoinstitutional theory of trust. Handbook of trust research, pp. 223–233 (2006)

35. Donath, J.: Signals in social supernets. Journal of Computer-Mediated Communication 13(1), 231–251 (2007)

36. Thaler, R., Sunstein, C.: Nudge: improving decisions about health, wealth, and happiness. Yale University Press, New Haven (2008)

37. Castelfranchi, C., Falcone, R.: Trust Theory: A Socio-Cognitive and Computational Model. Wiley (2011)

Trust Management Framework for Attenuation of Application Layer DDoS Attack in Cloud Computing

Dipen Contractor and Dhiren R. Patel

Department of Computer Engineering, NIT Surat
India 395007
contractor.dipen@yahoo.co.in,
dhiren29p@gmail.com

Abstract. There is a new breed of denial-of-service attacks intended to misuse resources and drive up the cost of cloud computing. Although the impact is less widespread than a traditional Network layer DDoS. Crashing a server is not always easy in the cloud because additional resources can be made available as needed to support sharp spikes in demand. However those resources are not free and an attack could make it economically prohibitive to keep the attacked cloud or its services running.

In this paper, we propose a Trust Management Framework as a partial solution to this problem. It is a lightweight mitigation mechanism that uses trust to differentiate legitimate users from attackers. The trust is evaluated on the basis of clients' visiting history, and used to schedule the service to their requests to access cloud. It uses a new feature called a license (composed of three parameters; client ID, IP address of the client, and computed Trust), for user identification (even beyond NATs) and store the trust information at clients. The license is cryptographically secured against forgery or replay attacks.

Keywords: DDoS attack, Cloud Computing, Trust Management.

1   Introduction

DoS/DDoS attacks are not new and are not directly related to the use of cloud computing. The issue with these attacks and cloud computing is an increase in an organization's risk at the network level due to some increased use of resources external to your organization's network. For example, there continue to be rumors of DDoS attacks on AWS, making the services unavailable for hours to AWS users [14].

However, when using IaaS [9], the risk of a DDoS attack is not only external but there is also the risk of an internal DDoS attack. That internal (non-routable) network is a shared resource, used by customers for access to their non-public instances (e.g., Amazon Machine Images or AMIs[15]) as well as by the provider for management of its network and resources (such as physical servers). If I become a rogue customer, there would be nothing to prevent me from using my customer access to this internal network to find and attack other customers, or the IaaS provider's infrastructure.

T. Dimitrakos et al. (Eds.): IFIPTM 2012, IFIP AICT 374, pp. 201–208, 2012.

Provider would probably not have any detective controls in place to even notify it of such an attack.

Application layer DDoS attack [7] is a DDoS attack that sends out requests following the communication protocol and thus these requests are indistinguishable from legitimate requests in the network layer. Most application layer protocols, for example, HTTP1.0/1.1, FTP and SOAP [10], are built on TCP and they communicate with users using sessions which consist of one or many requests (and hence the requester does not use spoofed IP addresses). An application layer DDoS attack may be of one or a combination of the following types [7, 8]: (1) session flooding attack sends session connection requests at a rate higher than legitimate users; (2) request flooding attack sends sessions that contain more requests than normal sessions and (3) asymmetric attack sends sessions with more high-workload requests.

In this paper, we focus on how to mitigate the session flooding attack in cloud. In this paper, we propose a lightweight mechanism, named Trust Management Framework that uses trust management to mitigate session flooding DDoS attack. For every established connection it records four aspects of trust to the user: short-term trust, long-term trust, negative trust and misusing trust which are used to compute an overall trust that helps in determining whether to accept a client's next connection request. These values are stored as part of a license at clients and when a client revisits the cloud; he attaches his license to the session connection request. Based on the license computes the client's overall trust, updates his license, and decides whether to accept his request. The license is designed such that the framework can easily identify the client and verify his associated trusts, but license forgery or replay is computationally infeasible. We can also extend Trust Management Framework to collaborative trust management in Hybrid Cloud [2].

The organization of this paper is as follows. In Section 2, we describe the legitimate user model and attacker model. In Section 3 we propose our design considerations. Then defense mechanism in Section 4 and in Section 5, we concluded.

2   Basic User Models

Before proposing the mitigation mechanism, behaviors of both normal and abnormal users should be investigated and described carefully. In this section, we build the legitimate user model. Firstly, we would like to make two assumptions.

Assumption 1. Under session flooding attacks, the bottleneck is the maximal number of simultaneous session connections, called as *MaxConnector*. It depends not only on the bandwidth of the server, but also on other resources of the server, e.g. CPU, memory, maximal database connections.

Assumption 2. Without attacks, the total number of session connections of the server should be much smaller than *MaxConnector*, e.g., smaller than 20% of *MaxConnector*, as a cloud controller [3] would set the threshold much higher to tolerate the potential burst of requests.

2.1   Legitimate User Model

In contrast to attackers, legitimate users are people who request services for their benefit from the content of the services. Therefore, the interarrival time of requests from a legitimate user would form a certain density distribution *density(t)* [5]. With this insight, we build the user model in the following way:

1. Use traces of Internet accesses to build an initial model $density_0(t)$, where t is a inter-arrival time and *density(t)* is the probability a legitimate user will revisit the service after t seconds. Many traces has been done by researchers, e.g. F. Douglis et al. [5] traced web users to investigate caching technique in World Wide Web, and M. Ar-litt et al. [1] presents a workload characterization study for Internet Web servers.
2. Rebuild user model $density_{i+1}(t)$ with the newly collected inter-arrival times of all legitimate users after Framework runs d days under model $density_i(t)$, where d is randomly chosen from [*dmin , dmax*]. It means that $density_{i+1}(t)$ is tightly de-rived from $density_i(t)$ and hence is difficult to be fooled by attackers.

As a practical legitimate user model, it should satisfy the following properties: firstly, it should converge fast to the users' accesses interval distribution; secondly, it should be dynamic as the distribution may change from time to time; and most importantly, it should be lightweight to be easily implemented and monitored in the defense mechanism.

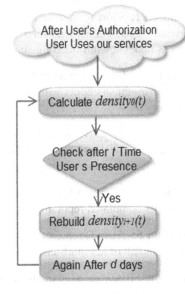

Fig. 1. Basic Flow chart

2.2   Attacker Model

The goal of an attacker is to keep the number of simultaneous session connections to cloud's resources as large as possible to stop new connection requests from legitimate users being accepted. So, an attacker may consider using the following strategies.

He controls a lot of zombie machines or can misuse P2P network as an attack platform

1. Send session connection requests at a fixed rate, without considering the response or the service ability of victim.
2. Send session connection requests at a random rate, without considering the re-sponse or the service ability of victim.
3. Send session connection requests at a random rate and consider the response or the service ability of victim by adjusting request rate according to the proportion of accepted session connection requests by the cloud provider [3]. Note that this behavior is different from legitimate behavior, since the random range and ran-dom model are different.

4. First send session connection requests at a rate similar to legitimate users to gain trust from server, then start attacking with one of the above attacking strategies.

3 Design Considerations

We have considered the following properties in designing our mitigation mechanism:

(1) It should be deployed at the server for incentive and performance reasons [6].
(2) It should be lightweight, to reduce the processing delay and to avoid being a new target of attacks.
(3) It should be easy to deploy and independent to the details of servers. The defense mechanism need not know what services the server runs or what configuration it uses. (4) It should be adaptive to the server's resource consumption and differentiate between concurrent requests.

Here we define several components of it before defining trust.

Definition 1: Short-term trust T_s, estimating the recent behavior of a client. It is used to identify those clients who send session connection requests at a high rate when the server is under session flooding attacks.

Definition 2: Long-term trust T_l , estimating the long-term behavior of a client. It is used to distinguish clients with normal visiting history and those with abnormal visiting history.

Definition 3: Negative trust T_n, cumulating the distrust to a client. Distrust means each time the client's overall trust falls below the initial value T_0. It is used to penalize a client if he is less trustworthy than a new client.

Definition 4: Misusing trust T_m, cumulating the suspicious behavior of a client who misuses its cumulated reputation.

Definition 5: Trust T, representing the overall trustworthiness of a client, which takes into account all of his short-term trust, long-term trust, negative trust and misusing trust.

Definition6: Blacklist, a list of clients whose trust value is below some minimum level.

Definition7: Whitelist, a list of clients whose trust value is above some threshold value.

When a client's trust T drops below defined minimum, that client moves into the blacklist with an expiration time. That client is then banned from accessing the services until his blacklist record expires. When session connection request reaches trust management framework (as shown in fig-2), it checks whether the client is blacklisted; if not, it computes the new trust T and use trust-based scheduling to schedule the connection request.

When trusted client starts behaving as an attacker, the number of sessions requested by that client differs. Such client can be moved from whitelist to blacklist.

4   Trust Management Framework Architecture

This architecture is not a monolithic solution that can be easily deployed to gain capabilities immediately. Our proposed architecture as depicted in Fig-2 is a collection of technology components, processes, and standard practices for cloud computing. Standard enterprise access architecture encompasses several layers of technology, services, and processes. Broadly categorized as follows:

1. User management Activities for the effective governance and management of identity life cycles [11]
2. Authentication management Activities for the effective governance and management of the process for determining that an entity is who or what it claims to be.
3. Authorization management Activities for the effective governance and management of the process for determining entitlement rights that decide what resources an entity is permitted to access in accordance with the organization's policies
4. Access management Enforcement of policies for access control in response to a request from an entity (user, services) wanting to access and IT resource within the organization
5. Data management and provisioning of identity and data for authorization to IT resources via automated or manual processes
6. Monitoring, auditing, and reporting compliance by users regarding access to resources within the organization based on the defined policies. Authenticate user records are stored parentally in cloud for future user through Legitimate User Model.

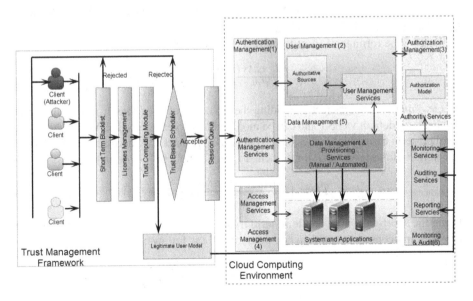

Fig. 2. Fundamental proposed model and with its components

4.1   License Management

The identification information and trust states can be stored at clients and verified by the server. We call the information stored at clients as *license*. It contains the following: 64-bit identifier *ID*, *IP* address of client IP, the overall trust *T* to the client, negative trust T_n, missus trust T_m, last access time *LT*, average access interval *AT*, the total number of accesses *AN*, and a keyed hash *H* of the concatenation of all the above, with a 128-bit server password *SP* as the key. *SP* is private to the server. We identify a client by his public IP and the server assigned identifier. If IP address alone is used, clients behind NATs cannot be distinguished, because they share the same public IP address.

A license serves two functions for user identification and trust computation. The identification information, such as *ID* and *IP*, must be stored at the client license. The state variables for trust computation can be stored at the client or at the server. Each has its advantages and drawbacks. Keeping licenses at a server largely prevents attackers from tempering them, but it is a single point of data failure.

4.2   Adaptive Trust Computing

The computation of trust T' employs T, T_n, T_m, *LT*, *AT* and *AN* in license, current time *now*, and *usedRate* (i.e., the percentage of connected sessions over *MaxConnector*) of the server. Based on Assumption 2 in Section 3 *usedRate* is much lower than 1. As we explained, a server should give priority to protect the connectivity of good users during session flooding attacks, instead of identifying all the attack requests. Since a higher trust value means a request is more likely to be accepted, it is desired to satisfy: $T_{legitimate\ user} > T_{new\ client} > T_{attacker}$

We give the formula of short-term trust as follows:

$$T_s' = \left(\frac{density(now-LT)}{e^{alpha \times usedRate}} \right) \qquad (1)$$

Where *alpha* is a weight factor deciding the influence of *usedRate*. It is a positive real number with default value 1 and can be modified by servers as needed. When $alpha \approx 0$, the short-term trust mainly relies on the interval of the latest two accesses of the client.

Similarly long-term behavior of a client. The formula of long-term trust is:

$$T_l' = \left(\frac{lg(AN) \times density(AT)}{e^{T_n}} \right) \qquad (2)$$

Using the short-term trust and long-term trust computed above and the misusing trust provided in license, we can then compute trust T' as follows:

$$T' = min \left(2 \times \frac{\beta \times T_s' + (1-\beta) \times T_l'}{e^{T_m}}, 1 \right) \qquad (3)$$

Where $\beta \in [0, 1]$ with default value 0.5, it decides the weight of short-term trust and long term trust in the overall trust computation. For a client accessing the server for the First time, its initial value of the overall trust is 0.1, and its initial value of negative trust and misusing trust are both 0, i.e. $T_0 = 0{:}1$, $T_{n0} = T_{m0} = 0$.

4.3   Trust-Based Scheduler

When a session connection request is made, this framework firstly validates the license of that client. If passed, it will compute the client's new overall trust, negative trust and misusing trust and then update this information into the license. Afterwards, the scheduler in Framework decides whether to redirect it to the server based on the trust values. It schedules session connection requests once every time slot. If the total number of the on-going sessions and the sessions waiting to be connected is not larger than the *MaxConnector* of the server, the scheduler will redirect all requests to the server. Otherwise, suppose there are N session connection requests waiting to be connected and the percentage of requests should be dropped is μ.

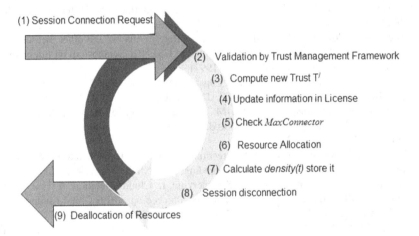

(1) Session Connection Request

(2)   Validation by Trust Management Framework

(3)   Compute new Trust T'

(4) Update information in License

(5) Check *MaxConnector*

(6)   Resource Allocation

(7) Calculate *density(t)* store it

(8)   Session disconnection

(9) Deallocation of Resources

Fig. 3. Flow of Operations

We propose the following scheduling policies to drop suspicious requests:

Foot-n: sort all requests in current time slot by the clients' trusts in the decreasing order. For clients that have the same overall trust, sort them by their misusing trusts in the increasing order. We then drop the last $n = \theta \times N$ requests.

5   Conclusion and Future Work

Defending against application DDoS attacks is a pressing problem of the Internet. Motivated by the fact that it is more important for the cloud service provider to accommodate good users when there is a scarcity of resources. Our proposed mechanism Trust Management Framework will mitigate session flooding attack using trust evaluated from user's history. We will try to compare this to with other defense mechanism. Trust Management Framework is lightweight, independent to the service details, adaptive to the Cloud's resource consumption and extendable to allow collaboration among different clouds.

References

1. Arlitt, M.F., Williamson, C.L.: Web Server Workload Characterization: The Search for Invariants. In: Proceedings of the ACM SIGMETRICS 1996 Conference, Pennsylvania, pp. 126–137 (1996)
2. Mell, P., Grance, T.: The NIST Definition of Cloud Computing (Draft). NIST Special Publication 800-145, pp. 6–10 (2011)
3. Nurmi, D., Wolski, R., Grzegorczyk, C., Obertelli, G., Soman, S., Youseff, L.: The Eucalyptus Open-Source Cloud-Computing System. In: Cluster Computing and Grid 9th IEEE ACM Proceedings, pp. 124–131. IEEE Press (2009)
4. Cornelli, F., Damiani, E., Vimercati, S., Paraboschi, S., Samarati, P.: Choosing reputable servents in a p2p network. In: Proceedings of the 11th International Conference, pp. 65–69 (2002)
5. Douglis, F., Feldmannz, A., Krishnamurthy, B.: Rate of change and other metrics: a live study of the World Wide Web. In: Proceedings of USENIX Symposium on Internetworking Technologies and Systems, pp. 1–13 (1997)
6. Natu, M., Mirkovic, J.: Fine-Grained Capabilities for Flooding DDoS Defense Using Client Reputations. In: Proceedings of LSAD 2007, Japan, pp. 105–112 (2007)
7. Ranjan, S., Swaminathan, R., Uysal, M., Knightly, E.: DDoS-Resilient Scheduling to Counter Application Layer Attacks under Imperfect Detection. In: Proceedings of INFOCOM 2006, pp. 1–13 (2006)
8. Yu, J., Li, Z., Chen, H., Chen, X.: A Detection and Offense Mechanism to Defend Against Application Layer DDoS Attacks. In: Proceedings of ICNS 2007, pp. 54–56 (2007)
9. Khajeh-Hosseini, A., Greenwood, D., Sommerville, I.: Cloud Migration: A Case Study of Migrating an Enterprise IT System to IaaS. In: Proceedings IEEE Cloud Computing 3rd Conference, pp. 55–65. IEEE Press (2010)
10. Curbera, F., Duftler, M., Khalaf, R., Nagy, W., Mukhi, N., Weerawarana, S.: Unraveling the Web Services Web: An Introduction to SOAP, WSDL, and UDDI. IEEE Internet Computing 6(2), 86–93 (2002)
11. Gopalakrishnan, A.: Cloud Computing Identity Management. SETLabs Briefings 7(7), 45–55 (2009)
12. Xie, Y., Yu, S.-Z.: A Novel Model for Detecting Application Layer DDoS Attacks Computer and Computational Sciences. In: IMSCCS 2006 First International Multi-Symposiums (2006)
13. Houle, K.J., Weaver, G.M., Long, N., Thomas, R.: Trends in Denial of Service Attack Technology CERT, Issue (October 2008)
14. Article: Rumor Amazon Hit With Denial-of-Service Attack, Again. posted June 6 (2008), http://www.appscout.com/2008/06/rumor_amazon_hit_with_denialof.php
15. Amazon machine images, http://en.wikipedia.org/wiki/Amazon_Ma-chine_Image

An Incentive Mechanism to Promote Honesty in E-marketplaces with Limited Inventory

Yuan Liu, Jie Zhang, and Qin Li

School of Computer Engineering
Nanyang Technological University, Singapore
{yliu3,zhangj,qin.li}@ntu.edu.sg

Abstract. In e-marketplaces with limited inventory where buyers' demand is larger than sellers' supply, promoting honesty raises new challenges: sellers may behave dishonestly because they can sell out all products without the necessity of gaining high reputation; buyers may provide untruthful ratings to mislead other buyers in order to have a higher chance to obtain the limited products. In this paper, we propose a novel incentive mechanism to promote buyer and seller honesty in such e-marketplaces. More specifically, our mechanism models both buyer and seller honesty. It offers higher prices to the products provided by honest sellers so that the sellers can gain larger utility. Honest buyers also have a higher chance to do business with honest sellers and are able to gain larger utility. Experimental results confirm that our mechanism promotes both buyer and seller honesty.

1 Introduction

In electronic marketplaces, lack of trust and reliability has been frequently cited to be one of the key factors that discourage buyers from participating. A reputation system, which predicts sellers' future behavior based on ratings given by buyers, is an effective way to help buyers to select good sellers [6]. It also creates incentives for sellers to behave honestly in order to be chosen by buyers. However, buyers may provide untruthful ratings to promote some sellers or drive some other sellers out of the market. To address this problem, incentive mechanisms, e.g. [5,3], have been designed to supplement reputation systems, by creating an incentive for buyers to provide truthful ratings. One common but perhaps implicit assumption in these reputation systems and incentive mechanisms is that sellers can provide a large number of products in e-marketplaces. However, In the real world, e-marketplaces with limited inventory exist in many scenarios. One example is the hotel booking system for a famous tourism area during a peak season since booking a satisfactory hotel is often difficult. We call a marketplace in which the demand outweighs the supply *a marketplace with limited inventory.*

New challenges are imposed on promoting buyer and seller honesty in e-marketplaces with limited inventory. Sellers with limited inventory, given that other sellers also hold limited inventory compared to buyer demand, may behave maliciously in their transactions, by not delivering promised products or reducing the quality of delivered products. Even though their reputation would decrease due to the negative ratings from the buyers cheated by them, the sellers may still be willing to increase their profit by sacrificing

T. Dimitrakos et al. (Eds.): IFIPTM 2012, IFIP AICT 374, pp. 209–216, 2012.

reputation, because they may not have as a strong desire to maintain a very high reputation as in the marketplace where the supply outweighs the demand. Therefore, in the e-marketplaces with limited inventory, reputation itself cannot give sellers enough incentives to behave honestly. Buyers may also have incentives to report dishonest ratings. After a successful transaction with a seller, the buyer knows that the seller is a good seller. If the buyer provides a truthful (positive) rating about the seller, then the buyer reduces her own opportunity of doing business with the seller in the future, due to the limited inventory that the seller has. If the transaction is unsuccessful, reporting a truthful (negative) rating also reduces the buyer opportunity of doing business with other good sellers because other buyers will be less likely to do business with the bad seller but with the other good sellers, after taking the buyer's advice.

To address those challenges, we propose an incentive mechanism to promote buyer and seller honesty in e-marketplaces with limited inventory. In our mechanism, buyer honesty is measured by a *normalized proper scoring rule*, where a buyer can and only can gain maximal scores by providing truthful ratings. The higher score brings the buyer a higher expected utility. Seller honesty is measured by the ratings provided by buyers so that honest sellers are able to gain a high reputation. The products of sellers with a higher reputation are offered higher prices. This idea of the price premium is well supported by economic studies. Empirical evidence reveals that prices of products sold by honest sellers are generally higher [4]. The buyers' purchase intention would not be affected by the price premium provided to honest sellers [1]. Also, buyers with larger scores have more opportunities to conduct transactions with more reputable sellers. We conduct experiments to confirm that our mechanism promotes both buyer and seller honesty.

2 Our Incentive Mechanism

The e-marketplace employing our mechanism runs periodically. During each transaction period, each seller can only sell one product and each buyer can only buy one product. In the beginning of each transaction period, sellers post the products they want to sell and buyers post buying requests specifying the products they want to buy. The e-marketplace center gathers together the sellers who sell the same kind of products and the buyers who want to buy those products. It is assumed that in each transaction period, buyers' demand for the products is larger than sellers' supply of those products, meaning that the e-marketplace has limited inventory, and thus some buyers may not be able to do business with sellers. For the same products, their prices will then be determined by the e-marketplace center and these products will be allocated to some buyers. After each transaction, the buyer can provide a rating in $[0, 1]$ for the seller from whom the buyer receives the product, reflecting the buyer's satisfaction about the transaction, i.e. the ratio of the quality of the received product to that of the product promised by the seller. As the central component of the e-marketplace, our incentive mechanism is composed of a *normalized proper scoring rule*, a *reputation model*, a *pricing algorithm* and an *allocation algorithm*. More specifically, in our incentive mechanism, we measure buyer honesty by a *score* and seller honesty by *reputation*, which are updated after each transaction period. Buyer score will be updated after the buyer submits a rating according to the normalized proper scoring rule, making sure that truthful ratings provided by buyers could bring maximum scores. The seller reputation is calculated by the reputation model which aggregates ratings of the seller provided by buyers weighted by the scores of these buyers. The pricing algorithm sets higher prices for the products provided by sellers with higher reputation. The allocation algorithm ranks buyers according to their scores, and allocates products of honest sellers to buyers with the highest scores.

2.1 Modeling Buyer Honesty

Buyer honesty is measured as scores by *normalized proper scoring rules*. In this section, we provide a class of normalized proper scoring rules where buyers providing truthful ratings about sellers will be able to gain the maximal scores.

Given a binary event with two outcomes e and e', p is the actual probability of e and the actual probability of e' is $1 - p$. Let x be a predicted probability of e. If the outcome of the event is e, the agent having predicted the probability as x will be rewarded the scores $\mathbf{S}(x)$, while if the outcome is e', the agent will be rewarded $\mathbf{S}(1 - x)$ scores. The expected amount of scores of the agent is denoted as $E(\mathbf{S}, x, p) = p\mathbf{S}(x) + (1-p)\mathbf{S}(1-x)$. The scoring function $\mathbf{S}(x)$ is a proper scoring rule, if and only if $E(\mathbf{S}, p, p) \geq E(\mathbf{S}, x, p)$ and the equality is true only when $x = p$ [2]. Based on the concept of proper scoring rules, we extend them to be normalized proper scoring rules, which are comparable, even when the scores are gained from the transactions with sellers having different honesty levels in delivering promised products.

Definition 1. *(Normalized Proper Scoring Rule $\overset{\bullet}{\mathbf{S}'}$) Given a proper scoring rule $\mathbf{S}$, $Max(p) = \max_x E(\mathbf{S}, x, p)$ and $Min(p) = \min_x E(\mathbf{S}, x, p)$, a normalized proper scoring rule is defined as $\mathbf{S}'(x) = \frac{\mathbf{S}(x) - Min(p)}{Max(p) - Min(p)}$.*

From Definition 1, normalized proper scoring rules are bounded in $[0, 1]$. It is also essential that they have the same properties of the proper scoring rules, that is $E(\mathbf{S}', x, p) = p\mathbf{S}'(x) + (1-p)\mathbf{S}'(1-x)$, $E(\mathbf{S}', p, p) \geq E(\mathbf{S}', x, p)$, and equality is true only when $x = p$.

In our mechanism, the honesty of a seller s in delivering promised products is modeled by the seller's reputation R_s, which will be introduced in detail in the next section. Thus, the probability of s being dishonest is $1 - R_s$. In the end of the current transaction period t, a buyer b involved in the transaction with seller s can provide a rating indicating the buyer's satisfaction about the transaction. Once the rating is given, the buyer's score towards seller s measured by a normalized proper scoring rule as defined by Definition 1 will be updated. In consequence, the buyer's overall scores towards all sellers will also be updated.

Before we measure a buyer b's honesty $R_b(t)$, we first calculate the expectation value (denoted as $\bar{r}_b^s(t)$) of the distribution of the ratings provided by the buyer b towards seller s, including the rating given in the current transaction period. The buyer b's scores towards seller s can then be measured as follows:

$$R_b^s(t) = R_s(t-1)\mathbf{S}'(\bar{r}_b^s(t)) + (1-R_s(t-1))\mathbf{S}'(1-\bar{r}_b^s(t)) \tag{1}$$

where $\mathbf{S}'$ is a normalized proper scoring rule and $R_s(t - 1)$ is the reputation of seller s up to the previous transaction. We also count the total number of ratings given by b

towards s, denoted as $N_b^s(t)$. By weighted averaging the scores gained towards different sellers, the buyer b's overall score is calculated as follows:

$$R_b(t) = \frac{\sum_{s \in S} R_b^s(t) \times N_b^s(t)}{\sum_{s \in S} N_b^s(t)} \tag{2}$$

where S is a set of all sellers whom the buyer b has done transactions with before and provided ratings for.

2.2   Modeling Seller Honesty

The honesty of a seller s is modeled by aggregating the ratings provided by buyers (who have previously conducted transactions with s) towards the seller s based on the respective buyers' scores reflecting the buyers' honesty in providing ratings. More formally, in the end of the transaction period t, given the expectation of the distribution of a buyer b's ratings $\bar{r}_b^s(t) \in [0, 1]$ towards seller s, buyer b's score $R_b(t)$ measured by Equation 2, and the number of transactions between buyer b and seller s denoted as $N_b^s(t)$, the reputation value (in $[0, 1]$) of seller s can be calculated as follows:

$$R_s(t) = \mathbf{F}(R_s(t - 1), N_{b \in B}^s(t), R_{b \in B}(t - 1), \bar{r}_{b \in B}^s(t)) \tag{3}$$

where B is a set of all buyers whom the seller s has done transactions with before and received ratings from, and $R_s(t - 1)$ is seller reputation in the end of the previous transaction period $(t-1)$. $\mathbf{F}$ is a reputation model which can truly measure seller honesty in delivering promised product, and in this paper, we do not specify the form of $\mathbf{F}$, since it is application dependent and many reputation modeling approaches have been proposed, such as [6].

2.3   Pricing and Allocating Products

In this section, we introduce the proposed pricing algorithm and allocation algorithm. For the purpose of simplicity, we focus on one kind of products[1], and assume that buyers' valuation of the products follows some distribution in the interval $[V_*, V^*]$ where V^* and V_* are the maximal and minimal valuation of buyers towards the products provided by sellers, respectively. We also assume that sellers have the same cost C of producing that same kind of products with the highest quality, and $V_* > C$, to make sure that honest sellers are profitable.

As we analyzed in the Section 1, sellers with limited inventory generally lack of the incentive to behave honestly even with reputation mechanisms employed because reputation information about sellers cannot impose competition among sellers in such markets, and sellers with relatively low reputation can still have the chance to do business with buyers because of the limited available products in the markets. The consequence is that sellers will decrease the quality of their delivered products (also reputation) to the point where buyers' utility is minimized (i.e. approaches 0) and at the same time maximize their own profit. In our mechanism, the pricing algorithm associates sellers' profit with their behavior. More specifically, it offers higher prices to products of sellers with

---

[1] Pricing and allocating is repeated for each kind of products.

higher reputation. In this way, it creates incentives for sellers to behave honestly. At the same time, the pricing algorithm makes sure that buyers can gain sufficient utility.

In our pricing algorithm, product prices are determined by a pricing function $\mathbf{P}(R)$, where R is seller reputation modeled by Equation 3. The pricing function should satisfy the some basic requirements: 1) $\mathbf{P}(R) > 0$ for $R \in (0, 1]$; 2) $\mathbf{P}(0) = 0$; 3) $\mathbf{P}(\delta) = C$; 4) $\frac{d\mathbf{P}(R)}{dR} > 0$; 5) $\mathbf{P}(R_0) = R_0 \times C$. Requirement 1 ensures that the price set for seller with positive reputation is larger than 0. In the extreme case where sellers never deliver products at all, the price for the sellers' products should be set 0 as in Requirement 2. In Requirement 3, δ is a reputation value set by our mechanism so that the price of products provided by sellers with reputation δ is exactly equal to C. Also, the price should increase with sellers' reputation (that is a monotonically increasing function), because sellers with higher reputation bear higher cost for delivering promised products. Since $\mathbf{P}(0) = 0$ and $\mathbf{P}(\delta) = C$, there should exist a reputation value R_0 so that $\mathbf{P}(R_0) = R_0 C$, according to the continuity property of the pricing function $\mathbf{P}(R)$. Thus, when a seller's reputation $R = R_0$, the seller's profit would be $\mathbf{P}(R_0) - R_0 C = 0$. In other words, R_0 is the minimum reputation with which sellers can gain non-negative profit. Sellers with reputation lower than R_0 will not be profitable. The purpose is to disappoint those sellers who intend to take advantages of the limited inventory situation by behaving dishonestly. By setting the lowest profitable reputation R_0, sellers with reputation lower than R_0 will generally leave the market.

To come up with a proper but simple pricing function, we started with a linear function for $\mathbf{P}(R)$, however it is impossible to satisfy all the basic requirements listed above. Thus, we choose a quadratic function in the general form $\mathbf{P}(R) = aR^2 + bR + c$. Given Requirement 2 ($\mathbf{P}(0) = 0$), we have $c = 0$. Given Requirements 3 and 5, we can derive $a = \frac{C(1-\delta)}{\delta(\delta - R_0)}$ and $b = \frac{C(\delta^2 - R_0)}{\delta(\delta - R_0)}$. According to Requirement 4, we can also derive that $2aR + b > 0$, which can be satisfied by setting the constraint $\delta \geq \sqrt{R_0}$. The pseudo code summary of the pricing algorithm is shown in Algorithm 1.

Algorithm 1: The Pricing Algorithm

Input   : S, a set of sellers offering the products;
R_s, reputation of a seller $s \in S$ before the current transaction period;
C, δ, R_0, which are introduced above;

Output   : P, the price for a seller's product;

1   $a = \frac{C(1-\delta)}{\delta(\delta - R_0)}$;

2   $b = \frac{C(\delta^2 - R_0)}{\delta(\delta - R_0)}$;

3   **foreach** $s \in S$ **do**

4   $\quad\lfloor\ P_s = \mathbf{P}(R_s) = aR_s^2 + bR_s$;

In addition, our pricing algorithm has two nice properties. The first property is that buyers' profit is positive when R_0 and δ are set properly, ensuring that the buyers allocated with products of sellers will be willing to carry out the transactions with the sellers (see Proposition 2 in the next section). The second property is that buyers allocated products from sellers with higher reputation will be able to gain larger profit even though the prices of these products are higher. Therefore, buyers are willing to buy products from sellers with higher reputation (see Proposition 2). Due to the first property and the fact that not all buyers can be allocated with products (limited inventory), our allocation algorithm ensures that honest buyers (i.e. buyers with larger scores) will have higher probabilities of being allocated with products. Due to the second property, we make sure that honest buyers will also likely be allocated with products provided by sellers with higher reputation, so that honest buyers will be able to gain more profit. These create incentives for buyers to behave honestly by providing truthful ratings.

Algorithm 2: The Allocation Algorithm

Input   : B, buyers who want to buy products;

              S, a set of sellers offering the products;

              η, the exploration factor;

Output   : Allocation of products to some buyers;

1 $S_r \leftarrow$ Randomly choose η percentage of S (products);
2 $S_g \leftarrow$ The rest $1 - \eta$ percentage of S (products);
3 Sort S_g based on seller reputation in descending order;
4 Sort B based on buyer scores in descending order;

5 **foreach** $s \in S_g$ **do**
6 | Allocate product of s to ranked top buyer $b \in B$;
7 |__   Remove b from B;

8 **foreach** $s \in S_r$ **do**
9 | Allocate product of s to random buyer $b \in B$;
10 |__   Remove b from B;

Following the two properties of the pricing algorithm, we come up with the allocation algorithm whose pseudo code summary is shown in Algorithm 2. More specifically, the algorithm sets an exploration factor $\eta \in [0, 1]$. The η percentage of randomly selected products among all available products will be randomly allocated to some buyers (excluding the most honest buyers with the largest scores who will be allocated with another $1 - \eta$ percentage of products) (see Lines 8-10 in Algorithm 2). This is to make sure that new buyers will also have a fair chance to do business with sellers and later provide truthful ratings to gain scores. The η factor is set relatively high in the beginning of the operation of an e-marketplace when a large number of new buyers join the market, but will be decreased when the market becomes more mature and stable and not many new buyers will join the market. Another $1 - \eta$ percentage of all available products will be allocated to the most honest buyers (i.e. the buyers with the largest scores). in a greedy manner. To be specific, these products are sorted according to their sellers' reputation in a descending order. The buyers are also ranked in a descending order according to their scores. The products are then allocated to the buyers one by one according to the descending order, so that the products of sellers with higher reputation are given to the buyers with larger scores (see Lines 5-7 in Algorithm 2). Note that each buyer is allocated with one product in each transaction period.

3   Experimental Validation

In this section, we carry out a set of experiments to evaluate our incentive mechanism. We conduct our experiments in a dynamic setting. In the dynamic setting, some new sellers and buyers join the marketplace during the experiment.

We simulate an e-marketplace environment involving sellers and buyers exchanging the same kind of products. The total number of products provided by the sellers is less than that of the buyers' demand, i.e. a market with the limited inventory. We set $R_0 = 0.6$, $\delta = 0.85$ the cost in producing promised quality product $C = 1$, the minimal valuation of buyers towards the product $V_* = 2$ and maximal valuation of buyers towards the product $V^* = 2.5$, allocation exploration factor $\eta = 0.1$, reputation learning rate $\alpha = 0.5$, the maximal error rate of reputation model $\xi = 0.5$ and confidence level of reputation model $\gamma = 0.5$. Note that a set of simulations with variant settings has been experimented, and the results are similar.

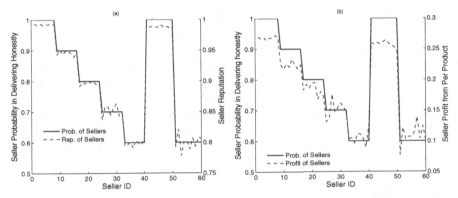

Fig. 1. The relationship between probability of sellers (a) seller reputation, (b) seller profit in selling one product. New buyers and sellers dynamically join the marketplace.

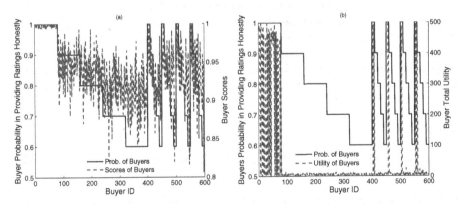

Fig. 2. The relation between buyer honesty and (a) buyer score, (b) buyer total utility

In our simulation, if a seller behaves honestly in one transaction, she delivers a quality product or a product with 50% quality. We set that the sellers have various probabilities in honest delivery and compare their average profit. For a buyer, if she behaves honestly, then she provides 1 for sellers who delivered quality products and 0.5 for sellers who deliver products with 50% quality. If the buyer is dishonest, then she provides 1 for sellers who delivered products with 50% quality and 0.5 for those who have delivered quality products. In the simulation, we allow new buyers and sellers join the marketplace during the simulation. In order to maintain our market constrain, i.e. e-marketplace with limited inventory, when a new seller joins, we allow 10 new buyers join into our system at the same time. After the boost-strapping, we let 5 new sellers and 50 new buyers (buyer honesty follows the same distribution with the existing 400 buyers) join into our simulation in every 100 transaction period. After 400 transaction periods, there are 20 new sellers (seller reputation follows the same distribution with the existing 80 sellers), and 200 new buyers participate into our market. After such a dynamic process, we simulate another 1000 transaction periods to observe seller profit and reputation. We obtain the results as shown in Figures 1 and 2.

In Figure 1, seller reputation and profit in selling one product (60 sellers in total) is shown. We observe that new honest sellers still gain the same reputation and profit as the sellers who previously existing in the e-marketplace. These results are shown in Figures 1(a) and 1(b), respectively. It means that honest sellers can always gain higher reputation and more profit no matter when they join our e-marketplace. In addition, more honest buyers gain higher scores and more utility, and these are shown in Figures 2(a) and 2(b). Therefore, the incentives of buyers and sellers in behaving honestly are still maintained when new sellers and buyers dynamically join into our e-marketplace. To conclude, our incentive mechanism ensures the sustainability of the e-marketplace by allowing new sellers and new buyers enter into our e-marketplace and our mechanism still works in such dynamic environment.

4   Conclusion

In this paper, we proposed an incentive mechanism to promote buyer and seller honesty in e-marketplaces with limited inventory. More specifically, a pricing algorithm is proposed to give high prices for products provided by honest sellers. In this way, sellers are incentivized to be honest. An allocation algorithm is proposed to allocate products of honest sellers to honest buyers. Conducting transactions with honest sellers will bring larger profit. Because of limited inventory, dishonest buyers may not be allocated any product. In this way, buyers are incentivized to be honest. We provide experimental verification for our mechanism.

References

1. Choe, Y.C., Park, J., Chung, M., Moon, J.: Effec of the food traceability system for building trust: Price premium and buying behavior. Information System Frontiers 11(2), 167–179 (2009)
2. Fang, F., Stinchcombe, M.B., Whinston, A.B.: Proper scoring rules with arbitrary value functions. Journal of Mathematical Economics 46(6), 1200–1210 (2010)
3. Jurca, R.: Truthful Reputation Mechanisms for Online Systems. Ph.D. thesis, EPFL (2007)
4. Mai, B., Menon, N.M., Sarkar, S.: No free lunch: Price premium for privacy seal-bearing vendors. Journal of Management Information Systems 27(2), 189–212 (2010)
5. Zhang, J., Cohen, R.: Design of a mechanism for promoting honesty in e-marketplaces. In: Procedings of the Conference on Artificial Intelligence, AAAI (2007)
6. Zhang, J., Cohen, R.: Evaluating the Trustworthiness of Advice about Selling Agents in E-Marketplaces: A Personalized Approach. Electronic Commerce Research and Applications 7(3), 330–340 (2008)

How Events Affect Trust: A Baseline Information Processing Model with Three Extensions

D. Harrison McKnight, Peng Liu, and Brian T. Pentland

Michigan State University
{mcknight,liup,pentland}@bus.msu.edu

Abstract. This article addresses how trust changes over time. We introduce a social psychology-based Information Processing Model (IPM) that explains how trust changes over time based on three cognitive mechanisms: attention, attribution, and judgment. This model is contrasted with the traditional incremental progression model of trust change. We also explain three extensions of the model. These models are then simulated and the results suggest that incremental progression may be inconsistent with established psychological theory.

Keywords: Trust, attention, attribution, threshold, risk, illusion, change.

1   Introduction

We define trust as the extent to which one is willing to depend on, or become vulnerable to another with a feeling of security despite situational risk. Based on social-psychological theory, this paper introduces a baseline information processing model (IPM) of how trust changes in response to external events. We then extend the baseline model in three ways and do simulations. The simulations suggest trust changes much less frequently, but in larger chunks, than in an incremental change model. We employ a process theory lens. Process theories specify which temporally-ordered occurrences are necessary for other occurrences to happen. They address how a phenomenon changes over time. Current trust change models offer a simple view of how trust changes, such as growth in small incremental steps as parties interact (e.g., [1]).

These "incremental step-by-step" trust progression models indicate interactional events lead to changes in trust levels. This helps specify the general trust change dynamic. Each positive event increases trust. However, they address the behavioral level and do not connect to the underlying cognitive processes by which humans process events. These models treat actors' detailed cognitive processes as a black box.

By contrast, Newell [9] presents a powerful example of detail-level theorizing. Newell argues that our knowledge at the biological level (e.g., neuron firing rates) should be predictive of phenomena observed at the cognitive or behavioral level (e.g., reaction time). The more detailed biological level helps explain how the cognitive level phenomenon works. Similarly, we believe that processes at the cognitive level should help explain how the process of trust changes work at a behavioral level. One

T. Dimitrakos et al. (Eds.): IFIPTM 2012, IFIP AICT 374, pp. 217–224, 2012.

reason this approach is needed is that empirical work often does not support the step-by-step trust progression models. For example, Jarvenpaa and colleagues [3] find almost no difference in virtual class team trust levels between T1 and T2. Rather, high trust teams maintained high trust and low trust teams maintained low trust. Incremental trust progression theory would predict small changes would occur based on experience. The lack of support suggests better theories of trust progression are needed.

Our IPM model builds on cognitive social psychology research because trust between people is primarily a social, mental construct [6] embodying perceptions. We focus on one person's trust perceptions with respect to one other party, either another person or a technology partner. Some of what we argue may not apply to a technology trusting a technology. The model is especially appropriate for soft trust situations or for studying reputation effects. The IPM contributes to theory by ordering the cognitive events needed to produce trust changes, an aspect of process theorizing. While the steps occur in a set temporal order, the outcome of the steps is not deterministic.

First, model action initiates when an event takes place that may have trust ramifications (Figure 1, Node 1.). The event is typically an interaction with the trustee. The model proceeds clockwise. Node 2. on Figure 1 (attention module) refers to whether the trusting person notices or pays attention to the event, which is important to trust (e.g., [7]). If the event is not noticed (2. "No" path), no subsequent steps are completed, trust stays the same, and the process awaits the next event. Attention necessarily precedes inference/attribution: "If events are noticed, people make sense of them; and if events are not noticed, they are not available for sensemaking" [4: 58-59].

Scholars posit that trust is updated through a mental attribution process [5]. After attribution, the trusting person assesses whether the attributed contradiction is serious enough to exceed the threshold cost of updating the trust level (node 4.). If not, the trust level is not updated and processing awaits the next event. If so, the update node is initiated, which increases / decreases the trust level. The person then brings a new level of trust to the perceptual system that encounters the next event. Not only is the trust level updated, but the likelihood of attending to and attributing about an event are also updated. We now briefly justify the model.

2   The Baseline Information Processing Model

By attention, we mean the person expends cognitive effort on the event instead of ignoring it. The mind only consciously processes a small percentage of stimuli. People often ignore information that does not match what they believe. An event passes through the trustor's perceptual / memory module before they pay attention to it (Figure 1). Thus attention is a necessary mental process that occurs before a trust change takes place. Although attention is necessary, it is not sufficient to change trust. Instead, the trustor must go through attribution and judgment subprocesses first [5].

Assumption 1: Trustor attention to a behavioral event is a necessary but not sufficient condition for the change in a trustor's level of trust.

Attribution means how a person makes sense of an event. One ascribes underlying qualities or enduring motivations to the other based on observable evidence. Because

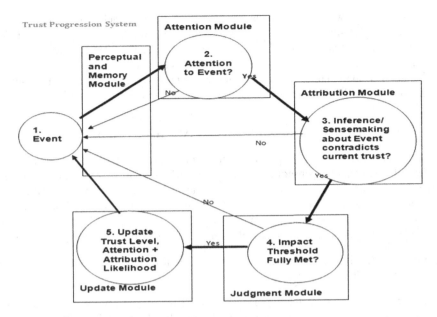

Fig. 1. Trust Development: A Baseline Information Processing Model (IPM)

attributions are subjective and affected by mood, their outcomes are hard to predict. Only when the cause of an event is decided can trust be updated, and only when the event's attribution contradicts one's existing trust perceptions is an update made. A trustor must perceive a clear contradiction between the existing trust level and event-implied trustworthiness before trust is updated. Even after a contradictory attribution takes place, a threshold judgment must still take place. Hence, attribution is necessary but not sufficient for a change in trust.

Assumption 2: Trustor attribution that a behavioral event contradicts current trust levels is a necessary but not sufficient condition for the change in the level of trust.

After making an attribution, a trustor judges whether it meets the threshold for revising trust levels. This is termed a judgment module because it compares the reasons or benefits for updating trust with the costs of updating trust. Judgment is defined as making a size comparison between two objects, which we argue are the perceived costs and benefits of a trust level change. Changing trust is cognitively expensive because trust is a central, highly connected relationship concept. If you alter trust, you have to change a number of other beliefs, such as liking and respect of O. It costs less to maintain existing beliefs and consider the event a quirk. Holmes [2] and Luhmann [5] discuss how trust changes involve thresholds.

Assumption 3: Exceeding a cost-versus-benefit threshold for changing trust is a necessary condition for the change in a trustor's level of trust.

Once the threshold is exceeded, the trust level is updated by some amount. The likelihood of attending to and attributing about the next event will also be affected. If trust goes down, one will be more likely to notice and attribute about the next event.

The IPM shows why trust changes are hard to predict [5]. Each of three sequential, probabilistic, inter-related process mechanisms (attention, attribution, threshold judgment) must operate consecutively for trust to change. The IPM also suggests that trust trends will tend to be "sticky." Once a trust level is firmly fixed, it may be hard to change. The incremental progression model suggests that small, frequent changes occur. Instead, the IPM suggests changes will be relatively infrequent and large.

3   Three Model Extensions—Risk, Negative Change, Illusion

Perceived situational risk is important to trust attribution. Situational risk means the likelihood that negative consequences will occur in the context. The higher the perceived situational risk, the more one will attend to an event and make attributions about it. Low risk situations do not get one's attention like high risk ones do. Similarly, attribution takes mental energy that will not be expended unless one thinks the risk justifies it. Thus, low risk situations will produce less effortful attribution.

Assumption 4: Higher perceived situational risk will increase the likelihood of both attention and attribution to events.

Will trust decreases be greater in magnitude than trust increases? The literature suggests the answer is "yes." Trust is easier to destroy than build, and cognitive research suggests negative trust-related events are easier to remember and have a greater relative effect than do positive events.

Assumption 5: Negative changes to trust will be significantly greater in magnitude than will positive changes in trust.

In committed romantic relationships people idealize their partner and use that idealized perception to dispel the effects of negative events [7]. This may also occur in business relationships. Illusion means the extent to which a partner is more optimistic about their relationship's future than rationally merited. When one has positive illusions, a set of positive/negative events will continue those illusions. Such a pattern provides equivocal evidence about O. However, when negative evidence is consistent across events, the evidence will be considered less equivocal. Then the illusionary "bubble" will burst and the pattern will stop until a consistent positive pattern occurs.

Assumption 6: Illusionary partners will reinterpret negative events as positive events. An accumulation of negative events will remove this reinterpretation effect, which will continue until an accumulation of consistently positive events reinstates it.

4   Method

4.1   Baseline Model

We simulate the above using MATLAB 7.11, as follows.

Events (E). A positive value means a good event and a negative value a bad event. Event values follow a normal distribution with zero as mean and one as standard deviation ($E \sim N(0, 1)$). The total number of events is $N = 1000$.

Memory (M). In this model, we assume M=10 which means a person remembers the most recent past ten events. When a new event is remembered, the oldest event is "forgotten." Memory will decay over time, as the value of events in the memory decreases by 10% as every new event happens ($E_T = E_{T-1} \times 0.9$).

Attention (A). Attention is the probability that one notices an event. Assuming a low baseline risk level, we set the probability at 30% chance that one will attend to an event. As trust increases, attention decreases (in proportion as trust changes), because people who feel secure pay less attention. When trust decreases, attention increases.

Attribution (R). The probability of full attribution about the event is Attribution (R). Because of the complex issues for Assumption 2 above, we set the initial probability of attribution at 0.3. An increase in trust leads to a lower probability of attribution about the next event. A decrease in trust leads to a higher probability.

Threshold (Th). To model this, we put a threshold of 0.5 for the baseline model. If the absolute value of the sum of the event values in memory is greater than the threshold, trust will be updated; otherwise trust will remain the same.

Trust (T). This model keeps track of the trust level (T) of a person and how it changes when a person experiences a stream of random events. Trust ranges from 0.0 to 1.0. Initially, we set the trust level to 0.5. This reflects the assumption that people give each other the benefit of the doubt when they first start to deal with each other [5]. When trust is being updated, the change of trust is one half the difference between the absolute value of the sum of the event values in memory and the threshold value. For example, if the sum is positive and 20% higher than the threshold, then trust will increase by 10%; and attention and attribution will decrease by 10%. If the sum is negative and the absolute value of the sum is 15% higher than the threshold, then trust will decrease by 7.5%; and attention and attribution will increase by 7.5%.

4.2   Three Extensions That Affect the Baseline Model

4.2.1   Situational Risk Model

There are high risk, medium risk and low risk situations (0.9, 0.6, and 0.3). The baseline model has low risk, with initial attention and attribution at 0.3, and memory effect at 10. The starting values of attention (A) and attribution (R) are equal to the value of the event risk (ER). When risk is high, there is no change in the attention and attribution; when risk is medium, the change of attention and attribution is 50% of what the baseline model says they should change; when risk is low, the change of attention and attribution is governed by the baseline model. Higher risk has a long memory effect (20 events recalled), medium risk has a medium memory effect (15 events), and low risk has a short memory effect (10).

4.2.2   Negativity Asymmetry Model

In the stronger negativity effect model, a negative event has twice the effect on trust as a positive event. So when a negative effect triggers the trust change, trust will change double what it would change in the baseline model; the baseline model governs the effects of a positive event.

4.2.3   Illusion Model

When the illusion effect is on (including initially), trust will keep increasing by taking the absolute value of the difference between the sum of the entire event values in memory and the threshold, even if a negative event triggers the trust change. But when there are three negative events in a row, the illusion effect is turned off, and the model becomes the baseline model and trust goes either up or down. If three positive events occur in a row, this turns back on the illusion effect.

5   Results

The following tables display simulation results. The incremental progression model simulates trust changing after each event, with the change magnitude equaling the event size ($E \sim N(0, 0.1)$). Table 1 also depicts medians of the magnitude, frequency, and trend of the trust level across 1000 events. Magnitude means the average size of the change in trust level for an event. Table 1 shows that the median baseline model magnitude of change is over twice that of the incremental progression model. Frequency means the number of changes in trust that have occurred divided by the number of events. Frequency of trust change is significantly lower for the baseline model and its extensions than for the incremental progression model. Trend means the average number of times trust changes in the same direction (e.g., increase) before it starts changing in the other direction (e.g., decrease). Note that the direction changes often for the incremental progression model, yielding a low trend figure (1.99), while in the other models trust progresses longer without changing direction.

Table 2 shows the first 200 events of three randomly selected simulations to illustrate the shape of the trust progression curve. The incremental progression model shows that trust changes often in small random increments. The baseline model shows a more infrequent change pattern with higher magnitude of the average trust change. The negativity asymmetry shows a similar trend, but with a decreasing direction. The medium and high situational risk models have even wider swings, both up and down.

Table 1. Medians for Simulated Model Instances

n = 1000	Magnitude	Frequency	Trend
Incremental Progression Model	0.023	0.835	1.998
Baseline Model (Low Risk)	0.049	0.097	4.280
Negativity Asymmetry Model	0.044	0.124	5.000
Medium Risk Model	0.055	0.146	4.567
High Risk Model	0.056	0.526	7.725
Illusion Model	0.054	0.096	5.875

6   Discussion

The simulation results are quite striking. First, as shown in Table 1, the magnitude of trust changes is much higher in every version of the IPM model than for the conventional incremental change model. The difference is particularly pronounced in high risk situations, where trust is most important. Qualitatively, this is a good fit with empirical results, which show that trust levels can make wide, sudden swings.

Table 2. Random Sample Displays of Trust Progression under Different Assumptions

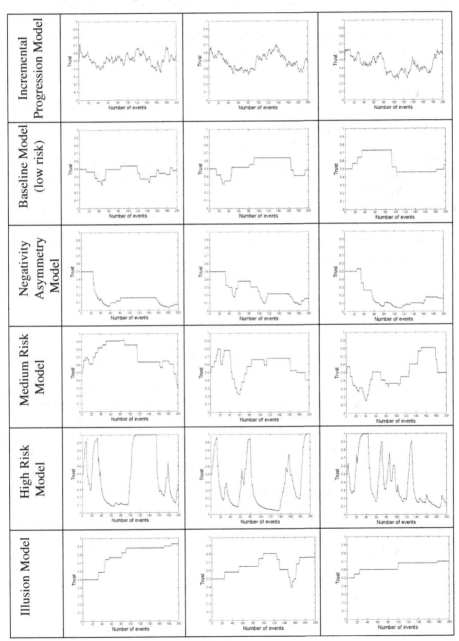

Second, as shown in Table 1, the frequency of change is much lower in every version of the IPM model than for the conventional incremental change model. This matches empirical findings that once it reaches a stable state, trust tends to be "sticky" and difficult to change. People do not notice or react to every little event.

Third, the IPM model predicts that trust changes will have momentum: when a change in trust level occurs, subsequent changes trend in the same direction. In the incremental progression model, random events generate two similar changes in a row, on average. In the IPM-based models, the same stream of events generates between 4 and 8 consecutive changes in the same direction (Table 1, Trend column).

7   Conclusion

The IPM contributes by providing a process theory of trust change that is grounded in social psychology's cognitive information processing. First, the model addresses the mental mechanisms people use as they are confronted by trust-related events. The Information Processing Model suggests these mechanisms must each be engaged for trust to change. Second, the model illustrates several reasons trust does not change under many circumstances that one might think warrant change. The model indicates that trust may be "sticky" or resistant to change, but that change can and will occur. The model is especially applicable to studies of reputation, soft trust, social networking, and e-commerce/mobile commerce.

References

1. Blau, P.M.: Exchange and Power in Social Life. John Wiley & Sons, New York (1964)
2. Holmes, J.G.: Trust and the Appraisal Process in Close Relationships. In: Jones, W.H., Perlman, D. (eds.) Advances in Personal Relationships (2), pp. 57–104. Jessica Kingsley, London (1991)
3. Jarvenpaa, S.L., Knoll, K., Leidner, D.E.: Is Anybody Out There? Antecedents of Trust in Global Virtual Teams. Journal of Management Information Systems 14, 29–64 (1998)
4. Louis, M.R., Sutton, R.I.: Switching Cognitive Gears: From Habits of Mind to Active Thinking. Human Relations 44, 55–76 (1991)
5. Luhmann, N.: Trust and Power. John Wiley, New York (1979)
6. Marsh, S.P.: Formalising trust as a computational concept, Ph.D. Thesis, University of Stirling (1994)
7. Muir, B.M.: Trust in Automation: Part I. Theoretical Issues in the Study of Trust and Human Intervention in Automated Systems. Ergonomics 37, 1905–1922 (1994)
8. Murray, S.L., Holmes, J.G.: A Leap of Faith? Positive Illusions in Romantic Relationships. Personal and Social Psychology Bulletin 23, 586–604 (1997)
9. Newell, A.: Unified Theories of Cognition. Harvard University Press, Cambridge (1990)

Improvements over Extended LMAP+: RFID Authentication Protocol

Jitendra B. Gurubani, Harsh Thakkar, and Dhiren R. Patel

Department of Computer Engineering, NIT Surat-395007, India
{jitendra.gurubani,harsh9t,dhiren29p}@gmail.com

Abstract. Radio Frequency Identification (RFID) systems are increasingly being deployed in a variety of applications. Widespread deployment of such contactless systems raises many security and privacy concerns due to unauthorized eavesdropping reader, de-synchronization between reader and tag etc. In this paper, we propose a light weight mutual authentication protocol which is an improvement over Li's extended LMAP+ protocol. In mutual authentication, the tag and the reader of the RFID systems will authenticate each other before transmitting unique ID of tag. The proposed protocol provides protection over traceability and de-synchronization attacks.

Keywords: RFID, Pseudonym, LMAP, Mutual Authentication Protocol.

1   Introduction

Radio Frequency Identification (RFID) systems are used for automated identification of objects and people. Applications that use RFID technology include warehouse management, logistics, railroad car tracking, product identification, library books check-in/check-out, asset tracking, passport and credit cards, etc. Most of the RFID systems comprise of three entities: the tag, the reader and the back-end database. The tag is a highly constrained microchip (with antenna) that stores the unique tag identifier and other related information about an object. The reader is a device that can read/modify the stored information of the tags and transfer these data to a back-end database, with or without modification. Back end database stores this information and will keep track of the data exchanged by the reader [1].

The possible security threats to RFID systems include denial of service (DoS), man in the middle (MIM), counterfeiting, spoofing, eavesdropping, traffic analysis, traceability, de-synchronization etc.

The low cost deployment demand for RFID tags forces the lack of resources for performing true cryptographic operations to provide security. Typically, tags can only store few hundred bits and have very limited number of logic gates, out of which very few can be devoted to security tasks. Considering these resource constraints, we aimed for authentication protocol that uses light weight primitives.

The rest of the paper is organized as follows: Background and related work are discussed in section 2. Section 3 describes system design considerations and the proposed protocol. Section 4 shows defense against traceability and de-synchronization attacks with conclusions and references at the end.

T. Dimitrakos et al. (Eds.): IFIPTM 2012, IFIP AICT 374, pp. 225–231, 2012.

2   Related Work

Providing light weight security in RFID systems is not a trivial task. Vajda and L. Buttyan [2] have proposed a set of extremely lightweight challenge response authentication algorithms. These can be used for authenticating the tags, but they may be easily attacked by a powerful adversary. Juels [3] proposed a solution based on the use of pseudonyms, without using any hash function. The RFID tag stores a short list of pseudonyms, which indexes a table (row) where all the information about a tag is stored: it is rotated releasing a different index on each reader query. After a set of authentication sessions, the list of pseudonyms will need to be reused or updated through an out-of-band channel, which limits the practicality of this scheme. In addition to this there are other lightweight mutual authentication protocols proposed in the literature [4-6]. Attacks have been successfully mounted on all of these as demonstrated in literature [7-9].

Peris *et al.* in [10], Proposed a Lightweight Mutual Authentication Protocol called LMAP. They also proposed an extension of this protocol LMAP+. These protocols are extremely lightweight and use only simple bitwise operations. However, attacks are mounted on this as well. It has been discovered that these protocols do not achieve the security they claim [11]. Later, following the LMAP designing strategy, Li [12] proposed a new lightweight protocol which is extension of LMAP proposed by Peris *et al.* in [10]. After that, Safkhani *et al.* in [14] presented two possible attacks on protocol which is extension of LMAP+.

We propose an improvement over Li's protocol [12] LMAP+ - incorporating better security and without compromising performance. Proposed protocol follows the structure and design of LMAP+ [12]; extended to provide defense against traceability and de-synchronization attacks.

3   Proposed Protocol: Improved LMAP+

3.1   Design Considerations

Fig.1 shows three main entities (tag, reader and database) of the RFID systems which are involved in the mutual authentication scenarios. Database and reader are connected through a secure wired channel while the tag and reader are connected through wireless channel which is insecure and is our main focus. We will consider database and reader as one unit responsible for maintaining the database where all the tag records are stored in a central table and tag as another unit which is to be authenticated. Before the tags are attached to the objects of the RFID applications, its Unique ID and Pseudo-ID are written in its ROM and EEPROM respectively together with several secret values (for authentication purpose).

The properties of the proposed protocol (Improved LMAP+) are:

- **Privacy:** A tag's Unique ID is never disclosed to an unauthorized reader. Only the authorized reader will identify the Tag by its Pseudo-ID along with its corresponding tag entry in the database. Pseudo-ID and the keys used will be changed after every successful protocol round.

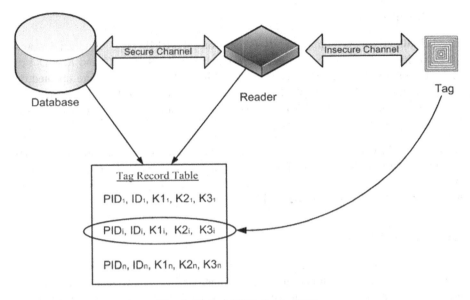

Fig. 1. Typical RFID System [12]

- **Security:** The scheme defends against various attacks like: sniffing attack, spoofing attack, active man-in-the-middle attack, traceability attack and desynchronization attack etc.
- **Compactness:** The proposed protocol uses only ultra-lightweight functions like X-OR and mod 2^m addition as used by Li in [12], whose hardware implementations is very simple.

3.2   Protocol Notations

In the proposed protocol, costly operations such as multiplications and hash evaluations are not used at all, and random number generation is only done at the reader end. Frequently used notations in this paper are listed below:

$ID_{tag(i)}$: Tag's unique identifier.

$PID_{tag(i)}^n$: Tag's dynamic pseudonym at the nth successful run of protocol.

$K1_{tag(i)}^n$, $K2_{tag(i)}^n$ and $K3_{tag(i)}^n$: Tag's secret keys at the nth successful run of protocol.

   r   : Reader generated pseudorandom number.

A, B, C : Messages transferred between reader and tag.

$\oplus$: XOR operation.

$\|$: concatenation operator.

$+$: addition mod 2^m.

$(X)_n$: n^{th} Bit of x

All parameters (i.e. ID, PID, K1, K2, K3, r, A, B, C) in the protocol are of 96-bit size as per EPC class 1 Gen2.

3.3   Initialization

Tag Initialization: Assuming 96-bits as one word, the RFID tag is assigned 5 words which include a Pseudo-ID, a tag unique ID and three keys ($K1$, $K2$ and $K3$). Out of these, tag unique ID is static (should be stored in ROM) and the rest are updated on every successful run of protocol (should be stored in EEPROM). Thus, tag requires 96 bits of ROM and 384 bits of EEPROM (4*96). Considering L as word size the tag has 5L bits of storage requirement.

Database Initialization: A central database is built in order to store all the information relevant to the RFID Tags. For each tag, it stores a row [*PID, ID, K1, K2, K3*]. All rows are listed in a single database table. If we have N tags, there will be N records and the total database size will be 5*N*L bits.

3.4   Protocol Description

The protocol has three main stages: tag identification, mutual authentication and updating. These stages are shown in table 1. Equations in first two stages are same as proposed in LMAP+ [12], except last equation in stage 2 – Mutual Authentication.

Table 1. Improved LMAP+: n^{th} Protocol Run between Tag and Reader (* shows modified or improved equations)

Tag Identification Reader → Tag: Hello Tag   → Reader: $PID^n_{tag(i)}$
Mutual Authentication Reader → Tag: $A \ // \ B$ Tag   → Reader: C Where, $A = PID^n_{tag(i)} \oplus K1^n_{tag(i)} + r$ $B = PID^n_{tag(i)} + K2^n_{tag(i)} + r$ $C = PID^n_{tag(i)} \oplus (K3^n_{tag(i)} + r) *$
Updating By both Reader and Tag $PID^{n+1}_{tag(i)} = PID^n_{tag(i)} \oplus r + (K1^n_{tag(i)} + K2^n_{tag(i)} + K3^n_{tag(i)}) *$ $K1^{n+1}_{tag(i)} = K1^n_{tag(i)} \oplus r + (PID^{n+1}_{tag(i)} + K2^n_{tag(i)}) *$ $K2^{n+1}_{tag(i)} = K2^n_{tag(i)} \oplus r + (PID^{n+1}_{tag(i)} + K3^n_{tag(i)}) *$ $K3^{n+1}_{tag(i)} = K3^n_{tag(i)} \oplus r + (PID^{n+1}_{tag(i)} + K1^n_{tag(i)}) *$

- **Tag Identification:** To start the protocol for mutual authentication, the reader has to identify the tag. The reader will initiate the protocol by sending a hello message to the tag, which will be responded by the tag sending its current pseudonym (PID). By means of this PID, only an authorized reader is able to search the database and access the tag's corresponding secret keys ($K = K1/K2/K3$), which are needed to carry out the next authentication stages.
- **Mutual Authentication:** Initially the reader generates a random number r. Using r along with the keys $K1$ and $K2$; the reader generates the messages A and B, and then sends them to the tag. Thus, the reader actually conveys a random challenge to the tag. At the tag side, upon receiving the messages A and B, the tag can calculate two random numbers ($r1$ from A and $r2$ from B) using secret keys $K1$ and $K2$ respectively. If $r1$ equals to $r2$, the tag can obtain r correctly and prepare the response message C as detailed by Li in [12]. On the reader side it calculates the value of C according to the equation in the table 1, as it has all required parameters and compares the calculated C value with the one received from the tag. If both are equal, the tag is authenticated. Then using the PID value, the reader retrieves the unique tag ID from the database table and considers the tag with this ID as detected. Hereafter that reader proceeds with update operations. If the reader is not authenticated, the authentication protocol is aborted. This makes the tag identification by the reader without actually transmitting the unique ID of the tag.
- **Updating:** Major improvements over LMAP+ are incorporated in this stage. After the reader and the tag have authenticated each other, they carry out the pseudonym and keys updating operations at both sides synchronously as mentioned by the equations in table 1.

The mechanism for synchronization is same as described by Li [12]. Both reader and tag contain a status bit in the protocol denoted by s. In each run, if the protocol is successfully completed, s will be initialized with 0 otherwise it is set to 1. Hence, $s = 1$ indicates that the protocol was aborted. So it should be reset or restarted.

4   Security against Traceability and De-synchronization Attacks

According to Li's protocol in [12]:

$$A = PID_{tag(i)}^{n} \oplus K1_{tag(i)}^{n} + r \tag{1}$$

$$B = PID_{tag(i)}^{n} + K2_{tag(i)}^{n} \oplus r \tag{2}$$

$$C = (PID_{tag(i)}^{n} + ID_{tag(i)} \oplus r) \oplus (K1_{tag(i)}^{n} + K2_{tag(i)}^{n} + r) \tag{3}$$

Our protocol reflects improvements as indicated by * in table 1.

4.1   Traceability Defense

According to Safkhani *et al.* [14], if we consider only last significant bit (LSB) then the modular additions mod 2^{m} can be replaced by bitwise XOR. Therefore, any adversary can extract and trace the last significant bit of tag unique ID by knowing $PID_{tag(i)}^n$, A, B and C as follows:

$$(ID_{tag(i)})_0 = (A)_0 \oplus (B)_0 \oplus (C)_0 \oplus (PID_{tag(i)}^n)_0$$

Our proposal (Improved LMAP+) provides defense against this attack as the actual unique ID of the tag is not transmitted and hence it will not be extracted by the adversary.

4.2   De-synchronization Defense

The main aim in this attack is to convince the tag and reader to update their common parameters to different values. With different values of common parameters; tag and reader will not be able to authenticate each other for future transactions. According to Safkhani *et al.* [14], if we assume that $(PID_{tag(i)}^n)_0$, $(K1_{tag(i)}^n)_0$, $(K2_{tag(i)}^n)_0$ and $(ID_{tag(i)})_0$ are zero then adversary can mount the attack by toggling the LSBs of A, B and r. It will have no impact on the correctness of above equations 1, 2 and 3. Only the random number retrieved at tag side will be different than the one sent by the reader. Tag and reader will authenticate each other and update their common parameters to different values as both have different r value which will be used in updating stage.

In our proposal, the random number r is used only once in the formation of equation C. Therefore, if the adversary changes the LSBs of A, B and r then the calculated value of C from tag will differ from the expected C value. Reader will not authenticate this tag and the transaction will be aborted. So, the de-synchronization attack is defended.

5   Conclusion

Improvements in Mutual authentication protocol for low cost RFID systems are proposed in this paper.

As it is an extension over LMAP+ protocol, it inherits security against tag cloning, spoofing and man in the middle attack as provided by LMAP+ protocol. In addition it is secure against traceability and de-synchronization attacks for which LMAP+ was not secure as shown by Safkhani *et al.* in [14]. The improved protocol is secure (more trustworthy than LMAP+) and uses ultra light weight bitwise operations.

References

1. Hunt, V.D., Puglia, A., Puglia, M.: RFID: A Guide to Radio Frequency Identification. Wiley-Inter science (2007)
2. Vajda, I., Buttyan, L.: Lightweight authentication protocols for low-cost RFID tags. In: Proc. of UBICOMP 2003 (2003)

3. Juels, A.: Minimalist Cryptography for Low-Cost RFID Tags (Extended Abstract). In: Blundo, C., Cimato, S. (eds.) SCN 2004. LNCS, vol. 3352, pp. 149–164. Springer, Heidelberg (2005)
4. Sadighian, Jalili, R.: Afmap: Anonymous forward-secure mutual authentication protocols for rfid systems. In: Third IEEE International Conference on Emerging Security Information, Systems and Technologies (SECURWARE 2009), pp. 31–36 (2009)
5. Sadighian, Jalili, R.: Flmap: A fast lightweight mutual authentication protocol for rfid systems. In: 16th IEEE International Conference on Networks (ICON 2008), New Delhi, India, pp. 1–6 (2008)
6. Chien, H.-Y.: SASI: A New Ultralightweight RFID Authentication Protocol Providing Strong Authentication and Strong Integrity. IEEE Transactions on Dependable and Secure Computing 4(4), 337–340 (2007)
7. Safkhani, M., Naderi, M., Bagher, N.: Cryptanalysis of AFMAP. IEICE Electronics Express 7(17), 1240–1245 (2010)
8. Safkhani, M., Naderi, M., Rashvand, H.: Cryptanalysis of AFMAP. International Journal of Computer & Communication Technologys 2(2), 182–186 (2010)
9. Bárász, M., Boros, B., Ligeti, P., Lója, K., Nagy, D.: Passive Attack Against the M2AP Mutual Authentication Protocol for RFID Tags. In: First International EURASIP Workshop on RFID Technology, Vienna, Austria (2007)
10. Peris-Lopez, P., Hernandez-Castro, J.C., Estevez-Tapiador, J.M., Ribagorda, A.: Lmap: A real lightwight mutual authentication protocol for low-cost rfid tags. In: Proceedings of RFIDSec 2006 Workshop on RFID Security, Graz, Austria, July 12-14 (2006)
11. Li, T., Wang, G.: Security Analysis of Two Ultra-Lightweight RFID Authentication Protocols. In: IFIP SEC 2007, Sandton, Gauteng, South Africa (2007)
12. Li, T.: Employing lightweight primitives on low-cost rfid tags for authentication. In: VTC Fall, pp. 1–5 (2008)
13. Niu, B., Li, H., Zhu, X., Lv, C.: Security Analysis of Some Recent Authentication Protocols for RFID. In: 2011 Seventh International Conference on Computational Intelligence and Security (CIS), pp. 665–669 (2011)
14. Safkhani, M., Bagheri, N., Naderi, M., Sanadhya, S.K.: Security analysis of LMAP++, an RFID authentication protocol. In: 2011 International Conference for Internet Technology and Secured Transactions (ICITST), pp. 689–694 (2011)

Automated Evaluation of Annotators
for Museum Collections Using Subjective Logic

Davide Ceolin, Archana Nottamkandath, and Wan Fokkink

VU University Amsterdam
De Boelelaan 1081a, 1081HV Amsterdam, The Netherlands
{d.ceolin,a.nottamkandath,w.j.fokkink}@vu.nl

Abstract. Museums are rapidly digitizing their collections, and face a huge challenge to annotate every digitized artifact in store. Therefore they are opening up their archives for receiving annotations from experts world-wide. This paper presents an architecture for choosing the most eligible set of annotators for a given artifact, based on semantic relatedness measures between the subject matter of the artifact and topics of expertise of the annotators. We also employ mechanisms for evaluating the quality of provided annotations, and constantly manage and update the trust, reputation and expertise information of registered annotators.[1]

1 Introduction

Cultural and heritage preserving organizations such as museums are rapidly digitizing their collections, and at the same time migrating digitized collections to the Web. Thus, there is a growing need for seeking experts world-wide for providing high quality annotations for digitized artifacts. This paper presents an architecture for finding such experts.

Unlike online content collaboration sites such as Wikipedia, museums cannot risk anyone say anything about a particular topic. Annotations should be provided only by trusted sources, and should be validated by museum experts or peers who have sufficient proven expertise in the same topic. We assume that a generic initial classification of the artifact is already available in the form of specific set of tags or keywords by digital curators, (e.g. indicating the period of production or the type of artifact). Most museums use a standard thesaurus (such as Iconclass [11]), which serves as a basis for deriving relations between the various artifacts, and forms a controlled vocabulary for annotations. The selection of experts who can provide an annotation for a certain topic is based on a proper average of an expert's reputation and the "semantic similarity" between the requested topic and the recorded expertise areas of the expert. Thus we select experts who can be trusted to provide quality annotations.

Moreover, we employ mechanisms for evaluating the quality of provided annotations. We constantly manage and update the trust, reputation and expertise

---

[1] This research is carried out as part of a Dutch FES COMMIT project entitled Socially Enriched Access To Linked Cultural Media (SEALINC).

T. Dimitrakos et al. (Eds.): IFIPTM 2012, IFIP AICT 374, pp. 232–239, 2012.

information of registered annotators by employing trust algorithms based on subjective logic [14], which is a probabilistic logic that takes into account uncertainty and belief ownership, to model and analyze situations that involve incomplete knowledge. This work extends previous work on determining the quality of annotations using (Semantic) Web sources [4] by combining subjective logic with measures of semantic relatedness, thereby providing an extensive model for managing annotations.

2 Related Work

Cultural heritage organizations are opening up their archives to external user contributions mainly classified as: (1) *Social tagging*, where users link artifacts with "tags", i.e, words generically related to them (see for instance the "Steve Social Tagging Project" [13] and the "Uncovering Nation's Art Collection" project [1] from BBC); (2) *Collaborative authoring*, mainly in case of encyclopedias (see [8]); (3) *Annotations*, where the requested "tags" specifically describe one aspect of the artifact [4].

Recommender systems are widely employed in media-related systems to provide valuable suggestions to the users (e.g. [10,20]). In collaborative communities such as Wikipedia, the correct allocation of tasks is done by intelligent task routing systems [7]. User participation increased up to four-fold when online tasks were mapped to user interests (see [5]). In cultural heritage organizations, the quality and trustworthiness of contributions play a vital role. There is a considerable amount of research on finding experts (as trustworhty contributors) in online communities such as Wikipedia [2] and online forums [22].

Semantic relatedness is a concept where sets of terms are assigned a metric based on the likeness of their meaning/semantic content. User interests are recorded and various thesauri are employed for deriving semantically related interests in content-based recommender systems for museums (e.g. [19]). Recent standardization efforts, such as SKOS [17], have lowered the technical boundaries to publish thesauri on the Web.

3 Adopted Methods and Technologies

Semantic Relatedness. This is a measure that indicates how closely two concepts relate in a taxonomy, given all existing relations between them. We use a WordNet [15] based similarity relatedness measure. WordNet is a large lexical database of English, often used by museums and similar to the models that they use to categorize and describe their artifacts.

Semantic Web Technologies. They include a wide range of formats and technologies aimed at enhancing the Semantic Web vision (which may be summarized with the slogan "moving from a Web of documents to a Web of data"). We use some of them, in particular:

- URIs: Uniform Resource Identifiers offer unique references to any possible entity (e.g.: annotators, artifacts, concepts).
- RDF: the Resource Definition Framework is basically a language for representing graphs. RDF statements are "triples" (Subject, Predicate, Object), where each of these elements can be either a URI or a literal value (with some restrictions).
- Ontologies: defined using RDFS/OWL language, ontologies define types, properties, etc., of URIs in particular contexts. For example, they allow to distinguish URIs referring to sets of users from those representing concepts. We use the following ontologies:
  - Friend Of A Friend (**foaf**) [3]: for representing people and connections among them.
  - Simple Knowledge Organization System (**skos**) [17]: for representing "concepts" and semantic relations among them.
  - Hoonoh (**hoonoh**) [9]: for representing expertise.
  - RDF Data Cube (**qb**) [6]: for representing multi-dimensional data.
  - Dublin Core Terms (**dcterms**) [12]: for representing meta-data.
  - PROV (**prov**) [18]: for representing provenance information.

Subjective Logic. Evidence about the expertise and reliability of annotators is handled by means of a probabilistic logic named subjective logic which represents the estimated truth value of propositions by means of subjective opinions. An opinion $\omega_{subject}^{object}(belief, disbelief, uncertainty, apriori)$ is defined by (1) and (2).

$$belief + disbelief + uncertainty = 1, \qquad apriori \in [0...1] \qquad (1)$$

$$belief = \frac{p}{p+n+2} \quad disbelief = \frac{n}{p+n+2} \quad uncertainty = \frac{2}{p+n+2} \qquad (2)$$

$$E = belief + apriori \cdot uncertainty \qquad (3)$$

p and n are the amount of positive and negative evidence respectively. *apriori* is the prior knowledge owned about the expertise, which does not change over time; its influence on the trust value computation lowers as we collect new evidence. In case of a lack of prior knowledge, the default value for *apriori* is 0.5, which is equally far from zero (*false*) and one (*true*).

The expected value of an opinion (3), which corresponds to the trust value we want to represent, is an expected value in the statistical sense, since it is the expected value of the Dirichlet distribution equivalent to the opinion. The distribution describes the probability of each value between zero and one to be the right trust value and its shape depends on the value of the opinion.

4   Model

Our model aims at obtaining trustworthy annotations through crowdsourcing. It is composed of two parts, strongly interlinked: data representation and algorithm. These two parts are connected by subjective opinions: the first part provides a representation for the expertise, i.e., the "object" of our opinions, whereas the algorithm computes the trust levels and outputs the most trustworthy annotations.

4.1   Data Representation

The expertise of each annotator is recorded, through the hoonoh ontology, by linking the URI representing the user to the one representing the concept of expertise. In RDF statements, it is represented as follows:

eg:T1 a **hoonoh**:Topic , **skos**:Concept.
eg:user a **foaf**:Person .
eg:E1 a **hoonoh**:ExpertiseRelationship ;
    hoonoh:from **eg**:user ;
    hoonoh:toTopic **eg**:T1 .

We define a data structure representing a subjective opinion, we link it to the corresponding hoonoh:ExpertiseRelationship and then populate it with observations, i.e., opinion instances:

eg:Opinion a **qb**:DataStructureDefinition ;
    qb:component
        [**qb**:measure **eg**:belief;] ,
        [**qb**:measure **eg**:disbelief;] ,
        [**qb**:measure **eg**:uncertainty;] ,
        [**qb**:measure **eg**:apriori;] .

eg:dataset a **qb**:DataSet ;
    qb:structure **eg**:Opinion ;
    dcterms:subject **eg**:E1 .

eg:obs1a a **qb**:Observation , **prov**:Entity ;
    qb:dataSet **eg**:dataset ;
    prov:wasAttributedTo **eg**:Museum;
    eg:belief 0.4;
    eg:disbelief 0.2;
    eg:uncertainty 0.4;
    eg:apriori 0.5.

Museum artifacts are annotated objects of type skos:Concept. E.g.:

eg:item1 **dcterms**:subject **eg**:T1.

4.2   Trust (Expertise) Management

We are interested in determining the user expertise about a given topic, so, if eg:E1 is of type **hoonoh**:ExpertiseRelationship, an opinion is:

$$expertise(user, T1) = \omega \ \substack{\textbf{eg}:E1 \ \textbf{hoonoh}:from \ \textbf{eg}:user \\ \textbf{eg}:E1 \ \textbf{hoonoh}:toTopic \ \textbf{eg}:T1}^{(b, d, u, a)} \qquad (4)$$

We assume that users are evaluated (e.g. through a questionnaire) when registered. This evaluation is represented by the *apriori* component, which provides an initial indication of the user expertise. As the user provides candidate values for annotations and these are evaluated, the weight of the *apriori* on the trust value will decrease. When evaluating the expertise of the user about a topic T1, the opinion is computed as in (2) but, before summming them, each piece of evidence is weighed on its semantic similarity with T1.

4.3   Algorithm

We introduce a pseudo-code algorithm that computes the trust levels and outputs the most trustworthy annotations, and we provide a qualitative description of it.

> **for all** *request* **do**
>   *users* ← *select_users*(*request*)
>   **for all** *users* **do**
>   *result* ← *append_value*(*user*, *request*)
>   **end for**
>   *output* ← *evaluate_results*(*result*)
>   *update_expertise*(*users*)
>   **return** *output*
> **end for**

select_users. This function selects a set of annotators to whom we forward an input *request*. A *request* should contain:
  - A reference to the artifact to be annotated.
  - A first, high-level classification of the item, that facilitates the annotators selection (e.g., the century when it was made)
  - The requested "facet", necessary to obtain comparable candidate values (e.g., the "what" facet, i.e. the artifact content).

The selection procedure depends on internal policies of the museum deploying the system, so we do not make it explicit. Some examples:
  - Select the n highest ranked experts about the requested topic.
  - Consider all the experts. Weigh their reputation with regards to the distance from the request. Order and select them.
  - Consider also the belief and uncertainty (and impose some conditions on them) when selecting annotators.

append_value. Collects the contributions obtained from the selected annotators. *result* is a list of couples like (*value*, *annotators_opinions*).

evaluate_results. Aggregates results and takes a decision about them. Subjective logic's cumulative fusion operator is a possible aggregation function. A possible decision strategy is to choose the highest-rated value. A decision strategy has to select a candidate value, while reducing the risk of taking a wrong decision and solving possible controversies, such as when multiple candidate values all share the highest rank.

update_expertise. After having evaluated the candidate values for the annotation, annotators will be "rewarded" (if their candidate was selected) or "penalized" (otherwise). In principle, this means adding a positive evidence to the first ones and a negative evidence to the last ones, but once again, this may depend on museum policies.

Output. The annotation selected can be directly accepted by the museum, or ranked qualitatively according to its trust level (e.g. "accept" when trust level is higher than 0.9, "review" otherwise), so that appropriate actions are taken.

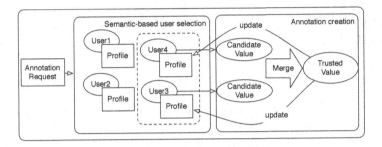

Fig. 1. Algorithm workflow

5   Evaluation

This section describes some analyses performed on the "Steve Social Tagging Project" [13] dataset, for validating our proposed approach. For this experiment, we computed the semantic relatedness by using the Wu & Palmer measure [21] on WordNet using an online service [16]. This gave us a *measure* $\in]0..1]$.

The "Steve Social Tagging Project" is a collaboration of museum professionals and others aimed at enhancing social tagging. We used the small portion of the data available as part of a 2006 project entitled "Researching social tagging and folksonomy in the ArtMuseum". This dataset comprises 1784 images from the museums which are open for tagging by the users. Each image is tagged by a single user with multiple tag words. There are 15,167 distinct tags. The 45,859 tag reviews of only 11 users are available as open source. Tag evaluations from the museum (e.g. "useful", "non-useful") are used as evidence in the training part and as a *gold standard* in the prediction evaluation.

A first empirical overview of the dataset hinted at the presence of possible semantic clusters. We then manually selected the candidate set of single words and proved that the semantic relatedness among those words is high. An example of clusters found is available in Fig. 2. After having shown the existence of these semantic clusters, we compared the expertise of people using words from those clusters and noticed that people having a high amount of positive (or negative) evidence regarding one word in a particular cluster also had a high amount of positive (or negative) evidence about the other words in the same cluster. Positive and negative evidence is derived from the evaluation by the museum:

tags evaluated as useful are counted as positive evidence, non-useful as negative. This manual and empirical analysis gave us a first concrete evidence about the relatedness between reputation based on evidence and semantic similarity.

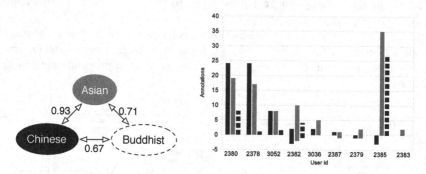

Fig. 2. Cluster and corresponding positive/negative evidence per user

We also built each user's reputation using a subset of the evaluations made by the museum and, based on this, we predicted the usefulness of future tags inserted by each user[2]. The prediction is performed as described in Section 4.2. Tags having a trust level of at least 0.7 are labelled as "useful". As a side effect of weighing, *uncertainty* of reputations rises, since weighing reduces the amount of evidence considered. However, often, this consequence did not worsen our results, especially when the reputation was already quite high (e.g., the reputation of an annotator reduced to 0.92 from 0.97). On the contrary, our approach allowed us to be prudent in our evaluations, so we could avoid accepting as useful tags with high *uncertainty*. Weighing improved the performance of subjective logic in a statistically significant manner, as proven by applying the sign test with a confidence interval of 95% on the compared errors.

6   Conclusion and Future Work

We demonstrate the potentials of combining subjective logic, semantic related-ness measures and Semantic Web technologies for handling users expertise and annoations trustworthiness.This work is an initial step in a promising direction that will be further explored. For instance, we plan to extensively deploy the described architecture and to extend the range of semantic relatedness measures and vocabularies adopted.

References

1. BBC. Uncovering Nation's art collection (January 2012)
   http://www.bbc.co.uk/yourpaintings
2. Breslin, J.G., Bojars, U., Aleman-meza, B., Boley, H., Nixon, L.J., Polleres, A., Zhdanova, A.V.: Finding experts using internet-based discussions in online com-munities and associated social networks. In: FEWS 2007. CEUR-WS.org (2007)

---

[2] The complete set of analyses is available at: http://bit.ly/y3uz1P

3. Brickley, D., Miller, L.: Foaf vocabulary specification 0.98 (January 2012), `http://xmlns.com/foaf/spec/`
4. Ceolin, D., Van Hage, W., Fokkink, W.: A trust model to estimate the quality of annotations using the Web. In: WebSci 2010 (2010)
5. Cosley, D., Frankowski, D., Terveen, L., Riedl, J.: SuggestBot: using intelligent task routing to help people find work in wikipedia. In: IUI 2007, pp. 32–41. ACM (2007)
6. Cyganiak, R., Reynolds, D., Tennison, J.: The RDF Data Cube vocabulary (February 2012), `http://publishing-statistical-data.googlecode.com/svn/trunk/specs/src/main/html/cube.html`
7. Demartini, G.: Finding experts using wikipedia. In: FEWS 2007, pp. 33–41. CEUR-WS.org (2007)
8. Emigh, W., Herring, S.C.: Collaborative authoring on the web: A genre analysis of online encyclopedias. In: HICSS 2005, p. 99a. IEEE (2005)
9. Heath, T., Motta, E.: The hoonoh ontology for describing trust relationships in information seeking. In: PICKME 2008. CEUR-WS.org (2008)
10. Hollink, L., Schreiber, G., Wielinga, B.: Patterns of semantic relations to improve image content search. Journal Web Semantics 5(3), 195–203 (2007)
11. IconClass. A multilingual classification system for cultural content (January 2012), `http://www.iconclass.org/`
12. Dublin Core Metadata Initiative. Dcmi metadata terms (February 2012), `http://dublincore.org/documents/dcmi-terms`
13. U.S institute of Museum and Library Services. Steve Social Tagging Project (January 2012)
14. Jøsang, A.: A logic for uncertain probabilities. Intl. Journal of Uncertainty, Fuzziness and Knowledge-Based Systems 9(3), 279–212 (2001)
15. Princeton University. A lexical database for English (January 2012), `http://wordnet.princeton.edu/`
16. Princeton University. Wordnet::Similarity (February 2012), `http://marimba.d.umn.edu/cgi-bin/similarity/similarity.cgi`
17. W3C. SKOS Simple Knowledge Organization System Primer (January 2012), `http://www.w3.org/TR/skos-primer/`
18. W3C. The PROV Ontology: Model and Formal Semantics (February 2012), `http://www.w3.org/TR/prov-o`
19. Wang, Y., Stash, N., Aroyo, L., Gorgels, P., Rutledge, L., Schreiber, G.: Recommendations based on semantically-enriched museum collections. Journal Web Semantics 6(4), 283–290 (2008)
20. Wang, Y., Stash, N., Aroyo, L., Hollink, L.: Using semantic relations for content-based recommender systems in cultural heritage. In: WOP 2009, pp. 16–28. CEUR-WS.org (2009)
21. Zhibiao, W., Palmer, M.: Verbs semantics and lexical selection. In: ACL 1994, pp. 133–138. ACL (1994)
22. Zhou, Y., Cong, G., Cui, B., Jensen, C.S., Yao, J.: Routing Questions to the Right Users in Online Communities. In: ICDE 2009. IEEE (2009)

A New Data Integrity Checking Protocol with Public Verifiability in Cloud Storage

Mihir R. Gohel and Bhavesh N. Gohil

Department of Computer Engineering, NIT - Surat, Surat-395007, India
{mihirgohel,bngohil06}@gmail.com

Abstract. Cloud computing is the long dreamed vision of computing as a utility, where users can remotely store their data into the cloud so as to enjoy the on-demand high quality applications and services from a shared pool of configurable computing resources. By data outsourcing, users can be relieved from the burden of local data storage and maintenance. It also eliminates their physical control of storage dependability and security, which traditionally has been expected by both enterprises and individuals. This unique paradigm brings about many new security challenges, which need to be clearly understood and resolved. This work studies the problem of ensuring the integrity of data storage in Cloud Computing. To ensure the correctness of data, we consider the task of allowing a third party auditor (TPA), on behalf of the cloud consumer, to verify the integrity of the data stored in the cloud. This scheme ensures that the storage at the client side is minimal which will be beneficial for thin clients.

Keywords: cloud storage, data integrity, public verifiability, Trusted Third Party Auditor (TPA).

1 Introduction

A new computing technology in today's world, called *cloud computing*, has been enabled to reality because of the rapid development of processing and storage technologies, ubiquitously available Internet, cheaper and more powerful computing resources than ever before. In this cloud computing technology, computing resources (e.g., CPU and storage) are provided as general utilities that can be leased or released by users in an on-demand fashion. In a cloud computing environment, the role of service provider is divided into two: the *infrastructure providers* who manage cloud platforms and lease resources according to a usage-based pricing model, and *service providers*, who rent resources from one or many infrastructure providers to serve the end users. The emergence of cloud computing has made a immense impact on the Information Technology (IT) industry over the past few years, where large companies such as Google, Amazon and Microsoft, IBM endeavor to provide more powerful, reliable and cost-efficient cloud platforms, and small and medium business (SMB)-enterprises try to reshape their business models to gain benefits from this new paradigm.

The cloud computing offers several benefits like scalability, rapid elasticity, ubiquitous network access, rapid deployment, pay-as-you go lower cost, low cost disaster

T. Dimitrakos et al. (Eds.): IFIPTM 2012, IFIP AICT 374, pp. 240–246, 2012.
© IFIP International Federation for Information Processing 2012

recovery and data storage solutions. While cloud offers these advantages, it also must ensure that they get the security aspects right.

One fundamental facet of this computing model is that data is being centralized or outsourced into the cloud. From the data owners' perspective, storing data remotely in a cloud brings the new and challenging security threats to the outsourced data. Since cloud providers (CP) are separate, data outsourcing actually relinquishes the owner's ultimate control over the fate of their data. As a result, the correctness of the data in the cloud is put at risk due to the various reasons. Although the infrastructures under the cloud are much more powerful and reliable than personal computing devices, they still face a broad range of both internal and external threats to data integrity.

For benefits of their own, there are various motivations for CPs to behave unfaithfully toward Cloud Consumers regarding the status of their outsourced data. For example, the storage service provider, which experiences Byzantine failures occasionally, may decide to hide the data errors from the clients. Other examples include CPs, for monetary reasons, reclaiming storage by discarding data that has not been or is rarely accessed [1], or even hiding data loss incidents to maintain a reputation [2].

As data owners no longer physically possess the storage of their data, traditional cryptographic primitives for the purpose of data security protection cannot be directly adopted [1, 2]. In particular, simply downloading the data for its integrity verification is not a practical solution due to the high cost of I/O and transmission across the network. Considering the large size of the outsourced data and the owner's constrained resource capability, the tasks of auditing the data correctness in a cloud environment can be expensive for data owners [1, 2]. Moreover, from the system usability point of view, data owners should be able to just use cloud storage as if it is local, without worrying about the need to verify its integrity.

In this paper, we are dealing with the problem of implementing a protocol for Public verifiable remote data integrity check, where data owners can resort to an external third party auditor (TPA) to verify the integrity of outsourced data when needed. Third party auditing provides a transparent yet cost-effective method for establishing trust between data owner and cloud server. Public verifiable remote integrity check relaxes users from the computation and online burden for periodical integrity check, especially desirable when the user is equipped with a low end computation device (e.g. smart phone, PDA) or is not always connected to the Internet.

- We propose a data integrity checking protocol for cloud storage, which can be viewed as an adaption of Sravan Kumar et al.'s protocol [3]. The proposed protocol inherits the protocol for data integrity verification, and supports public verifiability.
- The problem is further complicated by the fact that the owner of the data may be a small device, like a PDA or a mobile phone, which have limited CPU power, battery power and communication bandwidth. Hence a data integrity proof that has to be developed needs to take the above limitations into consideration. The scheme should be able to produce a proof without the need for the server to access the entire file or the client retrieving the entire file from the server. Also the scheme should minimize the local computation at the client as well as the bandwidth consumed at the client.

2   Related Work

The simplest Proof of data integrity can be made using a keyed hash function $h_k(F)$. In this scheme the Cloud Consumer (CC), before archiving the data file F in the cloud storage server (CSS), pre-computes the cryptographic hash of F using $h_k(F)$ and stores this hash as well as the secret key K. CC transfers this key and pre-computed hash value to Trusted Third Party Auditor (TPA), to verify the integrity of the file F at regular interval. To check if the integrity of the file F is lost the TPA releases the secret key K to the cloud archive and asks it to compute and return the value of $h_k(F)$. By storing multiple hash values for different keys the verifier can check for the integrity of the file F for multiple times, each one being an independent proof. Though this scheme is very simple and easily implementable the main drawback of this scheme are the high resource costs it requires for the implementation. At the verifier side this involves storing as many keys as the number of checks it want to perform as well as the hash value of the data file F with each hash key. Also computing hash value for even a moderately large data files can be computationally burdensome for some clients (PDAs, mobile phones, etc). At the archive side, each invocation of the protocol requires the archive to process the entire file F. This can be computationally burdensome for the archive even for a lightweight operation like hashing [3].

Recently, much of growing interest has been pursued in the context of remotely stored data verification [1–5]. Zhang and Chen have proposed an Integrity check scheme based on well-known RSA Security assumption called A RSA-based Assumption Data Integrity Check without Original Data [4]. In which they uses the concept of Random Oracle Model and RSA to verify the intactness of data. The proposed scheme is proven to be secure in Random oracle model.

Surya et al. have also proposed a protocol for the same called Data Integrity as a Service (DIaaS) [5]. The proposed protocol needs to have complex infrastructure to be implemented. i.e., Trust Management Service (TMS), Cloud Storage Service (CSS), Key Management Service (KMS) and Integrity Management Service (IMS). The proposed protocol also performs more no. of encryptions and hashing to verify the integrity.

Ari Juels and Burton S. Kaliski Jr. proposed a scheme called Proof of retrievability for large files using "sentinels" [1]. In this scheme, unlike in the key-hash approach scheme, only a single key can be used irrespective of the size of the file or the number of files whose retrievability it wants to verify. In this scheme special blocks (called sentinels) are hidden among other blocks in the data file F. To make the sentinels indistinguishable from the data blocks, the whole modified file is encrypted and stored at the archive. As this scheme involves the encryption of the file F using a secret key it becomes computationally cumbersome especially when the data to be encrypted is large. Hence, this scheme proves disadvantages to small users with limited computational power (PDAs, mobile phones etc.) [3]. The schematic view of this approach is shown in Figure 1.

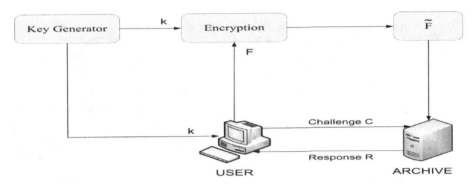

Fig. 1. Schematic views of a proof of retrievability based on inserting random sentinels in the file F [1]

Sravan Kumar R and Ashutosh Saxena have proposed scheme for data integrity proof [3], which does not involve the encryption of the whole data but encrypts only few bits of data per data Block, thus reducing the computational overhead on the clients. The client storage overhead is also minimized as it does not store any data with it. So the scheme suits well for thin clients. But the proposed scheme restricts the remote data verifiability to private only. It doesn't allow any third party auditor to verify the integrity of data, on behalf of client. The clients themselves need to devote their computation resources to perform frequent integrity checks. Hence, this scheme burdensome the client.

3   The Proposed Data Integrity Checking Protocol in Cloud Storage with Public Verifiability

In our proposed data integrity protocol, we inherit the support of data integrity from [3], and support of TPA from Qian Wang et al. [6]. In our proposed data integrity protocol, the client doesn't need to store any data with it. Verifier needs only a single cryptographic key and two functions which generate a random sequence. The client before storing the file at the archive, preprocesses the file and appends some meta data to the file and stores at the archive. The client then transfers the key and functions to the TPA to audit the file frequently. At the time of verification the TPA uses this meta data to verify the correctness of data. Our proposed scheme neither prevents the archive from modifying or deletions data nor preserves data privacy against TPA. Representative network architecture for cloud data storage with TPA is illustrated in Fig. 2.

3.1   Setup Phase

Let the client C wishes to the store the file F with the archive. Let this file F consist of n file blocks. We initially preprocess the file and create metadata to be appended to the file. Let each of the n data blocks have m bits in them. The initial setup phase is represented in Fig 3 and can be described in the following steps:

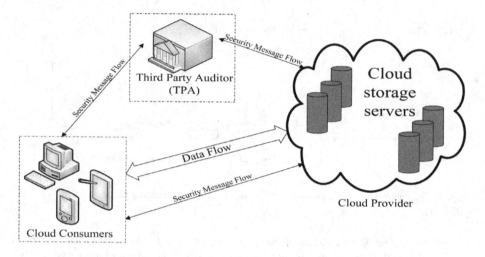

Fig. 2. Cloud Data Storage Architecture with TPA [6]

1)   Generation of metadata: Let g be the function defined as

$$g(i, j) \rightarrow \{1..m\}, i \in \{1..n\}, j \in \{1..k\} \tag{1}$$

Where k is the number of bits per data block which we wish to read as meta data. The function g generates for each data block a set of k bit positions within the m bits that are in the data block. Hence $g(i, j)$ gives the jth bit in the ith data block. The value of k is in the choice of the client and is a secret known only to him. Therefore for each data block we get a set of k bits and in total for all the n blocks we get $n*k$ bits. Let mi represent the k bits of meta data for the ith block.

2)   Encrypting the meta data: Each of the meta data from the data blocks m_i is encrypted by using a suitable algorithm to give a new modified meta data M_i. Without loss of generality we show this process by using a simple XOR operation. Let h be a function which generates a k bit integer α_i for each i.

$$h : i \longrightarrow \alpha_i, \alpha_i \in \{0.. \ 2^k\} \tag{2}$$

For the meta data (m_i) of each data block the number α_i is added to get a new k bit number M_i.

$$M_i = m_i + \alpha_i \tag{3}$$

In this way we get a set of n new meta data bit blocks.

3)   Appending of meta data: All the meta data bit blocks that are generated using the above procedure are to be concatenated together. This concatenated meta data should be appended to the file F before storing it at the cloud server. The file F along with the appended meta data $\breve{F}$ is archived with the cloud.

4)   Transferring the meta data attributes to TPA: Client now transfers the two functions g and h to trusted TPA. TPA audits the file F archived with cloud by using these two functions g and h at the time of data integrity verification.

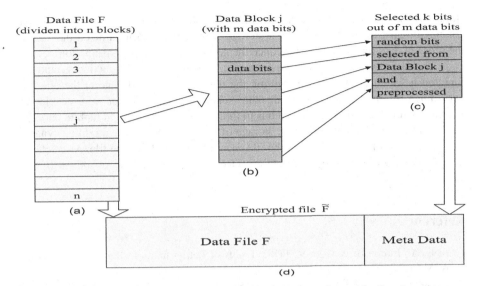

Fig. 3. (a) A data file F with n data blocks (b) a data block j, having m bits, is selected to pre-process (c) randomly selected k bits outcome of function g (d) preprocessed k bits are appended to data file F, the encrypted file F̃ will be stored at cloud

3.2   Verification Phase

Let the TPA want to verify the integrity of the file F. It throws a challenge to the archive and asks it to respond. The challenge and the response are compared and the TPA accepts or rejects the integrity proof. Suppose the TPA wishes to check the integrity of nth block. The TPA challenges the cloud storage server by specifying the block number i and a bit number j generated by using the function g. The TPA also specifies the position at which the meta data corresponding the block i is appended. This meta data will be a k bit number. Hence the cloud storage server is required to send $k + 1$ bits for verification by the client. The meta data sent by the cloud is decrypted by using the Number $\propto_i$ and the corresponding bit in this decrypted meta data is compared with the bit that is sent by the cloud. Any mismatch between the two would mean a loss of the integrity of the clients' data at the cloud storage.

4   Conclusions and Future Works

To ensure cloud data storage security, it is critical to enable a third party auditor (TPA) to evaluate the service quality from an objective and independent perspective. Public verifiability also allows clients to delegate the integrity verification tasks to TPA while they themselves can be unreliable or not be able to commit necessary computation resources performing continuous verifications.

In this paper we have worked to facilitate the client in getting a proof of integrity of the data. Our proposed scheme is developed to reduce the computational and storage overhead of the client with public verifiability as well as to minimize the computational overhead of the cloud storage server. We also minimized the size of the proof of data integrity so as to reduce the network bandwidth consumption.

At the client we only store two functions, the bit generator function g, and the function h which is used for encrypting the data. Hence the storage at the client is very much minimal compared to all other schemes [1-2, 4-5] that were developed. Hence this scheme proves advantageous to thin clients like PDAs and mobile phones.

Our scheme applies only to static storage of data. If archived file modifies dynamically, then client has to preprocess the file each time he modifies the file. Also scheme doesn't preserve privacy of data against TPA. Hence developing on this will be a future challenge.

References

1. Juels, A., Burton, J., Kaliski, S.: PORs: Proofs of Retrievability for Large Files. In: Proc. ACM CCS 2007, pp. 584–597 (October 2007)
2. Ateniese, G., et al.: Provable Data Possession at Untrusted Stores. In: Proc. ACM CCS 2007, pp. 598–609 (October 2007)
3. Kumar, S., Saxena, A.: Data integrity proofs in cloud storage. In: Proc. COMSNETS 2011, pp. 1–4 (January 2011)
4. Zhang, J., Chen, H.: Secuirty storage in the Cloud Computing: A RSA-based assumption data integrity check without original data. In: Proc. ICEIT 2010, pp. 17–19 (September 2010)
5. Nepal, S., Chen, S., Yao, J., Thilakanathan, D.: DIaaS: Data Integrity as a Service in the Cloud. In: Proc. IEEE Cloud Computing CLOUD 2011, pp. 308–315 (July 2011)
6. Wang, Q., Wang, C., Li, J., Ren, K., Lou, W.: Enabling Public Verifiability and Data Dynamics for Storage Security in Cloud Computing. In: Backes, M., Ning, P. (eds.) ESORICS 2009. LNCS, vol. 5789, pp. 355–370. Springer, Heidelberg (2009)

Document and Author Promotion Strategies in the Secure Wiki Model

Kasper Lindberg and Christian Damsgaard Jensen

Department of Informatics and Mathematical Modelling
Technical University of Denmark
Christian.Jensen@imm.dtu.dk

Abstract. Wiki systems form a subclass of the more general Open Collaborative Authoring Systems, where content is created by a user community. The ability of anyone to edit the content is, at the same time, their strength and their weakness. Anyone can write documents that improve the value of the wiki-system, but this also means that anyone can introduce errors into documents, either by accident or on purpose.

A security model for wiki-style authoring systems, called the *Secure Wiki Model*, has previously been proposed to address this problem. This model is designed to prevent corruption of good quality documents, by limiting updates, to such documents, to users who have demonstrated their ability to produce documents of similar or better quality. While this security model prevents all user from editing all documents, it does respect the wiki philosophy by allowing any author who has produced documents of a certain quality to edit all other documents of similar or poorer quality. Moreover, authors who consistently produce top quality documents will eventually be allowed to edit all documents in the wiki.

Collaborative filtering is used to evaluate the quality of documents that an author has contributed to the system, thus determining what other documents that the author can edit. This collaborative filtering mechanism, determines the promotion and demotion of documents and authors in the Secure Wiki Model. The original Secure Wiki Model only considers explicit promotion and demotion of documents, authors are implicitly promoted/demoted depending on the promotion/demotion of the documents that they contribute. In this paper, we revisit the question of promotion of documents and authors and propose a new security policy with explicit promotion of authors. This policy also incorporates a new collaborative filtering mechanism with a higher degree of parametrisation, so that the new policy can be adapted to the specific needs of a particular wiki.

1 Introduction

A *wiki* is a system that relies on user contribution to generate the content it provides. Wikis can be used by any group of people such as friends doing small projects, colleagues needing knowledge sharing in companies, companies engaging with their user base through crowd-sourcing and worldwide knowledge sharing between strangers. The open nature of wiki systems makes them ideal as a knowledge sharing platform to which everyone can contribute a small piece of the bigger picture. However, the strength of such an Open Collaborative Authoring System (OCAS) is also its weakness since it

T. Dimitrakos et al. (Eds.): IFIPTM 2012, IFIP AICT 374, pp. 247–252, 2012.

is equally easy to delete good content or for malicious or incompetent people to add erroneous information to the OCAS.

This problem has been addressed by the *Secure Wiki Model*, which has been proposed to ensure the correctness and accuracy of documents in wiki-style systems [3]. The secure wiki model introduces a classification of both documents and authors into a set of *integrity levels*, which indicate the quality of the documents or the quality of the authors based on their previous contributions to the wiki (the Secure Wiki Model is introduced more formally in Section 2). The model combines ideas from two classic multi-level access control mechanisms: a *static integrity model* that governs authors' ability to update documents based on the well known Biba integrity model [1], and a *dynamic integrity model* that governs the promotion and demotion of documents and authors among the different integrity levels inspired by a watermark based access control mechanism [5].

In the original model, the dynamic integrity model only considers explicit promotion of documents – authors are implicitly promoted, according to the watermark model, along with the promotion of documents that they have authored. Promotion is explicit and is normally initiated by one of the authors in the wiki. The promotion is based on a vote between a set of randomly selected authors with integrity levels higher than the integrity level of the considered document; this protects the voting mechanism against the Sybil attack [2]. One problem with this approach is that voters are being explicitly asked to evaluate the quality of a document, but this evaluation is implicitly used to determine the integrity level of the author who is the main contributor to the document, i.e. voters are asked a single question, but their answer is used for two separate purposes. In order to make promotion more transparent, we need to make promotion of both documents and authors explicit.

In this paper, we revisit the question of promotion of documents and authors and propose a new policy for the dynamic integrity model that explicitly promotes authors. This new policy then leaves it to the discretion of the authors to explicitly promote documents that they have improved to an appropriate integrity level, up to and including their own integrity level.

The rest of this paper is organised in the following way: Section 2 gives a brief description of the original Secure Wiki Model which forms the basis for the new policy proposed in this paper. In Section 3, we revisit the question of document and author promotion and analyse the requirements for a successful policy in relation to wiki-systems. Based on this analysis, we propose our new policy in Section 4 and discuss this policy in Section 5.

2   The Secure Wiki Model

The Secure Wiki Model[3] combines existing assessment techniques, based on collaborative filtering, with computer security integrity control mechanisms. The integrity control mechanism is based on the Biba integrity model, which defines a Simple Security Property (*No Read Down*) and * (star) property (*No Write Up*).

The proposed system recognises that the simple security property cannot be enforced due to the fact that the security mechanism does not have complete mediation over authors' access to information. The primary contribution of the Biba integrity model to this system is therefore the star property. The system requires every author to have an identifier that allows the system to recognise authors and assign quality confidence values (QCV) to them. The QCV indicates the general level of correctness, completeness and lack of bias in documents by that author. Similarly, the system assigns integrity levels (IL) to each document. The IL of a document is an indication of the correctness, completeness and lack of bias for that particular document as perceived by the community.

2.1 Access Control

The static integrity model is the component of the Secure Wiki Model that controls the access to the edit-feature of documents and thereby ensures that authors do not corrupt high-quality documents. The static integrity model is based on the sets $\mathbb{A}, \mathbb{D}$ and $\mathbb{I}$, where $\mathbb{A}$ is the set of identifiers of authors who have registered to use the system, $\mathbb{D}$ is the set of documents that are managed by the system and $\mathbb{I}$ is a totally ordered set of integrity levels. Using these sets, two functions are defined, that allow the system to compare the QCV of authors to the IL of documents, using the total order of $\mathbb{I}$. These functions are $qcv(a : \mathbb{A})$ which returns the quality confidence value of the author $a \in \mathbb{A}$ and $il(d : \mathbb{D})$ which returns the integrity level of the document $d \in \mathbb{D}$. These functions are used to define the predicate:

$$can\_edit(a : \mathbb{A}, d : \mathbb{D}) = {}'1' \text{ iff } il(d) \leq qcv(a)$$

which returns '1' if the author a is allowed to edit the document d ('0' otherwise) and thus prevents authors with a low(er) QCV from editing documents with a high(er) IL.

2.2 Dynamic Integrity Model

The dynamic integrity model is responsible for dynamically changing the IL of documents such that authors with a low QCV cannot corrupt a document that have been improved by an author with a higher QCV. The dynamic integrity model uses a variant of the watermark model [5], which says that when a subject reads an object with a label with a lower classification, the label of the object increases to the level of the subject, i.e., when an author with a QCV higher than the IL of a document edits the document, the resulting document will have its IL set to that of the authors QCV. The system does this on the assumption that authors that, in the past, have written accurate, complete and unbiased documents are likely to do so in the future.

Review Process. The description above shows how the integrity level of documents are raised. To raise the QCV of authors, the system uses a document review model that allows a contributor to submit a document for a review that will determine if the IL of the document should be raised. If the IL of the document is raised, so is the QCV of the *principal author*. To prevent denial of service through spurious document review requests, the proposed system limits the number of people that can request a promotion-review to the authors that contributed to the document, while allowing all authors, for which the can_edit predicate is '1', to request a demotion-review.

In order to analyse the security of the original model, it is assumed that each level L_i in the hierarchy contains $|A_i|$ registered users, of which z_i are assumed to be malicious and in collusion with each other. When reviewing a document, a number of users (r_i) of the $|A_i|$ registered users, from each of the levels that are participating in the review, are randomly selected to perform the review. The set of reviewers at level L_i defines a subset $A_{R_i} \subseteq A_i$. When reviewing a document d, each reviewer j makes his decision $\delta_j(d)$ on whether to promote a document or not. A yes-vote is represented as the value '1' and a no-vote is represented as the value '0'.

In the original policy, referred to as Π_1, the authors at each integrity level independently reach a decision. A simple majority of these decisions then decides the overall outcome of the vote.

3 Policy Analysis

In the following, we examine two problems that arise in the policy Π_1, namely the lack of transparency surrounding the promotion of authors and the problem of quorum.

3.1 Author and Document Promotion

The dynamic integrity model governs the promotion and demotion of both documents and authors. It is assumed that high level authors will work to improve the quality of the documents in the wiki, so the original model automatically promoted documents when they had been edited by a high level author. Work with the first prototype implementation of the secure wiki model [4], made us realise that authors will often make minor contributions, e.g. correct a spelling error, which in itself does not justify promotion, so it was left to the discretion of authors to promote documents that they edited. After editing a document, the author is allowed to increase the integrity level of the document up to and including her own integrity level; the default is to leave the document at its current integrity level. The resulting mechanism now has two explicit ways to promote documents, but only an implicit mechanism to promote authors. We therefore propose a new policy for the dynamic integrity model, which uses the voting mechanism to promote authors instead of documents – promotion of documents will be done explicitly by higher level authors who contribute to the document using the mechanism from the first prototype.

3.2 Voter Participation

The original policy Π_1 suggests that promotion of a document at level $i \in [0, 1, 2]$, would require two out of the three levels L_i, L_{i+1}, L_{i+2} to have a simple majority for the promotion, but it does not specify any conditions on voter-participation which raises some interesting issues, e.g. does one positive vote out of 100 authors, who were asked to vote but did not respond, represent a sufficient majority?

This suggests that there is the need for a critical mass of reviewers that must be met or the vote should be rejected due to the result being unreliable. One way to mitigate the risk of having too few participating reviewers will be to select only active contributors to perform a review. This will have the added benefit that dormant malicious users would not participate in reviews. If a user is malicious, with the intent of compromising reviews, the user would have to be active and potentially expose himself as malicious.

Despite mitigating actions, some reviewers will fail to participate in a review. It is assumed that the number of reviewers, at each level, that fails to vote on a review is equal, such that it does not skew the vote inappropriately. This can however be checked and guarded against.

4 New Promotion Policy

The original policy proposed for the secure wiki model is called Π_1, so we decided to call the new policy proposed here Π_2.

To promote an author from level L_i to L_{i+1}, a set of randomly selected members of the levels L_i, L_{i+1}, L_{i+2} perform a review to decide if the author should be promoted. Each vote is weighed according to the weight of the integrity level of the member who cast the vote and the weighted sum of the votes must reach a level-specific threshold. In order to increase the security of the higher integrity levels, this threshold increases as the levels gets higher.

For each reviewer j at level L_i, the review decision ($\delta_j(a)$) is multiplied by the weight of the level ($\mathcal{W}_i$). The resulting score, for each level L_i, will be termed $\mathcal{S}_i(a)$ and calculated as shown in (1).

$$\mathcal{S}_i(a) = \sum_{j \in \Lambda_{R_i}} \delta_j(a) \cdot \mathcal{W}_i \tag{1}$$

For the purpose of determining the percentage of approval, the term $\mathcal{S}_i^{\max}(a)$, defined in (2), will be used to denote the maximum score possible for a given level L_i.

$$\mathcal{S}_i^{\max}(a) = |\Lambda_{R_i}| \cdot \mathcal{W}_i \tag{2}$$

In Π_2, τ_i is used to denote the threshold of weighted yes-votes to reach for a promotion vote to be successful. To promote author a from level L_i to L_{i+1}, Π_2 uses the condition that the score of yes-votes is greater than the score of no-votes and that the score of yes-votes exceeds the threshold τ_i. This condition is denoted as $\mathcal{D}(a)$ and shown in (3).

$$\mathcal{D}(a) = \mathcal{S}_i(a) + \mathcal{S}_{i+1}(a) + \mathcal{S}_{i+2}(a) \geq$$
$$\left(\mathcal{S}_i^{\max}(a) + \mathcal{S}_{i+1}^{\max}(a) + \mathcal{S}_{i+2}^{\max}(a) \right) \cdot \tau_i \tag{3}$$
$$\text{for } i \in \{0, 1, \ldots, |\mathbb{I}| - 2\}$$

A third condition for the success of a review, is that the participation percentage must be sufficiently high to ensure the reliability of the review. If the participation percentage is not met, the result of the review must be considered as failed due to the unreliability of the result.

One extra author level is needed to be able to control documents at the highest integrity level using the common case condition. This extra level is there to control voting only and does not gain any extra privileges. In order for an author a to be promoted above the normal document integrity levels, the condition in (4) will be used with an especially high value of τ_i to preserve the integrity and security of the vote.

$$\mathcal{D}(a) = \mathcal{S}_i(a) + \mathcal{S}_{i+1}(a) \geq \left(\mathcal{S}_i^{\max}(a) + \mathcal{S}_{i+1}^{\max}(a)\right) \cdot \tau_i \tag{4}$$
$$\text{for } i = |\mathbb{I}| - 1$$

If an author no longer deserves the QCV currently associated with her, a demotion of the author is necessary. In general, demotion of authors works in the same way as promotion, but τ_i is replaced with τ_i^{dem}.

If all users at a given level has been promoted, so the level becomes empty, the members needed at that level will be selected from the next level above. With a system administrator at the top-most level, who can be trusted not to act maliciously, this also allows the system to securely populate the levels with users from the lowest levels, during the bootstrapping phase of the system.

5 Discussion

Controlling access without restricting it is difficult. The secure wiki model suggests how controlling the authors in Open Collaborative Authoring Systems, such as a wiki, can be done without restricting authors' ability to improve documents. The contribution of this paper is the presentation of an alternative security policy for explicit promotion of authors and documents in the secure wiki model.

The policy Π_2 has been designed for systems that are sufficiently populated. Small systems with only a few authors at each level will be able to use Π_2, but they may not get the full benefit of the policy since the small number of authors will all be asked to vote every time their level is involved in a promotion. However, the high degree of adaptability of Π_2 should provide even small systems with a useful policy.

In addition to the promotion policy, we have made references to a demotion policy, without specifying the demotion conditions explicitly. Specifying and analysing the formal policy for demotion is left for future work as well as an actual implementation of the proposed policy in a system using the secure wiki model.

References

1. Biba, K.J.: Integrity considerations for secure computer systems. Technical Report MTR-3153, The MITRE Corporation, Bedford, Massachusetts, U.S.A. (1977)
2. Douceur, J.R.: The Sybil Attack. In: Druschel, P., Kaashoek, M.F., Rowstron, A. (eds.) IPTPS 2002. LNCS, vol. 2429, pp. 251–260. Springer, Heidelberg (2002), http://portal.acm.org/citation.cfm?id=646334.687813
3. Jensen, C.D.: Security in Wiki-Style Authoring Systems. In: Ferrari, E., Li, N., Bertino, E., Karabulut, Y. (eds.) IFIPTM 2009. IFIP AICT, vol. 300, pp. 81–98. Springer, Heidelberg (2009)
4. Sander, P.: Sikkerhed i wiki-lignende systemer. Master's thesis, Technical University of Denmark, Department of Informatics & Mapthematical Modelling (2009) (in Danish)
5. Weissman, C.: Security controls in the adept-50 time-sharing system. In: Proceedings of the Fall Joint Computer Conference, Las Vegas, Nevada, U.S.A., November 18-20, pp. 119–133 (1969)

Robustness of Trust and Reputation Systems: Does It Matter?

Audun Jøsang

University of Oslo, Norway
josang@mn.uio.no

Abstract. Trust and reputation systems provide a foundation for security, stability, and efficiency in the online environment because of their ability to stimulate quality and to sanction poor quality. Trust and reputation scores are assumed to represent and predict future quality and behaviour and thereby to provide valuable decision support for relying parties. This assumption depends on two factors, primarily that trust and reputation scores faithfully reflect past observed quality, and secondly that future quality will be truly similar to that represented by the scores. Unfortunately, poor robustness of trust and reputation systems often makes it relatively easy to manipulate these factors, so that the fundamental assumption behind trust and reputation systems becomes questionable. On this background we discuss to what degree robustness against strategic manipulation is important for the usefulness of trust and reputation systems in general.

This paper is the printed version of the inaugural William Winsborough Commemorative Address at the IFIP Trust Management Conference 2012 in Surat.

1 Introduction

Online markets and communities are commonly moderated by trust and reputation systems, called TRS hereafter. The explosion in the use of collaborative trust and reputation propagation was triggered primarily by the speed and efficiency of the Internet and modern computers for collecting and propagating reputation information, and secondly by the emergence of Web 2.0 platforms and people's active engagement in them. Through collaborative effort members of the community provide ratings and reviews about targets which e.g. can be online services and resources as well as other community members and physical world goods and service, for example hotels, universities and medical doctors[10]. Cumulated ratings and reviews about a given target can assist other parties in deciding whether or not to use, transact with or connect with that target in the future. Introducing such systems in a community or market has multiple interrelated effects. The most direct effect is that it provides decision support for relying parties, by choosing the targets with the best scores or reviews. Targets that want to attract the business of relying parties in the future know that they need a high reputation score for that. The principle that future reputation depends on present behaviour typically influences present behaviour through the *"shadow of the future"* effect [21], meaning that anticipated future reputation casts a controlling shadow on present behaviour.

T. Dimitrakos et al. (Eds.): IFIPTM 2012, IFIP AICT 374, pp. 253–262, 2012.

A *trust scope* refers to the specific function or quality that the target is assumed to have for the purpose of the trust relationship. In other words, the target is relied upon to have certain qualities, and the scope is what the relying party assumes those qualities to be. For example, providing financial advice and providing medical advice represent two different scopes for which trust and reputation should be considered separately. Trust and reputation also exist within a context. It should be noted that the term context is sometimes used in the sense of scope in the literature.

The term "context" generally means the surroundings, circumstances, environment, background or settings which determine, specify, or clarify the meaning of something. We therefore define *trust context* to cover elements such as the legal and cultural environment, the domain policy, ethics and social attitudes of participants. A specific online market or social community such as eBay or facebook is always embedded in a wide context that consists of the above mentioned elements as well as others. The context of a TRS can therefore take a rather general meaning that would difficult to specify exhaustively. It would be practical to consider a domain identity such as "eBay" or "facebook" as an attribute of, or maybe the name/identifier of the context itself, because it indirectly refers to all its elements such as those elements mentioned above.

Another aspect of trust context is that two communities might use the same term for a specific trust scope such as "politeness", but the meaning could have different qualitative and semantic value if the two communities have different cultures. A simple way to convey this fact might be to include the name of the community/context as metadata or as an attribute of specific reputation scores. Another issue worth considering when comparing different TRS domains is the possibility that participants deliberately behave differently in specific different communities, so that it would not be meaningful to compute an average/federated reputation score for a specific participant who behaves in that way. In fact the community name becomes an attribute of the behaviour, i.e. the participant consciously behaves in a specific way in each different community and context. It would be possible for the participant to use the same name in the different communities so that relying parties would be aware of the difference in behaviour, or the participant could use different pseudonyms so that relying parties would ignore that two separate pseudonyms represent the same participant.

In relation to trust systems the term "recommendation" is often used in the sense of a trust measure passed between entities, whereas the term "rating" is often used with relation to reputation systems. In this presentation we will use the term "rating" to denote both. The term "score" primarily refers to a measure of trust or reputation derived by a TRS function based on the received ratings.

Many web sites allow participants to write reviews in natural language, not just as a numerical rating. For generality we will use the term "rating" also in the sense of a review. Similarly, we let the term "'score" also represent the collection of reviews that are presented to the public through a website, not just a numerical trust or reputation score.

Attempts to misrepresent quality and to manipulate reputation are commonplace in human societies, and probably also in animal societies. Con artists employ methods to appear trustworthy, e.g. through skillful acting or through the fabrication and presentation of false credentials. Analogous types of attacks are being used in online communities and markets. In case of online TRSs, vulnerabilities in the systems themselves can open up additional attack vectors. From that perspective TRSs should be robust against attacks that could lead to misleading trust and reputation scores. In the worst case, a vulnerable reputation system could be turned around and used as an attack tool to maliciously manipulate the computation and dissemination of scores. The consequence of this could be a total loss of community trust caused by the inability to sanction and avoid low quality and deceptive services and agents.

Attacks against TRSs are not normally committed by computer hackers breaking into the server where the TRS functions are being hosted, although of course this could happen. Attacks against TRSs typically consist of playing the role of relying parties and/or service provider, and of manipulating the TRS through specific behaviour that is contrary to policy and/or to assumed ethical behaviour. For example, a malicious party that colludes with the service provider, or simply an unethical service provider, could provide fake or unfair positive ratings to a reputation system with the purpose of inflating the service provider's score, thereby increasing the probability of that service provider being selected by other relying parties, which in turn would lead to increased profit. Alternatively, an unethical service provider could engage in unfair badmouthing of competitors in order to reduce their business and profit, with in turn would result in increased own business and profit.

Many other attack scenarios can be imagined that, if successful, would give unfair advantages to the attackers. All such attacks have in common that that they result in the erosion of community trust, with damaging consequences for services and applications in the affected market or community. The robustness of TRSs can therefore be crucial for the quality of markets and communities where a TRS is being applied.

A TRS must not only be robust against intentional attacks, but should produce quality trust and reputation scores under changing conditions and in the presence of unsophisticated participants. Assuming that ratings provided by the community are fair one would expect that a quality service provider always is represented as such through its trust and reputation scores published through the TRS. If that is not the case, i.e. if a reliable service provider is represented with a low score and bad reviews, or an unreliable service provider is represented with a high score and good reviews, then the TRS does not fulfill its most basic role, which could be very damaging for the community. In economic terms, this could cause severe inefficiencies similarly to those resulting from corruption. A second important TRS requirement is that it must react swiftly when the rating trend changes in the positive or negative direction, by immediately producing correspondingly more positive or more negative scores [21].

A TRS can be attacked from multiple angles, meaning that designing adequate defence against possible threats can be a daunting challenge. This presentation focuses on the need for robustness in real implementations of TRS i communities and markets. We do not focus on traditional security threats such as hacking and denial of service, although such defences must of course also be included in any practical implementation. Given that each community has its own specific characteristics the need for TRS robustness will different in each case. At the same time, there are some fundamental requirements for robustness that should be satisfied in general.

2 Threat Analysis and Proposed Solutions

Fig.1 illustrates potential attack vectors related to a TRS integrated with targets and relying parties in a community or market. Note that Fig.1 represents a functional view, not an architectural view. It is for example possible that the TRS function is distributed among all the relying parties as in case of a TRS for P2P networks. It is also possible that there is no distinction between relying parties and service providers.

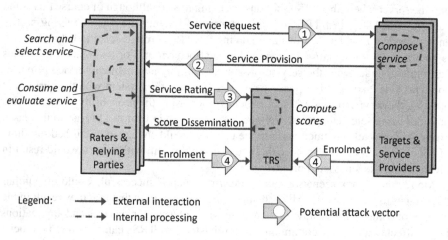

Fig. 1. Potential attack vectors related to a TRS environment

The combination of a TRS and a large number of participants (relying parties and targets) represents a highly dynamic and complex feedback system with many potential vulnerabilities. Making such systems robust against malicious manipulation represents a daunting challenge. The attack vectors in Fig.1 are briefly describe in Table 1.

Table 1. TRS attack vectors with reference to Fig1

Attack Vector	Brief Description
(1) Service Request	Malicious relying parties, possibly colluding with the service provider, could request services for the sole purpose of being entitled to rate. For example on eBay, ratings can only be provided after a registered transaction, which provides a ticket to rate.
(2) Service Provision	Malicious service providers could deliberately provide low quality services. Alternatively, low quality service could simply be the result of incompetent or unreliable service providers.
(3) Service rating	Ratings or reviews could be false or could unfairly misrepresent the actual service received.
(4) Enrollment	Relying parties and service providers can e.g. enroll multiple times in order to strategically manipulate the TRS.

The research literature on TRSs (Trust and Reputation Systems) is relatively mature, where the PhD thesis of Marsh (1994) [16] represents an early study of computational trust systems and the article by Resnick *et al.* (2000) [21] represents an early introduction to reputation systems. This literature is currently substantial and is still growing fast [8,12]. A large number of TRS designs and architectures have been and continue to be proposed and implemented. Commercial implementations of TRSs are now part of mainstream Web technology which has resulted in general textbooks on how to build TRSs in real applications, such as Farmer & Glass (2011) [6].

However, the literature specifically focusing on the robustness of TRSs is much more limited and still in an early stage. It should be noted that publications on TRSs usually analyse robustness to a certain extent, but typically only consider a very limited set of attacks. The text book by Farmer & Glass [6] also offers advice on robustness. However, many studies on robustness in the research literature suffer from the authors' desire to put their own TRS designs in a positive light, with the result that the robustness analyses often are too superficial and fail to consider realistic attacks. Publications providing comprehensive robustness analyses are rare.

Hoffmann, Zage and Nita-Rotaru (2009) [9] provide a taxonomy and analysis framework for TRSs proposed for P2P networks, and then give an analysis of 24 of the most prominent TRSs based on 25 different attributes. Out of the 24 TRSs, 6 were analysed in more detail because of the representativeness of their characteristics. General challenges for the building robustness into TRSs are presented in Jøsang & Golbeck (2009) [11]. They give an overview of typical attacks described in the literature, such as those listed in Table 2.

Table 2. Various strategies for attacking trust and reputation systems

Attack type	Short Description
Playbooks	Planned sequence of actions in order to manipulate and deceive
Unfair Ratings	Ratings that do not correctly reflect the actual experience
Review Spam	(aka. opinion spam) False reviews, often in conjunction with unfair ratings
Discrimination	Deliberately providing different quality services to specific relying parties
Collusion	Coordinated actions among participants in order to manipulate and deceive
Proliferation	Multiple offerings of the same service in order to obscure competing services
Reputation Lag	Abuse multiple buyers before the TRS reacts to their negative feedbacks
Re-entry	Take new identity, in order to eliminate bad reputation of old identity
Value Imbalance	Exploit reputation from many low value services, for one high value fraud
The Sybil Attack	Take on multiple identities in order to generate rating and review spam

Early proposals for strengthening the robustness of TRSs were typically based on the assumption that false or unfair ratings could be detected statistically, and focused on detecting patterns and outlayers among the ratings, e.g. Dellarocas (2000) [3], Yu & Singh (2003) [26], and Withby & Jøsang (2004) [23]. While these approaches could be characterised as simplistic and relatively easy to bypass for determined attackers, they present the idea of using data mining and reasoning to detect and protect against such attacks.

Kerr (2009) [13] provides independent robustness analyses of a set of proposed TRSs, and thereby represents a step in the right direction for TRS research. They also propose a testbed for evaluating TRSs in [14].

Large commercial TRSs have attracted, and continue to attract, the attention of independent third party analysts. For example, the robustness of Google's PageRank algorithm has been analysed by Zhang *et al.* (2004) [27] and by Clausen (2004) [2], and the robustness of eBay's Feedback Forum has been analysed by several authors, including Resnick *et al.* (2006) [22] and Dini & Spagnolo (2009) [4].

The relative simplicity of writing false reviews of goods and services, and the lack of sanctioning of this practice, currently is a significant problem and a major challenge for review sites such as epinions.com and tripadvisor.com. The problem of false reviews seems difficult to solve because it is in principle impossible to read people's minds and verify whether a review really reflects their inner thoughts. There are nevertheless techniques based on data mining and natural language processing for analysing the consistency of reviews against specific criteria, which can provide an indication of whether a given review is genuine or malicious spam. The goal of this research is to design the equivalent of a lie detector for ratings and reviews.

Analysis and detection of review spam (aka. opinion spam) is a relatively recent research trend, so the literature is still relatively limited, but some studies show promising results. Studies include Benevenuto *et al.* (2009) [1], Lim *et al.* (2010) [15], Gilbert & Karrie (2010) [7], Wu *et al.* [25,24], Ott *et al.* (2011) [19], and Duan & Liu (2012) [5].

As with traditional security solutions, it is to be expected that attackers will adapt to robustness solutions implemented in TRSs, thereby resulting in a endless cat-and-mouse game. This phenomenon can already be observed with regard to Google's search engine where the first version of the PageRank algorithm was attacked by link spam, which consists of inserting links to a specific page on open web fora such as discussion groups and wikis. A fix to the link spam problem was to introduce the no-follow tag in 2005 which from then on has been automatically added by web server software to every URL inserted in publicly editable web pages. The no-follow tag instructs search engines to ignore the link, thereby eliminating the effect of link spam. SEO (Search Engine Optimalization) is to influence search engines to get the highest possible position of a specific web page on the SERP (Search Engine Results Page). In SEO, almost anything goes, and search engines such as Google and Bing must constantly change the way their SERP ranking is computed, in order to prevent strategic manipulation.

2.1   Regulatory and Social Context for Online Reputation

It is important to look beyond purely technical aspects of TRS robustness when prevention of TRS manipulation is the goal. A real TRS is always embedded in a real community or market with its policy and legal context. Even if there are no technical barriers to manipulating a TRS, the fact that it is forbidden by policy or legislation might have a significant preventive effect on potential attackers. As an analogy, there is nothing that physically can stop a car driver for speeding if he really wants to do it. However, the possibility of a fine, or simply knowing the danger that it poses to people is sufficient to prevent most motorists from speeding. As an alternative to technical robustness mechanisms, it could be useful to define adequate regulation and policies for the deployment and usage of TRSs in online communities.

The simplicity of manipulating TRSs is in many ways paradoxical when considering that that TRSs often have considerable impact on economic performance. A hotel owner can be tempted to use a TRS to gain an advantage over competitors and to maximise profit in the following ways:

(a) Write false positive reviews and artificially inflate own reputation score.

(b) Write false negative reviews and give unfairly negative ratings to competitors.

While activity (a) would appear unethical to most people it would be difficult to define it as directly illegal. Activity (b) on the other hand would not only be considered unethical, but could be considered illegal under most jurisdictions on the basis of legislation regarding defamation.

Defamation is when someone makes a false claim implied to be true which may give a negative image to a person, business, product, group, government, or nation. In order for a complaint against defamation to succeed it is normally required that the defaming claim can be proven false and that the claim is communicated to someone other than the defamed entity. Slander and libel are specific categories of defamation, where slander typically refers to a malicious, false, and defamatory spoken statements, while libel refers to any other form of communication such as written words or images. Online defamation can therefore be characterised as libel. Most jurisdictions allow legal actions, civil and/or criminal, to deter various kinds of defamation and retaliate against groundless criticism.

In the case of Roger M. Grace vs. eBay (2004) [18] the plaintiff, Roger Grace, an eBay buyer, sued eBay and the seller Tim Neely after the seller had posted negative comments about Grace. According to court filings, Neely's comments about Grace were: *"Complaint: SHOULD BE BANNED FROM EBAY!!!! DISHONEST ALL THE WAY!!!!"*. The Superior Court of Los Angeles County held that Section 230 of the US Communications Decency Act of 1996 and the User Agreement on eBay's Web site relieve eBay of liability for libel with respect to comments posted by a seller on the eBay Web site. The user agreement on eBay's website contained the the following section: *"Because we are a venue, in the event that you have a dispute with one or more users, you release eBay (and our officers, directors...) from claims, demands and damages (actual and consequential) of every kind and nature, known and unknown, suspected and unsuspected, disclosed and undisclosed, arising out of or in any way connected with such disputes"*. The court also dismissed the suit against the seller Neely after eBay removed the challenged comments from its website.

While the above case released the owner of the TRS itself from liability, it does leave open the possibility of upholding complaints of libel against the party who produces an alleged defaming statement. Leaving baseless negative feedback and reviews can thus lead to legal prosecution. Not only that, even when users genuinely feel that there is an objective basis for leaving negative reviews, the user still faces the risk of legal action from the target of the negative reviews. This creates risk for anybody who wants to leave negative feedback, which by itself represents a disincentive against leaving negative feedback, even when it is warranted.

TRSs are so widespread in online communities and markets that one can speak about the *reputation society* as a new significant dimension of modern society [17]. Reputation is an asset that can be won and lost, just like real money. We have strict laws governing how money is exchanged, but very little legal regulation regarding reputation. While legislation about defamation provides protection against unfair damage to reputation, there seems to be no typical legislation against unfair inflation of own reputation. From a general point of view, unfair inflation of own reputation can have a negative economic impact on other parties similarly to damaging their reputation. One could therefore argue that there currently is a hole in most legislations in that respect. Participants in online communities thus face little risk when engaging in unfair inflation of own reputation. It is then up to the TRS owner to define specific policies and sanctions against this practice.

Since TRSs often cannot be considered robust, it seems surprising that they still can provide significant value and that they have become so widespread. One might therefore say that TRSs follow the paradoxical "Yhprums Law," which is the inverse of Murphys Law, expressed by: *"Something that shouldnt work sometimes does work."*.

One possible explanation of why TRSs are useful despite their weaknesses is that in many situations, a TRS does not necessarily need to be robust. Resnick & Zeckhauser (2002) [20] consider two explanations: (a) Even though a reputation system is not robust it might serve its purpose of providing an incentive for good behaviour if the participants think it works, and (b) even though the system might not work well in the statistical normative sense, it may function successfully if it reacts swiftly to bad behavior and imposes costs for a participant to get established.

Finally, it could be argued that the TRS in an online community serves as a kind of social glue. A TRS provides an interface through which participants can communicate and relate to each other, which in itself is valuable. Any TRS with user participation will depend on how people can use it to better connect to other participants and to the community as a whole, and must be designed with that perspective in mind.

3   Conclusion

The online world is somewhat analogous to the US Wild West of the 19th century where legislation was unclear and law enforcement was weak. In this context of relative lawlessness, trust and reputation systems represent alternative methods for moderating and regulating online communities. However, the informal and collaborative mechanisms of trust and reputation systems will inevitably come under pressure and attack whenever there is significant financial or political value at stake. In that case, malicious manipulation of a reputation system can only be prevented or mitigated if either 1) there exists regulation or policy that prohibits malicious manipulation with credible sanctioning options, or 2) there are technical mechanisms that can detect and block manipulation attempts. Ideally, both protection principles should be implemented simultaneously. In addition, adequate security mechanisms must be in place in order to prevent hacking attempts against trust and reputation systems or against participants' networks. If adequate robustness can be achieved, well functioning trust and reputation systems will become catalysts for healthy growth in online markets and communities.

References

1. Benevenuto, F., Rodrigues, T., Almeida, V., Almeida, J., Gonçalves, M.: Detecting spammers and content promoters in online video social networks. In: Proceedings of the 32nd International ACM SIGIR Conference on Research and Development in Information Retrieval, SIGIR 2009, pp. 620–627. ACM, New York (2009)
2. Clausen, A.: The Cost of Attack of PageRank. In: Proceedings of the International Conference on Agents, Web Technologies and Internet Commerce (IAWTIC 2004), Gold Coast (July 2004)
3. Dellarocas, C.: Immunizing Online Reputation Reporting Systems Against Unfair Ratings and Discriminatory Behavior. In: ACM Conference on Electronic Commerce, pp. 150–157 (2000)
4. Dini, F., Spagnolo, G.: Buiyng reputation on eBay: Do recent changes help? International Journal of Electronic Business 7(6), 581–598 (2009)
5. Duan, H., Liu, F.: Building and Managing Reputation in the Environment of Chinese E-commerce: A Case Study on Taobao. In: Kerkar, R., Badica, C. (eds.) Proc. of the 2nd International Conference on Web Intelligence, Mining and Semantics (WIMS 2012), Craiova, Romania (June 2012)
6. Farmer, R., Glass, B.: Building Web Reputation Systems. O'Reilly Media / Yahoo Press (March 2010)
7. Gilbert, E., Karahalios, K.: Understanding deja reviewers. In: Proceedings of the 2010 ACM Conference on Computer Supported Cooperative Work, CSCW 2010, pp. 225–228. ACM, New York (2010)
8. Golbeck, J.: Trust on the World Wide Web: A Survey. Foundations and Trends in Web Science 1(2) (2008)
9. Hoffman, K., Zage, D., Nita-Rotaru, C.: A Survey of Attack and Defense Techniques for Reputation Systems. ACM Computing Surveys 42(1) (December 2009) (to appear)
10. Jøsang, A.: Online Reputation Systems for the Health Sector. Electronic Journal of Health Informatics 3(1), e8 (2008)
11. Jøsang, A., Golbeck, J.: Challenges for Robust of Trust and Reputation Systems. In: Proceedings of the 5th International Workshop on Security and Trust Management (STM 2009), Saint Malo (September 2009)
12. Jøsang, A., Ismail, R., Boyd, C.: A Survey of Trust and Reputation Systems for Online Service Provision. Decision Support Systems 43(2), 618–644 (2007)
13. Kerr, R.: Smart Cheaters Do Prosper: Defeating Trust and Reputation Systems. In: Proceedings of the 8th Int. Joint Conference on Autonomous Agents & Multiagent Systems, AAMAS (July 2009)
14. Kerr, R., Cohen, R.: An Experimental Testbed for Evaluation of Trust and Reputation Systems. In: Ferrari, E., Li, N., Bertino, E., Karabulut, Y. (eds.) IFIPTM 2009. IFIP AICT, vol. 300, pp. 252–266. Springer, Heidelberg (2009)
15. Lim, E.-P., Nguyen, V.-A., Jindal, N., Liu, B., Lauw, H.W.: Detecting Product Review Spammers Using Rating Behaviors. In: Huang, J., et al. (eds.) Proceedings of the 19th ACM International Conference on Information and Knowledge Management, pp. 939–948. ACM, New York (2010)
16. Marsh, S.: Formalising Trust as a Computational Concept. PhD thesis, University of Stirling (1994)
17. Masum, H., Newmark, C., Tovey, M.: The Reputation Society: How Online Opinions Are Reshaping the Offline World. The Information Society Series. MIT Press (2012)
18. Court of appeal of the state of California. Roger M. Grace vs. eBay. B168765, Los Angeles County, Super. Ct. No. BS288836 (2004)

19. Ott, M., Choi, Y., Cardie, C., Hancock, J.T.: Finding deceptive opinion spam by any stretch of the imagination. In: Proceedings of the 49th Annual Meeting of the Association for Computational Linguistics: Human Language Technologies, HLT 2011, vol. 1, pp. 309–319. Association for Computational Linguistics (2011)

20. Resnick, P., Zeckhauser, R.: Trust Among Strangers in Internet Transactions: Empirical Analysis of eBay's Reputation System. In: Baye, M.R. (ed.) The Economics of the Internet and E-Commerce. Advances in Applied Microeconomics, vol. 11. Elsevier Science (2002)

21. Resnick, P., Zeckhauser, R., Friedman, R., Kuwabara, K.: Reputation Systems. Communications of the ACM 43(12), 45–48 (2000)

22. Resnick, P., Zeckhauser, R., Swanson, J., Lockwood, K.: The Value of Reputation on eBay: A Controlled Experiment. Experimental Economics 9(2), 79–101 (2006),
    http://www.si.umich.edu/~presnick/papers/
    postcards/PostcardsFinalPrePub.pdf

23. Withby, A., Jøsang, A., Indulska, J.: Filtering Out Unfair Ratings in Bayesian Reputation Systems. In: Proceedings of the 7th Int. Workshop on Trust in Agent Societies (at AAMAS 2004). ACM (2004)

24. Wu, G., Greene, D., Cunningham, P.: Merging multiple criteria to identify suspicious reviews. In: Proceedings of the Fourth ACM Conference on Recommender Systems, RecSys 2010, pp. 241–244. ACM, New York (2010)

25. Wu, G., Greene, D., Smyth, B., Cunningham, P.: Distortion as a validation criterion in the identification of suspicious reviews. In: Proceedings of the First Workshop on Social Media Analytics, SOMA 2010, pp. 10–13. ACM, New York (2010)

26. Yu, B., Singh, M.P.: Detecting Deception in Reputation Management. In: Proceedings of the Second Int. Joint Conference on Autonomous Agents & Multiagent Systems (AAMAS), pp. 73–80. ACM (2003)

27. Zhang, H., Goel, A., Govindan, R., Mason, K., Van Roy, B.: Making Eigenvector-Based Reputation Systems Robust to Collusion. In: Leonardi, S. (ed.) WAW 2004. LNCS, vol. 3243, pp. 92–104. Springer, Heidelberg (2004)

transCryptFS: A Trusted and Secure File System

Rajat Moona

Department of Computer Science and Engineering, IIT Kanpur
moona@iitk.ac.in

Abstract. For the reasons of flexibility and availability, the data may be stored in the cloud. However security of sensitive data and the reliability of access of data are two major issues that become immediate concern. Trust on the services for the secure upkeep of data, its regular maintenance and mechanisms for seamless access are other issues related to such organization of data.

In this talk, we present an encrypting file system based on GNU/Linux based servers which can be accessed through standard protocols such as NFS over unsecured networks. At the same time, the data stored in the servers is always in encrypted form. With only a suitable key management protocol and access control mechanisms, it is ensured that data is made available only to right entities. In the trusted domain for the files, even the system administrators are not included which makes it highly robust yet providing mechanisms for routine administrative jobs such as backup, restoration, duplication and other similar functions on data.

We also present a few more applications for this same file system, such as the case where data on a portable device such as laptop can be protected against loss of information in case of thefts etc.

T. Dimitrakos et al. (Eds.): IFIPTM 2012, IFIP AICT 374, p. 263, 2012.

Operational Challenges in Deploying Trust Management Systems - A Practical Perspective

Sundeep Oberoi

Global Head – Niche Technologies Delivery Group
Tata Consultancy Services Ltd.
sundeep.oberoi@tcs.com

Extended Abstract

With the exponentially increasing number of transactions being performed online, it has become critical to ensure that any electronic transaction can be associated with the electronic persona who has carried out the transaction. Furthermore it is very important to ensure that this electronic persona can be associated with a real human persona. This need has been highlighted by the regularity with which security measures are breached. In the circumstance of a breach or a failure of security, it is very important to determine the real person associated with the transaction in question so that accountability can be fixed and appropriate follow up actions taken. This requirement of accountability must be fulfilled with the same degree of rigour that we are used to in traditional paper based systems where transactions are authorized and accountability fixed by the use of "wet" signatures. Unless we are able to practically achieve this same level of accountability in electronic systems, reliance on paper based systems will continue.

Associating a transaction with a real human person has two steps. First the transaction must be associated with an electronic identity. The most simple example of this is a user-name. The second step is associating the given electronic persona with a real human persona. This is usually a matter of policy although there are some technologies, like biometrics, which could help establish this association is deployed carefully. Both these associations must be made with the requisite level of rigour if they are to be used as the basis for accountability.

1 Associating Electronic Identities with Transactions

In order to associate an electronic identity with a transaction, the system must store the identity as a part of the transaction in some way. This could be manifest, i.e. a user name is stored as part of the transaction. Some systems may create session or transaction identifiers which can be associated with an electronic identity via log entries. In this case the association is inferred. In any properly designed system, it must be possible to associate each transaction with an electronic identity. Further is must not be possible for this association to be altered by any means. Even if it is possible to identity an electronic identity in relation to each transaction and there is reasonable assurance that this identity has not been changed, it is still required to establish that the

T. Dimitrakos et al. (Eds.): IFIPTM 2012, IFIP AICT 374, pp. 264–266, 2012.
© IFIP International Federation for Information Processing 2012

transaction was carried out by the person authorized to use that electronic identity. This is usually achieved by authentication.

In practical scenarios authentication may not be fine grained. Authentication might happen at the level of logon. In recent times online banking systems have increasingly begun to authenticate each transaction that transfers value. However barring such examples authentication remains largely coarse grained and most systems lack the integrity mechanisms to ensure that the identity association and fact of authentication are maintained in a manner that cannot be tampered with.

In this context many countries have adopted Electronic Signature legislation in order to standardize and increase the assurance that transactions may be reliably associated with electronic identities and that it may be established that the authorized bearers of those electronic identities actually authorized those transactions. The practical issues here are that

- These techniques may have to be retrofitted to systems which do not have a fine grained transaction authorization mechanism. This could have an impact on code as well as storage since the signature information may now have to be stored and in some way associated with the transaction.
- Not all electronic signature techniques can guarantee the integrity of the signed records. Thus trust is required in the policies under which these records are processed and stored.
- Electronic credentials may be stolen and used without the knowledge of the authorized holder of those credentials thereby casting doubt on the intent by the authorized holder to authorize the transaction in question.

In practical systems today there are a very large number of users. The user base and therefore user credentials is not common across even all applications being run by a particular organization, let alone across organizations. In this scenario it is unavoidable that some form of self service be provided in terms on allowing the user to generate credentials on their own after an initial verification. Thus although initial registration will require a lot of information and a password will be generated by a means under the control of an application owner, subsequent password resets are usually self service based on authentication against pre-registered information. While this appears to be a practical necessity, trust in such systems requires the rigorous application and constant monitoring of compliance to policies.

2   Associating a Human Persona with an Electronic Persona

Most traditional systems did not even attempt to do this. The systems worked at the level of issuing electronic identities to people and did not have any technical measures or policies that would generate assurance in the association of humans to their electronic identities.

With the increasing adoption of electronic signature legislation it is becoming increasingly important to have high assurance in associating a given electronic identity to a specific individual. This requires that the identity of an individual requesting an electronic credential be rigorously verified before the electronic credential is issued. The practical problems here are

- Identity verification is expensive and inconvenient since a face to face verification might be required
- In light of the cost, practicality demands that such credentials be widely usable
- Applications must be in a position to use these interoperable credentials
- There must be ways to ensure that a credential can only be used by the authorized holder of the credential

The practical problems faced in deploying such systems have been

- Government Mandates needed when user base is not large enough
- Use seen largely as a compliance measure
- High verification costs which lead to lack of rigour in the credentialing process
- Insufficient measures to control unauthorized use of credentials

3   Summary

Although certain good technologies like Digital Signature and Biometrics exist that are technically secure, operating such technologies at a large scale requires trust management processes if their use is to be considered reliable and achieve the level of accountability that we expect from our traditional paper based system. This aspect of ensuring that a specific human persona is associated with a given electronic persona is a very vital element in ensuring the trustworthiness of electronic systems. Currently there are practical challenges in terms of cost and convenience which must be overcome before these systems can scale and be adopted widely.

A Perspective on the Evolution of the International Trust Management Research Community in the Last Decade

Theo Dimitrakos

Security Futures Practice, BT Research & Technology, UK
theo.dimitrakos@bt.com

Abstract. Year 2012 completes a decade since the iTrust research network was established in Europe. The international research community associated with iTrust is the predecessor of the IFIP Working Group 11.11 on Trust Management, the organization largely behind events such as the IFIPTM conference series. The completion of a decade since the establishment of iTrust also marks the first time that an international conference on Trust Management takes place in India, and indeed the first time that such a conference takes place outside of the aging "old world" economies of Europe, North America and Japan. This combination offers an excellent opportunity for a review of how we got here: the evolution of the international research community on trust management from 2002 to 2012. This review also offers a pre-text for surveying a selection of research results, research papers and innovative solution demonstrators that have been produce by the trust management community in the last decade.

This paper is the printed version of an invited keynote in IFIPTM 2012 conference that took place in Surat, India.

1   Introduction

The concepts of Trust and Trust Management in information systems and computer science attracted some attention in the late 1980's and the mid 1990's by pioneers who based themselves in sociological analyses such as Gambetta [1] or later in socio-inspired information systems such as McKnight [2]. Soon after, the idea that it may be possible to treat trust as a computational concept has been put forward by Marsh in [3] while the idea that trust can be a mathematical framework to reason about aspects of trust in a social network appeared in the work of Jøsang in [4,5,6] and [7]. In parallel, the concept that by managing some symbolic representation of trust one can aid the automated verification of actions against security policies, was put forward by Blaze and his team in [8] and [9]. In this variant of access control, actions are allowed if sufficient credentials are presented, separating symbolic representation of trust from the actual person or its identity. Although in a different context and serving a different application, essentially the same concept that Blaze's team introduced in the late 1990's has found more recently a new home in the WS-Trust protocol [10] that underpins security token exchange in web services implementations. Blaze's concept is still how many researchers and practitioners in information security perceive "trust management" today, especially if they are unfamiliar with the wider, interdisciplinary body of research in trust and trust management.

T. Dimitrakos et al. (Eds.): IFIPTM 2012, IFIP AICT 374, pp. 267–280, 2012.

Reviewing the plethora of facets and definitions of "trust" and "trust management" is out of the scope of this short paper. Many informative surveys have written about trust and trust management definitions including an extensive one by Grandison [11] back in 2000, a shorter one by Ruohomaa in 2005 [12] and a more recent survey on reputation systems by Jøsang [13] in 2007. It is also out of scope to examine if the terms such as "trust" and "trust management" are meaningful without context and a pre-text or if indeed trust can be managed. My views on this have been already presented in [14] and in [16].

This paper and the associated keynote are about the formation and evolution of an international and interdisciplinary community in trust management. What triggered, in fact necessitated, the creation of this community was not only the results of the research mentioned above, but most notably a major event in the recent history of the developed world: a crisis often referred to as the (first) "dot com bubble burst" in 2000 - 2001. On Friday, March 10, 2000, the technology heavy NASDAQ Composite index, peaked at 5,048.62 (intra-day peak 5,132.52), more than double its value just a year before. The NASDAQ fell slightly after that, and continued until March 20, 2000, when the financial magazines shocked the market with cover stories reporting that, within a year, many highflying Internet upstarts will have used up all their cash and unless they scare up more cash, they will be facing a savage shakeout. For example an article in a highly reputable financial magazine reported a survey of the likely losers and highlighted that "America's 371 publicly traded Internet companies have grown to the point that they are collectively valued at $1.3 trillion, which amounts to about 8% of the entire U.S. stock market"[15]. By 2001, a majority of the dot-com "miracle" companies ceased trading after burning through their venture capital, many having never made a "net" profit. The cause of the burst is often attributed to a combination of bad financial management and, most importantly, loss of consumer confidence as a result of unmet expectations for announced and oversold features that never materialized, negligent security and of poor customer experience.

2   iTrust Working Group: Incubating of an International Trust Management Community in Europe

The beginning of the first decade of the 21st century was a time that governments, industry and academics in Europe and North America were concerned about an apparent loss of consumer confidence in on-line services. They came to realise that some stimulation was necessary in order to save the internet and on-line services economy, and to allow it to grow and excel again. During that period, I had moved on from Imperial College, London to work as a senior researcher for the Central Laboratory UK Research Councils; a research facilities laboratory that hosted the W3C Office for the UK and Ireland (in addition to some of the most advanced particle physics and space science facilities in Europe). At that time, I put forward the idea that trust in virtual communities and on-line services, and a framework to manage trust in these, is fundamental for re-building a strong on-line services economy [16,17].

The idea of research in trust and trust management in order to facilitate strengthening trust relationships in on-line communities and on-line service value networks was well received by the UK government, and found supporters among my colleagues in academia such as Professors Maibaum and Jones at King's College London, Professor Morris Sloman at Imperial College London, and Dr Simon Shiu in HP Labs Bristol.

At that time, I was already familiar with the work of Blaze's team, via the research of Grandison [18], then a PhD candidate in Sloman's group, as well as the relevance that Jøsang's ideas in automating trust-based decision making. I had also grown an interest in the interplay between trust and risk following joint work with Ketil Stolen on model-based security risk analysis, that was marked by the inception of the CORAS methodology in 2001 [24,25]. I was exposed to formal models and logic-philosophical investigations in trust via Maibaum [19], Jones [20], Falcone and Castelfranchi [21,22] as well as to legal analyses on trust via the work of a team researchers in law at the Norwegian Research Centre for Computer and Law (NRCCL). I was therefore convinced that a solution to the problem could not be simply technical (or mathematical) and that it could not ignore psychological, socio-technical, legal, operational and economic aspects.

At roughly the same period, other researchers in the Joint Research Centre of the European Commission were also concerned about the impact of trust in on-line services and markets [23]. Through my interactions with them and other European Commission officials, the concept of an international and truly multi-disciplinary network of researchers in trust and trust management for on-line community and on-line services was conceived, and the European Commission agreed to support such an initiative at least for an incubation period. The research network was to have a global reach from its birth, albeit a European core base, and it become truly global and self-sufficient once it matured. At that time colleagues alerted me that Professor Christos Nicolaou, then rector of the University of Crete, was also considering proposing a research network with a focus on computational trust in global computing infrastructures. After an initial discussion with Professor Nicolaou, it became clear to both of us that all these approaches and expertise to "trust" and "trust management" were complementary and should co-exist and co-evolve, cross-fertilize and eventually fuse in the same research community.

That was in essence the birth of the iTrust working group in 2001, the main predecessor of what is now the IFIP working group on Trust Management. The European Commission appreciated the interdisciplinary nature of the team that was attracted by the ambitious goals put forward, and agreed to support the creation of a research network in Trust Management from 2002 to 2005, under the short-name "iTrust" with the view that the community would have become global, self-funded and self-sufficient by 2005.

2.1   The Vision of an Early Working Group on Trust Management

The vision of the iTrust working group was to bring together researchers and practitioners from a range of disciplines (computer science, sociology, economics, law, and philosophy) to develop models and techniques for dealing with trust in open dynamic systems. The group's aims were to explore the role of trust, and its interactions with security and authorization concerns for on-line virtual communities, value networks of on-line services and other dynamic open systems. We believed that effective trust modelling is an enabler for a range of new computing services including e-commerce, ubiquitous computing, grid computing, social networks and probably a variety of collaborative/cooperative online activities that we couldn't even imagine at that time.

For example, it was clear to us, at that time, that the sheer scale of the emerging global infrastructure, combined with the need for fully autonomous operation, surpass the usefulness of the advanced security infrastructures of that time including authorization services, public key infrastructures and certificate issuance and validation services. Possessing a certified identity in a dynamic and open environment does not a priori guarantee an acceptable behaviour and performance. In such systems, one cannot make informed decisions on access restrictions and controls, on selection of potential candidates to link in and interact with, or on what services to consume and how to consume them, on solely the basis of a certified identity. Mere knowledge of a certified identity alone is even less adequate for reasoning about the expected behaviour and dependability of entities for which no prior knowledge is available. Entities need to be distinguished not only based on their certified identities (which are static) but also based on their (un)expected, dynamically varying qualities that are relevant to the specific interaction context. Furthermore, such judgments, by necessity subjective due to the requirement for fully autonomous operation, need to be reviewed and possibly revised on a regular basis. For on-line services to achieve the same levels of acceptance as their conventional counterparts, trust management had to become an intrinsic part of on-line service provision.

Virtual community management, access management, business or social network partner selection, engagement in on-line transactions and e-commerce, and on-line service provision were some of the areas where we saw a needed for a practical, scalable and adaptable technology to capture, measure and manage the trusting relationships that underlie the interaction of on-line entities. Paving the way for such technology requires transfer of knowledge and close collaboration not only between academia and industry but also between different disciplines.

2.2   First Steps of an International Research Community in Trust Management

The iTrust research community soon expanded from its European base to include researchers from Australia, and North America. Members included legal experts, philosophers, psychologists, economists, and information / network security experts.

In 2003 the first collection of research results were published by the iTrust community in [26], following a conference in Crete, Greece. Research covered already a good mix of areas:

- *Trust Models*: including, for example, a model for "Regularity-Based Trust in Cyberspace" by Minsky, and a model for "Integrating Trustfulness and Decision Using Fuzzy Cognitive Maps" by Castelfranchi.

- *Policy-based systems*: including, for example, a paper distilling the "Experience with the KeyNote Trust Management System: Applications and Future Directions" by Matt Balze and the KeyNote team, as well as a proposal of "Trust Management Tools for Internet Applications" by Grandison and Sloman.
- *Credential disclosure negotiation*: including an overview of trust negotiation principles and tools by Winslett in her paper "An Introduction to Trust Negotiation".
- *Authentication systems and identity-based access control*: including for example research on "Authenticated Dictionaries for Fresh Attribute Credentials" by William Winsborough and his team, and an "Implementation of an Agent-Oriented Trust Management Infrastructure Based on a Hybrid PKI Model" by Karabulut.
- *Reputation systems*: including for example work on "Simulating the Effect of Reputation Systems on E-markets" by Jøsang.
- *Computational trust*: including for example work on "Trusting Collaboration in Global Computing Systems" by Paddy Nixon and his team, as well as research on "Trust Propagation in Small Worlds" by Christian D. Jensen et al.
- *Computer systems*: including work on "Hardware Security Appliances for Trust" by Baldwin and Shiu, as well as work on "Managing Trust and Reputation in the XenoServer Open Platform" by Twigg et al.
- *Early applications*: including work "Towards the Intimate Trust Advisor" and a "Methodology to Bridge Different Domains of Trust in Mobile Communications" by Piotr Cofta et al.
- *Socio-technical analyses*: including for example an analysis on "Social Capital, Community Trust, and E-government Services" by Grimsley and Meehan, and a "A Trust Matrix Model for Electronic Commerce" by Yao-Hua Tan.
- *Formal modelling of legal aspects*: including for example an analysis on "Trust, Reliance, Good Faith, and the Law" by Giovanni Sartor et al.

The iTrust community continued to build on such works and produced more results that were published in [27] following a community event in Oxford, UK, in 2004. The event in Oxford emphasised on trust in large scale distributed systems and virtual organisations, on the use of recommendation and reputation systems in social networks and on-line services and included a mixture of technical results, application case studies and socio-technical and legal analyses.

- *Large-scale systems and virtual organisations*: included works such as "Engineering Trust Based Collaborations in a Global Computing Environment" by Terzis et al, "Towards Dynamic Security Perimeters for Virtual Collaborative Networks" by Djordjevic et al., "Trust, Security, and Contract Management Challenges for Grid-Based Application Service Provision" by Mac Randal et al., "Towards Trust Relationship Planning for Virtual Organizations" by Robinson, Haller et al., and "Deploying Trust Policies on the Semantic Web" by Matthews et al., and "W5: The Five W's of the World Wide Web" by Massimo Marchiori from the W3C.
- *Recommendation and reputation systems*: included, for example, "Using Trust in Recommender Systems: An Experimental Analysis" by Massa, et al, and "A Case for Evidence-Aware Distributed Reputation Systems: Overcoming the Limitations of Plausibility Considerations" by Philipp Obreiter.

- *Socio-technical analyses*: included works such as "Human Experiments in Trust Dynamics" by C.M. Jonker, et al., "Modeling Controls for Dynamic Value Exchanges in Virtual Organizations" by Yao-Hua Tan et al., "Analyzing Correlation between Trust and User Similarity in Online Communities" by C.N. Ziegler, et al., "Managing Internet-Mediated Community Trust Relations" by Meehan et al., and "Trust Mediation in Knowledge Management and Sharing" by Castelfranchi.
- *Legal analyses*: included for example work on "Addressing the Data Problem: The Legal Framework Governing Forensics in an Online Environment" by Ian Walden.

The iTrust event in Oxford also fostered pioneering research investigating the interplay between on-line trust, risk and privacy as well as the role of trust in systems analysis and requirements engineering:

- *Trust and risk*: included for example "Analysing the Relationship between Risk and Trust" by Audun Jøsang and Stéphane Lo Presti, and "Using Risk Analysis to Assess User Trust: A Net-Bank Scenario" by Ketil Stølen.
- *Trust and privacy*: included for example "Trading Privacy for Trust" by Jean-Marc Seigneur, Christian Damsgaard Jensen, "Supporting Privacy in Decentralized Additive Reputation Systems" by Elan Pavlov et al.
- *Trust in requirements engineering*: included "Requirements Engineering Meets Trust Management: Model, Methodology, and Reasoning" by Fabio Massacci, John Mylopoulos et al.

The event in Oxford was also marked by an accompanying collection of tutorials and solution demonstrations that intensified knowledge transfer by bringing the iTrust community together with TrustCoM [28] – a major industry driven research project that brought together innovators from Atos, BT, BAe Systems, IBM, Microsoft and SAP with the aim to implement a collection standards-based web services technologies to facilitate secure and compliant business operation in virtual organisations.

Research in the iTrust community continued to produce strong results in 2005. The main community event of iTrust took place in Paris, France, with an emphasis on to computational trust, socio-technical and legal analyses [29]:

- *Models of Computational trust*: included works such as "Trust, Untrust, Distrust and Mistrust - An Exploration of the Dark(er) Side" by Marsh and Dibben, "A Representation Model of Trust Relationships with Delegation Extensions" by Lopez et al., "Towards a Generic Trust Model - Comparison of Various Trust Update Algorithms" by Kinateder et al., and "Towards an Evaluation Methodology for Computational Trust Systems" by J.-M. Seigneur et al.
- *Socio-Technical analyses*: included "Affect and Trust" by Lewis Hassel, "On Deciding to Trust" by Maria Fasli et al., and "Foraging for Trust: Exploring Rationality and the Stag Hunt Game" by Steven O. Kimbrough.
- *Legal analyses*: included works such as "Security and Trust in the Italian Legal Digital Signature Framework" by S. Zanero, and "Specifying Legal Risk Scenarios Using the CORAS Threat Modelling Language" by Mahler, Stølen et al.

The iTrust event in Paris in 2005 included demonstrations of solution prototypes covering a wide range of security and trust applications. These included compliance enabling technology, trust assessment for grid computing and virtual organizations, trust and risk modeling tools, and requirements engineering environments. Short papers summarizing the innovative solutions being demonstrated were also published in [29].

Year 2006 was a decisive test for the trust management community as the iTrust working group had to prove its strength and maturity by continuing to operate as a self-funded research community without any formal subsidy or sponsorship by national governments or the European Union. That was when two colleagues from Italy, Fabio Martinelli and Fabio Massacci, offered to host an iTrust conference in Pisa, Italy supported by Ketil Stølen from Norway and William H. Winsborough from the USA. In recognition of the continuing quality of research produced within the iTrust community, Springer, who had been publishing the proceedings of all previous iTrust events, agreed to continue to publish. Results published in [30] included research in reputation systems, trust-based decision making, and socio-technical analyses:

- *Recommendation and reputation systems*: included for example "Generating Predictive Movie Recommendations from Trust in Social Networks" by Jennifer Golbeck, "PathTrust: A Trust-Based Reputation Service for Virtual Organization Formation" by Haller et al., and "Virtual Fingerprinting as a Foundation for Reputation in Open Systems" by A.J. Lee and M. Winslett.
- *Trust-based decision making in trust networks*: included for example "Exploring Different Types of Trust Propagation" by Jøsang and Marsh, "Gathering Experience in Trust-Based Interactions" by Terzis, "A Versatile Approach to Combining Trust Values for Making Binary Decisions" by Klos and Poutré, as well as "Provision of Trusted Identity Management Using Trust Credentials" by Pearson and Casassa Mont, and a "Bayesian Trust Framework for Pervasive Computing" by Quercia, Capra et al.
- *Socio-technical analysis*: included "Why We Need a Non-reductionist Approach to Trust" by Castelfranchi, "Modelling Trade and Trust Across Cultures" by C.M. Jonker et al., and "Being Trusted in a Social Network: Trust as Relational Capital" by Falcone et al.

Building on the tradition of previous events, iTrust 2005 included a collection of innovative solution demonstrations for a variety of applications including solutions for user classification, trust establishment, authorization services based on trust negotiation, and threat, vulnerability and risk assessment tools. Short papers summarizing these solutions were also published in [30].

3   A Global Trust Management Community under IFIP

At the side of iTrust 2006 event in Pisa, I met with Dr Fabio Martinelli, who was then leading the ERCIM European community on Trust and Security and with whom I was co-organizing a series of advanced, high-quality workshops on formal aspects of security and trust [31,32,33,34], and with Professor Javier Lopez, who was to become the first Chair of IFIPTM to exchange our views about facilitating a better future for the trust management research community after iTrust. We discussed ways for preserving the pace and securing the future growth of the trust management research community in Europe and methods to safeguard its progress towards self-sufficiency and globalization. We decided that, having succeeded the test of iTrust 2006, and given that the community members included a significant number of researchers based in north America and in Australasia, the time had come to formally recognize the global nature of the trust management community and propose the formation of a working group under the auspices of the International Federation of Information Processing (IFIP).

Beyond its good academic reputation, one of the reasons for looking at IFIP was its balanced and truly global reach including not only the established economies where iTrust was already strong but also many of the rapidly emerging internet economies in Asia, Middle East and Latin America, where we felt that on-line trust and trust management could be even more relevant in the future. At that critical time, Dr Steven Marsh contributed further to the establishment of an IFIP working group with a global reach, by facilitating a bridge between the iTrust community and a research community in North America who were running the PST event on Privacy, Security and Trust with the endorsement of the National Research Council of Canada.

In less than a year, IFIP agreed to form a working group on Trust Management under its technical committee on Security, while recognising and safeguarding the interdisciplinary nature of the trust management working group. In order to strengthen the bond between the iTrust and PST communities the first IFIP Trust Management conference took place in New Brunswick, Canada in 2007. The proceedings of that event were again published by Springer in [35], albeit under the IFIP (AICT) series instead of LNCS. The results in [35] included works on privacy, trust and legal analysis:

- *Legal analysis*: included "Pulling it all together...privacy, security, cybercrime and safety" by Parry Aftab.
- *Trust models and trust management*: included, for example, a paper presenting a "Private Distributed Scalar Product Protocol With Application To Privacy-Preserving Computation of Trust" by Danfeng Yao et al., research on "Trust Transfer in Distributed Systems" by Dulay et al., a "Content Trust Model for Detecting Web Spam" by Wang Wei and Zeng Guosun, and "A trust protocol for community collaboration" by S. Galice et al.
- *Recommendation and Reputation systems*: included "Exploiting Trust and Suspicion for Real-time Attack Recognition in Recommender Applications" by Bagheri and Ghorbani, research on "Self-Selection Bias in Reputation Systems" by M. Kramer and on "Resisting Sybils in Peer-to-peer Markets" by J. Traupman.
- *Security and Privacy*: such as "A Privacy-Aware Service Discovery Middleware for Pervasive Environments" by Issarny et al., and an "Analysis of the implicit trust within the OLSR protocol" by Adnane, et al., as well as "Negotiation for Authorisation in Virtual Organisations" by Paurobally and "A Geo Time Authentication System" by Mostarda, et al.

In 2008, the IFIP working group on Trust Management had its annual event in Europe (Norway) where the focus was on trust modeling, recommendation and reputation systems, trust and privacy and socio-technical analyses [36]:

- *Trust modeling*: included "A Trust Evaluation Method Based on Logic and Probability Theory" by Reto Kohlas et al., "An Intensional Functional Model of Trust" by Kaiyu Wan, and A UML-based Method for the Development of Policies to Support Trust Management" by Ketil Stølen et al.
- *Recommendation and reputation*: included "Trust-Based Collaborative Filtering" and "SOFIA: Social Filtering for Robust Recommendations" by Licia Capra et al., "Continuous Ratings in Discrete Bayesian Reputation Systems" by Audun Jøsang et al., "Modeling Trust for Recommender Systems using Similarity Metrics" by Georgios Pitsilis, and "A Robust and Knot-Aware Trust-Based Reputation Model" by Nurit Gal-Oz, et al.
- *Privacy and trust*: included "A Model for Reasoning About the Privacy Impact of Composite Service Execution in Pervasive Computing" by Valérie Issarny, "Protecting Location Privacy through Semantics-aware Obfuscation Techniques" by Elisa Bertino et al., and an "Automatic Verification of Privacy Properties in the Applied pi Calculus" by Mark Ryan et al.
- *Socio-technical analysis*: included "Cooperation in Growing Communities" by Rowan Martin-Hughes and "The North Laine Shopping Guide: A Case Study in Modelling Trust in Applications" by Anirban Basu.

A collection of new technology demonstrations were also shown in IFIPTM 2008 including a stochastic reputation service for virtual organizations, a solution for monitoring application services, and a trust-based personalized travel guide. Short papers presenting these solutions were also included in [36].

As the trust management community had already developed critical masses in northern Europe and North America, the third Trust Management community took place in Purdue University, West Lafayette, Indiana, USA. Research reported in [37] focused on social aspects and usability, trust reasoning, trust and risk, privacy and data security, and recommendation and reputation systems:

- *Social aspects and usability*: including "Spiral of Hatred: Social Effects in Buyer-Seller Cross-Comments Left on Internet Auctions" by Radoslaw Nielek, et al, and "Graphical Passwords as Browser Extension: Implementation and Usability Study" by Kemal Bicakci et al.
- *Trust reasoning*: including "Elimination of Subjectivity from Trust Recommendation" by Elisa Bertino, et al., and "Trust-Enhanced Recommender Systems for Efficient On-Line Collaboration" by Georgios Pitsilis, et al.
- *Privacy and Data security*: including "Security in Wiki-Style Authoring Systems" by Christian Damsgaard Jensen, "On Usage Control in Data Grids" by Fabio Martinelli et al., and "Detection and Prevention of Insider Threats in Database Driven Web Services" by Danfeng Yao et al.

- *Information sharing and trust negotiation*: including "A Framework for Trustworthiness-Centric Information Sharing" by Ravi S. Sandhu et al., and "A Reconfigurable Framework for Trust Negotiation" by Marianne Winslett, et al.
- *Recommendation and reputation systems*: including "Comparison of the Beta and the Hidden Markov Models of Trust in Dynamic Environments" by Marie Elisabeth Gaup Moe, et al., and "Evaluating the STORE Reputation System in Multi-Agent Simulations" by Yücel Karabulut et al., as well as "Employing Key Indicators to Provide a Dynamic Risk Picture with a Notion of Confidence" by Ketil Stølen et al.

Following a community meeting at IFIPTM 2009, a restructuring of the working group to its current form was implemented and that came together with a re-affirmation of the commitment of the trust management research community to pursue its goal of a truly global reach. Consequently, Professor Yuko Murayama offered to host a community event in Morioka, Iwate, Japan for 2010. This would be the first time that a trust management conference was held in Japan. The IFIPTM 2010 was the first conference in the series to take place in the Far East and, through its success, offered a unique opportunity for all relevant research communities in Japan to be exposed to, engage in, trust management research. Although the Japanese economy is very similar to those of Europe and North America, IFIPTM 2010 validated that trust management is also appealing to societies with a different structure and societal fabric than those of Europe and North America. Research results published in [38] included:

- *Privacy and trust*: including "Schemes for Privately Computing Trust and Reputation" by Nurit Gal-Oz et al., and "Self-service Privacy: User-Centric Privacy for Network-Centric Identity" by José M. del Álamo, et al.
- *Trust Models*: including "Non-monotonic Trust Management for Distributed Systems" by Naranker Dulay et al., and "Implementation and Performance Analysis of the Role-Based Trust Management System, RT^C" by William Winsborough et al.
- *Experimental and Experiential trust*: including "Leveraging a Social Network of Trust for Promoting Honesty in E-Marketplaces" by Kate Larson et al., "Does Trust Matter for User Preferences? A Study on Epinions Ratings" by Georgios Pitsilis, et al., and "Bringing the Virtual to the Farmers' Market: Designing for Trust in Pervasive Computing Systems" by Ian Wakeman, et al.
- *Security and trust*: including a "Visitor Access Control Scheme Utilizing Social Relationship in the Real World" by Gen Kitagata et al., and "Metric Strand Spaces for Locale Authentication Protocols" by Joshua D. Guttman et al., as well as "An Enterprise Service Bus for Access and Usage Control Policy Enforcement" by Gabriela Gheorghe, et al.

In 2011, IFIPTM returned to Europe and was hosted in Copenhagen, Denmark. The research published in [38] included works in trust models, reputation systems, social aspects and usability, and trust / privacy in the cloud:

- *Trust Modeling*: such as "From Access Control to Trust Management, and Back - A Petition" by Dieter Gollmann, and "Composing Trust Models towards Interoperable Trust Management" by Valérie Issarny, et al.
- *Recommendation and reputation systems*: such as "Detecting and Reacting to Changes in Reputation Flows" by Sini Ruohomaa et al., and "From Reputation Models and Systems to Reputation Ontologies" by Rehab Alnemr, et al.
- *Social aspects and usability*: such as "The Evolution of Trust" by Pam Briggs, "Why We Need More Effective Trust Signaling" by Angela Sasse, and "Identifying Knots of Trust in Virtual Communities" by Nurit Gal-Oz, et al.
- *Trust in the Cloud*: such as "Enhancing Data Privacy in the Cloud" by Gene Tsudik et al., and "Regulatory Impact of Data Protection and Privacy in the Cloud" by Srijith K. Nair et al.

In 2012 the IFIP working group of Trust Management took yet another risk. This has been the first time for the working group to organize an event in India. The main motive for hosting an IFIPTM conference in India has been to introduce the trust management discipline to the research, government and commercial innovation communities of the Indian subcontinent and engage them into the research fostered by IFIP on Trust Management. Part of the motivation has also been to illustrate the catalyst role that Trust Management methods, techniques and know-how can play in a rapidly emerging economy and to a society that has yet another significantly different fabric and foundation than those of Europe, North America and Japan. The impact of IFIPTM 2012 in India is yet to be experienced and analyzed but the first indications from the IFIPTM Winter School in Surat in early 2012 are encouraging and show a high level of interest and likely involvement from the local research communities.

4   Concluding Remarks

The mission of the IFIP Trust Management is even more relevant now than the beginning of the 21st century. Trust remains a fundamental consideration for the growth and stability of electronic markets and on-line communities. Trust guides decisions about on-line interactions between humans, decisions about which service to consume and how and decisions about how organizations conduct their business and how they engage in business partnerships. The emergence of Cloud computing the establishment of interconnected social networks, covering now most social activities in modern life, and the proliferation of personal devices, electronic media and smart appliances offering continuous connectivity to on-line services from mixed home and work environments, bring about a situation that necessitates a radical rethinking of old security and on-line interaction models to meet new challenges. These challenges are different than those of 2001 but still highlight how relevant and important it is to understand and manage trust and to make trust-based decisions. Nurturing this know-how is critical not only for improving our on-line experience, but also for avoiding another drop in consumer or corporate confidence in the new technologies and new ways of social and business conduct, of higher magnitude than the dot-com bubble burst of 2001.

Failure to assess trust in online environments may lead to multiple and diverse security problems: The exploitation of global network mechanisms can enable attackers to disrupt services on a massive scale. Individuals or organized groups of criminals may also use automated agents to exploit market platforms to commit fraud and gain unfair advantages. Cleverly designed deceptions can trick a significant percentage of online users into revealing sensitive information. Online media and communities can be manipulated to create unnatural opinion biases and to hijack democratic processes. There is still relatively little technology support available for assessing the reliability and good faith of entities and the quality of resources in online environment, while people have a higher tendency to deceive through online interactions (compared to interaction involving physical presence). This increases uncertainty and risk, and it is in this environment that online communities and markets grow rapidly these days.

Contemporary research in trust management has two main facets, aligned with the nature of trust relationships. Firstly, it is about the *relying* parties assessing the reliability and good faith of other parties, as well of assessing the security, reliability and quality of online services, and helping to make better decisions about which parties it is safe to transact with. Secondly, it is about designing reliable and secure systems and processes, and enabling participants in online markets and communities to establish themselves as worth being *trusted*. Contemporary research in trust management enables providing incentives for good faith and quality services and sanctioning low-quality services and deceptive behavior has the effect of stimulating the emergence of quality markets and communities. It continues to bring together methods and tools from multiple disciplines including policy, information and network security, artificial intelligence, law, and cognitive sciences.

Ten years after the dot com burst in the "developed" economies of northern Europe, North America, and the Far East, there are similarities between the challenges that these economies faced while rebuilding trust in their on-line services and their on-line communities and the challenges that the emerging mega-economies, such as this in the Indian subcontinent, and elsewhere in Asia, in the Middle East, in South Africa and in Latin America, face now and will continue to face in the near future.

I think that academics, professionals, and entrepreneurs in today's emerging mega-economies can benefit by understanding trust and trust management and by studying the achievements and pitfalls of the "old-world" ageing economies that had to rebuild trust in on-line communities and on-line services, once or more, over the last ten years. It is my hope and expectation that the IFIP working group on Trust Management will play a catalyst role in this evolution and help to pave a way for a free, robust and resilient on-line market as the dynamics of the global economy evolve and new opportunities appear and growth shifts from the mature and declining economies of the West to the immature but vibrant and rapidly growing economies of the East.

I wish that the IFIPTM 2012 event in Surat India plays a very fruitful and pioneering role in this direction.

References

1. Gambetta, D.: Can We Trust Trust? In: Gambetta, D. (ed.) Trust: Making and Breaking Cooperative Relations, electronic edn., Department of Sociology, pp. 213–237. University of Oxford (1998),
   http://www.sociology.ox.ac.uk/papers/gambetta213-237.pdf
2. McKnight, D.H., Chervany, N.L.: The Meanings of Trust. Technical Report MISRC Working Paper Series 96-04, University of Minnesota, Management Information Systems Research Center (1996), http://misrc.umn.edu/wpaper/
3. March, S.P.: Formalising Trust as a Computational Concept. In: Computing Science and Mathematics, p. 170. University of Stirling (1994)
4. Jøsang, A.: Artificial Reasoning with Subjective Logic. In: 2nd Australian Workshop on Commonsense Reasoning (1997),
   http://www.idt.ntnu.no/~ajos/papers.html
5. Jøsang, A.: A Subjective Metric of Authentication. In: Quisquater, J.-J., Deswarte, Y., Meadows, C., Gollmann, D. (eds.) ESORICS 1998. LNCS, vol. 1485, pp. 329–344. Springer, Heidelberg (1998), http://www.idt.ntnu.no/~ajos/papers.html
6. Jøsang, A.: The right type of trust for distributed systems. In: ACM New Security Paradigms Workshop (1996), http://www.idt.ntnu.no/~ajos/papers.html
7. Jøsang, A.: A Logic for Uncertain Probabilities. International Journal of Uncertainty, Fuzziness and Knowledge-Based Systems 9(3), 279–311 (2001)
8. Blaze, M., Feigenbaum, J., Lacy, J.: Decentralized Trust Management. In: IEEE Conference on Security and Privacy, Oakland, California, USA (1996),
   http://www.crypto.com/papers/policymaker.pdf
9. Blaze, M., Ioannidis, J., Keromytis, A.D.: Experience with the KeyNote Trust Management System: Applications and Future Directions. In: Nixon, P., Terzis, S. (eds.) iTrust 2003. LNCS, vol. 2692, pp. 284–300. Springer, Heidelberg (2003)
10. Anderson, S., et al.: Web Services Trust Language (WS-Trust) (2005),
    http://specs.xmlsoap.org/ws/2005/02/trust/WS-Trust.pdf
11. Grandison, T., Sloman, M.: A survey of trust in Internet applications. IEEE Communications Surveys and Tutorials 3, 2–16 (2000)
12. Ruohomaa, S., Kutvonen, L.: Trust Management Survey. In: Herrmann, P., Issarny, V., Shiu, S.C.K. (eds.) iTrust 2005. LNCS, vol. 3477, pp. 77–92. Springer, Heidelberg (2005)
13. Jøsang, A., Ismail, R., Boyd, C.: A Survey of Trust and Reputation Systems for Online Service Provision. Decision Support Systems 43(2) (2007)
14. Jøsang, A., Keser, C., Dimitrakos, T.: Can We Manage Trust? In: Herrmann, P., Issarny, V., Shiu, S.C.K. (eds.) iTrust 2005. LNCS, vol. 3477, pp. 93–107. Springer, Heidelberg (2005)
15. Willoughby, J.: "Burning Up", article in Barrons magazine, March 20 (2000)
16. Dimitrakos, T.: System Models, e-Risks and e-Trust. In: I3E 2001, pp. 45–58 (2001)
17. Dimitrakos, T.: A Service-Oriented Trust Management Framework. In: Falcone, R., Barber, S.K., Korba, L., Singh, M.P. (eds.) AAMAS 2002 Ws Trust, Reputation... LNCS (LNAI), vol. 2631, pp. 53–72. Springer, Heidelberg (2003)
18. Grandison, T., Sloman, M.: Specifying and Analysing Trust for Internet Applications. In: Proceedings of the 2nd IFIP Conference on e-Commerce, e-Business and e-Government (I3E 2002), Lisbon (2002)
19. Maibaum, T.S.E.: How Do I Trust Thee? Let Me Count The Ways. In: IEEE ICCI 2002, p. 23 (2002)

20. Jones, A.J.I., Firozabadi, B.: On the characterisation of a trusting agent - aspects of a formal approach. In: Castelfranchi, C., et al. (eds.) Trust and Deception in Virtual Societies, pp. 157–168. Kluwer Academic Publishers, Dordrecht (2001)
21. Falcone, R., Castelfranchi, C.: The Socio-Cognitive Dynamics of Trust: Does Trust Create Trust? In: Falcone, R., Singh, M., Tan, Y.-H. (eds.) Trust in Cyber-societies. LNCS (LNAI), vol. 2246, pp. 55–72. Springer, Heidelberg (2001)
22. Castelfranchi, C., Falcone, R.: Trust is Much More Than Subjective Probability: Mental Components and Sources of Trust. In: HICSS 2000 (2000)
23. Jones, S., Wilikens, M., Morris, P., Masera, M.: Trust Requirements in E-Business: A Conceptual Framework. Communications of the ACM 43 (December 2000)
24. Dimitrakos, T., Raptis, D., Ritchie, B., Stølen, K.: Model Based Security Risk Analysis for Web Applications. In: EuroWeb 2002, Workshops in Computing BCS 2002 (2002)
25. Fredriksen, R., Kristiansen, M., Gran, B.A., Stølen, K., Opperud, T.A., Dimitrakos, T.: The CORAS Framework for a Model-Based Risk Management Process. In: Anderson, S., Bologna, S., Felici, M. (eds.) SAFECOMP 2002. LNCS, vol. 2434, pp. 94–105. Springer, Heidelberg (2002)
26. Nixon, P., Terzis, S. (eds.): iTrust 2003. LNCS, vol. 2692. Springer, Heidelberg (2003)
27. Jensen, C., Poslad, S., Dimitrakos, T. (eds.): iTrust 2004. LNCS, vol. 2995. Springer, Heidelberg (2004)
28. Dimitrakos, T., Golby, D., Kearney, P.: Towards a Trust and Contract Management Framework for Dynamic Virtual Organisations. In: eAdoption and the Knowledge Economy: eChallenges 2004 (2004)
29. Herrmann, P., Issarny, V., Shiu, S. (eds.): iTrust 2005. LNCS, vol. 3477. Springer, Heidelberg (2005)
30. Stølen, K., Winsborough, W.H., Martinelli, F., Massacci, F. (eds.): iTrust 2006. LNCS, vol. 3986. Springer, Heidelberg (2006)
31. Dimitrakos, T., Martinelli, F.: Formal Aspects in Security and Trust: Second IFIP TC1 WG1.7 Workshop on Formal Aspects in Security and Trust (FAST), an event of the 18th IFIP World Computer Congress, Toulouse, France, August 22-27, 2004. Springer (2005)
32. Dimitrakos, T., Martinelli, F., Ryan, P.Y.A., Schneider, S. (eds.): FAST 2005. LNCS, vol. 3866. Springer, Heidelberg (2006)
33. Dimitrakos, T., Martinelli, F., Ryan, P.Y.A., Schneider, S. (eds.): FAST 2006. LNCS, vol. 4691. Springer, Heidelberg (2007)
34. Degano, P., Guttman, J., Martinelli, F. (eds.): FAST 2008. LNCS, vol. 5491. Springer, Heidelberg (2009)
35. Etalle, S., Marsh, S. (eds.): Trust Management. IFIP, vol. 238. Springer, Boston (2007)
36. Karabulut, Y., Mitchell, J., Herrmann, P., Jensen, C.D. (eds.): Trust Management II. IFIP, vol. 263. Springer, Boston (2008)
37. Ferrari, E., Li, N., Bertino, E., Karabulut, Y. (eds.): IFIPTM 2009. IFIP AICT, vol. 300. Springer, Heidelberg (2009)
38. Nishigaki, M., Jøsang, A., Murayama, Y., Marsh, S. (eds.): IFIPTM 2010. IFIP AICT, vol. 321. Springer, Heidelberg (2010)
39. Wakeman, I., Gudes, E., Jensen, C.D., Crampton, J. (eds.): IFIPTM 2011. IFIP AICT, vol. 358. Springer, Heidelberg (2011)

Author Index